Self to Self

Selected Essays

Self to Self brings together essays on personal identity, autonomy, and moral emotions by the philosopher J. David Velleman. Although the essays were written independently, they are unified by an overarching thesis – that there is no single entity denoted by "the self" – as well as by themes from Kantian ethics, psychoanalytic theory, social psychology, and Velleman's work in the philosophy of action. Two of the essays were selected by the editors of *Philosophers' Annual* as being among the ten best papers in their year of publication.

Self to Self will be of interest to philosophers, psychologists, and others who theorize about the self.

J. David Velleman was professor of philosophy at the University of Michigan, Ann Arbor, and is now professor of philosophy at New York University. He is the author of *Practical Reflection* and *The Possibility of Practical Reason*, and he co-edits the online journal *Philosophers' Imprint*. His articles have appeared in *The Philosophical Review, Ethics,* and *Mind,* among other publications.

Reviewed in
Ethics
Oct 2006

Self to Self

Selected Essays

J. DAVID VELLEMAN
New York University

CAMBRIDGE
UNIVERSITY PRESS

CAMBRIDGE UNIVERSITY PRESS
Cambridge, New York, Melbourne, Madrid, Cape Town, Singapore, São Paulo

Cambridge University Press
40 West 20th Street, New York, NY 10011-4211, USA

www.cambridge.org
Information on this title: www.cambridge.org/9780521854290

First published 2006

Printed in the United States of America

A catalog record for this publication is available from the British Library.

Library of Congress Cataloging in Publication Data
Velleman, James David.
Self to Self : selected essays / J. David Velleman.
p. cm.
Includes bibliographical references and index.
ISBN 0-521-85429-6 (hardcover) – ISBN 0-521-67024-1 (pbk.)
1. Self. 2. Self (Philosophy) 3. Kant, Immanuel, 1724–1804 – Ethics. I. Title.
BF697.V45 2005
126–dc22   2005008114

ISBN-13 978-0-521-85429-0 hardback
ISBN-10 0-521-85429-6 hardback

ISBN-13 978-0-521-67024-1 paperback
ISBN-10 0-521-67024-1 paperback

for my brothers,
Paul and Dan

Contents

Acknowledgments

As this book goes to press, I am approaching the end of my twenty-two-year affiliation with the Department of Philosophy at the University of Michigan. The book contains most of my writing from the last ten of those years. Belonging to the Michigan department has been a rare privilege; I hope that I have used it well.

Although several of the essays in this volume return to themes in the philosophy of action that occupied my previous books, most venture into new areas – personal identity, psychoanalytic theory, the moral emotions, Kantian ethics. My freedom to explore these areas was greatly enhanced by a fellowship from the National Endowment for the Humanities and a fellowship from the John Simon Guggenheim Memorial Foundation, both of which were generously supplemented by the Philosophy Department and the College of Literature, Science, and the Arts.

For excellent editorial assistance, I am grateful to David Dick at Michigan and Beatrice Rehl at Cambridge University Press, and to my manuscript editor, Ronald Cohen.

Sources

Chapter 1, "Introduction," appears here for the first time.

Chapter 2, "A Brief Introduction to Kantian Ethics," appears here for the first time.

Chapter 3, "The Genesis of Shame," first appeared in *Philosophy and Public Affairs*, 30 no. 1 (Winter 2001), 27–52, published by Blackwell, and is reprinted here with the permission of the publisher. Copyright © 2001 Blackwell.

Chapter 4, "Love as a Moral Emotion," first appeared in *Ethics* 109 (January 1999), 606–28, published by the University of Chicago Press, and is reprinted here with the permission of the publisher. Copyright © 1999 by the University of Chicago. All rights reserved.

Chapter 5, "The Voice of Conscience," first appeared in *Proceedings of the Aristotelian Society*, November 1999, vol. 99, no. 1, 57–76, published by Blackwell, and is reprinted here with the permission of the publisher. Copyright © 1998 Blackwell.

Chapter 6, "A Rational Superego," first appeared in *The Philosophical Review* 108 (1999), 529–58, published by Cornell University, and is reprinted here with the permission of the publisher. Copyright © 1999 Cornell University.

Chapter 7, "Don't Worry, Feel Guilty," first appeared in *Philosophy and the Emotions,* Royal Institute of Philosophy Supplement 52, edited by Anthony Hatzimoysis (Cambridge: Cambridge University Press, 2003), 235–48, and is reprinted here with the permission of the publisher. Copyright © 2003 Cambridge University Press.

Chapter 8, "Self to Self," first appeared in *The Philosophical Review* 105 (1996), 39–76, published by Cornell University. Reprinted here with the permission of the publisher. Copyright © 1996 Cornell University.

Chapter 9, "The Self as Narrator," first appeared in *Autonomy and the Challenges to Liberalism: New Essays,* edited by Joel Anderson and John Christman (Cambridge: Cambridge University Press, 2005), 56–76, and is reprinted here with the permission of the publisher. Copyright © 2005 Cambridge University Press.

Chapter 10, "From Self Psychology to Moral Philosophy," first appeared in *Philosophical Perspectives* 14 (October 2000), 349–77, published by Blackwell, and is reprinted here with the permission of the publisher. Copyright © 2000 Blackwell.

Chapter 11, "The Centered Self," appears here for the first time.

Chapter 12, "Willing the Law," first appeared in *Practical Conflicts: New Philosophical Essays,* edited by Monika Betzler and Peter Baumann (Cambridge: Cambridge University Press, 2004), 27–56, and is reprinted here with the permission of the publisher. Copyright © 2004 Cambridge University Press.

Chapter 13, "Motivation by Ideal," first appeared in *Philosophical Explorations* 5 (May 2002), 89–104, published by Taylor & Francis, Ltd., Abingdon, United Kingdom, and is reprinted here with the permission of the publisher. Copyright © 2002 Taylor & Francis, Ltd.

Chapter 14, "Identification and Identity," first appeared in *The Contours of Agency: Essay on Themes from Harry Frankfurt*, edited by Sarah Buss and Lee Overton (MIT Press, 2001), pp. 91–123, and is reprinted here with the permission of the publisher. Copyright © 2001 MIT Press.

1

Introduction

The title of this book comes from John Locke, who described a person's consciousness of his past as making him "self to himself" across spans of time. Implicit in this phrase is the view that the word 'self' does not denote any one entity but rather expresses a reflexive guise under which parts or aspects of a person are presented to his[1] own mind. This view stands in opposition to the view currently prevailing among philosophers – that the self is a proper part of a person's psychology, comprising those characteristics and attitudes without which the person would no longer be himself. I do not believe in the existence of the self so conceived.

To say that 'self' merely expresses a reflexive mode or modes of presentation is not to belittle it. The contexts in which parts or aspects of ourselves are presented in reflexive guise give rise to some of the most important problems in philosophy. They include the context of autobiographical memory and anticipation, in which we appear continuous with past and future selves; the context of autonomous action, in which we regard our behavior as self-governed; the context of moral reflection, in which we exercise self-criticism and self-restraint; and the context of the moral emotions, in which we blame ourselves, feel ashamed of ourselves, or want to be loved for ourselves. To understand what is presented to us under the guise of self in each of these contexts would be to gain some insight into personal identity, autonomy, the conscience, and the moral emotions – all important and complex phenomena.

---

[1] For an explanation of why I use 'he' to denote the arbitrary person, see my *Practical Reflection* (Princeton: Princeton University Press, 1989), p. 4, n. 1.

Many philosophers think that we can account for all of these phenomena at a stroke, by identifying a single thing that serves simultaneously as that which we have in common with past and future selves, that which governs our behavior when it is self-governed, that which we restrain when exercising self-restraint, and that which we blame, of which we feel ashamed, or for which we hope to be loved. I think that expecting a single entity to play the role of self in all of these contexts can only lead to confusion. Each context presents something in a reflexive guise, but not necessarily in the same guise, and certainly not the same thing.

That said, I still believe that there is much to be gained from a comparative study of selfhood in all of these contexts. Several of the essays in this volume undertake such a comparative study, while others confine themselves to selfhood in one context, with cross-references to essays about the others. The result is not a unified theory of the self, but it is, I hope, a coherent series of reflections on selfhood. In this Introduction, I will identify some of the subsidiary lines of argument uniting these reflections.

What Is a Reflexive Mode of Presentation?

Some activities and mental states have an intentional object: they are mentally directed at something. Of these, some can take their own subject as intentional object: they can be mentally directed at that which occupies the state or performs the activity. Of these, some can be mentally directed at their own subject conceived as such – conceived, that is, as occupying this very state or performing this very activity. A reflexive mode of presentation is a way of thinking that directs an activity or mental state at its own subject conceived as such.

The attitude of respect, for example, is directed at a particular person by some way of thinking about him. Sometimes it is directed at a person by the thought of him as the one holding this very attitude of respect. That way of thinking is a reflexive mode of presentation, and the resulting attitude is consequently called "self-respect." In the simplest case, the reflexive mode of presentation is a first-person pronoun: the object of some respectful thought is picked out in that thought as "me," and then the "self" in "self-respect" is just an indirect way of attributing an attitude that would be directly expressed with the first person. But there are also non-verbal modes of reflexive thought.

For example, a visual image represents things in spatial relation to an unseen point where its lines of sight converge. Insofar as vision implicitly alludes to that point as the position of its own subject, its geometry constitutes a reflexive mode of presentation. Being visually aware of things involves being implicitly self-aware, because it involves this implicit way of thinking about the subject of vision as such. The reflexivity implicit in this awareness would naturally be expressed in the first person, with a statement beginning "I see. . . ." But what makes the awareness reflexive, to begin with, is not a use of the first-person pronoun. What makes visual awareness implicitly reflexive is the perspectival structure of the visual image, which secures the implicit reference to the subject of vision so conceived.

Whenever the self is spoken of, some reflexive activity or mental state is under discussion, with the word 'self' standing in for the mode of presentation by which the state or activity is directed at its subject as such. Strictly speaking, then, reference to the self *sans phrase*, in abstraction from any reflexive context, is incomplete. Talk of "The Self" is like talk of "The Subject" in that theory-laden sense which refers to a person in the abstract. Just as The Subject must be the subject of some activity or mental state, so The Self must be the self of some activity or mental state directed at its subject so conceived.

Talk of the self *sans phrase* can be harmless, of course, if the relevant state or activity is salient in the context. And some reflexive states and activities are of such importance to our nature that they can be made salient by little more than reference to the self. But our failure to specify a reflexive context when speaking of the self should not be taken to indicate that there is nothing to specify.

I distinguish among at least three reflexive guises under which a person tends to regard aspects of himself. These three reflexive guises correspond to at least three distinct selves.

First, there is the self-image by which a person represents which person and what kind of person he is – his name, address, and Social Security number, how he looks, what he believes in, what his personality is like, and so on. This self-image is not intrinsically reflexive, because it does not in itself represent the person as the subject of this very representation; in itself, it represents him merely as a person. It is made reflexive by some additional indication or association that marks it as representing its subject. It is like a photograph in the subject's mental album, showing just another person but bearing on the reverse side "This is me."[2]

---

[2] I discuss this issue further in "The Centered Self" (Chapter 11). See especially Appendix A.

A person's self-image cannot be intrinsically reflexive, in fact, if it is to embody his sense of who he is. Conceiving of who he is entails conceiving of himself as one of the potential referents for the pronoun 'who', which ranges over persons in general. From among these candidates neutrally conceived, it picks out the one he is, thus identifying him with one of the world's inhabitants. It therefore requires a conception of someone *as* one of the world's inhabitants, who can then be identified as "me."

Because a person's sense of who he is must contain a non-reflexive conception of himself as one of the world's inhabitants, it is the vehicle for those attitudes by which he compares himself to others or empathizes with their attitudes toward him. When he feels self-esteem, for example, he feels it about the sort of person he is, and hence toward himself as characterized by his self-image. When he indulges in self-hatred, he hates the object of his self-image, a person whom others might hate. As the repository of the characterizations grounding these self-evaluations, the self-image is sometimes referred to as the person's ego – not in the psychoanalytic sense but in the colloquial sense in which the ego is said to be inflated by praise or pricked by criticism. An inflated ego, in this colloquial sense, is an overly positive self-image.

Finally, a person's self-image is the criterion of his integrity, because it represents how his various characteristics cohere into a unified personality, with which he must be consistent in order to be self-consistent, or true to himself. Failures of integrity threaten to introduce incoherence into the person's conception of who he is; and in losing a coherent conception of who he is, the person may feel that he has lost his sense of self or sense of identity. This predicament is sometimes called an identity crisis.

When someone suffers an identity crisis, he may feel that he no longer knows who he is. The reason is not that he has forgotten his name or Social Security number; it's rather that the self-image in which he stores information about the person he is has begun to disintegrate under the strain of incoherence, either with itself or with his experience. Often such strain appears around features of his self-image that distinguish him from other persons and underwrite his self-esteem. The result is that his self-image seems to lose its power to set him apart from others in his eyes; and this result is what he is speaking of when he says that he no longer knows who he is.

Yet to say that a person has undergone an identity crisis, or no longer knows who he is, does not imply that there is any doubt, in our minds or in his, as to whether he is still the same person. His identity crisis is a crisis in his sense of identity, as embodied in his self-image; it is not a crisis in his metaphysical identity – that is, in his being one person rather than another, or one and the same person through time. The qualities that are distinctive of the person, either descriptively or evaluatively, are crucial to his sense of who he is because that sense is embodied in a self-image representing him as one person among others, from whom he then needs to be distinguished by particular qualities. The fact that distinctive qualities are necessary to pick out the person who he is, and thus inform his sense of identity, does not indicate that those qualities play any role in determining his identity, metaphysically speaking.

Unfortunately, philosophers sometimes assume that the qualities essential to a person's sense of who he is are in fact constitutive of who he is and therefore essential to his remaining one and the same person, numerically identical with himself and numerically distinct from others. Here they conflate the self presented by a person's self-image with the self of personal identity, or self-sameness through time.

Self-sameness through time is the relation that connects a person to his past and future selves, as they are called. In my view, past and future selves are simply past and future persons in reflexive guise, or under a reflexive mode of presentation.[3] The task of identifying a person's past and future selves is a matter of identifying which past and future persons are accessible to him in the relevant guise, or under the relevant mode of presentation – in short, which past and future persons are reflexively accessible to him. Past persons are reflexively accessible via experiential memory, which represents the past as seen through the eyes of someone who earlier stored this representation of it; and future persons are accessible via a mode of anticipation that represents the future as encountered by someone who will later retrieve this representation of it. These modes of thought portray past and future persons reflexively by implicitly pointing to them at the center, or origin, of an egocentric frame of reference, as the unseen viewer in a visual memory, for example, or the unrepresented agent in a plan of action. The unseen viewer in a visual memory is the self or "I" of the memory; the unrepresented agent in a plan of action is the self or "I" of the plan. Past and future selves are simply the past and future persons whom the subject can represent as the "I" of a memory or the "I" of a plan – persons of whom he can think reflexively, as "me."

These reflexive modes of thought are significantly different from the self-image that embodies a person's sense of self. To begin with, they

---

3 This claim is the thesis of "Self to Self" (Chapter 8).

are intrinsically reflexive, in the sense that their representational scheme is structured by a perspective whose point of origin is occupied by the past or future subject, whereas a self-image is the representation of a person considered non-first-personally but identified as the subject by some other, extrinsic means. Another difference lies in the extent to which these modes of thought actually constitute the self.

I have long defended the view that a person's self-image is self-fulfilling to some extent: thinking of himself as shy, or as interested in jazz, or as aspiring to cure cancer can be a part or a cause of his actually being shy, or being interested in jazz, or aspiring to cure cancer. Including these characteristics in his self-image can be partly constitutive of, or conducive to, possessing them in fact; and to this extent, the person can define himself by defining his self-image. I elaborate on this view of self-definition in several of the essays in this volume.[4] As I point out, however, a person's powers of self-definition are limited. Although thinking that he has a characteristic can be one part or one cause of his actually having it, other parts and causes are invariably required. And although the self-image through which he defines himself can also be said to embody his sense of who he is, the fact of who he is lies strictly beyond his powers of self-definition. Thus, thinking that he is interested in jazz may or may not succeed in making him interested in jazz, while thinking that he is Napoleon will certainly fail to make him Napoleon.

By contrast, someone's first-personal memories and expectations determine which past and future persons are accessible to him in the guise of selves; and as Locke first pointed out, we have good reason to acknowledge connections of selfhood forged in this manner, whether or not they conform to the life history of a single human being. Such diachronic connections are the topic of the title essay in this volume (Chapter 8). There I argue, in support of Locke, that if a person could retrieve experiential memories that were stored by Napoleon at Auster-litz, then Napoleon at Austerlitz would genuinely be related to him as a past self; and when he reported one of those memories by saying "I commanded the forces at Austerlitz," he would be expressing a thought that helped to constitute its own truth, by giving him first-personal access to the relevant inhabitant of the past.

In sum, a person's identity is constituted by reflexive thought in two distinct instances. In the first instance, the person can to some extent

---

[4] Empirical evidence for this view is summarized in "From Self-Psychology to Moral Philosophy" (Chapter 10). The view also figures in "The Self as Narrator" (Chapter 9), "The Centered Self" (Chapter 11), and "Motivation by Ideal" (Chapter 13).

fashion his own identity, because he can fashion his self-image and at the same time fashion himself in that image. In the second instance, the person's identity is given to him by the psychological connections that make past and future persons accessible to his reflexive thought.

The third reflexive guise under which a person is presented with a self is the guise of autonomous agency.[5] Among the goings on in a person's body, some but not others are due to the person in the sense that they are his doing. When he distinguishes between those which are his doing and those which aren't, he appears to do so in terms of their causes, by regarding the former but not the latter as caused by himself. Yet even the latter goings-on emanate from within his own body and mind, and so when he disowns them, he ends up disowning parts of his own body and mind, as if the boundary between self and other lay somewhere inside the skin.

I think that in order to locate the self to whom autonomous actions are attributed, we have to ask which part or aspect of the person is presented to him in reflexive guise when he considers the causes of his behavior. Whatever is presented in reflexive guise to the agent's causal reasoning will be that to which such reasoning attributes his behavior when attributing it to the self. Clearly, what's presented in reflexive guise to causal reasoning is that which conducts such reasoning – that part or aspect of the person which seeks to understand events in terms of their causes. The self to which autonomous actions are attributed must therefore be the agent's faculty of causal understanding. Insofar as a person's behavior is due to his causal understanding, its causes will appear to that understanding in reflexive guise, and the behavior will properly appear as due to the self.

Most of my work prior to the essays in this volume was devoted to arguing that the actions traditionally classified as autonomous by philosophers of action are indeed due to the agent's causal understanding.[6] Autonomous actions are actions performed for a reason, and reasons for performing an action, I argued, are considerations in light of which the action would be understandable in the causal terms of folk psychology. To act for a reason is to do what would make sense, where the consideration in light of which it would make sense is the reason for

---

5 The self of autonomy is the topic of "The Self as Narrator" (Chapter 9) and "Identification and Identity" (Chapter 14).

6 See my *Practical Reflection* (Princeton: Princeton University Press, 1989) and *The Possibility of Practical Reason* (Oxford: Oxford University Press, 2000).

acting. Thus, for example, one's being interested in jazz would explain why one might frequent nightclubs, and so one can frequent nightclubs not only out of an interest in jazz but also on the grounds of that interest, regarded as explanatory of one's behavior. When one's behavior is guided by such considerations, it is guided by one's capacity for making sense of behavior, which is one's causal understanding and is therefore presented in reflexive guise to that very understanding, as the self that causes one's behavior.

The essays in this volume elaborate on this theory of autonomy in a few, fairly modest respects. First, I explore what social psychologists have written about the self, pointing out that their research supports the aspect of my theory that seems most far-fetched to philosophers – namely, the claim that people are generally guided in their behavior by a cognitive motive toward self-understanding.[7] Second, I point to this motive as effecting a crucial, hidden step in the process posited by Daniel Dennett to explain how a human being makes up or invents a self.[8] I agree with Dennett in thinking that a human being makes up or invents a self in one sense; but I argue that in making up a self in that sense, a human being also manifests his possession of a self in another sense, by exercising genuine autonomy. The self that a human being makes up is the individuating self-conception that embodies his sense of who he is; the self that he thereby manifests is his capacity for understanding his behavior in light of that self-conception.

Dennett frames his notion of self-invention in terms of self-narration: the self-conception that a person develops is a sketch for the protagonist in his own autobiography. In these terms, the person's capacity for causal understanding gets redescribed as his capacity for coherent narration, which I call the self as narrator. In two further essays, I go on to explore implications for moral philosophy flowing from this narrative-based theory of autonomy.[9]

This completes my summary of the three reflexive guises under which we are presented with selves: the self-concept, the guise of past or future self,

---

[7] "From Self Psychology to Moral Philosophy" (Chapter 10).

[8] "The Self as Narrator" (Chapter 9).

[9] "Willing the Law" (Chapter 12) and "Motivation by Ideal" (Chapter 13). In all of these essays, I assume that narrative is just a way of formulating our causal understanding of the narrated events. I have recently come to doubt this conception of narrative ("Narrative Explanation" *The Philosophical Review* 112 [2003]: 1–25). Although narrative conveys causal understanding of the narrated events, I have come to think that it also conveys a distinct mode of understanding as well. This conclusion complicates my view of practical reason in ways that remain to be explored.

and the guise of the self as cause of autonomous action. As I mentioned at the beginning, my strategy of identifying distinct selves, corresponding to these distinct reflexive guises, runs counter to the prevailing trend among philosophers, who prefer to theorize about a single, all-purpose self. I now turn to a summary of the arguments by which I attempt to resist this trend. I interpret the trend as a reaction against Kantian moral psychology, and so my arguments are largely interpretations and defenses of Kant.

In Kant's moral psychology, the governing *autos* of autonomy is rational nature, which a person shares with all persons. This rational nature includes none of the qualities that differentiate the person from others, none of the idiosyncratic attitudes and characteristics that inform his sense of individuality. It is therefore unfit to serve as the target of reflexivity in other contexts – as the target of self-esteem, for example – and so it strikes many philosophers as denuded, the mere skeleton of a self. These philosophers have consequently sought to flesh out a rival conception of the self that includes personal particularities, and they have then deployed this conception not only in contexts to which it is appropriate, in my view, but in others as well, including the contexts of personal identity and autonomy. I pursue three distinct strategies for resisting this trend, though I don't always distinguish among them.

First, I attempt to meet the trend head-on by arguing that it underrates the importance of bare personhood. I grant that each person has a detailed sense of his identity, representing those features of himself which he values as differentiating him from others. This individuating self-conception is that to which the person is true when he is true to himself, that which he betrays when he betrays himself, and that under which he esteems himself in feeling self-esteem. The distinctive features represented in this conception can even be said to define who the person is. Yet these features are not, for example, the object of the person's self-respect, since self-respect is an appreciation of his value merely as a person. Whereas self-esteem says "I am clever" or "I am strong" or "I am beautiful," self-respect says simply "I am somebody."

Of course, each person is not merely somebody but a concrete individual, and the qualities that flesh out his individuality are, as I have just granted, the focus of some reflexive attitudes, such as self-esteem. But the fact that some reflexive attitudes bear on the person's distinctive features does not entail that all such attitudes must do so as well, because there isn't a single thing on which all reflexive attitudes must bear. Assuming otherwise inevitably leads to underrating the importance of being somebody. Who I am, in particular, matters for many reflexive purposes;

but if all that mattered for reflexive purposes was who I am, then it would no longer matter that (as Dr. Seuss so wisely put it) I am a Who.

In two of these essays, I argue that the importance of being somebody is registered in human emotions that are often analyzed by philosophers as concerned with personal distinctiveness – namely, love and shame.[10] The ordinary thought about love, reflected in most philosophical work on the subject, is that we love one another and want to be loved for who we are, in the sense of the phrase that I have just been using to invoke the qualities that differentiate us from others. Those same qualities are thought to be the basis for the negative emotion of shame.

I agree that personal distinctiveness is often in our sights when we feel shame, and always when we feel love, and I try to analyze precisely how it figures in these emotions. I argue, however, that its role is dependent on, and indeed unintelligible without, the role of bare personhood.

In my view, shame is anxiety that we feel about a threat to our socially recognized status as self-presenting creatures, a status that ultimately rests on the structure of a free will, in virtue of which we qualify as persons. This threat can arise from the exposure of particular discreditable qualities, of which we are then said to be ashamed, but it can also arise in the absence of any perceived demerit. We can therefore feel shame without there being anything about us of which we are ashamed. Such inchoate shame, I argue, is what we felt as children when pressed to perform for household guests, what we felt as adolescents when seen by our peers in the company of our parents, and what we feel as adults when subjected to various kinds of unwelcome attention ranging from racist epithets to excessive praise. These instances of shame are possible, I claim, because the object of anxiety in shame is not our distinctive personality but rather our social standing merely as self-presenting persons. Hence understanding shame requires acknowledging the importance of being somebody – in this case, the importance of being somebody to others.

Being somebody to others is also at the bottom of being loved, in my view. We often say that we want to be loved for who we are, again using that phrase which alludes to our particularities. Yet there is an ambiguity in the preposition that introduces this phrase – the 'for' in "for who we are." Personal love is an essentially experiential emotion: it's a response to someone with whom we are acquainted. We may admire or envy people of whom we have only heard or read, but we can love only the people

[10] "Love as a Moral Emotion" (Chapter 4) and "The Genesis of Shame" (Chapter 3).

we know. So there is no question but that personal qualities experienced directly or indirectly – appearance, manner, words, actions, traits of character, and so on – are essential to eliciting love. The question remains, however, whether the love that's elicited by these qualities is an emotion felt toward or about those same qualities. Loving someone is a way of valuing him, but are we valuing him on the basis of those qualities that elicit our love? What is it to love someone *for* the way he walks and talks, the way he holds his knife and sips his tea, or (more loftily) for who he is?

I argue that to love someone for the way he walks or the way he talks is not to value him on the basis of his gait or his elocution; it's rather to value his personhood as perceived through them. The qualities that elicit our love are the ones that make someone real to us as a person – the qualities that speak to us of a mind and heart within – and the value that is registered in our love is therefore the value of personhood. Wanting to be loved is like wanting to be found beautiful: it's a desire that others be struck by our particularities, but in a way that awakens them to a value in us that is universal.

This account of love, like my account of shame, is an attempt to cope with paradoxes inherent in our ordinary understanding of the emotion. In the case of shame, the paradox is what I have called "inchoate shame," in which we are shamed without there being anything that we are ashamed of. The paradox in the case of love is that, although it is a way of valuing people, it doesn't conform to any readily intelligible evaluations of them or value judgments about them.

Thus, I love my own wife and children as no others, and yet I know that other women and children are equally worthy of being loved by their own husbands and fathers. I do not honestly believe that mine are better or preferable; I don't even believe that they are better or preferable for me, as romantic soul-mates are supposed to be. Yet I treasure them above all. How can I value them especially without perceiving a special value in them? How can I believe that everyone, in deserving to be loved, deserves to be valued as special, if no one is especially deserving in this respect?

I am well aware that my view of love can be made to sound soft-headed and silly. Readers of my view sometimes think they can simply dismiss it with the remark that everyone knows love isn't like *that* – as if I did not already acknowledge the initial implausibility of the view. My response to these readers is that what "everybody knows" about love is deeply problematic, as most children begin to suspect by the age of five or six, once they are told, for example, that everyone is special. If what we are taught to find plausible about love made any sense upon reflection, then philosophizing about love would be as pointless as philosophizing about humor or the weather. In fact, the truth about love had better be something fairly implausible to us, or the emotion itself will turn out to be absurd. Those who aren't troubled by the conventional wisdom will see no need for anything else; but then they should see no need for philosophy, either.

My second line of argument against the doctrine of a single, all-purpose self – which I interpret, in turn, as a reaction against Kantian moral psychology – is to humanize the latter theory. At the center of Kantian moral psychology is the attitude of respect for the law, which many readers and teachers of Kant interpret as deference to a purely formal rule of conduct, or the abstract concept of such a rule. This interpretation makes the moral agent appear to be fixated on a mere abstraction, as if lost in impersonal thought; and one natural reaction against this alienated conception of the moral agent is to insist that his attention be focused, not on abstract rules, but on particular people instead. I argue that Kant actually holds an intermediate view, which portrays the moral agent as attending neither to rules nor to particular people but to an ideal of the person.

In particular, I argue that respect for the law is respect for an ideal image of oneself: it's what Freud would describe as admiration for an ego-ideal.[11] The ego-ideal in Kantian ethics is that rational configuration of the will which is represented in the Categorical Imperative. The point is that admiring an ego-ideal is not a way of getting lost in thought; it's a way of finding oneself. The Kantian moral agent can therefore be seen as less of a space cadet and more of a well-centered person.

What's more, the Kantian moral motive – respect for the law – can be seen as a motive that would naturally develop out of our experience as particular people among others. According to Freud, admiration for an ego-ideal arises from love for the real people after whom the ideal was fashioned – parents or their surrogates, in most cases. My account of love enables me to explain how the love that we felt for our parents in

---

[11] I argue for this interpretation of Kant in "Love as a Moral Emotion" (Chapter 4) and "The Voice of Conscience" (Chapter 5).

childhood might give rise to respect for the rational will as represented in the Kantian ego-ideal. Love for our parents was our response to their loving care, in which they treated us as self-standing ends – a configuration of their wills that we then incorporated into an ego-ideal, for which we continue to feel the admiration that amounts, in my view, to Kantian respect for the law. Kantian respect for the law can thus be learned from the love between parent and child, which Freud was surely right to identify as the textbook for our moral education.[12]

In this second line of argument, I consider myself to be interpreting what Kant actually says. In the third line of argument, I propose a revision of Kant's moral theory, as I understand it, thus making a strategic concession to the current trend.[13]

Kant insists that immoral action is always contrary to practical reason, and this insistence seems insensitive to the many ways in which people's peculiar interests and commitments can give them reason to act immorally. If practical reason required the moral course of action on every occasion, it would sometimes require people to step outside the personal characteristics that define who they are. Although morality may demand such self-transcendence (or self-betrayal), practical reason does not, and so I propose to modify the Kantian view.

What practical reason requires, I argue, is that people develop interests and commitments that would not give them reason to act immorally; but if they develop their interests and commitments irrationally, then they may find themselves with reason to act immorally, after all. Self-transcendence is possible in such cases, with the help of ideals of the sort that are embodied in the moral law, according to my interpretation of Kant; but self-transcendence in these cases always involves some irrationality, contrary to orthodox Kantian doctrine.[14]

Note that in this third line of argument, I again grant that 'self' sometimes refers to a constellation of traits that, as I have put it, define who someone is. These traits constitute a person's identity in that understanding of the term in which a person's identity is his *sense* of identity, as embodied in his self-conception. In this context, I agree with the currently

[12] This is the ultimate conclusion of "A Rational Superego" (Chapter 6).
[13] I argue for this revision in "Willing the Law" (Chapter 12) and "A Brief Introduction to Kantian Ethics" (Chapter 2).
[14] See "Motivation by Ideal" (Chapter 13).

prevailing view that the self is rich in particularities, the qualities that differentiate one person from another. I merely deny that what serves as the self in this context is what serves as the self in all contexts.

My advocacy for Kantian moral psychology in some of these essays may seem to conflict with my advocacy in others for my own, more naturalistic theory of agency. Yet I believe that these two conceptions of ourselves, though different in spirit and vocabulary, are at bottom compatible and will eventually submit to unification. Let me conclude this Introduction by speculating as to how they might be unified.

To begin with, my theory of agency adopts the Kantian strategy of deriving normative conclusions in ethics from premises in the philosophy of action. I look for rational pressures toward morality in the nature of reasons for acting; and I explore the nature of reasons by considering what would make acting for reasons an exercise of self-governance, or autonomy.

As I mentioned earlier, I identify the self of self-governance with the faculty of causal reasoning, by which a person understands the determinants of his behavior. When the person's causal reasoning helps to determine his behavior, his understanding of its determinants becomes inescapably reflexive, so that his behavior turns out to be determined by something inescapably conceived as self.

The way in which a person's causal reasoning helps to determine his behavior, in my view, is by inclining him toward behavior of which he has an incipient causal understanding – behavior that he is already prepared to understand as motivated by his desires, expressive of his beliefs, guided by his intentions, and so on. That he has those desires, beliefs, and intentions is reason for him to do the things that he could understand as partly determined by them, because reasons for doing something are considerations in light of which doing it would make sense.

There is nothing remotely like this conception of reasons for acting in Kant's moral psychology. Yet the considerations that qualify as reasons, according to this conception, meet the Kantian requirement of being recognizable from a universally accessible perspective – namely, the perspective of causal understanding. What's more, they belong to a mode of reasoning that abhors exceptions, as does practical reason, according to Kant. In one of the following essays, I try to show how the causal self-understanding that guides practical reason, as I conceive it, militates against making an exception of oneself, by way of something like a Kantian contradiction in conception.[15] In another essay, I consider how the same mode of reasoning militates against something like a Kantian contradiction in the will.[16]

Naturalism in moral psychology has traditionally been associated with Hume. But we can be naturalists without settling for Hume's impoverished conception of human nature. I believe – though I don't pretend to have shown – that we can be naturalists while preserving the moral and psychological richness of Kant.

---

[15] "The Centered Self" (Chapter 11).
[16] "Willing the Law" (Chapter 12).

2

A Brief Introduction to Kantian Ethics

The Overall Strategy

The overall strategy of Kant's moral theory is to derive the content of our obligations from the very concept of an obligation. Kant thought that we can figure out what we are obligated to do by analyzing the very idea of being obligated to do something. Where I am using the word 'obligation,' Kant used the German word *Pflicht*, which is usually translated into English as "duty." In Kant's vocabulary, then, the strategy of his moral theory is to figure out *what our duties are* by analyzing *what duty is*.

A duty, to begin with, is a practical requirement – a requirement to do something or not to do something. But there are many practical requirements that aren't duties. If you want to read Kant in the original, you have to learn German: there's a practical requirement. Federal law requires you to make yourself available to serve on a jury: there's another practical requirement. But these two requirements have features that clearly distinguish them from moral obligations or duties.

The first requires you to learn German only if you want to read Kant in the original. This requirement is consequently escapable: you can gain exemption from it by giving up the relevant desire. Give up wanting to

This essay is an attempt to reconstruct Kantian moral theory in terms intelligible to undergraduates who have not yet read Kant. In the interest of commending to students those parts of Kant's theory which seem right to me, I have changed parts that seem wrong, usually with an explanation of my reasons for doing so. I have also chosen not to complicate the essay with references either to the Kantian texts or to the secondary literature, although my debts to others are numerous and not always obvious. I am especially indebted to the work of Elizabeth Anderson, Michael Bratman, Stephen Darwall, Edward Hinchman, Christine Korsgaard, and Nishi Shah.

read Kant in the original and you can forget about this requirement, since it will no longer apply to you. The second requirement is also escapable, but it doesn't point to an escape hatch so clearly, since it doesn't contain an "if" clause stating a condition by which its application is limited. Nevertheless, its force as a requirement depends on the authority of a particular body – namely, the U.S. Government. Only if you are subject to the authority of the U.S. Government does this requirement apply to you. Hence you can escape the force of this requirement by escaping the authority of the Government: immunity to the authority of the body entails immunity to its requirements.

Now, Kant claimed – plausibly, I think – that our moral duties are inescapable in both of these senses. If we are morally obligated to do something, then we are obligated to do it no matter what our desires, interests, or aims may be. We cannot escape the force of the obligation by giving up some particular desires, interests, or aims. Nor can we escape the force of an obligation by escaping from the jurisdiction of some authority such as the Government. Kant expressed the inescapability of our duties by calling them **categorical** as opposed to **hypothetical**.

According to Kant, the force of moral requirements does not even depend on the authority of God. There is a simple argument for denying this dependence. If we were subject to moral requirements because they were imposed on us by God, the reason would have to be that we are subject to a requirement to do what God requires of us; and the force of this latter requirement, of obedience to God, could not itself depend on God's authority. (To require obedience to God on the grounds that God requires it would be viciously circular.) The requirement to obey God's requirements would therefore have to constitute a fundamental duty, on which all other duties depended; and so God's authority would not account for the force of our duties, after all. Since this argument will apply to any figure or body conceived as issuing requirements, we can conclude that the force of moral requirements must not depend on the authority of any figure or body by which they are conceived to have been issued.

The notion of authority is also relevant to requirements that are conditional on wants or desires. These requirements turn out to depend, not only on the presence of the relevant want or desire, but also on its authority.

Consider the hypothetical requirement "If you want to punch someone in the nose, you have to make a fist." One way in which you might escape the force of this requirement is by not wanting to punch anyone in the nose. But there is also another way. Even if you find yourself wanting to punch someone in the nose, you may regard that desire as nothing more than a passing fit of temper and hence as providing no reason for you to throw a punch. You will then regard your desire as lacking authority over you, in the sense that it shouldn't influence your choice of what to do. The mere psychological fact that you want to punch someone in the nose doesn't give application to the requirement that if you want to punch someone in the nose, you have to make a fist. You *do* want to punch someone in the nose, but you *don't* have to make a fist, because the relevant desire has no authority.

All of the requirements that Kant called hypothetical thus depend for their force on some external source of authority – on a desire to which they refer, for example, or an agency by which they have been issued. And these requirements lack the inescapability of morality because the authority behind them is always open to question. We can always ask why we should obey a particular source of authority, whether it be a desire, the U.S. Government, or even God. But the requirements of morality, being categorical, leave no room for questions about why we ought to obey them. Kant therefore concluded that moral requirements must not depend for their force on any external source of authority.

Kant reasoned that if moral requirements don't derive their force from any external authority, then they must carry their authority with them, simply by virtue of what they require. That's why Kant thought that he could derive the content of our obligations from the very concept of an obligation. The concept of an obligation, he argued, is the concept of an intrinsically authoritative requirement – a requirement that, simply by virtue of what it requires, forestalls any question as to its authority. So if we want to know what we're morally required to do, we must find something such that a requirement to do *it* would not be open to question. We must find something such that a requirement would carry authority simply by virtue of requiring that thing.

Thus far I have followed Kant fairly closely, but now I am going to depart from his line of argument. When Kant derives what's morally required of us from the authority that must inhere in that requirement, his derivation depends on various technicalities that I would prefer to skip. I shall therefore take a shortcut to Kant's ultimate conclusion.

As we have seen, requirements that depend for their force on some external source of authority turn out to be escapable because the authority behind them can be questioned. We can ask, "Why should I act on this desire?" or "Why should I obey the U.S. Government?" or even "Why should I obey God ?" And as we observed in the case of the desire to punch someone in the nose, this question demands a reason for acting. The authority we are questioning would be vindicated, in each case, by the production of a sufficient reason.

What this observation suggests is that any purported source of practical authority depends on reasons for obeying it – and hence on the authority of reasons. Suppose, then, that we attempted to question the authority of reasons themselves, as we earlier questioned other authorities. Where we previously asked "Why should I act on my desire?" let us now ask "Why should I act for reasons?" Shouldn't this question open up a route of escape from *all* requirements?

As soon as we ask why we should act for reasons, however, we can hear something odd in our question. To ask "Why should I?" is to demand a reason; and so to ask "Why should I act for reasons?" is to demand a reason for acting for reasons. This demand implicitly concedes the very authority that it purports to question – namely, the authority of reasons. Why would we demand a reason if we didn't envision acting for it? If we really didn't feel required to act for reasons, then a reason for doing so certainly wouldn't help. So there is something self-defeating about asking for a reason to act for reasons.

The foregoing argument doesn't show that the requirement to act for reasons is inescapable. All it shows is that this requirement cannot be escaped in a particular way: we cannot escape the requirement to act for reasons by insisting on reasons for obeying it. For all that, we still may not be required to act for reasons.

Yet the argument does more than close off one avenue of escape from the requirement to act for reasons. It shows that we are subject to this requirement if we are subject to any requirements at all. The requirement to act for reasons is the fundamental requirement, from which the authority of all other requirements is derived, since the authority of other requirements just consists in there being reasons for us to obey them. There may be nothing that is required of us; but if anything is required of us, then acting for reasons is required.

Hence the foregoing argument, though possibly unable to foreclose escape from the requirement to act for reasons, does succeed in raising the stakes. It shows that we cannot escape the requirement to act for reasons without escaping the force of requirements altogether. Either we think of ourselves as under the requirement to act for reasons, or we think of ourselves as under no requirements at all. And we cannot stand outside both ways of thinking and ask for reasons to enter into one or the other, since to ask for reasons is already to think of ourselves as subject to requirements.

The requirement to act for reasons thus seems to come as close as any requirement can to having intrinsic authority, in the sense of being authoritative by virtue of what it requires. This requirement therefore comes as close as any requirement can to being inescapable. But remember that inescapability was supposed to be the hallmark of a moral obligation or duty: it was the essential element in our *concept* of a duty, from which we hoped that the *content* of our duty could be deduced. What we have now deduced is that the requirement that bears this mark of morality is the requirement to act for reasons; and so we seem to have arrived at the conclusion that "Act for reasons" is the content of our duty. How can this be?

At this point, I can only sketch the roughest outline of an answer; I won't be able to supply any details until the end of this essay. Roughly, the answer is that to act for reasons is to act on the basis of considerations that would be valid for anyone in similar circumstances; whereas immoral behavior always involves acting on considerations whose validity for others we aren't willing to acknowledge. If we steal, for example, we take our own desire for someone else's property as a reason for making it our property instead – as if his desire for the thing weren't a reason for its being his property instead of ours. We thus take our desire as grounds for awarding ownership to ourselves, while denying that his desire is grounds for awarding ownership to him. Similarly, if we lie, we hope that others will believe what we say even though we don't believe it, as if what we say should count as a reason for them but not for us. Once again, we attempt to separate reasons for us from reasons for others. In doing so, we violate the very concept of a reason, which requires that a reason for one be a reason for all. Hence we violate the requirement, "Act for reasons."

So much for a rough outline of Kant's answer. Before I can supply the details, I'll need to explore further what we feel ourselves required to do in being required to act for reasons. And in order to explore this requirement, I'll turn to an example that will seem far removed from morality.

Reasons that are Temporally Constant

Suppose that you stay in shape by swimming laps two mornings a week, when the pool is open to recreational swimmers. But suppose that when your alarm goes off this morning, you just don't feel like facing the sweaty locker room, the dank showers, the stink of chlorine, and the shock of diving into the chilly pool. You consider skipping your morning swim just this once.

(If you don't exercise regularly, you may have to substitute another example for mine. Maybe the exceptions that you consider making "just for this once" are exceptions to your diet, your drinking limit, or your schedule for finishing your schoolwork.)

When you are tempted to make an exception to your program of exercise, you are likely to search for an excuse – some reason for staying in bed rather than going off to the pool. You sniffle a few times, hoping for some signs of congestion; you lift your head to look out the window, hoping for a blizzard; you try to remember your calendar as showing some special commitment for later in the day. Excuse-making of this sort seems perfectly natural, but it ought to seem odd. Why do you need a reason for not doing something that you don't feel like doing?

This question can be understood in several different ways. It may ask why you don't already have a good enough reason for not swimming, consisting in the fact that you just don't feel like it. To this version of the question, the answer is clear. If not feeling like it were a good enough reason for not swimming, then you'd almost never manage to get yourself into the pool, since the mornings on which you're supposed to swim almost always find you not feeling like it. Given that you want to stay in shape by swimming, you can't accept "I don't feel like it" as a valid reason, since it would completely undermine your program of exercise. Similarly, you can't accept "That would taste good" as a reason for going over your limit of drinks, or you wouldn't really have a limit, after all.

Why not accept "I don't feel like it" as a reason on this occasion while resolving to reject it on all others? Again the answer is clear. If a consideration counts as a reason for acting, then it counts as a reason whenever it is true. And on almost any morning, it's true that you don't feel like swimming.

Yet if a reason is a consideration that counts as a reason whenever it's true, then why not dispense with reasons so defined? Why do you feel compelled to act for *that* sort of consideration? Since you don't feel like swimming, you might just roll over and go back to sleep, without bothering to find some fact about the present occasion from which you're willing to draw similar implications whenever it is true. How odd, to skip exercise in order to sleep and then to lose sleep anyway over finding a reason not to exercise!

Kant offered an explanation for this oddity. His explanation was that acting for reasons is essential to being a person, something to which you unavoidably aspire. In order to be a person, you must have an approach to the world that is sufficiently coherent and constant to qualify as a single, continuing point-of-view. And part of what gives you a single, continuing point-of-view is your acceptance of particular considerations as having the force of reasons whenever they are true.

We might be tempted to make this point by saying that you *are* a unified, persisting person and hence that you *do* approach practical questions from a point-of view framed by constant reasons. But this way of making the point wouldn't explain why you feel compelled to act for reasons; it would simply locate acting for reasons in a broader context, as part of what makes you a person. One of Kant's greatest insights, however, is that a unified, persisting person is something that you *are* because it is something that you *aspire to be*. Antecedently to this aspiration, you are merely aware that you are *capable* of being a person. But any creature aware that it is capable of being a person, in Kant's view, is *ipso facto* capable of appreciating the value of being a person and is therefore ineluctably drawn toward personhood.

The value of being a person in the present context is precisely that of attaining a perspective that transcends that of your current, momentary self. Right now, you would rather sleep than swim, but you also know that if you roll over and sleep, you will wake up wishing that you had swum instead. Your impulse to decide on the basis of reasons is, at bottom, an impulse to transcend these momentary points-of-view, by attaining a single, constant perspective that can subsume both of them. It's like the impulse to attain a higher vantage point that overlooks the restricted standpoints on the ground below. This higher vantage point is neither your current perspective of wanting to sleep, nor your later perspective of wishing you had swum, but a timeless perspective from which you can reflect on now-wanting-this and later-wishing-that, a perspective from which you can attach constant practical implications to these considerations and come to a stable, all-things-considered judgment.

If you want to imagine what it would be like never to attain a continuing point-of-view, imagine being a cat. A cat feels like going out and meows to go out; feels like coming in and meows to come in; feels like going out again and meows to go out; and so on, all day long. The cat cannot think, "I have things to do outside and things to do inside, so how should I organize my day?" But when you, a person, find yourself to-ing and fro-ing in this manner, you feel an impulse to find a constant perspective on the question when you should "to" and when you should "fro."

This impulse is unavoidable as soon as the availability of the more encompassing vantage point appears. As soon as you glimpse the possibility of attaining a constant perspective from which to reflect on and adjudicate among your shifting preferences, you are drawn toward that perspective, as you would be drawn toward the top of a hill that commanded a terrain through which you had been wandering. To attain that standpoint, in this case, would be to attain the single, continuing point-of-view that would constitute the identity of a person. To see the possibility of attaining it is therefore to see the possibility of being a person; and seeing that possibility unavoidably leads you to aspire toward it.

Of course, there is a sense of the word 'person' that applies to any creature capable of grasping the possibility of attaining the single, continuing perspective of a fully unified person. One must already be a person in the former, minimal sense in order to aspire toward personhood in the latter. I interpret Kant as having used words like 'person' in both senses, to denote what we already are and what we consequently aspire to become.

This Kantian thought is well expressed – believe it or not – by a word in Yiddish. In Yiddish, to call someone a *Mensch* is to say that he or she is a good person – solid, centered, true-blue.[1] But *Mensch* is just the German word for "person" or "human being," like the English "man" in its gender-neutral usage. Thus, a *Mensch* in the German sense is merely a creature capable of being a *Mensch* in the Yiddish.

To be a solid, centered human being of the sort that Yiddishers call a *Mensch* entails occupying a unified, persisting point-of-view defined by a constant framework of reasons. But to be a human being at all, according to Kant, is to grasp and hence aspire toward the possibility of attaining personhood in this sense. Hence the imperative that compels you to look for generally valid reasons is an imperative that is naturally felt by all *Menschen*: the imperative "Be a *Mensch*."

---

[1] I say more about what it is to be a *Mensch* in "The Centered Self," (Chapter 11).

The requirement "Be a *Mensch*" already sounds like a moral requirement, but I have introduced it by way of an example about exercise, which
we don't usually regard as a moral obligation. My example may therefore
seem ill suited to illustrate a requirement that's supposedly fundamental
to morality. On second thought, however, we may have to reconsider what
sort of a requirement we are dealing with.

If you do roll over and go back to sleep, in my example, you will be left
with an emotion that we normally associate with morality – namely, guilt.
You feel guilty when you shirk exercise, go over your drinking limit, put
off working, or otherwise make an exception "just for this once." Indeed,
your motives for seeking a reason on such occasions include the desire to
avoid the sense of guilt, by avoiding the sense of having made a singular
exception.

There is the possibility that the word 'guilt' is ambiguous, and that
self-reproaches about shirking exercise do not manifest the same emotion as self-reproaches about lying or cheating. Alternatively, there is the
possibility that the guilt you feel about shirking exercise is genuine but
unwarranted. I would reject both of these hypotheses, however. If you go
for your usual swim but stop a few laps short of your usual distance, you
might well accuse yourself of cheating; if asked whom you were cheating,
you would probably say that you were cheating yourself. Insofar as you
owe it to yourself to swim the full distance, your sense of guilt may be not
only genuine but perfectly appropriate.

Kant believed that moral obligations can be owed not only to others
but also to oneself. Defenders of Kant's moral theory often seem embar-
rassed by his notion of having obligations to oneself, which is said to be
odd or even incoherent. But I think that Kant's concept of an obligation
is the concept of something that can be owed to oneself, and that any
interpretation under which obligations to self seem odd must be a misinterpretation. That's why I have begun my account of Kantian ethics with
self-regarding obligations.

Thus far, I have explained how the natural aspiration toward a stable
point-of-view is both an aspiration to be a person, in the fullest sense,
and a motive to act on considerations that have the same practical implications whenever they are true – that is, to act for reasons. I have thus
explained how the felt requirement to be a person can deter you from
cheating on your drinking limit or program of exercise and, in that minor
respect, impel you to be a *Mensch*. What remains to be explained is how
the same requirement can impel you to be a *Mensch* by eschewing other,
interpersonal forms of cheating.

Reasons that are Universally Shared[2]

In Kant's view, being a person consists in being a rational creature, both cognitively and practically. And Kant thought that our rationality gives us a glimpse of – and hence an aspiration toward – a perspective even more inclusive than that of our persisting individual selves. Rational creatures have access to a shared perspective, from which they not only see the same things but can also see the visibility of those things to all rational creatures.

Consider, for example, our capacity for arithmetic reasoning. Anyone who adds 2 and 2 sees, not just that the sum is 4, but also that anyone who added 2 and 2 would see that it's 4, and that such a person would see this, too, and so on. The facts of elementary arithmetic are thus common knowledge among all possible reasoners, in the sense that every reasoner knows them, and knows that every reasoner knows them, and knows that every reasoner knows that every reasoner knows them, and so on.

As arithmetic reasoners, then, we have access to a perspective that is constant not only across time but also between persons. We can compute the sum of 2 and 2 *once and for all*, in the sense that we would only get the same answer on any other occasion; and each of us can compute the sum of 2 and 2 *one for all*, in the sense that the others would only get the same answer. What's more, the universality of our perspective on the sum of 2 and 2 is evident to each of us from within that very perspective. In computing the sum of 2 and 2, we are aware of computing it *for all*, from a perspective that's shared by all arithmetic reasoners. In this sense, our judgment of the sum is authoritative, because it speaks for the judgment of all.

This shared perspective is like a vantage point overlooking the individual perspectives of reasoners, a standpoint from which we not only see what everyone sees but also see everyone seeing it. And once we glimpse the availability of this vantage point, we cannot help but aspire to attain it. We are no longer satisfied with estimating or guessing the sum of two numbers, given the possibility of computing it once for all: we are ineluctably drawn to the perspective of arithmetic reason.

Note that the aspect of arithmetic judgments to which we are drawn in this case resembles the authority that we initially regarded as definitive of moral requirements: it's the authority of being inescapable. We

---

[2] For further elaboration on the material in this section and the next, see "The Voice of Conscience," (Chapter 5).

can compute the sum of 2 and 2 once for all because the answer we reach is the answer that would be reached from any perspective and is therefore inescapable. We can approach the sum of 2 and 2 from wherever we like, and we will always arrive at the same answer. The case of arithmetic reasoning shows that inescapability can in fact appeal to us, because it is the feature in virtue of which judgments constitute a stable and all-encompassing point-of-view. Perhaps, then, the authority of moral judgments, which consists in their inescapability, can appeal to us in similar fashion, by offering an attractive vantage point of some kind.

But what does arithmetic reasoning have to do with acting for reasons? Well, suppose that the validity of reasons for acting were also visible from a perspective shared by all reasoners – by all practical reasoners, that is. In that case, our aspirations toward personhood would draw us toward the perspective of practical reason as well.

Indeed, that may be the perspective toward which you were being drawn when you felt compelled to find a reason for not exercising. Your immediate concern was to find a set of considerations whose validity as reasons would remain constant through fluctuations in your preferences; but you would also have regarded those considerations as constituting reasons for other people as well, insofar as they were true of those people. In accepting an incipient cold as a reason to skip swimming, you would have regarded it as something that would count as a reason for anyone to skip swimming, in circumstances like yours. What you were seeking may thus have been considerations that could count as reasons not only for you, whenever they were true of you, but for other agents as well.

There is one important difference between practical and arithmetic reasoning, however. When you searched for reasons not to exercise this morning, no considerations just struck you as the ones that would strike any practical reasoner, in the way that 4 strikes you as being the answer that would strike any reasoner adding 2 and 2. Rather, you had to try out different considerations as reasons; and you tried them out by testing whether you would be willing to have them strike you as reasons whenever they were true. That's how you tested and then rejected "I don't feel like it" as a reason for not exercising.

This feature of the case suggests that you may not have access to a pre-existing perspective shared by all reasoners in practical matters as you do in arithmetic. Apparently, however, you were trying to *construct* such a perspective, by asking whether you would be willing for various considerations to count as reasons whenever they were true, as if their reason-giving force, or validity, were accessible from a shared perspective. You asked, "What if 'I don't feel like it' were generally valid as a reason for not exercising?" – as if you could choose whether or not to enshrine the validity of this consideration in a constant perspective of practical reasoning.

There is a sense in which you could indeed enshrine the validity of this consideration in a constant *individual* perspective. For if you had taken something as a sufficient reason for not exercising on this occasion, you would later have remembered doing so, and your deliberations on subsequent occasions might then have been guided by the precedent. Having once accepted a consideration as a reason for not exercising, you might later have felt obliged to accept it again, in other situations where it was true. Even so, however, you aren't capable of enshrining the validity of a consideration in a perspective that would be shared by all practical reasoners, since your taking something as a reason would not influence the deliberations of others as it would the deliberations of your future selves. Although you can construct a *temporally constant* perspective from which to conduct your own practical reasoning, you cannot construct a *universally shared* perspective.

And yet constructing a universally shared perspective of practical reasoning is precisely what Kant said that you must regard yourself as doing when you decide how to act. Kant expressed this requirement as follows: "Act only on a maxim that you can at the same time will to be universal law."

The clearest example of willing a maxim to be universal law – the clearest example that I know of, at least – is the train of thought that you undertake when considering whether to make an exception "just for this once," such as an exception to your diet or program of exercise. You think of potential reasons, in the form of true considerations such as "That would taste good" or "I don't feel like it," but then you realize that you aren't willing to grant these considerations validity as reasons whenever they are true, since doing so would completely undermine your regimen. Having found that you cannot consistently will these considerations to be generally valid as reasons, you refuse to act on them, as if in obedience to Kant's requirement.

According to Kant, however, you are required to act on considerations whose validity as reasons you can consistently will to be evident, not just to yourself on other occasions when they are true, but to other practical reasoners of whom they may be true as well. You are thus required to act only on considerations whose validity you could willingly enshrine in a universally accessible perspective of practical reasoning. That's what Kant meant by acting only on a maxim that you could will to be universal law.

Yet the force of Kant's proposed requirement remains elusive. Even if I have managed to direct your attention to your own sense of being required to construct a temporally constant perspective of practical reasoning, that requirement presupposes the possibility of your constructing such a perspective – a possibility that depends, in turn, on ties of memory between your current decision-making and your decision-making in the future. As we have seen, however, you aren't capable of constructing a perspective of practical reasoning that would be universally accessible to all reasoners. So how can you feel required to construct one?

I'm going to skip over this question for the moment, in order to describe how Kant's moral theory reaches its conclusions. I'll return to the question later, eventually offering two alternative answers to it. First, however, I want to show how substantive moral conclusions can issue from Kant's theory.

Two Examples

Suppose that we were required to act only on considerations whose validity as reasons we could willingly enshrine in a universally accessible perspective of practical reasoning, just as we feel required to act only on considerations whose validity we could enshrine in a temporally constant perspective. This requirement would decisively rule out some considerations. Here is an example from Kant's *Critique of Practical Reason*:

Suppose, for example, that I have made it my maxim to increase my fortune by every safe means. Now, I have a deposit in my hands, the owner of which is dead and has left no writing about it. This is just the case for my maxim. I desire then to know whether that maxim can also hold good as a universal practical law. I apply it, therefore, to the present case, and ask whether it could take the form of a law, and consequently whether I can by my maxim at the same time give such a law as this, that everyone may deny a deposit of which no one can produce a proof. I at once become aware that such a principle, viewed as a law, would annihilate itself, because the result would be that there would be no deposits.[3]

In this passage, Kant imagines considering whether a consideration such as "I want the money" can count as a reason for denying the receipt of a deposit from someone who has died without leaving any record of it.

---

[3] Immanuel Kant, *Critique of Practical Reason*, trans. by Lewis White Beck (Indianapolis: Bobbs Merrill, 1956), 27.

Much as you asked whether you were willing to make "I don't feel like it" valid as a reason for not exercising on all occasions when it is true, Kant asks whether he is willing to make "I want the money" valid as a reason for all trustees of whom it is true. Kant says, "The result would be that there would be no deposits." Why not?

The answer is that the validity of reasons for denying unrecorded deposits would have to be common knowledge among all practical reasoners. If a trustee's desire to keep a depositor's money were a valid reason for denying its receipt, then the validity of that reason would have to be known to prospective depositors, who have access to the common knowledge of practical reasoners, and who would then be deterred from making any deposits, in the first place. A trustee can therefore see that he would never receive a single deposit if wanting to keep it would be a valid reason for him to deny its receipt, just as the drinker sees that he wouldn't have a limit if his thirst were a valid reason for exceeding it.

A trustee can therefore see that if "I want the money" were a valid reason for denying the receipt of deposits, there would be no deposits whose receipt he could deny. And a consideration can hardly be a reason for an action that would be rendered unavailable by the validity of that very reason. "I want the money" couldn't be a universally accessible reason for defaulting because, if it were, there would be no opportunities for defaulting. And since it couldn't be a universally accessible reason, it isn't valid as a reason for defaulting, after all.

Actually, this example is an instance of a larger class, since defaulting on the return of a deposit would unavoidably involve lying, and lying also violates the fundamental requirement "Act for reasons." So let's examine this larger class of examples.

To lie is intentionally to tell someone a falsehood. When we tell something to someone, we act with a particular kind of communicative intention: we say or write it to him with the intention of giving him grounds for believing it. Indeed, we intend to give him grounds for belief precisely by manifesting this very communicative intention in our speech or writing. We intend that the person acquire grounds for believing what we say by recognizing that we are acting with the intention of conveying those grounds.

Now, suppose that our wanting to give someone grounds for believing something constituted sufficient reason for telling it to him, whether or not we believed it ourselves. In that case, the validity of this reason would be common knowledge among all reasoners, including him. He would therefore be able to see that, in wanting to give him grounds for believing the thing, as was manifest in our communicative action, we already had sufficient reason for telling it to him, whether or not we believed it. And if he could see that we had sufficient reason for telling it even if we ourselves didn't believe it, then our telling it would give him no grounds for believing it, either. Why should he believe what we tell him if we need no more reason for telling him than the desire, already manifest in the telling, to give him grounds for believing it? So if our wanting to give him grounds for believing something were sufficient reason for telling it to him, then telling him wouldn't accomplish the result that we wanted, and wanting that result wouldn't be a reason for telling him, after all. Wanting to convey grounds for belief can't be a sufficient reason for telling, then, because if it were, it would not be a reason at all.

I introduced these examples by asking you to imagine that you could construct a universally accessible perspective of practical reasoning, so that you could be required to act only on considerations whose validity you could enshrine in such a perspective. Yet it has now turned out that there already *is* such a perspective – or, at least, the beginnings of one – and it hasn't been constructed by anyone. For we have stumbled on one kind of practical result that anyone can see, and can see that anyone can see, and so on.

The kind of practical result that we have found to be universally accessible has the following form: that the validity of some putative reason for acting could not be universally accessible. The validity of "I want the money" as a reason for denying receipt of a deposit, or the validity of "I want him to believe it" as a reason for telling something to someone, could not be universally accessible, any more than the validity of "That would taste good" as a reason for going over your limit of drinks. The fact that the validity of these reasons could not be universally accessible – *this* fact is already universally accessible to practical reasoners, any of whom can perform the reasoning by which it has come to light.

Thus, the notion of sharing a perspective with all practical reasoners is not a pipedream, after all. You already share a perspective with all practical reasoners to this extent: *that it is common knowledge among all reasoners that the validity of certain reasons for acting could not be common knowledge among all reasoners.* This item of common knowledge constitutes a universally accessible constraint on what can count as a reason for acting and hence what can satisfy a requirement to act for reasons. A requirement to act for reasons would forbid acting on the basis of considerations whose validity as reasons could not be common knowledge among all reasoners, and in the case of some considerations, this impossibility is itself common knowledge.

Let me review the argument to this point, which can now be seen to implement the overall strategy of deriving the content of our duties from the very concept of a duty. We began with the idea that moral requirements must be inescapable, which led to the idea that they must be intrinsically authoritative, in the sense of having authority over us simply by virtue of what they require. We then found a requirement that came as close as possible to having such authority – the requirement to act for reasons, which cannot coherently be questioned and must be presupposed by all other practical requirements.

Next we saw how the requirement to act for reasons is experienced in ordinary life, when one looks for an exemption from some regular regimen or policy. In this example, the requirement to act for reasons is experienced as an impulse to act on a consideration from which one is willing to draw the same consequences whenever it is true, an impulse that militates against cheating oneself. And we found such an impulse intelligible as part of one's aspiration toward the unified, persisting point-of-view that makes for a fully integrated person.

Our next step was to observe that rational creatures can attain not only unified individual perspectives but a single perspective that is shared, in the sense that its deliverances are common knowledge among them. And with the help of examples drawn from Kant, we saw that a requirement to act on considerations whose validity was common knowledge would amount to a ban on cheating others. What remains to be explained is how the requirement to act for reasons in this sense is experienced in ordinary life and whether it, too, can be understood as part of the aspiration to be a person.

The Idea of Freedom[4]

In order to answer this remaining question, we must return to a problem that we considered earlier and set aside – the question why we feel compelled to think of ourselves as constructing a universally accessible framework of reasons for acting. We can't actually build a universally accessible

---

4 The material in this section and the next is developed further in "Willing the Law," (Chapter 12).

framework of reasons, although we do enjoy universal access to the fact that some reasons, in particular, couldn't be built into such a framework. The question is why we feel compelled not to act on reasons that couldn't be built into something that isn't for us to build, in the first place.

Kant's answer to this question was that in order to act, we must conceive of ourselves as free; and that in order to conceive of ourselves as free, we must conceive of ourselves as acting on reasons that owe their authority to us. Considerations have authority as reasons only if they have the sort of validity that is universally accessible to all reasoners; but we won't be free in acting on them, Kant believed, if they have simply been dictated to us from a universal perspective in which we have no say. We must think of them as reasons on which we ourselves confer authority, by introducing them into that perspective.

I think that Kant was simply wrong about the idea of freedom, insofar as he thinks that it requires us to be the source of the authority in our own reasons for acting. Roughly speaking, I think that we cannot be guided by reasons whose only authority is that with which we ourselves have endowed them.

To endow reasons with authority, as I have now conceived it, would be to *make* their status as reasons common knowledge among all reasoners – a feat that is simply beyond our power. More importantly, it's a feat that we cannot help but *think* is beyond our power. If we thought that something's being a reason could become common knowledge among all reasoners only by dint of our making it so, then we would have no hope of its ever being so. Hence if we thought that reasons owed their authority to us, we would have no hope of their ever having authority.

Why can't reasons owe their authority to us? The answer is that endowing reasons with authority would entail making their validity common knowledge among all reasoners. And if we could promote reasons to the status of being common knowledge among all reasoners, then we should equally be able to demote them from that status – in which case, the status wouldn't amount to rational authority. The point of a reason's being common knowledge among all reasoners, remember, is that there is then no way of evading it, no matter how we shift our point-of-view. No amount of rethinking will make such a reason irrelevant, because its validity as a reason is evident from every perspective. But if we could decide what is to be common knowledge among all thinkers, then a reason's being common knowledge would not entail its being inescapable, since we could also decide that it wasn't to be common knowledge, after all. Our power to construct a universally accessible framework of reasons would therefore undermine the whole point of having one.

I think that Kant's mistake was to claim that we must act under the idea of **freedom**; what he should have said, I think, is that we must act under the idea of **autonomy**. Let me explain the difference between these concepts.

'Autonomy' is derived from the Greek word for self-rule or self-governance. Our behavior is autonomous when it is self-governed, in the sense that we ourselves are in control of it; it is not autonomous – or, as Kant would say, it is **heteronomous** – when it is controlled by something other than ourselves. To say that behavior is controlled by something other than ourselves is not to say that it is controlled from outside our bodies or our minds. A sneeze or a hiccup is not under our control; neither is a startle or an impulsive cry of pain; but all of these heteronomous behaviors originate within us. What makes them heteronomous is that, while originating *within*, they don't originate *with us*: they aren't fully our doing. Only the behaviors that are fully our doing qualify as autonomous actions.

The fact that we act autonomously doesn't necessarily entail that we have free will – not, at least, in the sense that Kant had in mind. In Kant's view, our having free will would require not only that we sit behind the wheel of our behavior, so to speak, but also that we face more than one direction in which it would be causally possible that we steer it, so that our future course is not pre-determined. One might suspect that if our future course *were* pre-determined, then we wouldn't really be in control of our behavior, and hence that autonomy really does require freedom. Yet there is a way for us to follow a pre-determined course and yet steer that course in a meaningful sense. Our course might be pre-determined by the fact that there are reasons for us to do particular things and that we are rationally responsive to reasons. So long as we are responding to reasons, we remain autonomous, whether or not those reasons pre-determine what we do.

Consider here our autonomy with respect to our beliefs. When we consider the sum of 2 and 2, we ourselves draw the conclusion that it is 4. The thought $2 + 2 = 4$ is not dictated to us by anyone else; it is not due to an involuntary mental association, not forced on our minds by an obsession or fixed in our minds by a mental block; in short, it isn't the intellectual equivalent of a sneeze or a hiccup. When we consider the sum of 2 and 2, we make our own way to the answer 4. And yet there is no other answer that we could arrive at, given that we are arithmetically competent and that, as any reasoner can see, the sum of 2 and 2 is 4. So when we consider the sum of 2 and 2, we are pre-determined to arrive at the answer 4, but to arrive there autonomously, under our own intellectual steam. We aren't free to conclude that $2 + 2$ is 5, and yet we are autonomous in concluding that it is 4.

Perhaps, then, we can steer our behavior as we steer our thoughts, in directions that are pre-determined, not by exogenous forces, but by our rational ability to do what there is reason for doing, just as we think what there is reason for thinking. In that case, we could have autonomy without necessarily having free will.

Kant himself identified what is special about behavior that is ratio-nally necessitated. Whereas heteronomous behavior is determined by antecedent events under a law of nature, he observed, autonomous behav-ior is determined by *our conception* of a law. A law, in this context, is just a practical requirement of the sort with which this analysis of duty began, a requirement specifying something that we must do. What makes our behavior autonomous is that we do it, not just because our doing it is necessitated by prior events, but because we realize that doing it is required – a realization that constitutes our conception of a law, in Kant's terms. Our recognition of a practical requirement, and our responsive-ness to that recognition, is what makes the resulting action attributable to us, as our doing: it's what gets us into the act.

Kant thus explained why acting for reasons makes us autonomous. Acting for reasons makes us autonomous because "Act for reasons" is the ultimate requirement lying behind all other practical requirements, whose authority depends on there being reasons to obey them. When-ever our behavior is determined by our conception of law – that is, by our realization that some action is required – we are being governed at bottom by a recognition of reasons, either constituting or backing up that requirement.

Kant thought that being determined by our recognition of a prac-tical requirement, on the one hand, and being determined by prior events under a law of nature, on the other, are mutually exclusive alter-natives, at least in the sense that we cannot conceive of ourselves as being determined in both ways at once. (In fact, he thought that we can per-haps *be* determined in both ways at once but that we can't *conceive* of being so, because we can't reconcile these two modes of determination in our minds.) But I think that being determined by our recognition of a practical requirement can itself be conceived as a causal process, governed by natural laws. I express this possibility by saying that we can conceive of ourselves as autonomous without having to conceive of ourselves as free.

Because Kant thought that we cannot conceive of ourselves as autonomous without also conceiving of ourselves as free, he insisted that we must not conceive of practical requirements as externally dictated. That is, we must not find ourselves confronted with inexorable reasons for doing things, in the way that we find ourselves confronted with an inexorable answer to the calculation of $2 + 2$; for if we did, our action would be predetermined, and we wouldn't be free to choose it, just as we aren't free to choose a sum for $2 + 2$. Kant thought that we must regard the balance of reasons for acting as being up to us in a way that the sum of 2 and 2 is not.

Kant's insistence that we act under the idea of freedom thus led him to insist that we conceive of ourselves as constructing rather than merely finding a universally accessible framework of reasons for acting. As I have explained, I think that our constructing reasons would deprive them of the authority that universal accessibility is meant to provide. But as I have also explained, I think that Kant's insistence on our constructing them is unnecessary, because we can act under the idea of autonomy, without any pretensions of being free.

Even if we need only think of ourselves as autonomous when we act, we will still be required to act for reasons, since autonomy consists in being determined by authoritative considerations. The requirement to act for reasons can thus be felt to arise from the aspiration to be a person in a more profound form. Our earlier discussion directed our attention toward the general region of experience where the requirement to act for reasons can be found, but it didn't identify the fundamental manifestation of that requirement. We saw that the requirement to act for reasons can be felt to arise from our aspiration to be a person, but we traced it to a fairly specific instance of that aspiration, consisting in our aspiration toward a temporally constant point-of-view. And then we found that this specific aspiration cannot account for the moral force of the requirement in interpersonal cases. The present discussion suggests that the fundamental manifestation of the requirement to act for reasons is a different form of the aspiration to be a person: it's the aspiration toward autonomy. We feel required to act for reasons insofar as we aspire to be persons by being the originators of our own behavior.

Contradictions in the Will

Replacing Kant's references to freedom with references to autonomy needn't alter our analysis of the foregoing examples. The aspiration toward autonomy yields a requirement to act for reasons, and this require- ment will forbid us to act on considerations whose practical implications couldn't be common knowledge, as in the cases of cheating analyzed earlier.

Yet there are other cases in which Kant derived moral conclusions in a way that depends on the very aspect of freedom by which it differs from what I have called autonomy. In these examples, what rules out some considerations as reasons for acting, according to Kant, is not that they couldn't be universally accessible, as in the case of our grounds for stealing or lying, but rather that we couldn't consistently *make* them universally accessible. It is precisely our inability to build these considerations into a universally accessible framework of reasons that prevents them from being reasons, according to Kant. Yet our inability to build some consid- erations into a universally accessible framework of reasons would prevent them from being reasons only if such a framework depended on us for its construction – which is what I have just been denying, in contesting Kant's view of freedom. My disagreement with Kant on the subject of freedom therefore threatens to escalate into a disagreement about which consid- erations can be reasons and, from there, into a disagreement about what is morally required.

The clearest cases of this kind have the form of prisoners' dilemmas.[5] Prisoners' dilemmas get their name from a philosophical fiction in which two people – say, you and I – are arrested on suspicion of having com- mitted a crime together. The police separate us for interrogation and offer us similar plea bargains: if either gives evidence against the other, his sentence (whatever it otherwise would have been) will be shortened by one year, and the other's sentence will be lengthened by two. The expected benefits give each of us reason to testify against the other. The unfortunate result is that each sees his sentence shortened by one year in payment for his own testimony, but lengthened by two because of the other's testimony; and so we both spend one more year in jail than we would have if both had kept silent.

---

[5] I discuss prisoners' dilemmas further in "The Centered Self," (Chapter 11). See note 2 of that chapter for an explanation of how to coordinate it with what I say about prisoners' dilemmas here.

Let me pause to apologize for a misleading feature of this story. Because the characters in the story are criminals, and the choice confronting them is whether to tell the whole truth and nothing but the truth, turning state's evidence may seem to be the option that's favored by morality. But this story serves as a model for every case in which the choice is whether to join some beneficial scheme of cooperation, such as rendering aid or keeping commitments to one another. There are parts of morality whose basic point is to enjoin cooperation in cases of this kind, and philosophers use the prisoners' dilemma as a model for those parts of morality. In order to understand philosophical uses of the prisoners' dilemma, then, we have to remember that cooperating with one's fellow prisoner represents the moral course in this philosophical fiction, because it is the course of mutual aid and commitment.

Prisoners' dilemmas are ripe for Kantian moral reasoning because the two participants are in exactly similar situations, which provide them with exactly similar reasons. When each of us sees the prospect of a reduced sentence as a reason to testify against the other, he must also see that the corresponding prospect is visible to the other as a reason for doing like-wise, and indeed that the validity of these reasons is common knowledge between us.

Given that our reasons must be common knowledge, however, I ought to wish that the incentives offered to me were insufficient reason for testifying against you, since the incentives offered to you would then be insufficient reason for testifying against me, and both of us would remain silent, to our mutual advantage. And you must also wish that the incentives were insufficient reason for testifying against me, so that I would likewise find them insufficient for testifying against you. Furthermore, each of us must realize that the other shares the wish that the incentives were insufficient reason for turning against the other. The following is therefore common knowledge between us: we agree in wishing that what was common knowledge between us was that our reasons for turning against one another were insufficient.

Here, the power to construct a shared framework of reasons would cer-tainly come in handy, since you and I would naturally converge on which reasons to incorporate into that framework and which reasons to exclude. The power to construct a shared framework of reasons would thus trans-form our predicament, in a way that it would not have transformed the cases considered earlier.

In the case of lying, for example, we found that it was not just undesirable but downright impossible that our desire for someone to believe
something should be a sufficient reason for telling it to him. This desire
couldn't possibly be such a reason, we concluded, because its being a
reason would entail common knowledge of its being one, which in turn
would ensure that it wasn't a reason, after all. This conclusion did not
depend on the assumption that we could in any way affect the rational
import of wanting someone to believe something – that we could elevate
it to the status of a reason or demote it from that status. Even if reasons
were handed down to us from a universally accessible perspective that we
took no part in constructing, we would know in advance that the deliverances of that perspective would not include, as a sufficient reason for
telling something to someone, the mere desire that he believe it.

Hence our conclusion about lying is not at all threatened by the doubts
outlined earlier about the Kantian doctrine of freedom. But those doubts
do threaten the prospect of drawing any Kantian conclusions about the
prisoners' dilemma. For whereas some reasons for lying are rendered
impossible by the necessity of their being common knowledge, our reasons for turning against one another in the prisoners' dilemma are rendered merely undesirable. And if reasons are indeed handed down to
us from a universally accessible perspective that we take no part in constructing, then we have no guarantee against being handed undesirable
reasons, even if they were universally undesirable. Only if we construct
the shared framework of reasons can we expect it to exclude undesirable reasons, such as our reasons for turning against one another in the
prisoners' dilemma.

Our proposed reasons for lying are ruled out by what Kant called a **contradiction in conception**. This contradiction prevents us from conceiving
that the desire for someone to believe something should be a sufficient
reason for telling it to him. Kant thought that our proposed reasons for
turning against one another in the prisoners' dilemma can also be ruled
out, not because a contradiction would be involved in their *conception*,
but rather because a contradiction would be involved in their *construction* – a contradiction of the sort that Kant called a **contradiction in the
will**. Specifically, building these reasons into the universally accessible
framework would contradict our desire that what was common knowledge between us were reasons for cooperating instead. But if the framework of reasons is not for us to construct, then contradictions in the will
are no obstacle to anything's being a reason, and half of Kantian ethics is

in danger of failure. Securing Kantian ethics against this failure requires a substantial revision in the theory, in my opinion. I'll briefly outline one possible revision.

The prisoners' dilemma places you and me at odds not only with one another but also with ourselves. If you find that the incentives are a sufficient reason for turning state's evidence, you will wish that they weren't, given that their status as a reason must be common knowledge between us, which will persuade me to turn state's evidence as well. You therefore find yourself in possession of reasons that you wish you didn't have. Of course, you may often find yourself in such a position. As you drag yourself out of bed and head for the pool, for example, you may wish that you didn't have such good reasons for sticking to your regimen of exercise. These cases may not involve any contradiction in your will, strictly speaking, but they do involve a conflict, which complicates your decision-making and compromises the intelligibility of your decisions. Think of the way that you vacillate when confronted with unwelcome reasons for acting, and the way that you subsequently doubt your decision, whatever it is.

I have argued that you cannot simply will away unwelcome reasons for acting, but the fact remains that you can gradually bring about changes in yourself and your circumstances that mitigate or even eliminate the conflict. You can learn to relish early-morning swims, you can switch to a more enticing form of exercise, or you can find some other way to lower your cholesterol. You can also cultivate a disdain for advantages that you wouldn't wish to be generally available, such as the advantages to be gained in the prisoners' dilemma by turning against a confederate. You might even learn to regard an additional year in prison as a badge of honor, when it is incurred for refusing to turn against a confederate, and a shortened sentence as a mark of shame under these circumstances – in which case, the plea bargain offered to you would no longer be a bargain from your point-of-view, and the prisoners' dilemma would no longer be a dilemma. This attitude toward incarceration can't be called up at a moment's notice, of course; it may take years to cultivate. But when you adopted a life of crime, you could have foreseen being placed in precisely the position represented by the prisoners' dilemma, and you could already have begun to develop attitudes that would clarify such a position for you. (Surely, that's what lifetime criminals do, and rationally so – however irrational they may be to choose a life of crime, in the first place.)

Thus, if you find yourself confronted with unwelcome reasons for acting, you have probably failed at some earlier time to arrange your circumstances or your attitudes so as to head off conflicts of this kind. You can't change your personality or your circumstances on the spot; nor can you change their status as reasons for acting here and now. But with a bit of foresight and self-command, you could have avoided the predicament of acting on reasons that you wished you didn't have. Since you had reason for taking steps to avoid such a conflict, you have somewhere failed to act for reasons – not here and now, as you act on your unwelcome reasons, but at some earlier time, when you allowed yourself to get into that predicament.

Hence the requirement "Act for reasons" can favor morality in two distinct ways. First, it can rule out various actions, such as lying, that are based on considerations whose validity as reasons is inconceivable. Second, it can rule out acquiring reasons whose validity, though conceivable, is unwelcome. In the latter case, it doesn't rule out performing any particular actions; rather, it rules out becoming a particular kind of person, whose reasons for acting are regrettable, even from his own point-of-view.

Before I turn from the current line of thought, I should reiterate that it cannot be traced to the works of Kant himself. Kant would reject the suggestion that contradictions in the will are always such as to have occurred long before the time of action, and hence to be beyond correction on the spot. The resulting moral theory is therefore kantian with a small *k*.

Respect for Persons[6]

There is one more way in which the requirement to act for reasons constrains us to be moral, in Kant's view. Kant actually thought that this constraint is equivalent to the ones that I've already discussed – that it is one of the aforementioned contradictions viewed from a different angle or described in different terms. I disagree with Kant on this point, and so I'll present this constraint as independent of the others, thus departing again from Kant.

Many people take up a regimen of diet or exercise as a means of staying healthy, but some overdo it, so that they ruin their health instead. Most people accumulate money as a means of buying useful or enjoyable things, but some overdo it, grubbing for money so hard that they have no time to spend it. In either case, the overdoers are making a fundamental

---

[6] The material in this section is developed further in "Love as a Moral Emotion" (Chapter 4) and in "A Right of Self-Termination?" *Ethics* 109 (1999): 606–28.

mistake about reasons for acting: they are exchanging an end for the means to that end, thus exchanging something valuable for something else that is valuable only for its sake. Exercise is not valuable in itself but only for the sake of health (or so I am assuming for the moment); money is not valuable in itself but only for the sake of happiness. To sacrifice health for the sake of exercise, or to sacrifice happiness for the sake of money, is to stand these values on their heads. The prospect of gains in exercise or income can't provide reason for accepting a net loss in the ends for whose sake alone they are valuable.

Kant's greatest insight, in my view, was that we can commit the same mistake in practical reasoning with respect to persons and their interests. The basis of this insight is that the relation between a person and his interests is similar to, though not exactly the same as, the relation between an end, such as happiness, and the means to it, such as money. Kant believed that persons themselves are ends, and that they consequently must not be exchanged for the things that stand to them in the capacity analogous to that of means.

Some commentators interpret Kant as meaning that persons are ends in the same sense as health or happiness – that is, in the sense that we have reason to promote or preserve their existence. What Kant really meant, however, is that persons are things *for the sake of which* other things can have value.

The phrase 'for the sake of' indicates the subordination of one concern to another. To want money for the sake of happiness is to want money because, and insofar as, you want to be happy; to pursue exercise for the sake of health is to pursue it because, and insofar as, you want to be healthy. You may also care about things for the sake of a person. You may want professional success for your own sake, but you may also want it for the sake of your parents, who love you and made sacrifices to give you a good start. In the latter case, your concern for your happiness depends upon your concern for others; in the former, it depends upon your concern for yourself.

The dependence between these concerns is evident in the familiar connection between how you feel about yourself and how you feel about your happiness. Sometimes when you realize that you have done something mean-spirited, you come to feel worthless as a person. You may even hate yourself; and one symptom of self-hatred is a loss of concern for your own happiness. It no longer seems to matter whether life is good to you, because you yourself seem to be no good. Your happiness matters only insofar as *you* matter, because it is primarily for your sake that your happiness matters at all.

Now, to want money for the sake of happiness is to want the one as a means of promoting or preserving the existence of the other; but to want happiness for your own sake is not to want it as a means of promoting or preserving your existence. Happiness is not a means of self-preservation, and the instinct of self-preservation is not the attitude that underlies your concern for it. The underlying self-concern is a sense of your value as a person, a sense of self-worth, which is not at all the same as the urge to survive. Hence, wanting happiness for your own sake is both like and unlike wanting money for the sake of happiness. The cases are alike in that they involve the subordination of one concern to another; but they are unlike with respect to whether the objects of concern are related as instruments and outcomes.

When Kant referred to persons as ends, he was not saying that they lend value to anything that stands to them as instruments, or means. He was saying merely that they are things for the sake of which other things can have value, as your happiness is valuable for your sake. The dependence between these values, however, is enough to yield a rational constraint similar to the constraint on exchanging ends for means.

If your happiness is valuable for your sake, and matters only insofar as you matter, then you cannot have reason to sacrifice yourself for the sake of happiness, just as you cannot have reason to sacrifice happiness for the sake of money. Just as your concern for money is subordinate to your concern for happiness, so your concern for happiness is subordinate to self-concern, and the former concerns must not take precedence over the latter, as would happen if you pursued money at the sacrifice of your happiness, or happiness at the sacrifice of yourself.

Sacrificing yourself for the sake of happiness may sound impossible, but it isn't. People make this exchange whenever they kill themselves in order to end their unhappiness, or ask to be killed for that purpose. The requirement to act for reasons rules out such mercy killing, which exchanges a person for something that's valuable only for his sake. Because a person's happiness is valuable for his sake, it cannot provide a reason for sacrificing the person himself.

(Before I go further, I should point out that Kantian ethics does not, in my view, rule out suicide or euthanasia in every case. As we have seen, Kantian ethics rules out actions only insofar as they are performed for particular reasons. For example, it doesn't rule out false utterances in general but only those which are made for the sake of getting someone to believe a falsehood. Similarly, it doesn't rule out suicide and euthanasia in general but only when they are performed for the sake of ending unhappiness. With that qualification in place, let me return to my explanation of persons as ends.)

Kant thought that the status of persons as ends rules out more than sacrificing them for their interests; he thought that it rules out treating them in any way that would amount to using them merely as means to other ends. In his view, persons shed value on other things, by making them valuable for a person's sake; whereas means merely reflect the value shed on them by the ends for whose sake they are valuable. To treat a person as a means is to treat him as a mere reflector of value rather than a value-source, which is a confusion on the order of mistaking the sun for the moon. Indeed, Kant thought that a universe without persons would be pitch dark with respect to value.

Here let me remind you of the aspiration in which the requirement to act for reasons is manifested in our experience. Reasons for acting are considerations that are authoritative in the sense that their practical import is common knowledge among all reasoners, including not only other people but also ourselves at other times. Having access to such considerations enables us to act autonomously, as the originators of our own behavior. And being autonomous is essential to – perhaps definitive of – being a person. Hence the requirement to act for reasons expresses our aspiration to realize a central aspect of personhood – or, as I put it, the aspiration to "be a *Mensch*."

This alternative formulation of the requirement to act for reasons has implications for the current discussion of persons as ends-in-themselves. What it implies is that the felt authority of reasons is due, in part, to our appreciation of ourselves as persons. In acting for reasons, we live up to our status as persons, and we act for reasons partly as a way of living up to that status. The motivational grip that reasons have on us is subordinate to our appreciation for the value of being a *Mensch*.

If you think back to our initial search for an intrinsically inescapable requirement, you will recall that "Act for reasons," though close to being inescapable, was not perfectly so. We settled for it after reflecting that we are required to act for reasons if we are subject to any requirements at all. What we have subsequently discovered is that seeing ourselves as subject to practical requirements is essential to seeing ourselves as autonomous and, in that respect, as persons. Thus, although we are required to act for reasons only insofar as we are subject to practical requirements at all, we are obliged to conceive of ourselves as subject to requirements, and hence required to act for reasons, by our aspiration toward personhood.

The value of persons now emerges as paramount, not only over the value of what we do for someone's sake, but over the value of acting for any reason whatsoever. Acting for reasons matters because being a person matters.

What's more, the value of our individual personhood here and now is inseparable from the value of participating in personhood as a status shared with our selves at other times and with other people, whose access to the same framework of reasons is what lends those reasons authority. Only by sharing in the common knowledge of reasoners do we find ourselves subject to authoritative requirements, recognition of which must determine our behavior if we are to be autonomous persons. Being an autonomous person is thus impossible without belonging to the community of those with access to the same sources of autonomy. Insofar as being a person matters, belonging to the community of persons must matter, and the importance of both is what makes it important to act for reasons.

That's why it's irrational to treat any person merely as a means, for any reason whatsoever. No reason for acting can justify treating a person as a mere reflector of value, because the importance of acting for reasons depends on the importance of personhood in general as a source of value. Reasons matter because persons matter, and so we cannot show our regard for reasons by showing disregard for persons.

3

The Genesis of Shame

I

"And they were both naked, the man and his wife, and were not ashamed."
So ends Chapter 2 of Genesis. Chapter 3 narrates the Fall and its
aftermath: "The eyes of them both were opened, and they knew that
they were naked; and they sewed fig leaves together, and made themselves aprons." Presumably, they made themselves aprons to cover their
nakedness, because they were now ashamed.

Why were Adam and Eve ashamed? And why hadn't they been ashamed
before? The text of Genesis 3 suggests that they became ashamed because
they realized that they were naked. But what realization was that? They
were not created literally blind, and so they weren't seeing their own
skin for the first time. The realization that they were naked must have
been the realization that they were unclothed, which would have required
them to envision the possibility of clothing. Yet the mere idea of clothing would have had no effect on Adam and Eve unless they also saw
why clothing was necessary. And when they saw the necessity of clothing,
they were seeing – what, exactly? There was no preexisting culture to

This chapter originally appeared in *Philosophy and Public Affairs 30*, no. 1 (Winter 2001): 27–
52. It is reprinted by permission of Princeton University Press. Thanks to George Mavrodes,
Brian Slattery, and Dan B. Velleman for discussions of this topic, and to Elizabeth Anderson,
Nomy Arpaly, David Copp, Rachana Kamtekar, Dick Moran, Martha Nussbaum, Connie
Rosati, Andrea Scarantino, Jonathan Schaffer, and Nishi Shah for comments on earlier
versions. This paper was presented to the philosophy departments of the University of
Manitoba; Bowling Green State University; Massachusetts Institute of Technology; the Uni-
versity of California, Berkeley; the University of Minnesota; the University of Massachusetts
at Amherst; and to a conference on the emotions at the University of Manchester.

disapprove of nakedness or to enforce norms of dress. What Genesis suggests is that the necessity of clothing was not a cultural invention but a natural fact, evident to the first people whose eyes were sufficiently open.

Or, rather, this fact was brought about by their eyes' being opened. For when we are told at the end of Chapter 2 that Adam and Eve were naked but not ashamed, we are not meant to suppose that they had something to be ashamed of but didn't see it, like people who don't know that their fly is open or their slip is showing. The reason why Adam and Eve were not ashamed of their nakedness at first is that they had no reason to be ashamed; and so they must not have needed clothing at that point. But in that case, the opening of their eyes must have produced the very fact that it enabled them to see: their eyes must have been opened in a way that simultaneously made clothing necessary and enabled them to see its necessity. What sort of eye-opening was that?

According to the story, their eyes were opened when they acquired a knowledge of good and evil. But this description doesn't answer our question. Although a knowledge of good and evil prompted them to remedy their nakedness – as evil, we suppose – we are still not meant to suppose that their nakedness had been evil antecedently. So the knowledge of good and evil didn't just reveal some evil in their nakedness; it must also have put that evil there. The question remains, what item of knowledge could have had that effect?

I am going to propose an account of shame that explains why eating from the tree of knowledge would have made Adam and Eve ashamed of their nakedness. Ultimately, this account will yield implications for current debates about the shamelessness of our culture. The way to recover our sense of shame is not, as some moralists propose, to recover our former intolerance for conditions previously thought to be shameful. I will propose an alternative prescription, derived from my diagnosis of how Adam and Eve acquired a sense of shame.

II

The story of Genesis makes little sense under the standard philosophical analysis of shame as an emotion of reflected self-assessment. According to this analysis, the subject of shame thinks less of himself at the thought of how he is seen by others.[1]

---

[1] My characterization of the standard analysis is intended to be vague, so as to encompass the views of several philosophers, including John Deigh, "Shame and Self-Esteem: A Critique," *Ethics* 93 (1983): 225–45; Gabriele Taylor, *Pride, Shame, and Guilt; Emotions of*

The problem is to explain how the shame of Adam and Eve could have involved a negative assessment of themselves.

In modern society, of course, public nakedness violates social norms and consequently elicits social censure, which can be echoed by self-censure on the part of its object. But assessments of this kind would have been unknown in the pre-social conditions of Eden. Adam and Eve's shame might still have reflected an observer's assessment if they thought of themselves as being judged by a natural rather than social ideal, but what could that ideal have been? It couldn't have been, for example, an ideal of attractiveness: Adam and Eve didn't think of themselves as being unattractive to one another. In any case, shame is more likely to arise in someone who feels all too attractive to an observer, such as the artist's model who blushes upon catching a glint of lust in his eye.[2]

This famous example might be taken to suggest that the knowledge acquired by Adam and Eve was knowledge of sex. What they suddenly came to see, according to this interpretation, were the sexual possibilities of their situation, which put lust in their eyes and then shame on their cheeks at the sight of the other's lust. Unlike the artist's model, however, Adam and Eve had no pretensions to a professional or purely aesthetic role from which they might feel demoted by becoming sexual objects to one another. So the requisite assessment of the self remains elusive.

III

This last interpretation also requires the implausible assumption that what the Creator sought to conceal from Adam and Eve, in forbidding

Self-Assessment (Oxford: Clarendon Press, 1985), Chapter 3; Roger Scruton, *Sexual Desire; A Moral Philosophy of the Erotic* (New York: The Free Press, 1986), pp. 140–49; Simon Blackburn, *Ruling Passions* (Oxford: Clarendon Press, 1998), pp. 17–19; and Richard Wollheim, *On the Emotions* (New Haven: Yale University Press, 1999), Chapter 3. Other authors include only some of these elements in their accounts of shame. For example, some analyze shame in terms of a negative self-assessment, without reference to any real or imagined observer (e.g., John Rawls, *A Theory of Justice* [Cambridge: Harvard University Press, 1971], pp. 442–46; Michael Stocker and Elizabeth Hegeman, *Valuing Emotions* [Cambridge: Cambridge University Press, 1996], pp. 217–30; Jon Elster, *Strong Feelings: Emotion, Addiction, and Human Behavior* [Cambridge, Mass: MIT Press, 1999], p. 21). Others analyze shame as a response to the denigrating regard of others, without requiring a negative assessment of the self (e.g., Bernard Williams, *Shame and Necessity* [Berkeley: University of California Press, 1993], Appendix 2).

[2] This example is discussed by Gabrielle Taylor, *Pride, Shame, and Guilt*, pp. 60–61; and by Richard Wollheim, *On the Emotions*, pp. 159–63. Wollheim traces it to Max Scheler, "Über Scham und Schamgefühle," in *Schriften aus dem Nachlass* (Bern: Francke Verlag, 1957), Vol. 1.

them to eat from the tree, was the idea of using the genitals that He had given them. And God would hardly have created anything so absurd as human genitals if He intended them to have no more use than the human appendix. I don't deny that the knowledge initially withheld from Adam and Eve was sexual knowledge in some sense. But it must have been a special kind of sexual knowledge, involving more than the very idea of getting it on. I suggest that what they didn't think of until the Fall was the idea of not getting it on – though I admit that this suggestion will take some getting used to.

Here I am imagining that the knowledge gained from the tree was not physically extracted from the fruit itself; rather, it was knowledge gained in the act of eating the fruit. And this knowledge was gained in practice only after having been suggested in theory, by the serpent. What the serpent put into Eve's ear as a theory, which she and Adam went on to prove in practice, was the idea of disobedience: "You don't have to obey."

One might wonder how this piece of knowledge could have qualified as sexual. What was there for Adam and Eve to disobey when it came to sex? The Lord had already enjoined them to "[b]e fruitful and multiply," further explaining that "a man . . . shall cleave to his wife: and they shall be one flesh." And since the Lord expected Adam and Eve to cleave to one another in the fleshly sense, he must have equipped them with the sexual instincts required to make the flesh, so to speak, cleavable. With everything urging them toward sex, they would hardly have associated sex with disobedience.

But that's just my point. Everything urged them toward sex, and so there was indeed something for them to disobey – namely, the divine and instinctual demand to indulge. The serpent's suggestion that Adam and Eve didn't have to obey the Lord implied, among other things, that they didn't have to obey His injunction to be fruitful, or the instincts with which He had reinforced that injunction. So the serpent's message of disobedience did convey a piece of sexual knowledge, after all.

I may sound as if I'm saying, paradoxically, that the sexual knowledge imparted by the serpent was the idea of chastity: "You don't have to obey" could just as well be phrased "Just Say No." But I would prefer to say that the sexual knowledge imparted by the serpent amounted to the idea of privacy. What Adam and Eve hastened to cover up after the Fall would in some languages be called their "shameful" parts: their *pudenda* (Latin), *aidoia* (Greek), *Schamteile* (German), *parties honteuses* (French). But in English, those parts of the body are called private parts.[3] The genitals became shameful, I suggest, when they became private. And the advent of privacy would have required, if not the idea of saying "no" to sex, then at least the idea of saying "not here" and "not now." So the idea of disobeying their sexual instincts could well have been instrumental in the development of shame, via the development of privacy.

I am not going to argue that shame is always concerned with matters of privacy: matters of privacy are merely the primal locus of shame. Similarly, the genitals are the primal locus of privacy – which is why our creation myth traces the origin of shame to the nakedness of our first ancestors. After I interpret the myth, however, I will explain how privacy extends beyond the body, and how shame extends beyond matters of privacy, to express a broader and more fundamental concern. My analysis will thus proceed in stages, from the natural shamefulness of the genitals, to the shamefulness of matters that are private by choice or convention, to the shamefulness of matters that do not involve privacy at all.

IV

The philosopher who comes closest to understanding shame, in my view, is St. Augustine. According to Augustine, man's insubordination to God was punished by a corresponding insubordination to man on the part of his own flesh, and this punishment is what made our sexual organs shameful:[4]

[T]hese members themselves, being moved and restrained not at our will, but by a certain independent autocracy, so to speak, are called "shameful." Their condition was different before sin. For as it is written, "They were naked and were not ashamed" – not that their nakedness was unknown to them, but because nakedness was not yet shameful, because not yet did lust move those members without the will's consent; not yet did the flesh by its disobedience testify against the disobedience of man. For they were not created blind, as the unenlightened vulgar fancy; for Adam saw the animals to whom he gave names, and of Eve we

---

3 A recent report on the BBC World Service described a criminal defendant who appeared on the witness stand stark naked, "with nothing but a plastic clipboard to hide his shame." Here the reporter replaced the English "private parts" with a translation of the Latin, French, or German expressions.

4 *The City of God*, Book XIV, chapter 15, transl. Marcus Dods (New York: The Modern Library, 1950), p. 463: "[B]y the just retribution of the sovereign God whom we refused to be subject to and serve, our flesh, which was subjected to us, now torments us by insubordination." I am grateful to George Mavrodes for directing me to the passages discussed below.

read, "The woman saw that the tree was good for food, and that it was pleasant to the eyes." Their eyes, therefore, were open, but were not open to this, that is to say, were not observant so as to recognise what was conferred upon them by the garment of grace, for they had no consciousness of their members warring against their will. But when they were stripped of this grace, that their disobedience might be punished by fit retribution, there began in the movement of their bodily members a shameless novelty which made nakedness indecent: it at once made them observant and made them ashamed.

This passage has provided many of the elements in my discussion thus far. For reasons that I'll presently explain, however, I think that the passage puts these elements together backwards.

Augustine says that the genitals became pudenda when they produced the "shameless novelty" of moving against their owners' will – in other words, when Adam lost the ability to control his erections, and Eve her secretions. The idea of their ever having possessed these abilities may seem odd, but it has a certain logic from Augustine's point-of-view. Augustine thinks that Adam and Eve did not experience lust before the Fall.[5] Yet he also thinks that the Lord's injunction to be fruitful and multiply must be interpreted literally. The combination of these thoughts leaves Augustine with a sexual conundrum. How was copulation supposed to occur without lust, which serves nowadays to produce the necessary anatomical preparations? Augustine's answer is this: "The man, then, would have sown the seed, and the woman received it, as need required, the generative organs being moved by the will, not excited by lust."[6] And it was because of being governed by the will, according to Augustine, that the genitals of Adam and Eve were not initially shameful.[7] They subsequently became shameful because they were removed from their owners' voluntary control, in punishment for original sin.

Let me introduce my disagreement with Augustine by pointing out how we differ on the relation between shame and punishment in Genesis. According to Augustine, bodily insubordination to the will, and the resulting shame, were inflicted on Adam and Eve as retribution for their disobedience. In Genesis, however, the Lord discovered the disobedience

---

[5] Ibid., Chapter 21, p. 468: "Far be it, then, from us to suppose that our first parents in Paradise felt that lust which caused them afterwards to blush and hide their nakedness, or that by its means they should have fulfilled the benediction of God, 'Increase and multiply and replenish the earth'; for it was after sin that lust began."

[6] Ibid., Chapter 24, p. 472.

[7] Ibid., Chapter 19, p. 467: "[T]hese parts, I say, were not vicious in Paradise before sin, for they were never moved in opposition to a holy will towards any object from which it was necessary that they should be withheld by the restraining bridle of reason."

of Adam and Eve only by discovering that they were hiding from Him in shame; and so their shame must have preceded their punishment. Their punishment consisted rather in being banished from the garden and condemned to a life of toil and sorrow.

What's more, Augustine does not attribute Adam and Eve's shame to the knowledge that they acquired from eating the forbidden fruit. He attributes their shame to their loss of voluntary control over their bodies, which was inflicted on them as punishment for their disobedience, which involved the tree of knowledge only incidentally, because that tree happened to be the one whose fruit was forbidden to them. Thus, eating from the tree of knowledge led to their shame indirectly, by angering God, who then hobbled their wills in a way that made their nakedness shameful. According to the text of Genesis, however, Adam and Eve were told by the serpent that eating from the tree of knowledge would open their eyes by itself, and it really did open their eyes, whereupon they were instantly ashamed. That this progression was antecedently predictable is implicit in the Lord's detective work: seeing their shame, He knew that they must have disobeyed. The text thus suggests that their shame was a predictable result of their eating from the tree of knowledge, not the result of any subsequent reengineering of their constitutions.

Note that the constitutional alteration to which Augustine attributes the shame of Adam and Eve could not have been brought about by the mere acquisition of knowledge. Having their eyes opened would not in itself have caused Adam and Eve to lose voluntary control that they previously possessed. But a slightly different alteration could indeed have been brought about by the acquisition of knowledge – and, in particular, by that knowledge of good and evil which Adam and Eve acquired in eating from the tree. For suppose, as I have already suggested, that this episode taught them about good and evil by teaching them about the possibility of disobeying God and their God-given instincts.[8] In that case, they must previously have been unaware that disobeying God and Nature was a possibility, and so they must have been in no position to disobey. They would have slavishly done as God and their instincts demanded, because of being unaware that they might do otherwise. And if they slavishly obeyed these demands, without a thought of doing otherwise, then

[8] Presumably, good and evil corresponded to the will's obedience and disobedience, respectively. But how could the good have consisted in obedience to instinct? The answer, I assume, is that human instincts were adapted to the conditions of Paradise in such a way that their promptings were unfailingly good.

their free will would have been no more than a dormant capacity, which they wouldn't exercise until they discovered the possibility of alternatives on which to exercise it. That discovery, imparted by the serpent, would thus have activated the hitherto dormant human will, thereby making it fully effective for the first time since the Creation.

On this interpretation, the reason why Adam and Eve weren't ashamed of their nakedness at first is not that their anatomy was perfectly subordinate to the will but rather that they didn't have an effective will to which their anatomy could be insubordinate. In acquiring the idea of making choices contrary to the demands of their instincts, however, they would have gained, not only the effective capacity to make those choices, but also the realization that their bodies might obey their instincts instead, thus proving insubordinate to their newly activated will. Hence the knowledge that would have activated their will could also have opened their eyes to the possibility of that bodily recalcitrance which Augustine identifies as the occasion of their shame.

V

What remains to be explained is why the insubordination of the body to the will should be an occasion for shame. The explanation, I believe, is that the structure of the will provides shame with its central concern, of which the central instance is a concern for privacy.

Privacy is made possible by the ability to choose in opposition to inclination. To a creature who does whatever its instincts demand, there is no space between impulse and action, and there is accordingly less space between inner and outer selves. Because a dog has relatively little control over its impulses, its impulses are legible in its behavior. Whatever itches, it scratches (or licks or nips or drags along the ground), and so its itches are always overt, always public.

By contrast, our capacity to resist desires enables us to choose which desires our behavior will express. And we tend to make these choices cumulatively and consistently over time.[9] That is, we gradually compile a profile of the tastes, interests, and commitments on which we are willing to act, and we tend to enact that motivational profile while also resisting inclinations and impulses incompatible with it. This recension of our

---

[9] In this and the following paragraph, I draw on a conception of agency that I have developed elsewhere. See my *Practical Reflection* (Princeton: Princeton University Press, 1989); *The Possibility of Practical Reason* (Oxford: Oxford University Press, 2000), esp. Chapters 1, 7, and 9; and "The Self as Narrator," (Chapter 9 in the present volume).

motivational natures becomes our outward face, insofar as it defines the shape of our behavior.

Putting an outward face on our behavior sounds like an essentially social enterprise, but I think that this enterprise is inherent in the structure of the individual will. Even Robinson Crusoe chose which of his desires to act on, and his need to understand and coordinate his activities required him to make choices by which he could consistently abide. He therefore lived in accordance with a persona that he composed, even though there was no audience for whom he composed it. Or, rather, he composed this persona for an audience consisting only of himself, insofar as it was designed to help him keep track and make sense of his solitary life. So even Robinson Crusoe had distinct overt and covert selves – the personality that he acted out, and a personality that differed from it by virtue of including all of the inclinations and impulses on which he chose not to act.

VI

In order to make sense and keep track of his life, Robinson Crusoe had to engage in a solitary form of self-presentation – displaying, if only to himself, behavior that was predictable and intelligible as manifesting a stable and coherent set of motives. Self-presentation serves a similar function in the social realm, since others cannot engage you in social interaction unless they find your behavior predictable and intelligible. Insofar as you want to be eligible for social intercourse, you must offer a coherent public image.[10]

Thus, for example, you cannot converse with others unless your utterances can be interpreted as an attempt to convey a minimally consistent meaning. You can't cooperate with others, or elicit their cooperation,

---

[10] See Georg Simmel, "The Secret and the Secret Society," Part IV of *The Sociology of Georg Simmel*, transl. Kurt H. Wolff (Glencoe, Ill.: The Free Press, 1950), pp. 311–12:

> All we communicate to another individual by means of words or perhaps in another fashion – even the most subjective, impulsive, intimate matters – is a selection from that psychological-real whole whose absolutely exact report (absolutely exact in terms of content and sequence) would drive everybody into the insane asylum – if a paradoxical expression is permissible. In a quantitative sense, it is not only fragments of our inner life which we alone reveal, even to our closest fellowmen. What is more, these fragments are not a representative selection, but one made from the standpoint of reason, value, and relation to the listener and his understanding. . . . We simply cannot imagine any interaction or social relation or society which are *not* based on this teleologically determined non-knowledge of one another.

unless your movements can be interpreted as attempts to pursue minimally consistent goals. In sum, you can't interact socially unless you
present others with an eligible target for interaction, by presenting noises
and movements that can be interpreted as the coherent speech and action
of a minimally rational agent.

Indeed, fully social interaction requires that your noises and movements be interpretable, not merely as coherent speech and action, but
also as intended to be interpretable as such. Only when your utterances
can be recognized as aiming to be recognized as meaningful do they
count as fully successful contributions to conversation;[11] only when your
movements are recognized as aiming to be recognized as helpful do they
count as fully successful contributions to cooperation; and even a competition or a conflict is not full-blown until the parties are recognized by
one another as trying to be recognized as opponents. Full-blown social
intercourse thus requires each party to compose an overt persona for the
purpose, not just of being interpretable, but of being interpretable as
having been composed partly for that purpose.

Note, then, that self-presentation is not a dishonest activity, since your
public image purports to be exactly what it is: the socially visible face of a
being who is presenting it as a target for social interaction.[12] Even aspects
of your image that aren't specifically meant to be recognized as such are
not necessarily dishonest. There is nothing dishonest about choosing not
to scratch wherever and whenever it itches. Although you don't make all
of your itches overt, in the manner of a dog, you aren't falsely pretending
to be less itchy than a dog; you aren't pretending, in other words, that
the itches you scratch are the only ones you have. You know that the only
possible audience for such a pretense would never be taken in by it, since
other free agents are perfectly familiar with the possibility of choosing not
to scratch an itch. And insofar as your persona is a positive bid for social
interaction, you positively want it to be recognized as such. Not being
recognized as a self-presenter would entail not being acknowledged as a

---

[11] Here I am simply making the familiar Gricean point about the content of communicative
intentions; in the remainder of the sentence, I extend the point to other modes of social
interaction.

[12] See Thomas Nagel, "Concealment and Exposure," *Philosophy & Public Affairs* 27, no. 1
(Winter 1998): 3–30, p. 6: "The first and most obvious thing to note about many of the
most important forms of reticence is that they are not dishonest, because the conventions
that govern them are generally known."; "[O]ne has to keep a firm grip on the fact that
the social self that others present to us is not the whole of their personality . . . and that
this is not a form of deception because it is meant to be understood by everyone" (p. 7).

potential partner in conversation, cooperation, or even competition and conflict.

You thus have a fundamental interest in being recognized as a self-presenting creature, an interest that is more fundamental, in fact, than your interest in presenting any particular public image. Not to be seen as honest or intelligent or attractive would be socially disadvantageous, but not to be seen as a self-presenting creature would be socially disqualifying: it would place you beyond the reach of social intercourse altogether. Threats to your standing as a self-presenting creature are thus a source of deep anxiety, and anxiety about the threatened loss of that standing is, in my view, what constitutes the emotion of shame. The realm of privacy is the central arena for shame, I think, because it is the central arena for threats to your standing as a social agent. As Thomas Nagel has put it, "Naked exposure itself, whether or not it arouses disapproval, is disqualifying."[13]

VII

Because of your interest in being recognized as a social agent, failures of privacy can set off a sense of escalating exposure. When something private about you is showing, you have somehow failed to manage your public image, and so an inadequacy in your capacity for self-presentation is showing as well, potentially undermining your standing as a social agent. Stripped of some accustomed item of clothing, you may also feel stripped of your accustomed cloak of sociality, your standing as a competent self-presenter eligible to participate in conversation, cooperation, and other forms of interaction. This escalating exposure is implicit in Bernard Williams's description of shame when he says that "[t]he root of shame lies in exposure . . . in being at a disadvantage: in . . . a loss of power."[14] Failures of privacy put you at a disadvantage by threatening the power inherent in your role as a participating member of the community, and the resulting anxiety constitutes the emotion of shame.

I say "failures of privacy," not "violations." When people forcibly violate your privacy, no doubt is cast on your capacity for self-presentation. But then, violations of privacy do not properly occasion shame. If you learn that someone has been peeping through your bedroom keyhole, you don't feel ashamed at the thought of what he might have seen; or, at least,

---

[13] Ibid., p. 4.
[14] Williams, *Shame and Necessity*, p. 220.

you shouldn't feel ashamed: you should feel angry and defiant. Proper occasions for shame are your own failures to manage your privacy, as symbolized in childhood culture by open flies and showing slips. In the case of the bedroom keyhole, the one who should be ashamed is the peeping Tom, who lacks the self-possession to keep any of his curiosity covert.[15] His naked curiosity is what should occasion shame, not your properly closeted nakedness.

The same goes for your intentional violations of your own privacy, which do not qualify as failures, either. Deliberately exposing yourself in public would not cause you to feel shame if it represented an unqualified success at publicizing your privates rather than a failure at concealing them. (That's why people don't usually feel ashamed of having posed for *Playboy* magazine.) Deliberate self-exposure occasions shame only when it entails some unintentional self-exposure as well – when you take off more than you meant to, or your taking it off exposes impulses that you didn't mean to expose. For only then do you feel vulnerable to the loss of your standing as a self-presenting person.

Although deliberate self-exposure doesn't necessarily occasion shame, there remains a sense in which public nakedness is naturally suited to occasion it and can therefore be called naturally shameful. What makes nakedness naturally shameful, I think, is the phenomenon adduced by St. Augustine – namely, the body's insubordination to the will. And I'm now in a position to explain why I agree with this much of Augustine's analysis.

VIII

Why does our culture tolerate frontal nudity in women more than in men? The politically correct explanation is that the culture is dominated by men and consequently tends to cast women as sex objects. An alternative explanation, however, is that male nudity is naturally more shameful.

Male nudity is more shameful because it is more explicit, not only in the sense that the male body is, as Mr. Rogers used to sing, fancy on the outside, but also in the sense that a man's outside is liable to reveal his feelings in a particularly explicit way, whether he likes it or not. The unwanted erection is a glaring failure of privacy. The naked man is unable to choose which of his impulses are to be public; and so he is only

---

[15] The example is Sartre's, *Being and Nothingness*, transl. Hazel E. Barnes (New York: Philosophical Library, 1956), pp. 261–62.

partly an embodied will and partly also the embodiment of untrammeled instincts. In such a condition, sustaining the role of a social agent becomes especially difficult.

Equally explicit, I think, is the curiosity expressed in looking at the naked male body. Viewing the naked female can easily be, or at least purport to be, an aesthetic exercise; whereas it's fairly difficult to look at the male organ without the thought of its sexual role, and hence without experiencing an undeniably sexual curiosity.

Thus, our double standard about nakedness may confirm St. Augustine's hypothesis that what's shameful about nakedness is the body's insubordination to the will.[16] And my account of privacy may explain this hypothesis by explaining why the insubordinate body threatens to put its owner in a socially untenable position, by undermining his standing as a self-presenting person. What my explanation implies is that the impulse to cover one's nakedness out of shame is not, in the first instance, the impulse to hide something whose exposure might occasion disapproval. It's rather the impulse to guard one's capacity for self-presentation and, with it, one's standing as a social agent.

This explanation makes sense of my earlier suggestion that the sexual knowledge imparted to Adam and Eve by the serpent was the idea of not indulging. Only after Adam and Eve recognized the possibility of saying "no" – or, at least, "not now" – to their sexual impulses did they attain a standing that could be undermined if their genitals proceeded to signal "yes" instead. Hence only after they recognized their freedom with regard to sex could they find their nakedness inherently shameful.

IX

The relation between shame and bodily insubordination is also illustrated by the physiological response to shame, which is blushing. A familiar feature of this response is that one blush can set off a cascade of ever

---

[16] Here is a piece of ethnographic evidence. In some cultures, men wear almost nothing other than penis sheaths, which have the effect of making every penis look erect. This mode of dress represents an alternative solution to the problem of keeping male arousal private, since it entails that an erect-looking penis is no longer a sign of arousal (just as wearing a yellow star in occupied Denmark was not a sign of being Jewish). Of course, the sight of penis sheaths can be alarming to outsiders if they belong to a culture that favors outright concealment over camouflage. Another piece of evidence, I think, is that the traditional focus for women's shame about their bodies is not the genitals as such but rather menstrual blood, which is unlike female sexual arousal, but like male arousal, in being visibly insubordinate to the will.

deeper blushes. The reason is that the blush itself is insubordinate to the will: one's complexion foils any attempt to conceal one's impulse toward concealment, or to keep private one's inflamed sense of privacy. This response to failures of privacy is in itself a further failure of the same kind.[17]

Having blushed can therefore be an occasion for blushing again. Subsequent blushes don't express or reflect any disapproval of the previous ones: there's nothing wrong or bad about blushing. Subsequent blushes merely express the sense that the previous blushes have further compromised one's capacity for self-presentation.

Of course, the face often betrays many feelings, and the question therefore arises why a bare face isn't considered even more shameful than naked genitals. The answer is that the face is also the primary medium for deliberate self-presentation. The face is indeed shameful insofar as it defies the will and thereby foils self-presentation; but insofar as it is instrumental to self-presentation, the face is essential to the avoidance of shame – which may be why a shameful turn of events is described metaphorically as a loss of face.[18] Some cultures use veils or fans to cover the face in situations conducive to shame. But face is to be saved only for the sake of being effectively displayed; and most cultures therefore favor facial disciplines other than concealment.

X

My account bears a complex relation to the standard account of shame as an emotion of reflected self-assessment.[19] Mine might be assimilated to

---

[17] On this feature of blushing, and its relation to sexual arousal, see Scruton, *Sexual Desire*, pp. 63–68. Another aspect of the reflexive response to shame is a sudden sense of confusion and disorientation: one's head spins, one's ears ring, and the lights may seem to go dim. A way of describing this aspect of the shame-response would be to say that shame causes a loss of self-possession; but I would prefer to say that shame is the experience of self-possession already lost. The occasion for shame is a failure to compose oneself in the manner distinctive of persons, and this failure comes to be felt as a loss of composure.

[18] Also relevant here are various terms for shamelessness, such as 'barefaced,' 'cheek,' and 'effrontery.' The shameless person holds up his face in circumstances where self-presentation has been discredited and should therefore be withdrawn. (See also notes 26 and 28, below.)

[19] Of the existing accounts of shame, Sartre's is the one with which I most agree. For Sartre, the thought involved in shame is that "I *am* as the Other sees me." And this thought is in fact the recognition that I am an *object*: "I am put in the position of passing judgment on myself as on an object, for it is as an object that I appear to the Other" (*Being and Nothingness*, p. 222). Hence the reflected self-assessment in Sartre's analysis of shame is an assessment of the self as less than a freely self-defining person: thus far, I agree. As I

the standard account as an instance thereof, since I say that to feel shame is to feel vulnerable to a particular negative assessment, as less than a self-presenting person. But this assimilation of the two accounts would obscure an important difference. In my account, the essential content of shame has no place for an assessment of the self in terms of ethics, honor, etiquette, or other specific dimensions of personal excellence. Of course, one can be ashamed of being greedy, cowardly, rude, ugly, and so on. But these specific value judgments cannot play the role of the self-assessment that is involved in the very content of shame, according to my account. These judgments stand outside the content of the shame that may be associated with them; and so shame can also occur without them. Let me explain, then, how specific value judgments acquire their contingent association with shame.

These judgments are associated with shame because they often serve as grounds for relegating aspects of ourselves to the private realm. This connection has already made a brief appearance, in my description of the peeping Tom, who may feel shame at having exposed his sexual curiosity. Many of our moral failings consist in impulsive or compulsive behavior in which we fail to keep some untoward impulse to ourselves. To acknowledge such behavior is to realize that some untoward impulse is showing, such as our greed or our cowardice, and this realization can induce the anxiety that amounts to shame, in my view. If our reason for wanting to keep these impulses private is that we perceive or imagine disapproval of them, then our shame at their exposure will also be associated with a reflected assessment of the sort posited by the standard account. But shame would not be associated with that assessment in the absence of any sense of compromised self-presentation – for example, if we acted on the same impulses with abject resignation or brazen defiance.

Once we acquire the idea of privacy by learning that we can refuse to manifest some of our impulses, or manifest them only in solitude, we can think about excluding other, non-motivational facts from our self-presentation. We can think about omitting our ancestry or our income or our physical blemishes. Again, we wouldn't try to leave out these features of ourselves if we didn't think of them as somehow discreditable, and so our shame at their exposure is indeed associated with reflected disapproval. But if their exposure did not somehow compromise our

understand Sartre, however, he also thinks that this assessment includes the attribution of a specific flaw or failing, such as vulgarity, which is attributed to the self as to an object; and here I disagree, for reasons explained below.

efforts at self-presentation, they wouldn't cause us shame. If we humbly admitted to our discreditable ancestry, then our response to real or imagined disapproval of it would amount to no more than a feeling of frank inferiority.

The possibility of responding to denigrating regard with humility shows that the perception of facing such regard is not sufficient for shame. That perception doesn't lead to shame unless it leads to a sense of being compromised in our self-presentation. Humility preempts this sense of being compromised by deflating our pretensions and thereby rendering our self-presentation consistent with the criticism that we face. Feeling humbled is thus an alternative to, and incompatible with, feeling humiliated or ashamed.

What isn't incompatible with shame, however, is pride – which goes to show that a perception of denigrating regard is not necessary for shame either. We keep some things private not because we fear disapproval of them but rather because we fear approval of a sort that we would experience as vulgar or cheap.[20] Even if we think that others would admire our poetry, for example, we may not like the idea of exposing it to their undiscerning admiration. And then if we mistakenly leave it in view, we may feel shame and pride together – a mixture of feelings that is not at all incongruous, because we needn't feel denigrated in order to feel undermined in our self-presentation.

XI

As the foregoing examples have illustrated, we can feel shame at many kinds of exposure other than nakedness, because our natural sense of privacy can be extended by choice to cover many things other than our bodies. Conversely, we can go naked without shame, if our natural sense of privacy has been modified by social norms.

Although a free will necessarily draws a line between the public and the private, individuals have considerable latitude in drawing that line, and society may therefore lay down norms for how to draw it. Because norms of privacy dictate that particular things ought to be concealed, they are implicitly norms of competence at self-presentation. The awareness of being seen to violate such norms induces the sense of vulnerability

---

[20] Williams mentions this possibility: "people can be ashamed of being admired by the wrong audience in the wrong way" (*Shame and Necssity*, p. 82).

constitutive of shame – a sense of vulnerability, that is, to being discounted as a self-presenting social agent. Hence norms of privacy are implicitly norms of shame as well.

Such norms can modify or even nullify the natural shamefulness of things like nakedness or blushing.[21] These phenomena are naturally shameful only in the sense that they involve bodily insubordination, which is naturally suited to undermine self-presentation and thereby to cause the relevant sense of vulnerability. But which failures of self-presentation actually cause a subject to have or to feel this vulnerability can be modified by social norms. Just as a society may dictate privacy for things that aren't naturally shameful, so it may permit publicity for things that are. And if a society rules that particular bodily upheavals aren't incompatible with competent self-presentation, then they are unlikely to undermine the subject's status as a self-presenting person. So what naturally caused shame in Eden may not have caused shame at all in Sodom and Gomorrah.

XII

Moreover, failures of privacy are not the only occasion for shame, although I do believe that they are the central occasion. One's standing as a self-presenting agent can be threatened without the exposure of anything specific, or of anything that one had specifically hoped to keep private. The result may be that one feels shame about things that are quite public, or about nothing in particular at all.[22]

---

[21] Here is an example, which arose in discussion with members of the Philosophy Department at the University of Manitoba. It was pointed out that whereas men's locker rooms have communal showers, women's locker rooms have private showers, because women are less willing to be seen naked, even by other women. How can this difference be reconciled with my claim that male nakedness is naturally more shameful? The answer may be that our greater toleration for images of female nudity has resulted in more specific and more demanding standards of beauty for the naked female body than for the male. Although female nakedness is naturally less shameful, then, women are more likely to regard their bodies as ugly and to keep them private for that reason – a reason that applies in the locker room no less than elsewhere. Men generally keep their bodies private on account of their natural shamefulness, which is based in sexuality, whose relevance to the locker room is vehemently denied by social fictions of sexual orientation.

[22] The fact that one can feel shame without being ashamed of anything in particular entails that an analysis of the emotion cannot simultaneously be an analysis of the word and all of its cognates. Not every instance of shame can be described in terms of what the subject is ashamed of. By the same token, a subject need not feel shame in order to be described as ashamed of something, since it may be something that he tries and succeeds at keeping

Why does my sixteen-year-old son feel shame whenever his peers see him in the company of his parents? I don't think that he is ashamed specifically of us, in the sense of finding us especially discreditable as parents: we're no dorkier than the average mom and dad. The explanation, I think, is that being seen in the company of his parents tends to undermine the self-presentation that he has worked so hard to establish among his peers. Within his teenage milieu, he has tried to present himself as an independent and autonomous individual, and being seen with his parents is a public reminder that he is still in many ways a dependent child. Yet I think it would be wrong to say that his continuing subordination to parents is something that he has tried to keep private; rather, he has tried to relegate this unavoidably public fact about him to the background of his public image, while promoting to the foreground various facts that are in tension with it – facts such as his having a driver's license and a telephone. His efforts at self-presentation include not only separating what is to be public about him from what is to be private, but also, within the public realm, separating what is to be salient and what is to be inconspicuous. His self-presentation can therefore be undermined by failures of obscurity as well as by failures of privacy.

A person can be shamed even by aspects of himself that he accepts as conspicuous, if they are so glaring as to eclipse his efforts at self-presentation. Someone who is obviously deformed may experience shame if he senses that he is perceived solely in terms of his deformity, to the exclusion of any self-definition on his part. His shame doesn't depend on a sense that his deformity is unattractive, since he might similarly be shamed by any glaring feature, from bright red hair to unusual height or an extraordinary figure. Even great beauty can occasion shame in situations where it is felt to drown out rather than amplify self-presentation.

A similar effect can befall victims of social stereotyping. The target of racist remarks is displayed, not just as "the nigger" or "the hymie," but as one who has thus been captured in a socially defined image that leaves no room for self-presentation. When he responds by feeling shame, he may accuse himself of racial self-hatred, on the assumption that what he feels is shame about his race. Yet he needn't be ashamed of his race in order to feel shame in response to racism; he need only feel the genuine

private, with the result that it never occasions the emotion of shame. The words 'shame' and 'ashamed' have many uses that are related only indirectly to the emotion. I have not offered an account of the words, only an account of the emotion itself, as a sense of being compromised in one's standing as a self-presenting social agent.

vulnerability of being displayed as less than the master of his self-definition and therefore less than a socially qualified agent.[23]

As my account would predict, one defense against the shame of being stereotyped is to play the part, at the price of self-esteem. When someone paints blackface on his black face, he is trying to make the role his own, by incorporating the stereotype into a deliberate self-presentation; and he is thus trying to strike a compromise with racism, surrendering any positive image of his race in order to retain some shred of his role as a self-presenting person. Of course, observers may feel that performing in blackface is itself shameful, but their feeling rests on the belief that the performer is only deceiving himself about being left with any real scope for self-presentation.

A better defense against racist remarks is to muster a lively contempt for the speaker and hearers, since regarding others as beyond one's social pale is a way of excluding them from the notional audience required for the emotion of shame. If one doesn't care about interacting with particular people, then one will not feel anxiety about being disqualified in their eyes from presenting a target for interaction. Hence the victim of a racist remark can rise above any feelings of shame if he can disregard the present company as contemptible racists, so as not to feel vulnerable to their disregard. Unfortunately, this defense can be undermined by the presence of a sympathetic observer whose recognition the victim hopes to retain. A racist incident can therefore be rendered more shameful for the victim if a friend is present to see him stripped of his social agency.

No amount of racial pride can protect the target of racism from the shamefulness of his position. Pride would protect him from self-hatred,

---

[23] For a deeper discussion of this issue, with references to relevant literature, see Cheshire Calhoun, "An Apology for Moral Shame" (forthcoming in the *Journal of Political Philosophy*). Calhoun argues that shame experienced in the face of racism or sexism may be a perfectly legitimate response that does not betray self-hatred. But Calhoun reaches this conclusion from a rather different analysis of shame and its place in the practice of morality. Liz Anderson has directed me to an apt passage in Ralph Ellison's *Invisible Man*, where the narrator describes the shame he felt to find himself enjoying a yam: "What a group of people we were, I thought. Why, you could cause us the greatest humiliation simply by confronting us with something we liked. . . . This is all very wild and childish, I thought, but hell with being ashamed of what you liked. No more of that for me. I am what I am!" [*Invisible Man* (New York: New American Library, 1952), pp. 230–31]. The thought behind this shame is not that liking yams is wrong or bad; it is that liking yams is part of a stereotype that a black man must escape in order to be self-defining. Enjoying his yam, the narrator feels "I am as the Other sees me" – which is Sartre's formulation of the thought involved in shame. For further discussion of this formulation, see note 19, above.

but it can't protect him from shame, which is anxiety about disqualification rather than disapprobation, an anxiety that cannot be allayed by a sense of personal excellence, and especially not by a sense of racial excellence, which tends to be formulated in further stereotypes. What the victim of shame needs to recover is, not his pride in being African-American or Jewish, but his social power of self-definition, which he can hardly recover by allowing himself to be typed, even by his friends.[24]

XIII

The shame induced by racism is a case of utterly inchoate shame, whose subject is successfully shamed without being ashamed of anything in particular. Inchoate shame typically results, as in this case, from deliberate acts of shaming.

Consider, for example, the shaming carried out by the Puritans by means of the pillory. The standard account of shame would imply that the pillory shamed a wrongdoer by exposing him to his neighbors' disapproval of his wrongdoing. But he would have been exposed to that disapproval anyway, as he went about his daily business. And surely the pillory was designed to inflict shame on him even if – indeed, especially if – his neighbors' disapproval left him unashamed.[25] My account of shame

---

[24] Of course, positive stereotypes offer roles that are easier to play with that sense of conviction which feels like authorship. Hence people often fail to experience the shame that they ought to feel in letting themselves be co-opted into positive stereotypes, including such current favorites as The Good Liberal or The Right-Thinking Multiculturalist. But these stereotypes are only a further form of self-compromise, which might be described as putting on whiteface.

[25] Here I disagree with Nathaniel Hawthorne, who says: "There can be no outrage . . . more flagrant than to forbid the culprit to hide his face for shame; as it was the essence of this punishment to do." (*The Scarlet Letter* [New York: Bantam Books, 1986], p. 53). According to Hawthorne, the essence of the pillory was to prevent the culprit from alleviating shame that he already felt – presumably, for his wrongdoing. I believe that the pillory was designed to inflict shame even on wrongdoers who were not ashamed of what they had done: it was a device for teaching shame to the shameless. To be sure, the shamefaced culprit was prevented by the pillory from alleviating his shame, but only by being denied the means of self-presentation. Hiding one's face in shame is a symbolic act, since it neither hides one from view nor spares one the awareness of being viewed. It is rather a symbolic admission of having failed to manage one's public self: one withdraws one's botched self-presentation, symbolized by the face, as if to set it right before returning it to public view. The pillory prevented this gesture of withdrawal, thereby preventing the culprit from symbolically reestablishing his self-possession and, with it, his claim to socially recognized personhood. It was by preventing this restorative self-presentation that the pillory blocked the wrongdoer's recovery from shame. As I argue in the text, this was only one means of self-presentation that the pillory denied the wrongdoer.

suggests how the pillory could have had such an effect. The physical constraints of the pillory – applied to the head and hands, which are the primary instruments of self-presentation – ensured that the wrong-doer was simultaneously displayed to the public and disabled from presenting himself, so that he was publicly stripped of his social status as a self-presenting person. Forcibly displaying him in this position had the effect of shaming him whether or not he was ashamed of what he had done.[26]

This effect is illustrated by another practice, which survives today and may be the closest that any of us has come to the pillory. As children, many of us were forced to perform for household guests, and our shame on these occasions did not necessarily involve any negative assessment of our performance. Being exposed against our will, and hence displayed as less than self-presenting persons, was enough to make our position shameful. It never helped for our parents to say that we had nothing to be ashamed of, because we weren't ashamed of anything in particular: we were merely sensible of being shamed.[27]

---

[26] Another cultural practice of shaming is described by Jon Elster in *Strong Feelings*, pp. 100–101:

> In nineteenth-century Corsica, contempt for the person who failed to abide by the norms of vengeance was expressed by the *rimbecco*, "a deliberate reminder of the unfulfilled revenge. It could take the form of a song, a remark, a gesture or a look, and be delivered by relatives, neighbors or strangers, men or women. It was a direct accusation of cowardice and dereliction":
>
> > [...] In Corsica, the man who has not avenged his father, an assassinated relative or a deceived daughter can no longer appear in public. Nobody speaks to him; he has to remain silent. If he raises his voice to emit an opinion, people will say to him: "avenge yourself first, and then you can state your point of view." The *rimbecco* can occur at any moment and under any guise. It does not even need to express itself in words: an ironical smile, a contemptuous turning away of the head, a certain condescending look – there are a thousand small insults which at all times of the day remind the unhappy victim of how much he has fallen in the esteem of his compatriots. [Quoted from S. Wilson, *Feuding, Conflict, and Banditry in Nineteenth-Century Corsica* (Cambridge: Cambridge University Press, 1988), p. 203.]
>
> Elster interprets this practice as inducing shame in its victim by expressing the community's contempt. The practice does express contempt, of course, but it also conveys the victim's loss of credentials as a self-presenter. His every attempt to present himself to others is met with a reminder that their knowledge of his situation has rendered them deaf and blind to anything else about him.

[27] One might think that what is felt on these occasions is embarrassment rather than shame. Let me respond by explaining how I distinguish between the two. Note that 'embarrassment' is not, in the first instance, the name of an emotion at all. The primary meaning of the verb 'to embarrass' is "to impede or encumber," and the noun 'embarrassment'

Try to imagine a culture in which heroes and paragons are displayed to the public in a pillory, the better to receive their neighbors' admiration. I find such a culture impossible to imagine, because forcibly displaying someone cannot help but seem like a means of shaming him.[28] The only way to bear up under admiring attention is to receive it actively or at least voluntarily – preferably not by strutting and preening, of course, but at least by holding up a pleased or grateful or even a modest face. Those who are afraid of actively presenting themselves to admiring attention may experience the attention as pinning them down, and so they may experience praise itself as a kind of pillory.[29] That's why praise alone can make some people blush with shame, even though they have nothing to be ashamed of.

refers either to the encumbrance or the state of being encumbered. (Hence the concept of "financial embarrassments," which are not so called because they tend to make one blush.) Insofar as 'embarrassment' refers to a mental state, it refers to the state of being mentally encumbered or impeded – that is, baffled, confounded, or flustered. In this generic sense, embarrassment can be a component or concomitant of any disconcerting emotion, including shame. In recent times, 'embarrassment' has also come to denote a particular emotion distinct from shame. (This use of the term is little more than a hundred years old, according to the Oxford English Dictionary.) This emotion begins with the sense of being the focus of undue or unwelcome attention – typically, ridicule or derision – and it culminates in self-consciousness, the self-focused attention that hinders fluid speech and behavior (and that consequently counts as embarrassment in the generic sense). Being flustered in the face of laughter is the typical case of the emotion called embarrassment. This emotion differs from shame, first, because it involves self-consciousness rather than anxiety and, second, because it involves a sense of attracting unwelcome recognition rather than of losing social recognition altogether. Being ridiculed is an essentially social kind of treatment. Self-consciousness in the face of ridicule is therefore different from anxiety at the prospect of social disqualification. Whereas the subject of embarrassment feels that he has egg on his face, the subject of shame feels a loss of face – the difference being precisely that between presenting a target for ridicule and not presenting a target for social interaction at all. Returning to the example under discussion in the text, I grant that some children may suffer no more than embarrassment when forced to perform for guests, if they feel merely self-conscious about being the center of attention. But other children experience their position more profoundly, as a threat to their social selves, undermining their prospects of being taken seriously as persons.

[28] Several readers have pointed out that our culture has a pillory of just this kind: the tabloids. But then, celebrities feel shame about being displayed in the tabloids, insofar as they are displayed in ways that undermine rather than enable self-presentation on their part.

[29] Of course, these people may be afraid of actively receiving admiration because they would be ashamed of the vanity or exhibitionism that such a self-presentation would reveal. They consequently find themselves in a bind, with nowhere to turn without shame. Others may feel no more than embarrassment in the same circumstances: see note 27, above.

With these examples, I have completed the promised progression, from the natural shamefulness of the naked body, to the shamefulness of matters considered private by choice or convention, to the shamefulness of circumstances not involving privacy at all. In all of these cases, I have argued, shame is the anxious sense of being compromised in one's self-presentation in a way that threatens one's social recognition as a self-presenting person.

XIV

My account of shame has a present-day moral. We often hear that our culture has lost its sense of shame – an observation that I think is largely true. Some moralists take this observation as grounds for trying to re-scandalize various conditions that used to be considered shameful, such out-of-wedlock birth or homosexuality. These moralists reason that nothing is shameful to us because nothing is an object of social disapproval, and hence that reviving disapproval is the only way to reawaken shame.

In my view, however, nothing is shameful to us because nothing is private: our culture has become too confessional and exhibitionistic.[30] The way to reawaken shame is to revive our sense of privacy, which needn't require disapproval at all. To say that people should keep their sexual practices to themselves is not to imply that there is anything bad or wrong about those practices. "What!" exclaims St. Augustine, "does not even conjugal intercourse, sanctioned as it is by law for the propagation of children, legitimate and honorable though it be, does it not seek retirement from every eye?"[31]

What's responsible for the exhibitionism of our culture, I think, is a mistake that I warned against earlier, about the dishonesty of self-presentation.[32] People now think that not to express inclinations or impulses is in effect to claim that one doesn't have them, and that honesty therefore requires one to express whatever inclinations or impulses one has. What they forget is that the overt personas we compose are not interpreted as accurate representations of our inner lives. We have sex in private but – to quote again from St. Augustine – "Who does not know what passes between husband and wife that children may be born?"[33]

---

[30] This point is the main theme of Nagel's "Concealment and Exposure."

[31] *The City of God*, Chapter 18, p. 466.

[32] See the quotations from Nagel in note 12.

[33] *The City of God*, Chapter 18, p. 467. See again the quotations from Nagel in note 12.

No one believes that our public faces perfectly reflect our private selves, and so we shouldn't be tempted to pretend that they do, or to accuse ourselves of dishonesty when they don't.

XV

The moralists are wrong, in my view, not only about the means of reawakening shame, but also about its proper objects. Although sexual behavior calls for privacy, for example, the homosexual variety calls for no more privacy than the heterosexual and is therefore no more an occasion for shame.

That said, I should add that the moralist's view of homosexuality as inherently shameful strikes me as intelligible. The politically correct interpretation of this view is that it is a blatant prejudice if not in fact a mental illness diagnosable as a phobia. I do think that this view of homosexuality is a grievously harmful mistake, but I also think that it is an understandable mistake, given the nature of shame.

People who think that homosexuality is shameful tend to be people who don't know any homosexuals – or, more likely, don't realize that they do. For them, heterosexuality is very much the default condition, and homosexuality is therefore especially salient. The fact that someone is a homosexual, if it ever comes to their attention, tends to occupy their attention in connection with that person.[34] And this fact is, after all, a very private fact about the person, involving the anatomy of his bedmates and what passes between them in bed. If someone's sexual orientation is especially salient to people, then his very presence will cause them to think about his private life in ways that will occasion shame – vicarious shame on his behalf, for the imagined exposure of his sexuality, and shame on their own behalf, for the sexual curiosity aroused.

If they conclude that the homosexual ought to be ashamed, then the moralists (as I've called them) are behaving like outraged peeping Toms, mistaking their invasion of someone's privacy for a failure of privacy on his part. The mistake in this case is both less and more understandable: less, because the moralists are seeing the homosexual behavior only in their imaginations; more, because they cannot control

---

[34] As Liz Anderson has pointed out to me, this effect is aggravated by the moralists' tendency to think that homosexual relationships are all about sex and not at all about love and friendship, so that the social appearance of homosexual partners seems as indecent as the appearance of a heterosexual man with his prostitute.

their imaginations, which makes them feel that they are being forced to see, as if they were the victims of an exhibitionist.

The remedy for all of this shame, of course, is to get used to the fact of the person's homosexual behavior, so that it can be put out of mind. Moralists are simply wrong in thinking that they should induce the homosexual to share the vicarious shame that they feel on his behalf. For the homosexual to flaunt his sexuality, however, can at most be a means of forcing this error into the open; it cannot be part of the ultimate resolution, since the moralists have got at least this much right, that sexuality requires a realm of privacy.

To say that the homosexual should not, in the end, be flaunting his sexuality is not at all to suggest a return to the closet, since privacy is not the same as secrecy or denial. Everyone knows that most adults have sex with their dates or domestic partners (among others), and no reasonable norm of privacy would rule out discussion or display of who is dating or living with whom. But allowing people to know something should not be confused with presenting it to their view. There's a difference between "out of the closet" and "in your face," and what makes the difference is privacy.

In short, Adam and Eve were right to avail themselves of fig leaves. Although the term "fig leaf" is now a term of derision, I think that fig leaves are nothing to be ashamed of. They manifest our sense of privacy, which is an expression of our personhood.

4

Love as a Moral Emotion

Introduction

Love and morality are generally assumed to differ in spirit. The moral point of view is impartial and favors no particular individual, whereas favoring someone in particular seems like the very essence of love. Love and morality are therefore thought to place conflicting demands on our

This chapter originally appeared in *Ethics* 109 (January 1999): 338–374. It is reprinted by permission of the University of Chicago. Copyright © 1999 The University of Chicago. All Rights Reserved. The theme of this chapter was suggested to me by Harry Frankfurt's "Autonomy, Necessity, and Love" (in *Vernunftbegriffe in der Moderne*, ed. Hans Friedrich Fulda and Rolf-Peter Horstmann [Klett-Cotta, 1994], pp. 433–47). I first attempted to state the theme in a paper entitled "Frankfurt on Love and Duty," written for a conference organized by Rüdiger Bittner in the spring of 1996, at the Zentrum für interdiziplinäre Forschung, in Bielefeld, Germany. Some of that paper is reproduced here. Also contained here is material from a commentary on Henry S. Richardson's *Practical Reasoning about Final Ends* (Cambridge: Cambridge University Press, 1994); my commentary was presented at a session of the Society for Informal Logic at the 1995 meetings of the American Philosophical Association (APA) Eastern Division. Earlier versions of this chapter were read to the philosophy departments at Arizona State University; Harvard; Princeton; University of California, Los Angeles; University College London; and to a discussion group that meets at Oriel College, Oxford, under the auspices of David Charles. This essay was presented at the 1997 meetings of the APA Eastern Division, with commentaries by Harry Frankfurt and Thomas Hill. It has also had the benefit of comments from: Neera Badhwar, Marcia Baron, Paul Boghossian, Linda Wimer Brakel, Michael Bratman, Sarah Buss, Jennifer Church, Stephen L. Darwall, Elizabeth Fricker, Richard Heck, David Hills, Robert N. Johnson, Christine Korsgaard, Elijah Millgram, David Phillips, Peter Railton, Connie Rosati, Tamar Schapiro, Michael Smith, Michael Stocker, and Alec Walen. Work on this chapter was supported by a sabbatical leave from the College of Literature, Science, and the Arts, University of Michigan, and by a fellowship from the National Endowment for the Humanities.

attention, requiring us to look at things differently, whether or not they ultimately require us to do different things.[1]

The question is supposed to be whether a person can do justice to both perspectives. Some philosophers think that one or the other perspective will inevitably be slighted – that a loving person cannot help but be inattentive to his[2] moral duty, while a fully dutiful person cannot help but be unloving.[3] Other philosophers contend that a person can pass freely between these perspectives, tempering either with insights drawn from the other and thereby doing justice to both.

A Problem for Kantian Ethics

The latter arguments have been especially effective when pressed by consequentialists.[4] Consequentialism makes no fundamental demands on an agent's attention: it says that an agent ought to think in whatever way

---

[1] I will not be concerned in this chapter with the possibility of practical conflict between love and duty; my sole concern will be the supposed psychological conflict – what I have called the conflict in spirit. For the claim that love and duty conflict in practice, see Michael Slote, *Goods and Virtues* (Oxford: Clarendon Press, 1983), p. 86. Slote's example is discussed by Marcia Baron in "On Admirable Immorality," *Ethics* 96 (1986): 557–66, pp. 558 ff. An alternative version of Slote's example appears in Susan Wolf, "Morality and Partiality," *Philosophical Perspectives* 6 (1992): 243–59, 253.

[2] I explain my reasons for using 'he' to denote the arbitrary person in my *Practical Reflection* (Princeton, N.J.: Princeton University Press, 1989), p. 4, n. 1.

[3] Some philosophers see love as conflicting with morality only as the latter is conceived by a particular moral theory. See, e.g., Julia Annas, "Personal Love and Kantian Ethics in *Effi Briest*," in *Friendship; A Philosophical Reader*, ed. Neera Kapur Badhwar (Ithaca, N.Y.: Cornell University Press, 1993), pp. 155–73; and Neera Badhwar Kapur, "Why It Is Wrong to Be Always Guided by the Best: Consequentialism and Friendship," *Ethics* 101 (1991): 483–504. Annas and Badhwar think that love is compatible with morality, properly conceived; and so they reject Kantianism and consequentialism, respectively, for implying otherwise. Other philosophers see the conflict between love and morality as cutting across at least some differences among moral theories. These authors include: Bernard Williams, "A Critique of Utilitarianism," in J.J.C. Smart and Bernard Williams, *Utilitarianism For and Against* (Cambridge: Cambridge University Press, 1973), pp. 75–150; "Morality and the Emotions," in his *Problems of the Self* (Cambridge: Cambridge University Press, 1973), pp. 207–29; "Persons, Character and Morality," in his *Moral Luck: Philosophical Papers 1973–1980* (Cambridge: Cambridge University Press, 1981), pp. 1–19; Michael Stocker, "The Schizophrenia of Modern Ethical Theories," *Journal of Philosophy* 73 (1976): 453–66, and "Friendship and Duty: Some Difficult Relations," in *Identity, Character, and Morality: Essays in Moral Psychology*, ed. Owen Flanagan and Amélie Oksenberg Rorty (Cambridge, Mass.: MIT Press, 1990), pp. 219–33; Susan Wolf, "Morality and Partiality," and "Moral Saints," *Journal of Philosophy* 79 (1982): 419–39; John Deigh, "Morality and Personal Relations," in his *The Sources of Moral Agency: Essays in Moral Psychology and Freudian Theory* (New York: Cambridge University Press, 1996), pp. 1–17.

[4] See Henry Sidgwick, *The Methods of Ethics* (Indianapolis: Hackett, 1981), pp. 432 ff.; Sarah Conly, "Utilitarianism and Integrity," *Monist* 66 (1983): 298–311, and "The Objectivity of

would do the most good, which will rarely entail thinking about how to do the most good. Although the consequentialist standard is impartial and impersonal, its satisfaction allows, and probably requires, partial and personal attention to individuals.

Kantian moral theory cannot efface itself in this fashion, because it makes fundamental demands on an agent's practical thought. What morality demands of an agent, according to Kant, is that he act on a maxim that he can universalize – or, roughly, that he act for reasons of a type that he could regard as valid for anyone in similar circumstances.[5] Because Kantianism thus demands that an agent be able to take a particular view of his own reasons, it requires him to be morally minded and not just morally behaved.

This moral theory is sometimes misrepresented by those who claim that it conflicts with the spirit of love. For example, Kantian ethics has been said to require that one accord others "equal consideration" in a sense that entails "giving equal weight to the interests of all," which would seem incompatible with caring about some people more than others.[6] Yet equal consideration in Kantian ethics consists in considering everyone as having equal access to justifications for acting – which amounts to considering everyone's rights as equal, not everyone's interests. Caring about some people more than others may be perfectly compatible with according everyone equal rights.[7]

Even so, Kantian morality seems to require an agent to live with a nagging reservation, insofar as he is to act on no maxim that he cannot

---

Morals and the Subjectivity of Agents," *American Philosophical Quarterly* 22 (1985): 275–86; Peter Railton, "Alienation, Consequentialism, and the Demands of Morality," *Philosophy and Public Affairs* 13 (1984): 134–72. See also Alan Gewirth, "Ethical Universalism and Particularism," *Journal of Philosophy* 85 (1988): 283–302; and Frank Jackson, "Decision-Theoretic Consequentialism and the Nearest and Dearest Objection," *Ethics* 101 (1991): 461–82.

5 Here I am glossing over many exegetical issues in order to state a version of the Categorical Imperative that seems both intuitively plausible and faithful to Kant. I defend this version of the Categorical Imperative in my "The Voice of Conscience" (Chapter 5 in the present volume).

6 Lawrence A. Blum, *Friendship, Altruism and Morality* (London: Routledge & Kegan Paul, 1980), p. 44.

7 A similar reply can be made to the following remark by Robert C. Solomon: "On the Kantian model, the particularity of love would seem to be a form of irrationality – comparable to our tendency to make 'exceptions' of ourselves, in this case, making exceptions of persons close to us" ("The Virtue of (Erotic) Love," *Midwest Studies in Philosophy* 13 [1988]: 12–31, p. 18). The Kantian model forbids only those exceptions by which we act for reasons that we couldn't make generally accessible. It does not forbid differential

universalize. This reservation threatens to interfere with some of the motives and feelings generally regarded as essential to love. The Kantian moral agent cleaves to his loved ones only on the condition that he can regard cleaving to loved ones as reasonable for anyone, and he thereby seems to entertain "one thought too many " for cleaving to them at all.

This formulation of the problem comes from Bernard Williams, discussing the case of a man who can save only one of several people in peril and who chooses to save his own wife. Williams remarks, "It might have been hoped by some (for instance, his wife) that his motivating thought, fully spelled out, would be the thought that it was his wife, not that it was his wife and that in situations of this kind it is permissible to save one's wife."[8]

As Kantian moralists have hastened to point out, however, their theory allows an agent to act without expressly considering whether he could universalize his maxim, provided that he would notice and be deterred if he couldn't; and the motivational force of love not only can but should be conditional to this minimal extent.[9] Although Kant's impartial morality can never fully remove itself from the deliberative process, they argue, it can make itself sufficiently inconspicuous to allow for intimate personal relations. Conscience can stand by in the role of chaperone, and love need not feel inhibited by such unobtrusive supervision.

Effective as this solution may be, it concedes too much to the supposed problem. To argue that conscience can leave room for love by withdrawing into the background of our thoughts is implicitly to concede that it would interfere with love if permitted to share the foreground. A conflict in spirit is thus admitted but shown to be manageable, through segregation of the conflicting parties.

treatment of different people. (This point is also made, e.g., by Marcia Baron in "Impartiality and Friendship," *Ethics* 101 [1991]: 836–57, p. 851.)

8 Williams, "Persons, Character and Morality," p. 18.

9 See Henry E. Allison, *Kant's Theory of Freedom* (Cambridge: Cambridge University Press, 1990), pp. 191–98; Barbara Herman, *The Practice of Moral Judgment* (Cambridge, Mass.: Harvard University Press, 1993), esp. chapters 1, 2, and 9; Marcia Baron, "On Admirable Immorality" and *Kantian Ethics Almost without Apology* (Ithaca, N.Y.: Cornell University Press, 1995), chapters 4–6. See also H.J. Paton, "Kant on Friendship," *Proceedings of the British Academy* 42 (1956): 45–66; N.J.H Dent, "Duty and Inclination," *Mind* 83 (1974): 552–70; Mary Midgley, "The Objection to Systematic Humbug," *Philosophy* 53 (1978): 147–69; Adrian M.S. Piper, "Moral Theory and Moral Alienation," *Journal of Philosophy* 84 (1987): 102–18; and Cynthia A. Stark, "Decision Procedures, Standards of Rightness, and Impartiality," *Noûs* 31 (1997): 478–95.

If love and morality were even potentially at odds to this extent, then love would have to be, if not an immoral emotion, then at least non-moral. But love is a moral emotion. So if we find ourselves segregating love and morality in order to keep the peace, then we have already made a mistake.

We have made a mistake, I think, as soon as we accept the assumption of a conflict in spirit. Love is a moral emotion precisely in the sense that its spirit is closely akin to that of morality. The question, then, is not whether two divergent perspectives can be accommodated but rather how these two perspectives converge.

Possible Solutions

One way to bring them into convergence would be to reject the Kantian conception of morality as impartial. Lawrence Blum endorses the view, which he attributes to Iris Murdoch, that "the moral task is not to generate action based on universal and impartial principles but to attend and respond to particular persons."[10] The way to effect a convergence of spirit between love and morality, according to Blum, is to allow for greater partiality in our conception of morality.

I think that this view is the opposite of correct. The way to bring love into convergence with morality is not to stop thinking of morality as impartial but to rethink the partiality of love.

Here there is a danger of falling into "righteous absurdity," as Williams calls it, by getting too high-minded about love.[11] I'll try to avoid absurdity, but I won't entirely avoid the righteousness, I'm afraid, since I think that moral philosophers could stand to be more rather than less high-minded on the subject. The account of love offered by many philosophers sounds

---

[10] Lawrence Blum, "Iris Murdoch and the Domain of the Moral," *Philosophical Studies* 50 (1986): 343–67, p. 344. Blum draws this view from Murdoch's *The Sovereignty of Good* (New York: Routledge & Kegan Paul, 1970). Others who subscribe to this view include John Kekes, "Morality and Impartiality," *American Philosophical Quarterly* 18 (1981): 295–303; Andrew Oldenquist, "Loyalties," *Journal of Philosophy* 79 (1982): 173–93; John Cottingham, "Ethics and Impartiality," *Philosophical Studies* 43 (1983): 83–99; Annette Baier, "The Moral Perils of Intimacy," in *Pragmatism's Freud: The Moral Disposition of Psychoanalysis*, ed. Joseph H. Smith and William Kerrigan (Baltimore: Johns Hopkins University Press, 1986), pp. 93–101; Christina Hoff Sommers, "Filial Morality," *Journal of Philosophy* 83 (1986): 439–56; Seyla Benhabib, "The Generalized and the Concrete Other: The Kohlberg-Gilligan Controversy and Moral Theory," in *Women and Moral Theory*, ed. Eva Feder Kittay and Diana T. Meyers (Totowa, N.J.: Rowman & Littlefield, 1987), pp. 154–77; Lynne McFall, "Integrity," *Ethics* 98 (1987): 5–20. See also various contributions to a symposium published in *Ethics* 101, no. 4 (1991).

[11] Williams, "Persons, Character and Morality," p. 16.

to me less like an analysis of the emotion itself than an inventory of the desires and preferences that tend to arise in loving relationships of the most familiar kinds. Once we distinguish love from the likings and longings that usually go with it, I believe, we will give up the assumption that the emotion is partial in a sense that puts it in conflict with the spirit of morality.[12]

I can foreshadow my conclusion by pointing out that Murdoch's ethic of attending to the particular is not necessarily at odds with the ethics of impartiality. On the contrary, Murdoch emphasizes that the attention required is "impersonal" and "an exercise of *detachment*."[13]

To be sure, Murdoch equates attending to individuals with a form of love for them,[14] and a morality based on love might naturally be assumed to differ from any morality that is impartial. Yet the attention that embodies love, in Murdoch's view, is strictly objective and fair-minded:

Should a retarded child be kept at home or sent to an institution? Should an elderly relation who is a trouble-maker be cared for or asked to go away? Should an unhappy marriage be continued for the sake of the children?...The love which brings the right answer is an exercise of justice and realism and really *looking*.[15]

In Murdoch's language of impersonality, detachment, realism, and justice, there is no suggestion that particularity entails partiality.

Let me extend these remarks on Murdoch by noting that her term for that which constitutes love – that is, 'attention' – can be translated into German as *Achtung*, which was Kant's own term for the motive of morality.[16] This is a punning translation, of course, since *Achtung* can denote

---

[12] For a related attempt to rethink the partiality of love, see Jennifer Whiting, "Impersonal Friends," *Monist* 74 (1991): 3–29.

[13] Murdoch, *Sovereignty of Good,* p. 65.

[14] "Prayer is properly not petition, but simply an attention to God which is a form of love"; "the capacity to love, that is to *see*"; "attention to reality inspired by, consisting of, love" (ibid., pp. 55, 66, 67).

[15] Ibid., p. 91.

[16] Iris Murdoch herself draws this connection in "The Sublime and the Good," in *Existentialists and Mystics: Writings on Philosophy and Literature,* ed. Peter Conradi (New York: Penguin, 1997), pp. 205–20. In this essay, after asserting that "love is the extremely difficult realisation that something other than oneself is real" (p. 215), Murdoch says that this "exercise of overcoming oneself... is very like *Achtung*," adding: "Kant was marvelously near the mark" (p. 216). To be sure, Murdoch's primary concern in this essay is to criticize Kant for being "afraid of the particular" (p. 214). But I think that Murdoch underestimates the extent to which the object of Kantian *Achtung* can be a universal

not only attention but also a mode of valuation, and the latter is the meaning intended by Kant.[17] But these two meanings are not independent:
there is a deep conceptual connection between valuation and vision – a
connection evident in words like 'respect,' 'regard,' and even in Kant's
synonym for *Achtung*, the Latin *reverentia*.[18] If love is indeed a matter of

law embodied in a particular person, or the object of love can be a particular person
as embodying something universal. In short, I think that Murdoch underestimates how
near Kant was to the mark.

[17] On the concept of respect for persons in moral theory, see: Stephen L. Darwall, "Two
Kinds of Respect," *Ethics* 88 (1977): 36–49; William K. Frankena, "The Ethics of Respect
for Persons," *Philosophical Topics* 14 (1986): 149–67. As these discussions make clear,
Kantian respect is not the same as esteem. It is rather a kind of a practical considera-
tion paid to another person. See also Robin Dillon, "Respect and Care: Toward Moral
Integration," *Canadian Journal of Philosophy* 22 (1992): 105–32.

[18] Immanuel Kant, *The Metaphysics of Morals*, trans. Mary Gregor (Cambridge: Cambridge
University Press, 1996), 6:402. All references to Kant's works are given by the volume and
page number of the Royal Prussian Academy edition of his *gesammelte Schriften* (Berlin:
de Gruyter, 1902–). The Latin *vereor* is cognate with the Greek '*ορα'ω*,' "to see," as well
as the English 'beware.' On the connection between respect and attention, see
Dillon, "Respect and Care," pp. 108, 119–20, 124–27. The connection between love and
attention was attributed by Murdoch to Simone Weil(see Simone Weil, "Human Personality," in *The Simone Weil Reader*, ed. George A. Panichas [New York: David McKay, 1977],
pp. 313–39, p. 333). Similar connections are drawn by George Nakhnikian, "Love in
Human Reason," *Midwest Studies in Philosophy* 3 (1978): 286–317; Roger Scruton, *Sexual
Desire: A Moral Philosophy of the Erotic* (New York: Free Press, 1986), pp. 99–100; Martha
Craven Nussbaum, "'Finely Aware and Richly Responsible': Literature and the Moral
Imagination," in *Anti-Theory in Ethics and Moral Conservatism*, ed. Stanley G. Clarke and
Evan Simpson (Albany: SUNY Press, 1989), pp. 111–34; and Nathaniel Branden, "Love
and Psychological Visibility," in Badhwar, ed, pp. 64–72. David Hills has pointed out to
me that Stanley Cavell's essay on *King Lear* is primarily about our motives for avoiding the
visibility that comes with being loved (Stanley Cavell, "The Avoidance of Love: A Reading
of *King Lear*," in his *Must We Mean What We Say? A Book of Essays* [Cambridge: Cambridge
University Press, 1976], pp. 267–353). The psychoanalytic literature offers an especially
vivid instance of love as a form of attention. It is D. W. Winnicott's image of the mother's
face as a mirror ("Mirror-Role of Mother and Family in Child Development," in his *Playing and Reality* [New York: Routledge, 1989], pp. 111–18). Winnicott imagines that the
good-enough mother (as he calls her) expresses in her face the feelings that she sees
expressed in the baby's face, thus presenting the baby with an expression that mirrors
both its face and its state of mind. The mother looks at the baby in a way that enacts her
unclouded perception of what it feels: hers is a look that visibly sees. This image of "really
looking" is also, unmistakably, an image of motherly love. (On the application of Murdoch's views specifically to maternal love, see also Sara Ruddick, "Maternal Thinking,"
in *Women and Values: Readings in Recent Feminist Philosophy*, ed. Marilyn Pearsall [Belmont,
CA: Wadsworth, 1986], pp. 340–51, 347 ff.)

Winnicott's image may explain why Freud imagined the psychoanalyst as offering his
patient "a cure through love" while doing no more than holding up a mirror to him. (For
the former notion, see Freud's letter to Jung, December 6, 1906, *The Freud/Jung Letters:
The Correspondence between Sigmund Freud and C.G. Jung* [Princeton, N.J.: Princeton

"really looking," then it ought to resemble other instances of valuation-as-vision, including Kantian respect.

My aim in this chapter is to juxtapose love and Kantian respect in a way that is illuminating for both. On the one hand, I hope to show that we can resolve some problems in our understanding of love by applying the theory of value and valuation that Kant developed for respect. On the other hand, I hope that this application of Kant's theory will show that its stern and forbidding tone is just that – a tone in which Kant stated the theory rather than an essential characteristic of the theory itself, which is in fact well suited to matters of the heart.

Respect for the Law and Respect for Persons

A potential obstacle to this project is that Kantian respect is, in the first instance, respect for the law, an attitude whose object is widely assumed to consist in rules of conduct, or (in Blum's phrase) "universal and impartial principles." An attitude toward rules or principles would seem to have nothing in common with love for a person.

I shall argue, however, that Kantian respect is not an attitude toward rules or principles. It is rather an attitude toward the idealized, rational will, which qualifies as a law because it serves as a norm for the actual, empirical will – thus qualifying, in fact, as that law which the will is to itself. This rational will, in Kant's view, is also the intelligible essence of a person: Kant calls it a person's true or proper self. Respect for this law is thus the same attitude as respect for the person; and so it can perhaps be compared with love, after all.

Even within the confines of the *Groundwork*, Kant speaks of the law in several different senses. The English word 'law' is normally used to denote, first, particular rules of conduct; second, an abstract form or status that some rules exemplify (when, as we say, they have the force of law); and third, the associated social institutions that apply them (when, as we say, we call in the law).

Kant uses *das Gesetz* in something like the first sense when referring to the output of universalization, the "universal law" into which one must

University Press, 1974], pp. 12–13; for the latter, see Freud, "Recommendations to Physicians Practicing Psycho-Analysis," *The Standard Edition of the Complete Psychological Works of Sigmund Freud*, ed. James Strachey [London: Hogarth Press, 1958] [hereafter cited as *S.E.*], vol. 12, pp. 111–20, p. 118. This connection was suggested to me by Nina Coltart's essay "Attention," in her *Slouching towards Bethlehem* [New York: Guildford, 1992], pp. 176–93.)

imaginatively transform one's maxim in order to test its permissibility. He also refers to the Categorical Imperative as a law in this sense.[19]

To my knowledge, however, Kant never holds up the law in this first sense as the proper object of respect or reverence. The moral agent who imaginatively transforms his maxim into a universal law may subsequently act out of reverence for the law, but this reverence is not directed at the particular law he has imagined; nor is it directed at the rule requiring this imaginative exercise. Rather, the agent's engaging in this exercise – and his thereby obeying that rule – manifests his reverence for the law in some other sense.

Kant speaks of the law in something like the abstract, second sense when he gives this derivation of the Categorical Imperative: "For since besides the law this imperative contains only the necessity that our maxim should conform to this law, while the law, as we have seen, contains no condition to limit it, there remains nothing over to which the maxim has to conform except the universality of a law as such; and it is this conformity alone that the imperative properly asserts to be necessary."[20] Here the law to which the Categorical Imperative requires conformity is law in the abstract sense – the universal form of law – rather than any particular law, which would need some "condition to limit it." *Das Gesetz* in this context is the abstraction that's described in an earlier passage as "the idea of the law in itself."[21]

In that earlier passage, Kant seems to say that the idea of the law in itself is the proper object of reverence and hence the determining ground of the good will. But then he goes on to ask, "What kind of law can this be the thought of which ... has to determine the will if this is to be called good absolutely and without qualification?" In reply, he offers a more subtle formulation: "Since I have robbed the will of every inducement that might arise for it as a consequence of obeying any particular law, nothing is left but the conformity of actions to universal law as such, and this alone must serve the will as its principle."[22] The English version fails to make clear that what is said to determine the will, in this passage, is not the idea of the universal law but rather the idea of the conformity of actions to that law – the idea of "the universal-law–abidingness of actions"

[19] Immanuel Kant, *Groundwork of the Metaphysic of Morals*, trans. H.J. Paton (New York: Harper & Row, 1964), 4:420, 426, 437.
[20] Ibid., 4:421–22. See also 4:402.
[21] Ibid., 4:400–401.
[22] Ibid., 4:402.

(*die allgemeine Gesetzmässigkeit der Handlungen*). And shortly thereafter, Kant says that the object of reverence is "a possible enactment of universal law" – a *Gesetzgebung*, not a *Gesetz*.[23]

What determines the good will by commanding respect or reverence, then, is not exactly the idea of law in the abstract but rather the idea of law's being laid down for, and taken up in, a person's actions. This object of reverence remains as yet obscure, Kant says – and we can only agree.[24] We can seek clarification, however, by considering other senses in which Kant speaks of the law.

Kant says that the will is a law to itself.[25] In what sense is the will a law?

Kant explains: "The proposition 'Will is in all its actions a law to itself' expresses . . . only the principle of acting on no maxim other than one which can have for its object itself as at the same time a universal law."[26] This explanation is less than satisfactory, since it fails to make clear how "will is a law to itself" can express the principle of acting on lawlike maxims. Perhaps the connection is that the will is a law to itself insofar as it gives itself lawlike maxims on which to act, thereby functioning toward itself as a law-giving authority, which is the third of the senses canvassed above for the English word 'law.'

Yet there is a further respect in which the will is a law to itself. Kant says that when an agent considers himself as an inhabitant of the intelligible world "he is conscious of possessing a good will which, on his own admission, constitutes the law for the bad will belonging to him as a member of the sensible world."[27] Kant is not here envisioning one will causally governing another: after all, the intelligible and the sensible are supposed to be two different aspects of one and the same thing. Rather, Kant is envisioning the purely intelligible will as a paradigm or ideal established for the sensible will. The will is a law to itself in the sense that its own intelligible or noumenal aspect serves as an ideal for its sensible or phenomenal

---

[23] Ibid., 4:403. See also 4:436.

[24] Ibid., 4:403.

[25] Ibid., 4:440, 447.

[26] Ibid., 4:446.

[27] Ibid., 4:455. Also relevant here is this passage from Immanuel Kant, *Critique of Practical Reason*, trans. Lewis White Beck (Indianapolis: Bobbs-Merrill, 1956), 5:32. "One need only analyze the sentence which men pass upon the lawfulness of their actions to see in every case that their reason, incorruptible and self-constrained, in every action holds up the maxim of the will to the pure will, i.e., to itself regarded as a priori practical." Here the process of submitting a maxim to the test of the Categorical Imperative is equated with holding it up to a conception of the will itself, as a faculty of a priori practical reason.

self. In its capacity as an ideal, the noumenal will qualifies as a law in a fourth sense that is somewhat foreign to the English word.

The ideal will is one that acts on lawlike maxims, and this ideal is what commands our respect: "Our own will, provided it were to act only under the condition of being able to make universal law by means of its maxims – this ideal will which can be ours is the proper object of reverence."[28] Reverence for the law is therefore reverence for that intelligible aspect under which our will is an ideal, or law, to its empirical self. Since the intelligible aspect of the will is to give itself lawlike maxims, reverence for this ideal is also reverence for the will as a self-governing authority; and under either guise, it counts as reverence for the law. But reverence for the law, so understood, is directed neither at lawlike maxims nor at the Categorical Imperative, considered as a rule. Its object is rather that ideal which is held up to us by the Categorical Imperative – namely, the intelligible aspect of our will as a faculty of acting on lawlike maxims.

We can now understand why Kant said earlier that the proper object of reverence is a possible enactment of universal law, or the idea of actions conforming to universal law, rather than simply universal law itself. These notions of law-giving and -following are Kant's first approximations to the notion of the rational, self-governing will, which is indeed the proper object of reverence. Reverence for this object can also be called reverence for the law, but not because it is reverence for a rule, a body of rules, or even the abstract form of rules.[29] It can be called reverence for the

---

[28] Kant, *Groundwork*, 4:440. See 4:435: actions performed from duty "exhibit the will which performs them as an object of immediate reverence"; ibid., 4:436: "The law-making [*Gesetzgebung*] which determines all value must for this reason have a dignity – that is, an unconditioned and incomparable worth – for the appreciation of which, as necessarily given by a rational being, the word '*reverence*' is the only becoming expression"; Kant, *Critique of Practical Reason*, 5:73: "Since this law, however, is in itself positive, being the form of an intellectual causality, i.e., the form of freedom, it is at the same time an object of respect." In this last passage, the moral law is an object of respect insofar as it is "the form of an intellectual causality" – i.e., a conception of the free will. See also Kant, *Groundwork*, 4:410–11, where Kant explains how "the pure thought of duty, and in general of the moral law, has . . . an influence on the human heart so much more powerful than all the further impulsions capable of being called up from the field of experience." The explanation of this influence is that "in the consciousness of its own dignity reason despises these impulsions and is able gradually to become their master." Here the influence exerted by "the pure thought of the moral law" is equated with an influence exerted by reason's "consciousness of its own dignity." The motive by which we are influenced in contemplating the moral law is thus a response to an ideal conception of ourselves.

[29] As should already be clear from my survey of how Kant uses the term *das Gesetz*, I do not mean to deny that individual rules or the abstract form of rules plays a role in Kantian moral theory. In particular, the abstract form of rules plays a crucial role in the procedures followed by the will in living up to its self-ideal of being an autonomous legal

law because it is reverence for the authoritative self-ideal that the will's intelligible aspect constitutes for it, which is precisely its aspect as self-governing legal authority.[30]

Thus, respect for the law is an attitude toward the rational will. And a person's rational will must "think itself into the intelligible world" as the bearer of freedom, which cannot be found in the sensible order.[31] Rational will therefore constitutes the person as he is in himself rather than as he appears; it is, as Kant says, "sein eigentliches Selbst."[32] So if reverence for the law is in fact reverence for rational will, then it is reverence for that which constitutes the true or proper self of a person.

The result is that reverence for the law, which has struck so many as making Kantian ethics impersonal, is in fact an attitude toward the person, since the law that commands respect is the ideal of a rational will, which lies at the heart of personhood. This result puts us in a position to consider how Kantian reverence might resemble another moral attitude toward the person, the attitude of love.[33]

authority. My interest, however, is focused exclusively on the law as the proper object of *Achtung*. And I find strong textual evidence for the conclusion that the proper object of *Achtung* is not the abstract form of law but rather the idea of a will that constrains its dictates to be compatible with that form.

[30] This reading seems not to fit a statement in the footnote attached to Kant's initial discussion of reverence: "All reverence for a person is properly only reverence for the law (of honesty and so on) of which that person gives us an example" (*Groundwork*, 4:400). My interpretation says, on the contrary, that all reverence for the law is properly only reverence for the person.

The context of this statement is important to its interpretation. In the present footnote, Kant is forestalling an objection to the effect that reverence is "an obscure feeling" rather than "a concept of reason." Kant's answer to this objection is that "although reverence is a feeling, it is not a feeling *received* through outside influence, but one *self-produced* by a rational concept." He is therefore at pains to emphasize that reverence is a response to something in the rational order rather than to anything in the empirical world.

Kant's statement about the object of reverence must be read in this light. It is meant, I think, to rule out persons as proper objects of reverence *insofar as they are inhabitants of the empirical world*. Their serving as objects of reverence in their purely intelligible aspect, as instances of rational nature, is compatible with the point that Kant is trying to make. It is precisely in this aspect that persons embody the law that is the object of reverence, according to my interpretation. Thus, "the law ... of which that person gives us an example" is one and the same with the rational nature of which he gives us an example. (See also the material at 5:76 ff. of Kant's *Critique of Practical Reason*, which appears to support this interpretation.)

[31] Kant, Groundwork, 4:458.

[32] Ibid., 4:457–58. See also 4:461.

[33] My approach bears similarities to that of Gregory Vlastos, "Justice and Equality," in *Social Justice*, ed. Richard B. Brandt (Englewood Cliffs, N.J.: Prentice Hall, 1962), pp. 31–72. Vlastos draws a connection between love and the principles of social justice, as being

The Conative Analysis of Love

"Love... looks different after one has read Freud," says Richard Rorty.[34] It looks different, according to Rorty, because it has come to appear "morally dubious."[35] If we are to rethink our conception of love, as I have proposed, then we might as well begin with Freud.

Freud's Theory of Drives
One might think that Freud renders love morally dubious by reducing it to sex. Even brotherly love, of both the literal and figurative varieties, is regarded by Freud as "aim inhibited" libido, consisting of drives that "have not abandoned their directly sexual aims, but... are held back by internal resistances from attaining them."[36] Yet I think that what makes love morally dubious, when so conceived, is not that it is fundamentally sexual but that it takes the form of a drive.[37]

Freud conceives of a drive as a constant, internal stimulus that the subject is motivated to remove, whereupon he attains a temporary, repeatable satisfaction, toward which the drive is said to aim.[38] In addition to this aim, a drive also has an object, "the thing in regard to which or through which the [drive] is able to achieve its aim," but its attachment to this

---

    jointly grounded in the "individual worth" of a person. My approach also resembles that of Dillon in "Respect and Care," although I differ from Dillon in trying to retain a Kantian conception of respect. Finally, I also find similarities to Weil's "Human Personality," in which the disparagement of "the person" and "rights" strikes me as aimed at un-Kantian versions of these concepts, and hence as Kantian in spirit.

34 Richard Rorty, "Freud, Morality, and Hermeneutics," *New Literary History* 12 (1980): 177–85, p. 180. This passage is quoted by Baier, p. 93. Murdoch says that Freud "presents us with a realistic and detailed picture of the fallen man" (*Sovereignty of Good*, p. 51). My discussion of Freud is an attempt to make clear and explicit what is implicit in Murdoch's brief allusions to him (pp. 46–51).

35 Richard Rorty, "Freud, Morality, and Hermeneutics," p. 178.

36 Freud, "The Libido Theory," in *S.E.*, vol. 18, pp. 255–59, p. 258. See also Freud, *Civilization and Its Discontents, S.E.*, vol. 21, pp. 59–145, pp. 102–3; "Group Psychology and the Analysis of the Ego," *S.E.*, vol. 18, pp. 67–143, pp. 90–91, and 137–40; "The Dynamics of Transference," in *S.E.*, vol. 12, pp. 97–108, p. 105; "Three Essays on the Theory of Sexuality," *S.E.*, vol. 7, pp. 125–243, p. 200.

37 'Drive' is the literal translation of the word (*Trieb*) that is translated in *S.E.* as 'instinct'. For a critique of the latter translation, see Bruno Bettelheim, *Freud and Man's Soul* (New York: Vintage, 1984), pp. 103–12.

38 Freud, "Instincts and Their Vicissitudes," in *S.E.*, vol. 14, pp. 111–140, pp. 118–23. See also Freud, *New Introductory Lectures in Psychoanalysis*, in *S.E.*, vol. 22, pp. 3–182, 97. In what follows I substitute the word 'drive' for 'instinct' in the *S.E.* translation. Freud later modified the notion that drives aim at the removal of a "tension due to stimulus," but only by introducing the possibility of their aiming at a particular qualitative character in the stimulus ("The Economic Problem of Masochism," *S.E.*, vol. 19, pp. 156–70, pp. 159–61). This modification makes no difference for my purposes.

object is purely instrumental. The object "is what is most variable about a [drive] and is not originally connected with it, but becomes assigned to it only in consequence of being peculiarly fitted to make satisfaction possible."[39] Hence a drive is not in any sense a response to its object. It is a preexisting need,[40] individuated by its aim,[41] to which the object is an adventitious and replaceable means.[42]

The conception of love as a drive can have various unfortunate implications. One implication embraced by Freud is that love tends to cloud rather than clarify the lover's vision. For Freud, love is anything but an exercise of "really looking."

In Freudian theory, the satisfaction of a drive is entirely internal to the subject, because it consists in the removal or modification of an inner irritant. A drive therefore focuses on an object only insofar as it can be used as a source of inner relief – a scratch for the subject's felt itch. And an itchy mind has a way simply of imagining objects to be scratchy.

The consequence is that Freudian love, far from an exercise in perceiving the beloved, is often an exercise in misperceiving him. Misperception becomes extreme in the state of being in love, which is typically marked, according to Freud, by overvaluation and transference. In overvaluation, we project onto our object various excellences borrowed from our ego-ideal, setting up "the illusion . . . that the object has come to be sensually loved on account of its spiritual merits, whereas on the contrary these merits may really only have been lent to it by its sensual charm."[43] In transference, the affection we feel for one object is merely a repetition of feelings originally felt for other objects, so that we relate to our beloved, as one commentator has put it, "through a dense thicket of absent others."[44] Freud emphasizes that a patient's transference-love for the analyst regularly arises "under the most unfavourable conditions and where there are positively grotesque incongruities."[45] Yet he believes that the same

[39] Freud, "Instincts and Their Vicissitudes," p. 122.

[40] Freud himself offers the word 'need' for the motivating stimulus of a drive (ibid., pp. 118–19).

[41] See Freud, "Three Essays," p. 168.

[42] Freud, "Instincts and Their Vicissitudes," pp. 122–23: "[The object] may be changed any number of times in the course of the vicissitudes which the [drive] undergoes during its existence; and highly important parts are played by this displacement of [drive]."

[43] Freud, "Group Psychology," pp. 112–13. See also Freud, "Three Essays," pp. 150–51; "On Narcissism: An Introduction," in *S.E.*, vol. 14, pp. 67–102, pp. 88 ff.

[44] Janet Malcolm, *Psychoanalysis: The Impossible Profession* (New York: Vintage, 1980), p. 6.

[45] Freud, *Introductory Lectures on Psychoanalysis*, in *S.E.*, vol. 16, p. 442.

mechanism of misdirected affection is at work not just within the analytic relationship but whenever we are in love.[46]

Of course, the love that we feel when we are *in* love is that which is proverbially said to be blind. Overvaluation and transference are simply the mechanisms by which Freud explains the blindness of romantic love. And I do not want to claim that blind, romantic love has any special kinship with morality. When I say that love is a moral emotion, what I have in mind is the love between close adult friends and relations – including spouses and other life-partners, insofar as their love has outgrown the effects of overvaluation and transference.

Unfortunately, however, Freud offers no reason why the forces conducive to misperception in the case of romantic love should lead to any clearer perception in their aim-inhibited manifestations as love between parents and children, or as love among siblings or friends.[47] Aim inhibition just is a matter of pursuing something other than what one really wants, and so it is similar to those mechanisms by which "spiritual merits" are substituted for "sensual charms," or one love object for another. Freud's explanation for the blindness of romantic love thus gives us reason to expect love in all forms to suffer at least from blurred vision. Loving someone, we bring to bear on him our infantile needs and all of our imaginative resources for casting him as a source of their satisfaction. But we needn't see or be moved to see him as he really is.

I believe that it was by clouding the eyes of love in this fashion, not by uncovering its genitals, that Freud undermined its moral standing. As Murdoch says, "The chief enemy of excellence in morality...is personal fantasy: the tissue of self-aggrandizing and consoling wishes and dreams which prevents one from seeing what is there outside one."[48]

---

[46] Freud, "Observations on Transference-Love," in *S.E.*, vol. 12, pp. 157–71, p. 168. Indeed, Freud says that transference governs "the whole of each person's relations to his human environment" (*An Autobiographical Study*, in *S.E.*, vol. 20, pp. 3–74, p. 42). See also Freud, *Five Lectures on Psychoanalysis*, in *S.E.*, vol. 11, pp. 3–55, p. 51: "Transference arises spontaneously in all human relationships."

[47] See, e.g, Freud's explanation of parental love as a form of narcissistic overvaluation: "Parental love, which is so moving and at bottom so childish, is nothing but the parents' narcissism born again" ("On Narcissism," p. 91).

[48] Murdoch, *Sovereignty of Good*, p. 59. Murdoch is not here speaking specifically of Freud, though she has already noted that "Freud takes a thoroughly pessimistic view of human nature" in which "fantasy is stronger than reason" (p. 51; see also pp. 66–67). For a related discussion of the Freudian conception of love, see Marcia Cavell, "Knowing and Valuing: Some Questions of Genealogy," in *Psychoanalysis, Mind and Art: Perspectives*

Freud embedded love deep within the tissue of fantasy, thereby closing it off from the moral enterprise.

Analytic Philosophers on Love

Analytic philosophers might be expected to differ from psychoanalysts on the subject of love, and they have fulfilled this expectation insofar as they have deemphasized the sexual. But they are in unexpected agreement with Freud on the psychological form of love, since they tend to conceive of it as having an aim, in the manner of a Freudian drive.

Here are some examples. Henry Sidgwick: "Love is not merely a desire to do good to the object beloved, although it always involves such a desire. It is primarily a pleasurable emotion, which seems to depend upon a certain sense of union with another person, and it includes, besides the benevolent impulse, a desire of the society of the beloved."[49] Laurence Thomas: "Roughly (very roughly), love is feeling anchored in an intense and nonfleeting (but not necessarily permanent) desire to engage in mutual caring, sharing, and physical expression with the individual in question or, in any case, some idealized version of her or him."[50] Harry Frankfurt: "What I have in mind in speaking of love is, roughly and only in part, a concern specifically for the well-being or flourishing of the beloved object that is more or less disinterested and that is also more or less constrained."[51] Gabriele Taylor: "If x loves y then x wants to benefit and be with y etc., and he has these wants (or at least some of them) because he believes y has some determinate characteristics ψ in virtue of which he thinks it worth while to benefit and be with y."[52] William Lyons: "For X to love Y, ... X must not merely evaluate Y as appealing ..., but X must want certain things in regard to Y as well. X must want to be with Y, to please Y, to cherish Y, to want Y to return the love, to want Y to think well of him."[53] Patricia Greenspan: "Attachment-love is picked out as such by the justificatory completeness of its analysis, with personal evaluations taken as needed to support

  on Richard Wollheim, ed. Jim Hopkins and Anthony Saville (Oxford: Blackwell, 1992), pp. 68–86, esp. pp. 81 ff.

[49] Sidgwick, p. 244.

[50] Laurence Thomas, "Reasons for Loving," in *The Philosophy of (Erotic) Love*, ed. Robert C. Solomon and Kathleen M. Higgins (Lawrence: University of Kansas Press, 1991), pp. 467–76, p. 470.

[51] Frankfurt, "Some Thoughts about Caring," *Ethical Perspectives* 5 (1998): 3–14, p. 7.

[52] Gabriele Taylor, "Love," *Proceedings of the Aristotelian Society* 76 (1976): 147–64, p. 157.

[53] William Lyons, *Emotion* (Cambridge: Cambridge University Press, 1980), p. 64.

its characteristic desire: the desire to *be with* another person."[54] Robert
Nozick: "What is common to all love is this: Your own well-being is tied up
with that of someone (or something) you love.... When something bad
happens to one you love,... something bad also happens *to you*.... If a
loved one is hurt or disgraced, you are hurt; if something wonderful happens to her, you feel better off."[55] John Rawls: "Love clearly has among
its main elements the desire to advance the other person's good as this
person's rational self love would require."[56] Alan Soble: "When *x* loves *y*,
x wishes the best for *y* and acts, as far as he or she is able, to pursue the
good for *y*."[57]

The common theme of these statements is that love is a particular
syndrome of motives – primarily, desires to act upon, or interact with,
the beloved.[58] Before I elaborate on what these statements share with
Freudian theory, I want to register my dissent from the statements themselves.

In my opinion, the foregoing quotations express a sentimental fantasy –
an idealized vision of living happily ever after. In this fantasy, love necessarily entails a desire to "care and share," or to "benefit and be with."

But, surely, it is easy enough to love someone whom one cannot stand
to be with. Think here of Murdoch's reference to a troublemaking relation. This meddlesome aunt, cranky grandfather, smothering parent, or
overcompetitive sibling is dearly loved, loved freely and with feeling: one
just has no desire for his or her company. The same ambivalence can
occur in the most intimate relationships. When divorcing couples tell
their children that they still love one another but cannot live together,
they are telling not a white lie but a dark truth. In the presence of such
everyday examples, the notion that loving someone entails wanting to be
with him seems fantastic indeed.

[54] Patricia Greenspan, *Emotions and Reason: An Inquiry into Emotional Justification* (New York:
Routledge, 1988), p. 55.

[55] Robert Nozick, *The Examined Life* (New York: Simon & Schuster, 1989), p. 68.

[56] John Rawls, *A Theory of Justice* (Cambridge, Mass.: Harvard University Press, 1971),
p. 190. See also p. 487.

[57] Alan Soble, "Union, Autonomy, and Concern," in *Love Analyzed*, ed. Roger E. Lamb
(Boulder, Colo.: Westview, 1997), pp. 65–92, p. 65.

[58] Nozick diverges somewhat from this trend, but not very far from it. Nozick thinks that
love yokes together the welfare interests of lover and beloved, but these interests are also
formulable in terms of motives – if not the motives that the parties actually have then
the ones that they rationally would or ought to. Nozick goes on to speak about these
motives in much the same terms as the other authors.

There is only slightly more realism in the suggestion that loving some-one entails being moved to do him good. In this case, the authors quoted above seem to be thinking of a blissful family in which caring *about* others necessarily coincides with caring *for* them or taking care *of* them. Cer-tainly, love for my children leads me to promote their interests almost daily; yet when I think of other people I love – parents, brothers, friends, former teachers and students – I do not think of myself as an agent of their interests. I would of course do them a favor if asked, but in the absence of some such occasion for benefiting them, I have no continu-ing or recurring desire to do so. At the thought of a close friend, my heart doesn't fill with an urge to do something for him, though it may indeed fill with love.

In most contexts, a love that is inseparable from the urge to benefit is an unhealthy love, bristling with uncalled-for impingements. Love becomes equally unhealthy if too closely allied with some of the other desires mentioned in these passages – the desire to please or to be well-thought-of, and so on. Of course, there are occasions for pleasing and impressing the people one loves, just as there are occasions for caring and sharing. But someone whose love was a bundle of these urges, to care and share and please and impress – such a lover would be an interfering, ingratiating nightmare.

At this point the philosophical mischaracterization of love can no longer be set down to sentimentality: a deeper philosophical error appears to be at work. Let me offer a tentative diagnosis.

Suppose that one were committed to a conative analysis of love, as a motive toward a particular aim.[59] And suppose that one were unwilling to accept Freud's conative analysis, in which the aim of love is sexual union. What other aims might love be a motive to? Caring and sharing, benefiting and being with, are the obvious candidates. One is hard pressed to think of other aims motivation toward which might plausibly be identified with love.

[59] Why might philosophers be committed to a conative analysis of love? My suspicion is that this commitment reflects the extent to which the practical syllogism has come to monopolize moral psychology. Philosophers who are unduly impressed with the power of belief-desire explanation, and the associated instrumental reasoning, would like every psychological state or attitude to be analyzable as either a belief or a desire, or perhaps as some combination of the two. An especially clear case of this philosophical bias (as I would call it) can be found in O.H. Green, *The Emotions: A Philosophical Theory* (Boston: Kluwer, 1992) and "Is Love an Emotion?" in Lamb, ed., pp. 209–24.

These philosophical accounts of love can thus be read as aim-inhibited versions of Freud. They retain Freud's commitment to a conative analysis, in which love impels the lover toward an aim; they merely replace the sexual aim identified by Freud with the aims of desexualized charity and affection.[60]

The error in all of these theories, I think, is not their choice of an aim for love but their shared assumption that love can be analyzed in terms of an aim. This assumption implies that love is essentially a pro-attitude toward a result, to which the beloved is instrumental or in which he is involved. I venture to suggest that love is essentially an attitude toward the beloved himself but not toward any result at all.[61]

Having an Object but No Aim

Kant makes a similar claim about the moral motive of reverence, when he says that it orients the will toward ends consisting of persons rather than results to be achieved.[62] Kant's notion that the end of an action can be a person rather than an envisioned result is the model for my suggestion that love can have an object but no aim.

---

[60] Indeed, Freud names "such features as longing for proximity, and self-sacrifice" as charactertistic of aim-inhibited libido ("Group Psychology," pp. 90–91).

[61] Compare Scruton, pp. 101–2. Scruton considers and rejects the claim that love approaches its object with no aim. My argument for this claim will draw on Michael Stocker's "Values and Purposes: The Limits of Teleology and the Ends of Friendship," *Journal of Philosophy* 78 (1981): 747–65. Stocker's version of the claim reads as follows: "There are no ends, properly so-called, the seeking of which is, as such, to act out of friendship" (p. 756). Note that in denying that there is any particular aim attached to the motive of friendship, Stocker uses the term 'end' instead of 'aim.' I prefer to distinguish between ends and aims, however, because I want to say that acting from friendship does involve an end – namely, one's friend, who serves as one's end in the sense that one acts for his sake. Of course, the idea of a person's serving as an end comes straight out of Kantian moral psychology, as I shall explain later. In this application of Kantian theory, I am drawing on Elizabeth Anderson's *Value in Ethics and Economics* (Cambridge, MA: Harvard University Press, 1993), chapter 2. The departure from classical moral psychology in which I thus join Stocker and Anderson bears some resemblance to the departure from Freudian drive theory that was taken by objects-relations theorists, who asserted the priority of libidinal objects over libidinal aims. See especially the essays in part 1 of W.R.D. Fairbairn's *Psychoanalytic Studies of the Personality* (London: Routledge, 1990).

[62] Kant, *Groundwork*, 4:427 ff. As I mentioned in the preceding note, this application of Kantian moral psychology is indebted to Anderson, chapter 2. Also relevant here are R.S. Downie and Elizabeth Telfer, *Respect for Persons* (New York: Schocken, 1970), chapter 1; and Stephen Darwall, "Self-Interest and Self-Concern," *Social Philosophy and Policy* 14 (1997): 158–78, and "Empathy, Sympathy, Care," *Philosophical Studies* 89 (1998): 261–82.

Persons as Ends

The notion of persons as ends is puzzling to many philosophers, because they think that an end is an aim simply by definition.[63] Yet the concept of an end is not in fact equivalent with that of an aim, as becomes evident when philosophers attempt to nail down this equivalence. For example:

An end is an aim of action. It is something for the sake of which an action is to be done.... "Why did the chicken cross the road? To get to the other side!" "In order to get to the other side," we might explain, just in case someone did not get it. An end, in this broad sense, states a goal.[64]

There is a slight incongruity in this passage. If an end is anything *for the sake of which* an action is to be done, then it shouldn't have to be something that the action is done *in order to achieve*. Perhaps you ought to attend church or synagogue this weekend for the sake of your dear departed mother, or just for old times' sake. Old times aren't something that you act in order to achieve; neither is your mother. So 'for the sake of' and 'in order to' are not interchangeable constructions.

Perhaps some paraphrase with "in order to" can be cobbled together for every mention of a "sake." We might say that you ought to attend church or synagogue in order to fulfill your late mother's wishes, or in order to revive the memory of old times, rather than for your mother's or old times' sake. We shall then have identified an achievement corresponding to each of the "sakes" for which we described you as acting. But note that each of these achievements can in turn be re-expressed in terms of a "sake," since we might equally say that you ought to attend religious services for the sake of fulfilling your mother's wishes, or for the sake of reviving the memory of old times. And the question then arises whether these "sakes" are the same "sakes" with which we began. Is attending services for the sake of fulfilling your mother's wishes the same as attending services for the sake of your mother herself?

Not really. In doing something for the sake of fulfilling your mother's wishes, you would be acting on a motive that was once shared by all sorts of people – car mechanics, telephone operators – who didn't have any feelings for your mother herself. A stranger might have offered your mother his seat on the bus for the sake of accommodating her evident

---

[63] David Phillips has directed me to this quotation from Sidgwick (p. 390n): "The conception of 'humanity as an end in itself' is perplexing: because by an End we commonly mean something to be realised, whereas 'humanity' is, as Kant says, 'a self-subsistent end.'"

[64] Richardson, p. 50.

desire to sit down, but he needn't thereby have acted for her sake. His guilty awareness of a desire that he ought to accommodate need not have included any personal feelings about its subject. He might just have been in the habit of deferring to the wishes of elderly ladies.

Of course, you also want to fulfill a wish of your mother's: if she had never wanted you to attend religious services, you would never think of doing so for her sake. In this respect, you have a motive similar to that of the stranger on the bus. But you have an additional motive that he lacked, in that you want to fulfill your mother's wish for her sake, whereas he acted without any thought for her. He had no further end than to do what your mother wanted;[65] but you have a further end for which you want to do what she wanted – namely, your mother herself. So when you act, you act with the proximate end of fulfilling her wish, but ultimately for her sake.

If one is to act for the sake of a person, the person himself must be the object of a motive operative in one's action: he must be that with a view to which one is moved to act. 'That with a view to which one is moved to act' is nearly equivalent to 'that for the sake of which one acts', and either expression can serve as the definition of an end.[66] Hence every "sake" belongs to an end. By the same token, however, not every end is an aim – not, that is, if one can be moved to act, for example, with a view to a person, in being moved by an attitude that takes a person as its object.

Kant is emphatic in insisting on this possibility. His reason for insisting on it is his belief that a will actuated with a view to results cannot be unconditionally good, because the value of results is always conditional.[67]

---

[65] Of course, he might have had a further end – e.g., if he deferred to the elderly out of respect for his own mother, who taught him to do so. In that case, he might have given up his seat for the sake of his mother, not yours.

[66] One of these proposed definitions is not quite right. An end is that for the sake of which one acts, but it is not exactly that with a view to which one is moved to act; it is that with a view to whose (positive) value one is moved. Because I have not yet discussed the value of a person, I temporarily gloss over this particular wrinkle in the concept of an end. This wrinkle becomes important in cases of motivation by negative attitudes – at least, under some conceptions of those attitudes. I myself am inclined to think that hate, e.g., is not the mirror image of love because hate, unlike love, really is a drive: hating someone is not a response to his (negative) value but rather a matter of adopting him as the object of one's aggression. On this view, to act out of hate is to be motivated, in the first instance, with a view to an aggressive aim, not with a view to the person hated. But one might think, alternatively, that hate is the mirror image of love, in that it is a response to the disvalue of its object. On this view, actions motivated by hate are motivated with a view to the hated person. Yet they still aren't done for the sake of that person, nor with the person as their end, because they aren't motivated with a view to the positive value of anything. So conceived, hateful actions would be utterly pointless.

[67] Kant, *Groundwork*, 4:400, 428, 437.

If an unconditionally good will is to exist, Kant believes, there must be "something which is conjoined with my will solely as a ground and never as an effect"; there must be "a ground determining the will" that is "not an expected result."[68]

Kant's first candidate for this role is "the idea of the law in itself," but as I have already argued, this abstraction is quickly replaced in Kant's account by the rational will, which is both a law to itself and the true self of a person. Kant distinguishes this end from others by saying that it "must . . . be conceived, not as an end to be produced, *but as a self-existent* end."[69] That is, the rational nature of a person already exists, and so taking it as an end doesn't entail any inclination to cause or promote its existence. When Kant says that rational nature "exists as an end in itself,"[70] he is emphasizing that it is an end whose existence is taken for granted.

The existence of this end is taken for granted, in particular, by the motivating attitude of which it is the proper object. Because ends are motivational objects, what distinguishes some of them as self-existent lies in the distinctive relation by which they are joined to their associated motives. Self-existent ends are the objects of motivating attitudes that regard and value them as they already are; other ends are the objects of attitudes that value them as possibilities to be brought about. The fact that a person is a self-existent end just consists in the fact that he is a

---

[68] Ibid., 4:400–401.

[69] Ibid., 4:437. Paul Guyer notes that the word translated by Paton as 'self-existent' is *selbständig*, which can be translated idiomatically as 'self-sufficient' or 'independent' (Paul Guyer, "The Possibility of the Categorical Imperative," *Philosophical Review* 104 [1995]: 353–85, pp. 373–74, n. 17). According to Guyer, rational nature is *selbständig* only in the sense that it is "independent of particular, contingent ends."

I don't think that my interpretation of Kant rests on the translation of this term. What supports my interpretation is that it respects the sharp distinction that Kant draws between ends in themselves and ends that are the potential results of our actions. Guyer's interpretation tends to collapse this distinction, by treating ends in themselves as things that we are obliged to "promote" and "preserve."

Although my interpretation of Kant doesn't rest on the translation of this term, I still find Paton's translation preferable to Guyer's. *Selbständig* can perhaps be translated as 'self-sufficient' or 'independent,' but it is not strictly equivalent to either of these expressions. The literal German equivalent of 'independent' is *unabhängig*; the literal equivalent of 'self-sufficient' is *selbstgenügsam*. The root word *ständig* means 'fixed, constant, standing' – as in 'a standing committee.' *Selbständig* therefore suggests that an end so described is already in place, "standing" on its own two feet, not needing to be brought into existence. That's why *selbständig* is contrasted in this sentence with "to be produced." The translation 'self-existent' conveys this contrast while also echoing Kant's earlier statement that rational nature *existiert als Zweck an sich selbst* (*Groundwork*, 4:429).

[70] Ibid., 4:429.

proper object for the former sort of attitude. Specifically, he is a proper object for reverence,[71] an attitude that stands back in appreciation of the rational creature he is, without inclining toward any particular results to be produced.[72]

One might contend that such an attitude cannot motivate action except by way of a desire, whose object would then be some envisioned result. This contention implies that acting out of respect for a person entails

---

[71] Kant draws this connection in ibid., 4:428.

[72] I thus disagree with interpretations that treat respect for rational nature as requiring "the preservation and promotion of freedom," or efforts to "help others set their own ends and rationally pursue them." (The first quotation is from Guyer, p. 372; the second is from Thomas E. Hill, Jr., "Humanity as an End in Itself," in his *Dignity and Practical Reason in Kant's Moral Theory* [Ithaca, N.Y.: Cornell University Press, 1992], pp. 38–57, p. 54.) Insofar as we regard rational nature as something for us to promote, preserve, or facilitate, we regard it no differently from happiness, and our motive toward it is no different from desire. Hence these interpretations assimilate ends-in-themselves to ends that are projected results of our actions, collapsing a distinction on which Kant repeatedly insists.

  I grant that these interpretations seem to gain some support from the passage in which Kant applies the Formula of Humanity to his standard examples (*Groundwork*, 4:430). Here he says: "It is not enough that an action should refrain from conflicting with humanity in our own person as an end in itself: it must also *harmonize with this end*. Now there are in humanity capacities for greater perfection which form part of nature's purpose for humanity in our person. To neglect these can admittedly be compatible with the *maintenance* of humanity as an end in itself, but not with the *promotion* of this end." Yet I do not think that we can draw conclusions from this passage until we have attempted to reconcile it with the numerous passages in which Kant denies that humanity is a result to be produced. Consider, e.g, how Kant expands upon this denial only a few pages later: "The end must here be conceived, not as an end to be produced, *but as a self-existent* end. It must therefore be conceived only negatively – that is, as an end against which we should never act" (4:437). How can these two passages be rendered consistent?

  In the earlier passage, the first sentence says that our humanity, regarded as an end, requires us not only to avoid acts that would "conflict" with it but also to undertake acts that "harmonize" with it. I regard this statement as consistent with the later statement that humanity must be conceived negatively, as an end against which we mustn't act. The reason why we are required to undertake positive steps in cultivating our talents is that the alternative would be to neglect them, which would be to act against our humanity. The duty of self-cultivation, like all imperfect duties, is the positive requirement that results when some omission is forbidden – in this case, the omission that would constitute self-neglect. Thus, the fundamental requirement is the negative requirement not to act against our humanity by neglecting our talents.

  The question is whether self-cultivation also entails promoting our own humanity, as the final sentence of the first passage seems to say. A problem in reading this sentence is that Kant applies the Formula of Humanity, like the Formula of Universal Law, via the notion of a system of nature, which is "analogous" to the system of morality (*Groundwork*, 4:437). In the present case, nature is said to have a "purpose (*Zweck*) for humanity in our person," a purpose that is at most analogous

having not only the person as our end but also an additional end that isn't self-existent.[73]

I could accept a version of this claim, by conceding that self-existent ends such as persons must always have subordinate ends consisting in desired consequences – that they must always be ends for the sake of which one wants to accomplish some result. Yet even if I conceded that self-existent ends must always have subordinate ends consisting in desired outcomes, I would still deny that the one sort of end can be reduced to the other. Perhaps you cannot act for your mother's sake unless there is some outcome that, for her sake, you want to produce. Even so, your desiring the outcome for her sake entails your having a motive over and above simply desiring the outcome, or even desiring it under some description that mentions her.[74] It entails your having a motive that takes her as its object and that motivates your desire for the outcome, to which she consequently stands as an ulterior end. Your wanting the outcome for her sake consists in your wanting it out of this further attitude toward her.

Kant thinks that respect is an ulterior motive in this sense, but he thinks that it has a negative rather than positive relation to the motives subserving it. When considering the motivational force of respect, he says that its object "must . . . be conceived only negatively – that is, as an end

to the end (*Zweck*) consisting of our humanity itself. I think that Kant then glosses over the distinction between these two *Zwecke*. The sentence consequently abbreviates Kant's view, which is that promoting nature's purpose for humanity is an analog, or image, for the positive steps that we must take in order to avoid acting against our humanity as an end. What is to be promoted, then, is nature's purpose for humanity, not the self-existent end of humanity itself. (Paton gives a similar reading of this passage in his "Analysis of the Argument," [in Kant, *Groundwork*, p. 31], though he elsewhere suggests that Kant simply "forgets" the passage when saying that the end of humanity is to be conceived only negatively [p. 140, n. 1, which refers to p. 82 of the translation].) My reading of these passages is supported, I believe, by Kant's treatment of the topic in *The Metaphysics of Morals*. There he says a person has a duty to cultivate his faculties "so that he may be worthy of the humanity that dwells within him" (6:387). Humanity is "the capacity to set oneself an end," and the associated duty is "to make ourselves worthy of humanity by culture in general, by procuring or promoting the *capacity* to realize all sorts of possible ends" (6:392). What we are required to cultivate, then, is not our humanity, which already "dwells within" us, but rather the capacities that would make us worthy of our humanity, and whose neglect would be an affront to it.

73 For this point, see Michael Smith, "The Possibility of Philosophy of Action," in *Human Action, Deliberation and Causation*, ed. Jan Bransen and Stefaan Cuypers (Dordrecht: Kluwer Academic Publishers, 1998), pp. 17–41.

74 We can say that wanting to produce an outcome for her sake consists in the fact that a reference to her in the description of the outcome is motivationally relevant: you want to produce the outcome, say, as something that mattered to her, in particular. But what explains the motivational relevance of this reference to her in the description of the desired outcome? What explains it, I claim, is that you have some attitude toward her, out of which you desire the outcome.

against which we should never act, and consequently as one which in all our willing we must never rate *merely* as a means."[75] In other words, respect can motivate us, if not by impelling us to produce its object, then by deterring us from violating it; and the violation from which we are thus deterred can be conceived as that of using the object as a mere means to other ends.

Kant offers a further hint about the motivational potential of reverence. "Reverence," he says in a footnote, "is properly awareness of a value which checks my self-love."[76] Now, 'self-love' is a term that Kant uses for motivation by empirical motives and the associated prudential reasoning.[77] Such motivation aims at achieving empirical results, via the use of necessary means. As we have seen, reverence for a person exerts its negative motivational force by placing a constraint on our use of him as a means to desired ends. That's why it can be said to check our self-love: it arrests some of our empirical motives – in particular, the motives in whose service we might be tempted to put the person to use. Such a motive against having or acting on another motive is a negative second-order motive.[78]

The Beloved as an End

Could this model of a negative second-order motive apply to love? Let me return to Kant's description of reverence as the awareness of a value that arrests our self-love. I am inclined to say that love is likewise the awareness of a value inhering in its object; and I am also inclined to describe love as an arresting awareness of that value.

---

[75] Kant, *Groundwork*, 4:437. See also 4:428: "Their nature already marks them out as ends in themselves – that is, as something which ought not to be used merely as a means – and consequently imposes a limit on all treatment of them (and is an object of reverence)." This aspect of respect is discussed by Darwall in "Two Kinds of Respect."

[76] Kant, *Groundwork*, 4:400. I have substituted the verb 'checks' for 'demolishes' in Paton's translation. The verb used by Kant is *Abbruch tut*, and *Abbruch* means 'a breaking up' or 'breaking off' – a rupture. Causing an *Abbruch* to self-love would fall short of demolishing it. Compare Kant, *Critique of Practical Reason*, 5:73: "Pure practical reason merely checks selfishness. . . . But it strikes down self-conceit." The expression that Beck here translates as 'checks' is once again *Abbruch tut*, which is expressly contrasted with the more decisive 'striking down' in the next sentence.

[77] See Kant, *Groundwork*, 4:406. See also Kant, *Critique of Practical Reason*, 5:22.

[78] Some might argue that even this motive must be a desire, such as a desire not to use another person merely as a means. But I would reply, as before, that one can want not to use others, and consequently be moved not to use them, without so wanting or being so moved for their sake, since one can want and pursue such restraint for one's own sake, or for the sake of restraint itself – a project that is hardly moral. The moral project is to abstain from the use of others for their sake, which requires that one take them as an end, by virtue of having a motive, such as respect, that takes them as its object.

This description of love seems right, to begin with, as a piece of phenomenology, just as the conative analysis of love seems implausible, to begin with, on phenomenological grounds. Love does not feel (to me, at least) like an urge or impulse or inclination toward anything; it feels rather like a state of attentive suspension, similar to wonder or amazement or awe.

If respect arrests our self-love, as Kant asserts, then what does love arrest? I suggest that it arrests our tendencies toward emotional self-protection from another person, tendencies to draw ourselves in and close ourselves off from being affected by him. Love disarms our emotional defenses; it makes us vulnerable to the other.

This hypothesis would explain why love is an exercise in "really looking," as Murdoch claims. Many of our defenses against being emotionally affected by another person are ways of not seeing what is most affecting about him. This contrived blindness to the other person is among the defenses that are lifted by love, with the result that we really look at him, perhaps for the first time, and respond emotionally in a way that's indicative of having really seen him.

According to this hypothesis, the various motives that are often identified with love are in fact independent responses that love merely unleashes. They are the sympathy, empathy, fascination, and attraction that we feel for another person when our emotional defenses toward him have been disarmed. The hypothesis thus explains why love often leads to benevolence but doesn't entail a standing desire to benefit: in suspending our emotional defenses, love exposes our sympathy to the needs of the other, and we are therefore quick to respond when help is needed. The resulting benevolence manifests our heightened sensitivity to the other's interests rather than any standing interest of ours.

The responses unleashed by love for a person tend to be favorable because they have been unleashed by an awareness of value in him, an awareness that is also conducive to a favorable response. But these responses need not be exclusively favorable. Love also lays us open to feeling hurt, anger, resentment, and even hate.[79]

The present hypothesis thus discourages us from positing necessary connections between love and desires for particular outcomes. It applies to

---

[79] See D. W. Winnicott, "Hate in the Countertransference," *Through Paediatrics to Psychoanalysis* (London: Hogarth Press, 1975), pp. 194–203, p. 199. See also Jerome Neu, "*Odi et Amo:* On Hating the Ones We Love," in *Freud and the Passions*, ed. John O'Neill (University Park: Pennsylvania State University Press, 1996), pp. 53–72.

a lover's aim what Freud says about his object – namely, that it "is what is most variable about" his love "and is not originally connected with it."[80] Only vague generalizations can be drawn about what love can motivate the lover to do.

I suspect that those who see particular motives as necessary to love are simply imagining the lover in a narrow range of stereotypical situations, to which love has made him especially responsive. In reality, I think, love can occur in a far wider range of situations, calling for a wider range of motivational responses.

For example, I think that love naturally arises between student and teacher, but that when it opens one's eyes to what the other really is, one sees that he is one's teacher or student, who is to be dealt with professionally. Students and teachers may of course feel desires for intimacy with one another, but such desires are unlikely to be an expression of true love in this context; usually, they express transference-love, in which the other is a target of fantasies. When I say that I have had the good fortune to be loved by some of my students, I do not mean the students who have shown a desire to get next to me. Students who want to benefit and be with me seem not loving but confused, just as I do not strike myself as loving when I feel a desire to treat students otherwise than as students. Here is a relationship in which true love can manifest itself in an inclination to keep one's distance.

The Partiality of Love

I have suggested that love is an arresting awareness of value in a person, differing from Kantian respect in that its primary motivational force is to suspend our emotional self-protection from the person rather than our self-interested designs on him.[81] Yet if love is a way of valuing persons, then in loving some people but not others, we must value some people but not others. The upshot seems to be that love really is partial in a sense that conflicts with the spirit of morality, which insists that people are equally valuable.

How We Want to be Loved
This difficulty is best appreciated from the perspective of the beloved. That human beings are selective in love matters more to us in our capacity

---

[80] Quoted at n. 39.
[81] I discuss other differences between love and respect below.

as objects of love than in our capacity as subjects. We want to be loved, and in being loved, to be valued, and in being valued, to be regarded as special. We want to be prized, treasured – which seems to entail being valued discriminately, in preference to or instead of others. The love that we want to receive therefore seems to be precisely that discriminating love which threatens to conflict with impartial morality.

Notice, then, that when philosophers are trying to impress us with the supposed conflict between love and morality, they tend to shift from the perspective of the lover to that of the beloved. The perspective of the lover is where the conflict is supposed to arise, between two potential sources of motivation. So when philosophers tell us about the problem in the abstract, they speak to us in our capacity as lovers, by saying that morality threatens to interfere with our loving particular people. But when they want to get us worried about the problem, to make us feel what's problematic about it, they speak to us in our capacity as aspiring objects of love, by warning that morality threatens to interfere with our being loved. Thus, for example, the "one thought too many " that Williams detects in the husband of his story is, more specifically, one too many for the wife: it interferes with her being loved in the way that she would hope.[82]

One of the merits that I would like to claim for the present hypothesis about love is that it helps to explain why and how we want to be loved. There is little attraction in the prospect of being cathected by another's libido; but having another heart opened to us by a recognition of our true selves – well, that seems worth wanting. Yet if my hypothesis has captured what makes love desirable to receive, mustn't it also have captured the very partiality that sets love in conflict with morality?

I think that the question how we want to be loved provides one of our first exposures in childhood to that air of paradox which, for some of us, eventually condenses into philosophy. We are told by adults who love us, and who want us to feel loved, that we are special and irreplaceable. But then we are told by the same adults, now acting as moral educators, that every individual is special and irreplaceable. And we wonder: if everyone is special, what's so special about anyone?

Adults often confuse us further by saying that we're special because no one else is quite like us – as if the value attaching to us, and to everyone else as well, was that of being qualitatively unique. This explanation seems

---

[82] See also Stocker's example of the hospital visit in "The Schizophrenia of Modern Ethical Theories," p. 462.

to invoke scarcity as a standard of value, but it is easily defeated by the very same standard. How valuable can our uniqueness make us if everyone is unique? We sense a similar paradox in attempts to elicit our childish awe at individual snowflakes, of which (they say) no two are alike. Why get excited about any one unprecedented snowflake, when its lack of precedents is so well precedented?

Matters only get worse if adults start to detail the personal qualities for which we are loved, since these qualities fail to distinguish us completely, and they consequently feel like accidents rather than our essence. We are like the girl who wants to be loved but not for her yellow hair – and not, we should add, for her mind or her sense of humor, either – because she wants to be loved, as she puts it, "for myself alone."[83] What is this self for which she wants to be loved? What can it be, if not her particular bundle of personal qualities, which include the color of her hair?

By now it should come as no surprise that I find an answer to this question in Kantian moral theory.[84] Kant's theory of value reveals the philosophical error behind our confusion about being loved.

The Value of Self-Existent Ends

Kant says that the value of a person is different in kind from the value of other things: a person has a dignity, whereas other things have a price. The difference is this: "If [something] has a price, something else can be put in its place as an *equivalent*; if it is exalted above all price and so admits of no equivalent, then it has a dignity."[85]

---

[83] The reference is to Yeats's poem "For Anne Gregory," in *The Collected Poems of W.B. Yeats* (New York: Macmillan, 1956), p. 240. Note that by Anne's reckoning, the husband in Williams's example entertained, not one thought too many, but two. Since Anne wants to be loved for herself alone, she would have no use for either one of the premises adduced by a husband who reasoned "that it was his wife and that in situations of this kind it is permissible to save one's wife." She would no more want to be loved for being someone's wife than for her yellow hair. Yet Williams is surely right that the husband's first premise – that it was his wife – was appropriate in the circumstances, and that only the second was potentially problematic. Perhaps, then, the motivating thoughts that are appropriate in such cases aren't thoughts of love at all. I shall return to this possibility at the end of the chapter. For some recent discussions of the passage from Yeats, see Neil Delaney, "Romantic Love and Loving Commitment: Articulating a Modern Ideal," *American Philosophical Quarterly* 33 (1996): 339–56, pp. 345–46; and Roger E. Lamb, "Love and Rationality," in Lamb, ed., pp. 23–47.

[84] Here again I have benefited from Anderson's *Value in Ethics and Economics*. See also Scruton, pp. 104–5. Scruton considers the idea, which I shall defend, that to be loved for oneself is to be treated as an end in oneself. Scruton rejects this idea, but only because he doesn't adequately explore the Kantian notion of an end in itself (pp. 104, 111, 123).

[85] Kant, *Groundwork*, 4:434.

The distinction between price and dignity, in Kantian theory, corresponds to the distinction between ends that consist in possible results of action and ends that are self-existent.[86] The former ends are objects of preference and choice, which are comparative. Among the various outcomes that we could produce by acting, we must choose which ones to produce, given that we can't produce all of them. We therefore need a common measure of value for these ends, so that we can combine the values of those which are jointly producible and then compare alternative combinations. Values that allow for comparisons among alternatives also allow for equivalences, and so they qualify as prices in Kant's terminology.[87]

Yet a self-existent end, which is not to be produced by action, is not an alternative to other producibles. Its value doesn't serve as grounds for comparing it with alternatives; it serves as grounds for revering or respecting the end as it already is. What Kant means in calling this value incomparable is that it calls for a response to the object in itself, not in comparison with others.[88]

Kant's view is that the incomparable value of a person is a value that he possesses solely by virtue of his being a person – by virtue, in fact, of what Kant calls his rational nature. Do I mean to suggest that love is an awareness of this same value?

I don't want to say that registering this particular value is an essential feature of love, since love is felt for many things other than possessors of rational nature. All that is essential to love, in my view, is that it disarms our emotional defenses toward an object in response to its incomparable value as a self-existent end.[89] But when the object of our love is a person, and when we love him *as* a person – rather than as a work of nature, say,

---

[86] See Anderson's "pragmatic theory of comparative value judgments" (pp. 47ff.).

[87] Kant draws the connection between products and prices by speaking, in both cases, about the relativity of the values involved. That is, an end that consists in a possible product of action has a value relative to the strength of our desire for that product (*Groundwork*, 4:427); and relative value of this kind necessarily has the form of a price (4:434–35). This way of connecting products and prices is compatible with the way that I connect them. Strength of desire is the common currency to which we resort when forced to compare the values of alternative products.

[88] Ibid., 4:436.

[89] Kant himself says that "morality, and humanity so far as it is capable of morality, is the only thing which has a dignity" (ibid., 4:435). He thus seems to rule out the possibility of responding to objects other than persons as self-existent ends. I am inclined to differ from Kant on this point. See also Anderson, pp. 8–11.

or an aesthetic object – then indeed, I want to say, we are responding to
the value that he possesses by virtue of being a person or, as Kant would
say, an instance of rational nature.

Before balking at this statement, recall the following tenets of Kantian
theory: that the rational nature whose value commands respect is the
capacity to be actuated by reasons; that the capacity to be actuated by
reasons is also the capacity to have a good will; and that the capacity for a
rational and consequently good will is that better side of a person which
constitutes his true self. I find it intuitively plausible that we love people
for their true and better selves. Were we to speak of the yellow-haired girl
in German, we might well borrow Kant's phrase and say that she wished
to be loved for "ihr eigentliches Selbst."

Remember, further, that the capacity to be actuated by reasons is a
capacity for appreciating the value of ends, including self-existent ends
such as persons. For Kant, then, people have a capacity whose value we
appreciate by respecting them; and that capacity, at its utmost, is *their*
capacity for respect. I am suggesting that love is an appreciation for the
same value, inhering in people's capacity to appreciate the value of ends,
including self-existent ends such as persons. For me, then, people have a
capacity whose value we appreciate not only with respect but also sometimes with love; and that capacity, at its utmost, is their capacity not only
for respect but also for love. I find it plausible to say that what we respond
to, in loving people, is their capacity to love: it's just another way of saying
that what our hearts respond to is another heart.

The idea that love is a response to the value of a person's rational nature
will seem odd so long as 'rational nature' is interpreted as denoting the
intellect. But rational nature is not the intellect, not even the practical
intellect; it's a capacity of appreciation or valuation – a capacity to care
about things in that reflective way which is distinctive of self-conscious
creatures like us. Think of a person's rational nature as his core of reflective concern, and the idea of loving him for it will no longer seem odd.

I can now summarize my view of the relation between love and Kantian
respect, as follows. The Kantian view is that respect is a mode of valuation
that the very capacity for valuation must pay to instances of itself.[90] My
view is that love is a mode of valuation that this capacity *may* also pay to

---

[90] Here I am smuggling Kantian universalization into my account, by speaking in the
abstract of a capacity for valuation, and then speaking about the attitude of this abstract
capacity toward particular instances of itself. I would need to offer a fair amount of
argumentation in order to earn the right to this manner of speaking.

instances of itself. I regard respect and love as the required minimum and optional maximum responses to one and the same value.

Respect for others is required, in Kant's view, because the capacity for valuation cannot take seriously the values that it attributes to things unless it first takes itself seriously; and it cannot first take itself seriously if it treats instances of itself as nothing more than means to things that it already values.[91] That's why the capacity for valuation, when facing instances of itself, must respond in the manner constitutive of respect, by restraining its self-interested tendency to treat them as means.

In my view, love for others is possible when we find in them a capacity for valuation like ours, which can be constrained by respect for ours, and which therefore makes our emotional defenses against them feel unnecessary.[92] That's why our capacity for valuation, when facing instances of itself, feels able to respond in the manner constitutive of love, by suspending our emotional defenses. Love, like respect, is the heart's response to the realization that it is not alone.

Being Valued as Special

We now have both halves of a solution to our childhood puzzle about being loved. One half of the solution is that being loved does not entail being valued on the basis of our distinctive qualities, such as our yellow hair; on the contrary, it entails being valued on the basis of our personhood, in which we are no different from other persons. Of course, this half of the solution is by itself no solution at all, because it leaves us wondering how being valued on so generic a basis is compatible with being valued as special. But that's where the second half of the solution comes in. The second half is this: being valued merely as persons is compatible with being valued as special because our value as persons is a dignity rather than a price.

As we have seen, the distinction between price and dignity rests on a distinction between the responses that constitute their proper appreciation.[93] Preference and choice belong to one mode of appreciation, which is warranted by that kind of value which Kant calls a price.

---

[91] Note that this formulation of Kant's view treats the value of persons as one that rational nature doesn't *find in* but must *project onto* instances of itself. See Christine M. Korsgaard, *The Sources of Normativity* (Cambridge: Cambridge University Press, 1996), pp. 122–25.

[92] Thanks to Richard Heck for suggesting the first sentence of this paragraph, and to Christine Korsgaard for suggesting the last.

[93] This way of understanding the distinction is due to Anderson: "Things that differ in the kind of worth they have merit different kinds of appreciation" (chapter 1, p. 9).

Dignity is a different kind of value because it warrants a different mode of appreciation, consisting of motives and feelings in which we submit to the object's reality rather than strive toward its realization.

This distinction between modes of appreciation relies, in turn, on a prior distinction, between appreciating the value of an object and judging it to have that value.[94] When Kant says that an object with dignity "admits of no equivalents," he is speaking about how to appreciate such an object, not how to judge it. Kant himself believes that each person has a dignity in virtue of his rational nature, and hence that all persons should be judged to have the same value. What he denies is that comparing or equating one person with another is an appropriate way of responding to that value. The value that we must attribute to a person imposes absolute constraints on our treatment of him, thus commanding a motivational response to the person in and by himself. And the constraints that it imposes on our treatment of the person include a ban on subjecting him to comparisons, which would implicitly subordinate his value to some ulterior or overarching value.

Thus, the value that we must attribute to every person requires that we respond to each person alone, partly by refusing to compare him with others. The class of persons just is a class whose members must be appreciated as individuals rather than as members of a class.

There is a tendency to assume that attributing value to people as members of a class is incompatible with appreciating them as individuals. For example:

Although the Kantian formula of persons as ends in themselves is claimed to regard persons as irreplaceable, there is a sense in which Kantian respect does in fact view persons as intersubstitutable, for it is blind to everything about an individual except her rational nature, leaving each of us indistinguishable from every other. Thus, in Kantian-respecting someone, there is a real sense in which we are not paying attention to *her* – it makes no difference to how we respect her that she is who she is and not some other individual.[95]

94 Ibid., p. 2. I am using the verb 'to appreciate' where Anderson uses 'to value'.
95 Dillon, "Respect and Care," p. 121. This passage is discussed by Baron in *Kantian Ethics Almost Without Apology*, p. 10, n. 9. See also Robin S. Dillon, "Toward a Feminist Conception of Self-Respect," *Hypatia* 7 (1992): 52–69. For a similar point about love, see Neera Kapur Badhwar's "Friends as Ends in Themselves," *Philosophy and Phenomenological Research* 48 (1987): 1–25, p. 5: "If I love you unconditionally, I love you regardless of your individual qualities – your appearance, your temperament, your style, even your moral character. So you are no different from anyone else as the object of my love, and my love for you is no different from my love for anyone else. But then in what sense are *you* the object of my love?" See also Neu, p. 58.

But this reasoning confuses judgment and appreciation. In respecting someone, we are "blind to everything except her rational nature" only in the sense that we are responding to a value attributable to her on the basis of that nature, which is shared by others. But our response to a value attributable to her on a shared basis can still consist in "paying attention to *her*" in her own right.

For the same reason, we can judge the person to be valuable in generic respects while also valuing her as irreplaceable. Valuing her as irreplaceable is a mode of appreciation, in which we respond to her value with an unwillingness to replace her or to size her up against potential replacements. And refusing to compare or replace the person may be the appropriate response to a value that we attribute to her on grounds that apply to others as well.[96] The same value may be attributable to many objects without necessarily warranting substitutions among them.

Of course, some values do warrant substitutions among the objects that share them: that's the definition of a price. To assume that something will be irreplaceable only if it is uniquely valuable is thus to assume that its value is a price rather than a dignity.

No wonder, then, that we were suspicious of adults who said that we were irreplaceable in their love because of being qualitatively unique.[97]

---

[96] A similar point is made by Cynthia Stark, pp. 483–84.

[97] Versions of this thought can be found in many of the works quoted at nn. 49–57, including those of Taylor, Lyons, and Greenspan. Nozick is a complicated case. In Robert Nozick, *Anarchy, State, and Utopia* (New York: Basic Books, 1974), p. 168, he said: "An adult may come to love another person because of the other's characteristics; but it is the other person, and not the characteristics, that is loved. The love is not transferable to someone else with the same characteristics." But when Nozick seeks to understand the nontransferability of love in *The Examined Life*, he falls back on "the particularity of the qualities that you come to love." Nozick now explains that love isn't transferable because "no other person *could* have precisely those traits" (p. 81). Here Nozick expresses the view currently under discussion, that someone is valued as irreplaceable only if he is valued under a description that fits him uniquely. See also Kapur, "Why It Is Wrong to Be Always Guided by the Best," p. 483. In the text, I criticize this view as involving a confusion between value judgment and appreciation. Other confusions are common in the literature on this subject. One confusion is between "the basis and the object of love," as Alan Soble puts it (*The Structure of Love* [New Haven, Conn.: Yale University Press, 1990], pp. 225 ff.). In this case, loving someone for his qualities is equated with loving the qualities themselves. Another confusion is between the basis of love and the way in which love picks out its object. In this case, the qualities by which love picks out an object are assumed to be the same as those for which it values that object – as if it couldn't pick out an object by one set of qualities while valuing him for another. Love is therefore said to have as its object all of the people who share the qualities on which it is based. (See, e.g., the quotation from Badhwar in n. 95.) See also Robert Kraut, "Love *De Re*," *Midwest Studies in Philosophy* 10 (1986): 413–30; Amélie Oksenberg Rorty, "The Historicity of Psychological Attitudes:

These adults were implying that we would indeed be subject to replacement by anyone who shared the qualities grounding their love, and hence that our irreplaceability depended on our possessing qualities that no one shared. They were in effect conceding that their love for us established criteria of equivalence to us; they were merely asserting that these criteria were too narrow for anyone else to satisfy, like a job description so specific as to fit only one applicant.

But if there are criteria of equivalence to something, then it has a price. Extremely narrow criteria may make the price unaffordable, so to speak, but they cannot transmute it into what Kant calls a dignity. For they cannot prevent the thing's being replaceable in principle; they can only ensure that there will be no replacements in practice. What makes something truly irreplaceable is a value that commands appreciation for it as it is in itself, without comparison to anything else, and hence without substitutions.

If you were lucky, you were one of those children who learn about their worth from that Kindergarten Kantian, Dr. Seuss:

> Come on! Open your mouth and sound off at the sky!
> Shout loud at the top of your voice, "I AM I!
> ME!
> I am I!
> And I may not know why
> But I know that I like it.
> *Three cheers!* I AM I!"[98]

According to Dr. Seuss, your sense of deserving love needn't rest on any flattering self-description ("I may not know why"). It rests solely on your individuality as a person, your bare personal identity, as expressed in the statement "I am I."[99]

The fact that you are you is just the fact that you are a self-identical person – that you are an "I," or as Dr. Seuss says elsewhere, a "Who."[100]

Love Is Not Love Which Alters Not When It Alteration Finds," *Midwest Studies in Philosophy* 10 (1986): 399–412; Scruton, pp. 103–7; Delaney, p. 346; Lamb, "Love and Rationality"; Deborah Brown, "The Right Method of Boy-Loving," in Lamb, ed., pp. 49–63.

[98] *Happy Birthday to You!* (New York: Random House, 1959).

[99] Lest you feel tempted to celebrate being yourself instead of some other person, Dr. Seuss makes clear that being yourself is rather to be contrasted with being "a clam or a ham or a dusty old jar of sour gooseberry jam" – or, worse yet, being a "Wasn't." Being yourself is thus to be contrasted, not with being someone else, but with failing to exist as a person at all.

[100] Dr. Seuss, *Horton Hears a Who!* (New York: Random House, 1954). The refrain of this book is: "A person's a person, no matter how small."

This fact makes you eligible to be loved in just the way that you want to be loved, for yourself alone. To be loved for yourself alone is to be loved just for being you – for your bare individuality as a person, which you express by saying "I am I."

In being a self-identical person, of course, you are no different from anyone else: everyone can say "I am I." But Kant's theory of value reveals that being valued as a person is not a matter of being compared with others, anyway. If you assimilate Kant's insight, you will realize that being prized or treasured as special doesn't entail being compared favorably with others; it rather entails being seen to have a value that forbids comparisons. Your singular value as a person is not a value that you are singular in possessing; it's rather a value that entitles you to be appreciated singularly, in and by yourself.

In this sense, everyone can be singularly valuable, or special. The specialness of each person is a value of the kind that attaches to ends in themselves, which are to be appreciated as they are in themselves rather than measured against alternatives. It is therefore a value whose possession by one person isn't prejudicial to its possession by any other.

Once you realize that someone's love can single you out without basing itself on your distinguishing characteristics, you are in a position to realize, further, that the latter sort of love would in fact be undesirable. Someone who loved you for your quirks would have to be a quirk-lover, on the way to being a fetishist.[101] In order for his love to fit you so snugly, it would need so many angles as to be downright kinky. Of course, you may hope that love would open a lover's eyes to everything about you, including your quirks, and that he would see them in the reflected glow of your true, inner value. But if you learned that they were themselves the evaluative basis of his love, you would feel trivialized.

---

[101] See Whiting's complaint against "the fetish concern with uniqueness characteristic of modern discussions of friendship" (p. 8). Those moved by this concern sometimes go so far as to suggest that love for someone should be based not only on his merits but also on his flaws, because his flaws help to individuate him. (See, e.g., Gregory Vlastos, "The Individual as an Object of Love in Plato," in his *Platonic Studies* [Princeton, N.J.: Princeton University Press, 1973], pp. 3–42; Martha C. Nussbaum, "Beatrice's 'Dante': Loving the Individual?" in *Virtue, Love, and Form: Essays in Memory of Gregory Vlastos*, ed. Terence Irwin and Martha C. Nussbaum [Edmonton: Academic Printing & Publishing, 1993], pp. 161–78.) While I agree that we want to be loved warts and all, as the saying goes, I don't think that we want to be loved for our warts. Who wants to be the object of someone's wart-love? What we want is to be loved by someone who sees and isn't put off by our warts, but who appreciates our true value well enough to recognize that they don't contribute to it.

The Selectivity of Love

Why, then, do we love only some people? And why do we say that we love them for their distinctive qualities, such as their senses of humor or their yellow hair? Let me answer both of these questions by pointing out an important respect in which love differs, in my opinion, from Kantian respect.

Love for the Empirical Person

Kant says that respect is produced by the subordination of our will to a mere concept or idea.[102] Our respect for a person is a response to something that we know about him intellectually but with which we have no immediate acquaintance. According to my hypothesis, the value to which we respond in loving a person is the same as that to which we respond in respecting him – namely, the value of his rational nature, or personhood. But I have not said, nor am I inclined to say, that the immediate object of love is the purely intelligible aspect of the beloved. Love of a person is not felt in contemplation of a mere concept or idea.

The immediate object of love, I would say, is the manifest person, embodied in flesh and blood and accessible to the senses. The manifest person is the one against whom we have emotional defenses, and he must disarm them, if he can, with his manifest qualities. Grasping someone's personhood intellectually may be enough to make us respect him, but unless we actually *see* a person in the human being confronting us, we won't be moved to love; and we can see the person only by seeing him in or through his empirical persona.

Hence there remains a sense in which we love a person for his observable features – the way he wears his hat and sips his tea (in the lyrics of the jazz era), or the way he walks and the way he talks (in the lyrics of rock and roll). But loving a person for the way he walks is not a response to the value of his gait; it's rather a response to his gait as an expression or symbol or reminder of his value as a person.

Unfortunately, the philosophical tradition of reducing all motives to propositional attitudes has left us with no generally accepted vocabulary for describing most of the ways in which the value of one thing can be reflected in or refracted through another. This tradition treats all value

---

[102] See the footnote in Kant, *Groundwork*, 4:401 and my discussion of this passage in n. 30. See also 4:439.

as emanating from states of affairs, and as radiating only to other states related to them as means. The ways in which the value of a person can infuse his persona, and the ways in which we can respond to his value through that persona, are consequently beyond our ordinary powers of philosophical description. Maybe we need a language of "valuing as," analogous to our language of "seeing as," to describe how we respond to a person's looks or acts or works as conduits rather than sources of value. We might then feel more comfortable with the idea of appreciating these features as expressions or symbols of a value that isn't theirs but belongs instead to the inner – or, as Kant would say, merely intelligible – person.

The desire to be valued in this way is not a desire to be valued on the basis of one's distinctive features. It is rather a desire that one's own rendition of humanity, however distinctive, should succeed in communicating a value that is perfectly universal. (In this respect, it's like the desire to be found beautiful.) One doesn't want one's value as a person to be eclipsed by the intrinsic value of one's appearance or behavior; one wants them to elicit a valuation that looks through them, to the value of one's inner self.

One reason why we love some people rather than others is that we can see into only some of our observable fellow creatures. The human body and human behavior are imperfect expressions of personhood, and we are imperfect interpreters. Hence the value that makes someone eligible to be loved does not necessarily make him lovable in our eyes. Whether someone is lovable depends on how well his value as a person is expressed or symbolized for us by his empirical persona. Someone's persona may not speak very clearly of his value as a person, or may not speak in ways that are clear to us.

Another reason why we discriminate in love is that the value we do manage to see in some fellow creatures arrests our emotional defenses to them, and our resulting vulnerability exhausts the attention that we might have devoted to finding and appreciating the value in others. We are constitutionally limited in the number of people we can love; and we may have to stop short of our constitutional limits in order to enjoy the loving relationships that make for a good life.

We thus have many reasons for being selective in love, without having to find differences of worth among possible love objects.[103] We know that

---

[103] A similar point is made about selectivity in friendship by Diane Jeske in "Friendship, Virtue, and Impartiality," *Philosophy and Phenomenological Research* 57 (1997): 51–72, pp. 69 ff.

people whom we do not happen to love may be just as eligible for love as our own children, spouses, parents, and intimate friends. In merely respecting rather than loving these people, we do not assess them as lower in value. Rather, we feel one emotion rather than another in appreciation of their value. Loving some but not others entails valuing them differently but not attributing different values to them, or even comparing them at all.

Other Grounds for Partiality

Perhaps I can illustrate this point by returning briefly to Williams's story of a man who can save only one of several people in peril and wants to save his wife. Williams recognizes that the Kantian moral agent would save his wife, as any husband would. The problem, for Williams, is that he would save his wife only after reflecting impartially on the permissibility of doing so – a second thought that Williams regards as unloving. But I think that Williams overestimates the partiality that love would require of the agent in this case.

I do believe that the man's love for his wife should heighten his sensitivity to her predicament. But I cannot believe that it would leave him less sensitive to the predicament of others who are in – or perhaps alongside – the same boat. My own experience is that, although I may be insensitive to suffering until I see it in people I love, I cannot then remain insensitive to it in their fellow sufferers. The sympathy that I feel for my wife's difficulties at work, or my children's difficulties at school, naturally extends to their coworkers and classmates.

The idea that someone could show love for his own children by having less compassion for other children strikes me as bizarre. Whatever caused someone to favor his own children in this manner could hardly be love. Of course, a person's love for his children shouldn't necessarily lead him to *love* other children. Ideally, he will find his own children especially lovable – that is, especially expressive, in his eyes, of an incomparable value. But when his children awaken him to that value as only they can, they awaken him to something that he recognizes, or ought to recognize, as universal.

Of course the man in Williams's story should save his wife in preference to strangers. But the reasons why he should save her have nothing essentially to do with love.

The grounds for preference in this case include, to begin with, the mutual commitments and dependencies of a loving relationship. What the wife should say to her husband if he hesitates about saving her is not "What about me?" but "What about us?"[104] That is, she should invoke their partnership or shared history rather than the value placed on her by his love. Invoking her individual value in the eyes of his love would merely remind him that she was no more worthy of survival than the other potential victims, each of whom can ask "What about me?"

No doubt, the man also has nonmoral, self-regarding reasons for preferring to save his wife. Primary among these reasons may be that he is deeply attached to her and stands in horror at the thought of being separated from her by death. But attachment is not the same as love. Even a husband who long ago stopped loving his wife – stopped really looking or listening – might still be so strongly attached to her as to leap to her rescue without a second thought.

Conclusion

Maybe that's what Williams imagines the wife to be wishing for: a blind attachment, to which any critical reflection would be inimical. But then the wish that is disappointed by the Kantian agent in this story is not the wish for a loving husband; it's more like the wish for a trusty companion.

Insofar as the wife wants to be loved, however, she will want to be seen for the priceless creature that she is. She will therefore want to be seen, not in a way that tips the balance in her favor, but rather in a way that reveals the absurdity of weighing her in a balance at all.

Illustrating this absurdity is all that lifeboat cases are good for, in my opinion. These cases invite us to imagine situations in which we feel forced to make choices among things that cannot coherently be treated as alternatives, because their values are incomparable. Love does not help to overcome the absurdity in these cases: it doesn't help us to compare incomparables. On the contrary, love is virtually an education in this absurdity. But for that very reason, love is also a moral education.

---

[104] This way of putting the point was offered to me by Peter Railton, in a very helpful conversation about an earlier draft of this chapter.

5

The Voice of Conscience

How do you recognize the voice of your conscience? One possibility is that you recognize this voice by what it talks about – namely, your moral obligations, what you morally ought or ought not to do. Yet if the dictates of conscience were recognizable by their subject matter, you wouldn't need to think of them as issuing from a distinct faculty or in a distinctive voice. You wouldn't need the concept of a conscience, any more than you need concepts of distinct mental faculties for politics or etiquette. Talk of conscience and its dictates would be like talk of the mince-pie syllogism, in that it would needlessly elevate a definable subject matter to the status of a form or faculty of reasoning.[1]

Our having the concept of a conscience suggests, on the contrary, that ordinary practical thought does not contain a distinct, moral sense of 'ought' that lends a distinct, moral content to some practical conclusions.

---

[1] The mince-pie syllogism was the ironic invention of Elizabeth Anscombe. Anscombe objected to the notion that the practical syllogism was merely a syllogism on a practical topic, such as what one ought to do. She argued that if there were a distinct logical form for reasoning about what one ought to do, then there might as well be distinct forms for reasoning about every definable topic, including mince pies. (*Intention* [Ithaca, NY: Cornell University Press, 1957], 58.)

This essay was originally presented at a meeting of the Aristotelian Society, held in Senate House, University of London, on Monday, 23rd November, 1998, at 8.15 p.m.; and originally appeared in *Proceedings of the Aristotelian Society*, 1999, vol. 99, no. 1, pp. 57–76. It is reprinted by permission of Blackwell Publishing. In writing this essay, I have drawn on conversations and correspondence with Marcia Baron, Jennifer Church, Stephen Darwall, David Hills, David Phillips, and Connie Rosati. Work on this essay has been supported by a sabbatical leave from the College of Literature, Science, and the Arts, University of Michigan; and by a fellowship from the National Endowment for the Humanities.

The point of talking about the conscience and its voice is precisely to mark a distinction among thoughts that are not initially distinguishable in content. Among the many conclusions we draw about what we ought or ought not to do, some but not others resonate in a particular way that marks them as dictates of conscience. The phrase 'morally ought' is a philosophical coinage that introduces a difference of sense where ordinary thought has only a difference of voice – whatever that is.

But what is it? Conscience doesn't literally speak. The idea of its addressing you in a voice is thus an image, albeit an image that may infiltrate your experience of moral thought and not just your descriptions of it. Yet whether the dictates of conscience are somehow experienced as spoken or are just described as such after the fact, this image must represent something significant about them, or it wouldn't be used to identify them as a distinctive mode of thought. The question is what literal feature of these thoughts is represented by the image of their being delivered in a voice.

The answer, I think, is that the dictates of conscience carry an authority that distinguishes them from other thoughts about what you ought or ought not to do.[2] The voice of conscience is, metaphorically speaking, the voice of this authority. To recognize an 'ought' as delivered in the voice of conscience is to recognize it as carrying a different degree or kind of authority from the ordinary 'ought', and hence as due a different degree or kind of deference.

If the voice of conscience does represent a distinctive authority that accompanies some practical conclusions, then it is more than a curiosity of moral psychology: it symbolizes a fundamental feature of morality, regarded by some philosophers as *the* fundamental feature. Kant, in particular, thought that what morality requires can be deduced from the authority that must accompany its requirements. If Kant had written in the imagery of conscience, he might have put it like this: by reflecting on how the voice of conscience must *sound*, you can deduce what it must *say* – whereupon you will have heard it speak.

Of course, Kant didn't formulate his moral theory in these terms, but I think that they can be substituted for terms such as 'duty' and 'moral law' in Kant's own formulations, with some gain in clarity and persuasiveness

[2] The authority of conscience is the central theme of Butler's *Sermons*. For a recent discussion of Butler, see Stephen Darwall, *The British Moralists and the Internal 'Ought' 1640–1740* (Cambridge: Cambridge University Press, 1995), chapter 9.

for modern readers. My goal is to reconstruct Kant's categorical imperative in the terms of conscience and its voice.[3]

The idea of reconstructing the categorical imperative as the voice of conscience originated with Freud. Freud was interested in the voice of conscience because he thought that it could explain why paranoiacs heard
voices commenting on their behaviour;[4] and that it could in turn be
explained by the psychological origins of conscience in parental discipline 'conveyed . . . by the medium of the voice.'[5] In tracing conscience to
the voice of parental discipline, Freud also thought that he could explain
why its power 'manifests itself in the form of a categorical imperative.'[6]
This explanation showed, according to Freud, that 'Kant's Categorical
Imperative is . . . the direct heir of the Oedipus complex.'[7]

My view, which I cannot defend here,[8] is that the categorical imperative
can indeed be identified with the super-ego, at least in one of its guises.
For I think that the categorical imperative is what Freud would call an ego
ideal. The ego ideal, in Freudian theory, is that aspect of the super-ego
which represents the excellences of parental figures whom the subject
loved and consequently idealized when he was a child.[9] Although Kant
often framed the categorical imperative as a rule for the will to follow,
I think that it is better understood as an ideal for the will to emulate,
in that it describes an ideal configuration of the will itself. And I think

[3] There is at least one passage in which Kant uses the word 'conscience' in reference to the
activity of applying the categorical imperative: *Groundwork of the Metaphysic of Morals,* trans.
H. J. Paton (New York: Harper and Row, 1964), 89 (422). (Page numbers in parentheses
refer to the Prussian Academy Edition.)

[4] 'On Narcissism: An Introduction,' in *The Standard Edition of the Complete Psychological Works
of Sigmund Freud,* Vol. 14, ed. James Strachey (London: The Hogarth Press, 1957), 69–102,
at 95. See also *Group Psychology and the Analysis of the Ego, S.E.* 18: 67–143, at 110 [53];
New Introductory Lectures on Psycho-Analysis, S.E. 22: 3–182, at 59 [74]. (Page numbers in
brackets refer to the Norton paperback volumes of individual works from the Standard
Edition.)

[5] 'On Narcissism.' 14: 96.

[6] *The Ego and the Id, S.E.* 19: 3–66, at 35, 48 [31, 49]. Freud also uses this phrase in *Totem
and Taboo, S.E.* 13: ix-162, at 22.

[7] 'The Economic Problem of Masochism,' *S.E.* 19: 156–70, at 167. Freud also identified
the super-ego with the Kantian 'moral law within us' (*New Introductory Lectures,* 22:61, 163
[77, 202]).

[8] But see 'A Rational Superego' (Chapter 6 in the present volume).

[9] Freud's views on the relation between super-ego and ego ideal are clearly summarized in
Joseph Sandler, Alex Holder, and Dale Meers, 'The Ego Ideal and the Ideal Self,' 18 *The
Psychoanalytic Study of the Child* 139–58 (1963). See also Joseph Sandler, 'On the Concept
of the Superego,' 15 *The Psychoanalytic Study of the Child* 128–62 (1960).

that this ideal could indeed be internalized from parental figures as they appear to the eyes of a loving child.

This conception of the categorical imperative as an ego ideal will reappear at the end of this essay, but it is not my immediate concern. What concerns me here is Freud's suggestion that the categorical imperative can be identified with the voice of conscience.

The image of conscience as having a voice is potentially misleading in one respect. Taken literally, the image may lead us to think of conscience as an external intelligence whispering in our ears, like Socrates's *daimon*. Even when taken figuratively, the image still suggests that the dictates of conscience occur to us unbidden, as thoughts that we don't actively think for ourselves, and hence as external to us, in the sense made familiar by the work of Harry Frankfurt.[10]

Conscience is most likely to seem external in this sense when it opposes temptation: conscience and temptation can seem like parties to a dispute on which we sit as independent adjudicators. Yet even this judicial image is misleading, since the disputing parties do not appear as distinct from ourselves. We ourselves play each role in the mental courtroom, now advocating the case of temptation, now that of conscience, representing each side *in propria persona*. In short, we vacillate – which entails speaking in different voices, not just hearing them.

Thus, hearing the voice of our conscience is not really a matter of hearing voices. It's rather a matter of recognizing a voice in which we sometimes speak to ourselves.

Freud's theory of the super-ego might seem to favor the image of conscience as an independent agency, distinct from and in opposition to the self. Freud certainly thought that in cases of mental illness, the super-ego could become the source of voices heard involuntarily, and hence from outside the self in Frankfurt's sense.[11] Yet in the normal subject, the super-ego bears an ambiguous relation to the self. It is 'a differentiating grade in the ego',[12] and the process of introjection by which it is formed is a way of identifying with other people, which is necessarily a deployment of the self. So another description of what happens when the

---

[10] *The Importance of What We Care About* (Cambridge: Cambridge University Press, 1988), especially chapters 2, 5, 7, and 12.

[11] See the passages cited in note 5.

[12] This is the title of Chapter XI of *Group Psychology*.

super-ego addresses the ego is that the self identifies with others in addressing itself.

Although Kant doesn't tend to speak of the conscience *per se*, his moral philosophy also reflects the complexity of its relation to the self. On the one hand, Kant says that the moral law is necessary and inescapable; on the other hand, he describes it as a law that we give to ourselves. For Kant, giving ourselves the moral law represents both our exercise of an autonomous will and our subjection to a necessity larger than ourselves; just as, for Freud, conscience is the ego addressing itself in the voice of external authority.[13]

This analogy reveals what is right about Freud's claim that the voice of the super-ego is the voice of Kant's categorical imperative. The necessity to which we submit in the law that we give to ourselves can be imagined as the authority we recognize in a voice with which we address ourselves – namely, the voice of conscience. I want to show that Kant's attempt to derive the content of the moral law from the very concept of its practical necessity can be restaged as an attempt to derive the words of conscience from the authoritative sound of its voice.

An example of rational authority. The first step in this reconstruction of Kantian ethics is to analyze the authority that Kant would attribute to the conscience. Whereas Freud thought of the conscience as the seat of internalized parental authority, Kant would think of it – if he thought in such terms at all – as a seat of rational authority. But what sort of authority is that?

Consider, by way of analogy, the authority of cognitive judgments whose propositional content is self-evidently true. You make such a judgment, for example, when you confirm for yourself that $2 + 2 = 4$. To say that such a judgment is authoritative is to say that it merits deference. But why should anyone defer to your judgment on matters of elementary arithmetic?

The answer is not that you're especially well positioned to think about such matters. When it comes to adding 2 and 2, all thinkers are in the same position. But for that very reason, a computation performed by you here and now can take the place of anyone's, including your own on future occasions. That is, you can compute the sum of 2 and 2 *once*

---

[13] Kant seems to reject the image of an external voice of conscience at *Groundwork* 93 (425–26), where he insists that moral philosophy cannot serve 'as the mouthpiece of laws whispered to her by some implanted sense or by who knows what tutelary nature. . . .'

and for all, in that you would only compute it similarly in the future; and you can also compute it *one for all,* in that others would only compute it similarly, too. Your judgment is thus authoritative because it can serve as proxy for anyone's, including your later selves'. To see yourself as judging authoritatively is to see yourself as judging for all in this sense – in the sense, that is, of judging as anyone would.

But what if your judging as anyone would were, in turn, a matter on which judgments might differ? In that case, your arithmetic judgment might only seem authoritative to you. Surely, however, you recognize your judgment as having an authority that anyone would recognize. You must therefore see yourself as judging, not just as anyone would, but as anyone would judge that anyone would.

And now an infinite regress rears its head. For what if judgments could differ as to whether you were judging as anyone would judge that anyone would – and so on? Fortunately, there is independent reason to expect such a regress in the present context, and also to regard it as benign.

The reason is that the facts of elementary arithmetic are common knowledge among those who consider them, and common knowledge involves a regress of the present form. Anyone who adds 2 and 2 sees, not just that it's 4, but also that anyone who added 2 and 2 would see that it's 4, and that such a person would see this, too, and so on. The facts of elementary arithmetic are like objects in a public space, where everyone sees whatever everyone else sees, and everyone sees everyone else seeing it. Unlike publicly visible objects, however, the facts of arithmetic are common knowledge among all possible thinkers rather than a finite population of actual viewers.

As a participant in this common knowledge, you have higher-order knowledge about the judgments of all other thinkers, and about their judgments about the judgments of all. This higher-order knowledge constitutes a perception of authority in your own judgment that $2 + 2 = 4$, since it represents this judgment as that which anyone would think, and would think that anyone would think, and so on.

So it's just as we might have expected: the voice of authority is the one with the reverb. But now we know the source of the reverberations. A judgment resounds with authority when it is perceived as echoing and re-echoing in the minds of all other thinkers, as it does when its content is a matter of common knowledge.

This authority attaches, as we have seen, to items of *a priori* knowledge, such as the judgment that $2 + 2 = 4$. Items of *a priori* knowledge would seem to be the only bearers of this authority, in fact, since only the *a priori* can be regarded as what anyone would think, or be thought to think, and so on.

The authority of the moral law. I suspect that the form of common knowledge among all thinkers – of that which anyone would think, and would think that anyone would think, and so on – is the form that Kant attributes to the moral law in calling it universal. Of course, Kant thinks that the moral law is universal in the sense that it applies to all rational creatures; and the most economical way of representing a universally applicable law is with a universal quantifier, as in 'All rational creatures must keep their promises' or 'No rational creature may lie.' But serious problems, both textual and philosophical, stand in the way of reading Kant's talk of universal law as referring to universally quantified rules.

Consider, to begin with, these two passages from the *Groundwork:*

> Everyone must admit that a law, if it is to hold morally – that is, as the ground of an obligation – must carry with it absolute necessity; that the command 'Thou shalt not lie' does not hold just for men, without other rational beings having to heed it, and similarly with all the other genuine moral laws; and that consequently the ground of obligation here must be sought, not in the nature of man or in the circumstances of the world where he is located, but solely *a priori* in the concepts of pure reason.[14]

> It may be added that unless we wish to deny to the concept of morality all truth and all relation to a possible object, we cannot dispute that its law is of such widespread significance as to hold, not merely for men, but for all *rational beings as such* – not merely subject to contingent conditions and exceptions, but *with absolute necessity.* . . . And how could laws for determining *our* will be taken as laws for determining the will of a rational being as such – and only because of this for determining ours – if these laws were merely empirical and did not have their source completely *a priori* in pure, but practical reason?[15]

These passages are central to the *Groundwork,* because they introduce the conceptual connections among morality, universality, and the *a priori* – the connections through which Kant hopes to derive the content of the

---

[14] *Groundwork* vi (389), my translation. For reasons that will be explained later, I have brought this passage into conformity with Paton's translation of the following passage, in which 'gelten für' is translated as 'hold for.'

[15] *Groundwork* 76 (408).

categorical imperative from the very concept of morality. The passages argue that the concept of morality entails that its laws carry 'absolute necessity'; which entails that they hold not only for men but for all rational creatures; which entails that they hold *a priori*.

Suppose that we interpret this argument as using the word 'laws' to denote general rules, and as contrasting rules that quantify over men with rules that quantify over rational creatures. We must then wonder why the former rules are any less necessary than the latter, since the former apply necessarily to anything insofar as it is a man, just as the latter apply necessarily to anything insofar as it is rational, and either represent some conduct as necessary for the relevant agents. 'All men must keep their promises' and 'All rational creatures must keep their promises' would seem to be equally necessary, each within its specified domain. We may also wonder why the concept of morality calls for laws of the latter form. Couldn't there be a distinctively human morality, in which 'All men must keep their promises' would count as a law? Finally, we may wonder why such a law could not follow *a priori* from the concept of a man, just as a rule quantifying over rational creatures might follow from the concepts of reason and rationality.

Note, however, that Kant's example of absolute necessity is not a general rule that quantifies over all rational creatures. His example is rather a second-person command, 'Thou shalt not lie.' And what Kant says about such a requirement is not that it must refer to all rational creatures but that it must 'hold for' them – an expression that he repeats throughout the *Groundwork*, as we shall see.

Of course, the pronoun in 'Thou shalt not lie' might be standing in for a universal quantifier, and what's at issue could be the domain of that implicit quantifier. Yet if the issue were whether 'thou' referred to all men or to all rational creatures, then Kant wouldn't ask for whom the rule holds. The rule, fully spelled out, would be either '(All) thou (men) shall not lie' or '(All) thou (rational creatures) shall not lie,' and in either case it would have to hold or not hold, without limitation. 'All men shall not lie' cannot hold only locally or selectively, any more than 'All men are mortal.'

Suppose, however, that 'Thou shalt not lie' were a type of which various tokens were addressed to various agents, with corresponding variance in the reference of the pronoun. Commands of this type could be said to 'hold for' particular agents in two related senses: they might be authoritative from the perspectives of particular agents as addressees, and they might consequently be valid in application to those agents. To ask for whom the rule holds would be to ask who finds himself addressed by an authoritative command of this type.

According to this interpretation, Kant isn't thinking of moral requirements as universally quantified rules; he's thinking of them as personally addressed practical thoughts, of the form 'Thou shalt not lie.' We can now extend the interpretation so as to explain Kant's chain of inferences.

For suppose, next, that when Kant insists on the 'absolute necessity' of moral requirements, he means that the corresponding thought must be absolutely authoritative from the perspective of the addressee: an agent should not be able to exempt himself from the force of such a thought. Absolute necessity, so understood, can indeed be said to follow from the very concept of a moral requirement. So we have accounted for the first link in Kant's chain.

Now suppose that 'Thou shalt not lie' would be absolutely authoritative, in the requisite sense, if and only if it were what any agent would think to himself upon considering whether to lie, and would think that any agent would think, and so on. If it were such a thought, then an agent considering whether to lie would not only think to himself 'Thou shalt not lie' but would also think of himself as *having nothing else to think*, because this thought would strike him as what anyone would think on the subject, including himself on other occasions. He would therefore think of the question as having been settled once and for all – or, in other words, authoritatively. By contrast, if 'Thou shalt not lie' weren't such a thought, then even an agent who thought it would regard it as optional, there being other things that anyone, including himself, might think on the subject. He would therefore find it lacking in authority. Here is a sense in which the absolute authority entailed in the very concept of moral requirements can be seen to consist in their 'holding for' all rational agents – that is, by constituting what anyone would think, or would think that anyone would think, and so on. We have now accounted for the second link in Kant's chain.[16]

The third link follows without further suppositions. The form of what anyone would think, and would think that anyone would think, and so on – the form, if you like, of that than which there is nothing else *to* think – is the form of *a priori* knowledge. When it attaches to a thought

---

[16] See also *Groundwork* 92–3 (425): '[D]uty has to be a practical, unconditioned necessity of action; it must therefore hold for all rational beings . . . .'

such as 'Thou shalt not lie,' it yields a thought that is simultaneously *a priori* and practical. Hence the very concept of a moral requirement can be seen to entail an absolute authority that is found only in *a priori* practical thought.[17] Kant's argument is now complete.

I have embroidered this interpretive hypothesis on two mere swatches of text. How it will look against the broader fabric of Kantian ethics remains to be seen. First, however, I want to register an important qualification.

My hypothesis is that moral laws, for Kant, are not universally quantified rules but rather personally addressed practical thoughts, whose universality and authority both consist in their being what anyone would think, and would think that anyone would think, and so on. Yet if 'Don't lie' is universal in this sense, then everyone in the relevant circumstances will find himself with nothing else to think; and if everyone in the relevant circumstances finds himself with nothing else to think but 'Don't lie,' then there will, in effect, be a universal rule of not lying.

For this reason, my hypothesis cannot be that moral laws, for Kant, aren't universally quantified rules at all; it must be that they aren't universally quantified rules in the first instance. Moral laws, as I understand them, can be expressed in universally quantified rules, provided that those rules are understood as expressing the authority of personal practical thoughts, whose authority just consists in their being what anyone would think that anyone would think.

Let me emphasize, then, that I do not mean to ignore or dismiss the many passages in which Kant himself enunciates laws as universally quantified rules of behaviour. I merely suggest that the universal rules enunciated by Kant should be understood as summaries of something more complex, or as the outer surfaces of something deeper – namely, a state of affairs in which practical thoughts, in personal form, are common knowledge among all agents.

How universalization works. With this qualification in mind, I want to apply my interpretive hypothesis to Kant's account of universalization, the procedure by which maxims are tested under the categorical imperative. Here, too, the hypothesis helps to resolve both textual and philosophical problems.

---

[17] See *Groundwork* 93 (426): 'These principles must have an origin entirely and completely *a priori* and must at the same time derive from this their sovereign authority....'

Consider this instance of universalization:[18]

[A person] finds himself driven to borrowing money because of need. He well knows that he will not be able to pay it back but he sees too that he will get no loan unless he gives a firm promise to pay it back within a fixed time. He is inclined to make such a promise; but he has still enough conscience to ask 'Is it not unlawful and contrary to duty to get out of difficulties in this way?' Supposing, however, he did resolve to do so, the maxim of his action would run thus: 'Whenever I believe myself short of money, I will borrow money and promise to pay it back, though I know that this will never be done.' Now this principle of self-love or personal advantage is perhaps quite compatible with my own entire future welfare; only there remains the question 'Is it right?' I therefore transform the demand of self-love into a universal law and frame my question thus: 'How would things stand if my maxim became a universal law?' I then see straight away that this maxim can never hold as a universal law of nature and be self-consistent, but must necessarily contradict itself. For the universality of a law that every one believing himself to be in need can make any promise he pleases with the intention not to keep it would make promising, and the very purpose of promising, itself impossible, since no one would believe he was being promised anything, but would laugh at utterances of this kind as empty shams.

The target of universalization in this passage is what Kant calls a maxim of action: 'Whenever I believe myself short of money, I will borrow money and promise to pay it back, though I know that this will never be done.' We might think that the way to make this maxim universal is to replace the first-person pronoun with quantified variables ranging over all rational creatures.[19] Kant seems to suggest such a procedure when he refers to 'the universality of a law that every one believing himself to be in need can make any promise he pleases. . . .' But Kant also suggests a different procedure, when he considers whether his maxim itself 'can . . . hold as a

---

[18] *Groundwork* 90 (422). I have brought Paton's version of this passage into conformity with his translation of the preceding passage, by rendering 'gelten' as 'to hold.' (See note 15.)

[19] For an interpretation of universalization along these lines, see, e.g., Onora O'Neill, *Acting on Principle: An Essay on Kantian Ethics* (New York: Columbia University Press, 1975), esp. Chapter Five, 59–93; and 'Consistency in Action,' in *Constructions of Reason: Explorations of Kant's Practical Philosophy* (Cambridge: Cambridge University Press, 1989), 81–104. See also Christine Korsgaard, 'Kant's Formula of Universal Law,' in *Creating the Kingdom of Ends* (Cambridge: Cambridge University Press, 1996), 77–105. According to Korsgaard, universalization 'is carried out by imagining, in effect, that the action you propose to perform in order to carry out your purpose is the standard procedure for carrying out that purpose' (92). In the present case, then, the agent 'imagines a world in which everyone who needs money makes a lying promise and he imagines that, at the same time, he is part of that world, willing his maxim' ('Kant's Analysis of Obligation: the Argument of *Groundwork I*,' in *ibid.*, 43–76, at 63). Finally, see Roger J. Sullivan, *Kant's Moral Theory* (Cambridge: Cambridge University Press, 1989), 168–69.

universal law.' Kant's maxim is framed in the first person, and so it – the maxim itself – can 'hold' as a universal law only if first-personal thoughts can somehow be universal.

Kant's framing his maxim in the first person is no accident. He could not have restated it, for example, as 'Immanuel Kant will make lying promises when he is in need.' Such a third-personal thought would not be a maxim of action, since it could not be acted upon by the thinker until he reformulated it reflexively, in the first person. Insofar as the target of universalization is a practical thought, it is essentially first-personal.[20]

This first-personal thought should remind us of the second-personal injunction considered above, 'Thou shalt not lie,' which was there regarded as being addressed by the agent to himself. So regarded, 'Thou shalt not lie' was couched in what might be called the reflexive second-person – the second-person of talking to oneself. And when it is thus addressed to oneself, 'Thou shalt not lie' is just the contradictory of 'I shall lie,' the maxim that is currently up for universalization. Our earlier reflections on how the second-personal injunction could be a universal law are thus directly relevant to the universalization of the first-personal maxim.

As before, we might consider transforming the maxim into a universal law, by substitution of a quantifier for the first-person pronoun. But Kant speaks more often of maxims' *being* laws themselves than of their being *transformed into* laws. In addition to asking whether a maxim can 'hold as a universal law,'[21] he asks: whether maxims can 'serve as universal laws,'[22] whether they have 'universal validity . . . as laws'[23] or 'the universality of a law';[24] whether a maxim 'at the same time contains in itself its own universal validity for every rational being'[25] or is constrained 'by the condition that it should be universally valid as a law for every subject';[26] whether it 'can have for its object itself as at the same time a universal law'[27] or can 'have as its content itself considered as a universal law.'[28] All of these expressions call for a single thought to be regarded simultaneously as the maxim of one agent and as a law for all.

---

[20] On this topic, see John Perry, *The Problem of the Essential Indexical and Other Essays* (New York: Oxford University Press, 1993).

[21] Also at 103–4 (438).

[22] 94 (426).

[23] 126 (458); see also 129 (461).

[24] 128 (460).

[25] 105 (437–38).

[26] 105 (438).

[27] 114 (447).

[28] 115 (447).

According to my interpretation, however, a single thought can simultaneously be a first-personal maxim and a universal law, if it is what anyone would think in response to the relevant practical question, and would think that anyone would think, and so on. It is then a type of thought whose tokens would be authoritative for any agent. And imagining that 'I will make false promises' would be authoritative for anyone is a way of imagining a universal law of making false promises.

This interpretation explains how an individual maxim can 'have as its content itself considered as a universal law'[29] or 'contain in itself its own universal validity for every rational being.'[30] Universalizing a first-personal maxim ('I will make false promises') is not, in the first instance, a process of conjoining it with some universally quantified variant of itself ('Everyone will make false promises'). Universalizing this maxim is rather a matter of regarding the maxim itself as what anyone would think, or would think that anyone would think, and so on. The universalized maxim is more like this – 'Obviously, I will make false promises' – where 'obviously' indicates that the following thought would occur to anyone, as would occur to anyone, and so on. That's how a first-personal maxim can contain its own universal validity within itself.

Kant says that a universal law of making false promises would have the result that 'no one would believe he was being promised anything, but would laugh at utterances of this kind as empty shams.' If we think of this law as a universally quantified rule, to the effect that everyone may or will make false promises when in need, then we shall have to wonder why it would have the results predicted.

The answer might be that people's adherence to such a law would entail the issuance of so many false promises that everyone would eventually learn to distrust everyone else.[31] But this answer would be a piece

---

[29] 115 (447).

[30] 105 (437–38).

[31] For this interpretation, see O'Neill, 'Universal Laws and Ends-in-Themselves,' in *Constructions of Reason*, 126–44, at 132: 'The project of deceit requires a world with sufficient trust for deceivers to get others to believe them; the results of universal deception would be a world in which such trust was lacking, and the deceiver's project was impossible.' See also Korsgaard, 'Kant's Formula of Universal Law,' 92: 'The efficacy of the false promise as a means of securing the money depends on the fact that not everyone uses promises this way. Promises are efficacious in securing loans only because they are believed, and they are believed only if they are normally true.' Finally, see Sullivan, *Kant's Moral Theory*, 171: 'Truthful assertions cannot survive any universal violation of the essential point of such speech. Once everyone lies for what each considers a "good" reason, we can never know when any verbal behavior counts as "telling the truth."'

of empirical reasoning, about how social interactions would evolve in response to a particular pattern of conduct; whereas Kant says that the requirements of morality must be derivable *a priori*. This piece of empirical reasoning would therefore be out of place in the process of universalization, by which the specific requirements of morality are derived.

What's more, the same empirical reasoning wouldn't apply to a law licensing promises whose falsity would go undetected, since the proliferation of undetectably false promises would not undermine people's trust; yet Kant reaches the same conclusion about a law of undetectable falsehoods. He imagines a case in which 'I have in my possession a deposit, the owner of which has died without leaving any record of it.' Moral reflection in these circumstances raises the question 'whether I could . . . make the law that every man is allowed to deny that a deposit has been made when no one can prove the contrary.' Kant's conclusion is 'that taking such a principle as a law would annihilate itself, because its result would be that no one would make a deposit.'[32] This conclusion cannot be an empirical prediction of what would happen under a universally quantified rule of denying unrecorded deposits. General adherence to such a rule would not in fact discourage prospective depositors, precisely because there would be no record of the deposits involved.

In my view, however, the way to imagine a universal law of denying unrecorded deposits is to imagine that the maxim 'I will deny unrecorded deposits' is authoritative, in that it is what anyone would think, and would think that anyone would think, and so on. This law would indeed undermine the faith of prospective depositors – not empirically, through the pattern of conduct it produced; but rationally, through the *a priori* practical thinking that it embodied, which would be common knowledge among all agents. *No one would make unrecorded deposits if stealing them were all there was to think of doing with them.*

If the maxim of denying unrecorded deposits were a law in this sense, then the authority of that maxim would be evident to prospective depositors no less than it was to their intended trustee, since the maxim would be what anyone would think that anyone would think. Depositors would only have to reason about the case from the perspective of their trustee in order to see what his maxim for dealing with their deposits

[32] *Critique of Practical Reason*, trans. Lewis White Beck (Indianapolis: Bobbs Merrill, 1956), 27 (27). The same case appears, with embellishments, in the essay 'On the Proverb: That May be True in Theory, But Is of No Practical Use,' in *Perpetual Peace and Other Essays*, trans. Ted Humphrey (Indianapolis: Hackett Publishing, 1983), 61–92, at 69–70 (286–287).

would be, since there would be nothing else to think of doing with them. That the trustee would deny having received their deposits isn't something that depositors would have learned from past experience of his or anyone else's behaviour; it's something that would be evident to them through their own practical reasoning, as proxy for his. They would consequently be deterred from making unrecorded deposits.

This interpretation simply assumes that the connections fundamental to Kant's conception of morality – the connections among universality, necessity, and the *a priori* – hold for all of the laws involved in universalization, including: (1) the categorical imperative, in which the procedure of universalization is prescribed; (2) the specific requirements derived by means of that procedure; and, finally but crucially, (3) the laws imagined within it. In this last instance, imagining one's maxim to be a universal law must entail imagining it to have all three connected properties – that is, to be universally inescapable *a priori*. Hence universalization is a procedure of imagining one's maxim to constitute practical but *a priori* and hence common knowledge.

The nature of maxims. Thus far I have avoided inquiring into the nature of maxims, choosing instead to work with simple expressions of intent, such as 'I'll make false promises' or 'I'll deny unrecorded deposits.' Now that I have offered an hypothesis as to how maxims are universalized, however, I can no longer avoid the question of what they are and, more importantly, why they might be subject to such a procedure. And I don't think that maxims are simply intentions or expressions of intent.

Kant says that maxims are 'principles of volition.'[33] Many interpreters have noted that Kant usually formulates maxims of action so as to specify both a type of behavior and a purpose to be served by it – or, in other words, an end as well as a means.[34] I think that maxims so often connect end and means, and do so in the form of general principles, because they state the connection between reasons and action.[35]

---

[33] *Groundwork* 68 (400).

[34] See O'Neill, *Acting on Principle*, 37–38; Korsgaard, 'Kant's Analysis of Obligation,' 57–58, and *The Sources of Normativity* (Cambridge: Cambridge University Press, 1996), 108.

[35] See Korsgaard, 'An Introduction to the Ethical, Political, and Religious Thought of Kant,' in *Creating the Kingdom of Ends*, 3–42, at 13–14: 'Your maxim must contain your reason for action: it must say what you are going to do, and why'; 'Kant's Analysis of Obligation,' 57: 'Your maxim thus expresses what you take to be a reason for action.' I am inclined to put a slightly finer point on this claim, by saying that the maxim states the rule of practical inference, from reason to action.

Consider again the maxim of a lying promise: 'Whenever I believe myself short of money, I will borrow money and promise to pay it back, though I know that this will never be done.' I interpret this maxim to mean that financial need is a reason for promising to return a loan, and that this reason outweighs the countervailing consideration that the promise would be false. The maxim is thus a principle of volition in the sense that it licenses a practical inference, from the premises 'I need money' and 'I'd be lying if I promised to repay a loan,' to the conclusion 'I'll promise to repay a loan.' The license for this inference is framed as a general principle because the validity of an inference-type cannot vary from one token to another.

More importantly, the validity of an inference is a logical relation that must be recognizable *a priori*. That's why a maxim is naturally subject to the test of universalization. If there is a valid inference from 'I need money' to 'I'll make a false promise,' then the validity of that inference must be such as anyone would recognize, and would recognize that anyone would recognize, and so on. The validity of a practical inference, like the validity of *modus ponens*, must hold for – and be common knowledge among – all thinkers.

In this case, the inference can't be valid, precisely because its validity would have to be common knowledge, which would undermine a presupposition of the inference itself – namely, that making false promises is a means of getting money.[36] If it were common knowledge that a decision to make false promises followed from a need for money, then nobody would lend on the basis of promises; promises wouldn't be a means of getting money; and a decision to make them would no longer follow. Thus, if 'I'll make false promises' did follow from 'I need money,' then it wouldn't follow, after all; and so it doesn't follow, to begin with. A desire for money isn't a valid reason for making false promises.

Its not being a reason is also *a priori*. And this point provides the most challenging twist in Kant's argument. Kant thought that we cannot wait passively to receive practical dictates with *a priori* authority, and hence that we cannot wait for the voice of conscience to speak.[37] We have to

[36] Here I follow what Korsgaard calls 'the practical contradiction interpretation' ('Kant's Formula of Universal Law,' 92). I differ from Korsgaard, however, in tracing the practical contradiction to an imagined piece of common knowledge rather than an imagined standard practice. (See note 20.)

[37] See again the passage quoted in note 14.

propose our own practical dictates and ask whether they could possibly carry *a priori* authority. And sometimes, when the answer is no, *that answer* turns out to carry the sought-for authority: *it* resounds with the voice of conscience.

The practical dictate in the present example is the maxim that making a false promise follows from circumstances of financial need. That the validity of this inference must be *a priori* is itself *a priori*, since validity is a matter of rationality, which is common to all thinkers. From the *a priori* requirement that the validity of an inference must be *a priori*, the impossibility of a valid inference from financial need to false promises follows *a priori* as well. Anyone can see, and can see that anyone can see, that the validity of this inference would have to be *a priori*, but that one of the inference's presuppositions would then be false, so that the inference wouldn't be valid, after all. The fact that the validity of such an inference would have to be common knowledge, which would invalidate the inference – this fact is itself common knowledge among all who care to reflect on the matter. So when the question is whether a need for money is a reason for making false promises, anyone can see that the answer is no, and that anyone can see it, and so on.

Here, finally, is a dictate of conscience, reverberating with the appropriate authority. Conscience tells us that the reasons we thought we had for doing something couldn't be reasons for doing it; and it tells us authoritatively, once and for all. They couldn't be reasons for doing it, conscience tells us, because their being reasons couldn't be seen, and be seen to be seen, by all. And what conscience here points out to us is something that can be seen, and seen to be seen, by all. Thus, conscience authoritatively reveals that our proposed reasons for acting couldn't be authoritative and consequently couldn't be reasons.

The role of autonomy. But isn't conscience supposed to forbid us from doing things rather than merely inform us that we don't have reason for doing them?

Kant's answer, I think, would be that by informing us of the absence of reasons for doing things, conscience rules out the possibility of our doing them for reasons and, with it, the possibility of our doing them autonomously – or, indeed, the possibility of *our* doing them, since we are truly the agents of the things we do only when we do them for reasons. And ruling out the possibility of our being the agents of the things we do is the way that conscience forbids us from doing them at all.

Kant says:[38]

[M]orality lies in the relation of actions to the autonomy of the will.... An action which is compatible with the autonomy of the will is *permitted*; one which does not harmonize with it is *forbidden*.

Kant could have put his point differently. An action that is incompatible with the autonomy of the will isn't, properly speaking, an action at all: it's a piece of behavior unattributable to an agent, a bodily movement in which there is nobody home. So put, of course, the point seems to be that we *won't* do the forbidden thing – or, at least, that *we* won't do it. Yet this point is compatible with the recognition that we might still do the forbidden thing in the weaker sense of 'do' that includes nonautonomous behaviour. As I interpret Kant, the recognition that we could do something only nonautonomously deters us from doing the thing even in this weaker sense. The deterrent force of this recognition derives from our reverence for the idea of ourselves as rational and autonomous beings.

Kant speaks of a 'paradox' with the following content: 'that without any further end or advantage to be attained[,] the mere dignity of humanity, that is, of rational nature in man – and consequently that reverence for a mere idea – should function as an inflexible precept for the will.'[39] In other words, the prescriptive force of moral dictates is a force registered in our reverence for the idea of ourselves as rational and autonomous beings. Conscience tells us that if we do something, we shall have to do it nonautonmously, without reason; and conscience thereby appeals to our reverence for this self-ideal as a motive against doing the thing at all.

The Kantian ego ideal. I have now returned to the idea that Kant resembles Freud in positing an ego ideal. This ideal is necessary to motivate our adherence to the conclusions that result from applying the categorical imperative – the conclusions that I have identified with the dictates of conscience. These conclusions authoritatively refute our proposed reasons for acting; but in order to deter us from acting, they must engage our respect for the conception of ourselves as acting only for reasons. Moral requirements thus motivate us via an ideal image of our obeying them.

---

[38] *Groundwork* 107 (439).
[39] 106 (439).

I believe that the ego ideal plays a similar role in Freudian theory.[40] Freud sometimes speaks as if the commands of the super-ego are backed by threats and obeyed by the ego solely out of fear. In fact, however, his descriptions of the relations between ego and super-ego depend heavily on the ego's admiration for the super-ego, as an internalized object of love. And it is in this latter capacity that the super-ego is described by Freud as being, or as including, an ego ideal.

I believe that Freud's theory of the ego ideal can help us to humanize Kant's ideal of ourselves as rationally autonomous. It can help us to see that what Kant called 'reverence for a mere idea' – reverence, that is, for 'the mere dignity of humanity'[41] – is in fact our response to something that we have internalized from real people in the course of our moral development. More specifically, I believe that the object of this reverence, the ideal of ourselves as rationally autonomous, is an ideal that we acquire in the course of loving our parents, in the manner described by Freud. But my reasons for this belief will have to wait for another occasion.

[40] The claims made in this paragraph are defended in 'A Rational Superego' (Chapter 6).
[41] Quoted at note 39.

6

A Rational Superego

Just when philosophers of science thought they had buried Freud for the last time, he has quietly reappeared in the writings of moral philosophers. Two analytic ethicists, Samuel Scheffler and John Deigh, have independently applied Freud's theory of the superego to the problem of moral motivation.[1] Scheffler and Deigh concur in thinking that although Freudian theory doesn't entirely solve the problem, it can nevertheless contribute to a solution.

Freud claims that the governance exercised over us by morality is a form of governance that was once exercised by our parents and that was subsequently assumed by a portion of our own personalities. This inner proxy for our parents was established, according to Freud, at the time when we were obliged to give up our oedipal attachment to them. Freud

---

[1] Scheffler, *Human Morality* (New York: Oxford University Press, 1992), chapter 5 ("Reason, Psychology and the Authority of Morality"); Deigh, *The Sources of Moral Agency: Essays in Moral Psychology and Freudian Theory* (Cambridge: Cambridge University Press, 1996), chapter 6 ("Freud, Naturalism, and Modern Moral Philosophy"). See also Scheffler's paper "Naturalism, Psychoanalysis, and Moral Motivation," in *Psychoanalysis, Mind and Art: Perspectives on Richard Wollheim*, ed. Jim Hopkins and Anthony Savile (Oxford: Blackwell, 1992), 86–109; and chapter 4 of Deigh's book ("Remarks on Some Difficulties in Freud's Theory of Moral Development").

From *The Philosophical Review* 108 (1999), 529–558. Copyright © 1999 Cornell University. Reprinted by permission of the publisher. In writing this essay, I have drawn on conversations and correspondence with Linda Wimer Brakel, Jennifer Church, Stephen Darwall, David Phillips, Connie Rosati, Nancy Sherman, and the editors of the *Review*. Work on this essay has been supported by fellowships from the National Endowment for the Humanities and the John Simon Guggenheim Memorial Foundation, together with matching leaves from the College of Literature, Science, and the Arts, University of Michigan.

therefore declares that "Kant's Categorical Imperative is . . . the direct heir of the Oedipus complex."²

Scheffler and Deigh are skeptical of Freud's claim to have explained the force of Kant's imperative. In Freud's thoroughly naturalistic account, our obedience to moral requirements owes nothing to their meriting obedience; it's due entirely to incentives that appeal to our inborn drives. Freud thus explains the influence of morality in a way that tends to debunk its rational authority, whereas the Categorical Imperative is supposed to carry all the authority of practical reason.

But Scheffler and Deigh believe that moral requirements can carry rational authority, as Kant believed, while still emanating from a distinct portion of the personality, formed out of identifications with other persons in the manner described by Freud. These philosophers consequently envision a rationalist version of Freudian theory. Scheffler describes this hybrid view as follows:

> [T]he suggestion that an authoritative aspect of the self may play a role in moral motivation is not obviously incompatible in itself with the rationalist position. Offhand, for example, there seems to be no reason why one could not take the view that the (generic) superego is part of the psychological apparatus whereby purely rational considerations succeed in motivating rational human agents. On this view, the superegos of rational human agents confer motivational authority on moral principles in recognition of their status as principles of pure practical reason.³

Deigh also envisions a rationalist version of Freudian theory, but he would locate the force of reason in the ego, as "the force of the ego's initiative in negotiating peace among the id, superego, and the requirements of reality."⁴ Of course, the ego's initiative in these matters is also attributed by Freud to the operation of natural drives. But Deigh finds this aspect of Freudian theory unsupported: "Nothing in the theory beyond its own antirationalist commitments . . . argues against a rationalist understanding" of the same phenomenon.⁵ Both philosophers thus think that Freud's conception of the personality could and perhaps should

---

² "The Economic Problem of Masochism," *The Standard Edition of the Complete Psychological Works of Sigmund Freud*, ed. James Strachey et al. (London: The Hogarth Press), 19:156–70, at 167. Freud also identified the superego with the Kantian "moral law within us" (*New Introductory Lectures*, S.E. 22:61, 163 [77, 202]). (Page numbers in brackets refer to the Norton paperback versions of the S.E.)
³ Samuel Scheffler, *Human Morality*, 96–97 n. 22.
⁴ *The Sources of Moral Agency*, 130.
⁵ Ibid.

make room for a seat of reason, though they differ as to where reason should sit.

I think that this marriage of Freud and Kant is worth pursuing, for several reasons. Freud's theory of the superego provides a valuable psychological model for various aspects of the Categorical Imperative, if not for its rational force. And Freud provides something that is missing from Kantian moral theory – namely, a story of moral development. If only Freud's theory could be purged of its antirationalism (as Deigh calls it), the result might be a valuable complement to Kant.

One feature of the Categorical Imperative that is reflected in Freudian theory is its dual status as a prescription and an ideal. On the one hand, the Imperative tells us what to do: "Act only on that maxim which you can simultaneously will to be a universal law." On the other hand, the imperative describes what a rational will does, and it thereby holds up the rational will as an ideal for us to emulate. In fact, the motive that induces us to obey the prescription is our reverence for the ideal that it conveys.[6] These two aspects of the Categorical Imperative are mirrored in Freudian theory by the concepts of the superego and ego ideal. The superego tells us what to do; the ego ideal gives us a model to emulate. A standard reading of Freud posits a division of labor between these two figures, but I shall argue that Freudian theory makes best sense if they are seen as unified, in the same manner as the corresponding aspects of the Categorical Imperative.[7] Our obedience to the demands of the superego must be seen as motivated by our admiration for it, in its alternate capacity as ego ideal.

Freud's moral theory also reflects the interplay between internal and external authority in Kantian ethics. On the one hand, Kant says that the moral law is necessary and inescapable; on the other hand, he describes it as a law that we give to ourselves. We are bound by the authority of morality, according to Kant, and yet we somehow exercise that authority in our own right. This combination, which sounds so paradoxical in the abstract, is made concretely imaginable by Freud. The external authority of morality is represented as the authority of another person, the parent; the autonomous exercise of that authority is represented as the assumption of the parent's role by a part of the self, in which the parent is internalized. Our ability to exercise moral authority over ourselves is thus explained by the familiar psychological process of internalizing other people.

---

[6] I argue for this claim in "The Voice of Conscience" (Chapter 5 in the present volume).
[7] See note 29.

One might think that personalizing the authority of morality in this fashion violates the spirit of Kantian ethics, which is often described as austerely impersonal. But here I disagree with the standard interpretation of Kant. The Categorical Imperative is not an impersonal rule but an ideal of the person, and our reverence for it is therefore akin to our feelings for persons whom we idealize. That's why respect for the moral law, in Kant, coincides with respect for persons.[8] Representing moral authority in the image of an idealized person is therefore compatible with Kantian ethics, as I interpret it.

Finally, this representation of moral authority yields a story of moral development that should be welcome to followers of Kant. Kantian ethics is an ethics of respecting persons, others as well as ourselves. But what awakens us to the personhood of others, to the fact that the creatures around us are persons like ourselves? Freud gives the only plausible answer to this question. The main theme of Freud's moral theory is that we are inducted into morality by our childhood experience of loving and being loved – the experience without which we would neither idealize nor internalize a parental figure. Love is our introduction to the fact that we are not alone in the world; and morality as formulated by Kant is our practical response to that fact.[9]

Of course, the Freudian story of moral development can thus be assimilated into Kantian ethics only if it is significantly revised. The ideal that we internalize from those we love must not be merely a representation of social respectability or conventional propriety; it must be an ideal of personhood as rational nature; otherwise, the result will not be an internal moral authority that Kant would recognize as "the moral law within." But I believe that Freudian theory needs to be revised in this direction anyway, and that the materials for such a revision are provided by Freud himself. My goal in this essay is to explain how this rationalist version of psychoanalytic theory emerges from the works of Freud.

Freud's Theory of Guilt: First Reading

Freud often presents his moral psychology as a theory of the moral emotions, especially guilt. He claims to explain what guilt is and how a sense of guilt is acquired. But Freud realizes that a theory of guilt must ultimately rest on a theory of moral authority, since a sense of having disobeyed that authority is prerequisite to feeling guilty.

---

[8] I argue for this claim in "Love as a Moral Emotion" (Chapter 4 in the present volume).
[9] This way of putting my point was suggested by Christine Korsgaard.

Freud introduces the connection between guilt and moral authority as follows:

> To begin with, if we ask how a person comes to have a sense of guilt, we arrive at an answer which cannot be disputed: a person feels guilty...when he has done something which he knows to be [wrong]. But then we notice how little this answer tells us.[10]

What tells us little, according to Freud, is the answer that traces guilt to self-criticism framed in moral terms, such as 'wrong.' This answer is uninformative, Freud explains, because it "presuppose[s] that one had already recognized that what is [wrong] is reprehensible, is something that must not be carried out." "How," he asks, "is this judgment arrived at?"[11]

What needs to be explained, in other words, is how some self-reproaches are recognized to be authoritative about what must or must not be done, so that they can occasion guilt. Saying that they are couched in moral terms simply raises the further question how these terms are known to bear the requisite authority.

Freud prefers to think of moral authority as vested, not in a particular vocabulary of self-criticism, but rather in a particular self-critical faculty. This inner faculty is the superego, which is established at the resolution of the Oedipus complex, when the child imaginatively takes his parents into himself, through a process known as introjection.

Freud hypothesizes that the introjected parent criticizes the subject's behavior and, like a real parent, threatens to punish him for it. The subject's fear of this inner disciplinarian constitutes his sense of guilt. Thus, "the sense of guilt is at bottom nothing else but a topographical variety of anxiety; in its later phases it coincides completely with *fear of the super-ego.*"[12] Freud often refers to this fear as "conscience anxiety": *Gewissensangst.*[13]

---

[10] *Civilization and Its Discontents*, S.E. 21:59–145, at 124 [71]. I have substituted the term 'wrong' for the translation in the *Standard Edition*, which is 'bad.' Freud's word is *böse*, which differs from the English 'bad' in that it is essentially a term of moral criticism. If Freud had wanted a word that was morally neutral, like 'bad,' he would have used *schlecht*. The difference is clearly marked by *Der Grosse Duden*, which defines *böse* as "sittlich schlecht" – "morally bad."

[11] Ibid.

[12] *Civilization and Its Discontents*, S.E. 21:135 [82]; see also 124–29 [71–75].

[13] Ibid., 124 [71]. For the term *Gewissensangst*, see the editor's note in *Inhibitions, Symptoms and Anxiety*, S.E. 20:77–175, at 128 [56]. Freud seems to equate the sense of guilt with *Gewissensangst* at "The Economic Problem of Masochism," S.E. 19:166–67. See also *The Ego and the Id*, S.E. 19:57 [60]; *New Introductory Lectures* S.E. 22:62 [77].

Here Freud equates the guilt induced by self-reproaches bearing moral authority with fear induced by reproaches bearing a threat. He thus appears to equate the authority of morality with the power to threaten. I do not believe that Freud's view can be reduced to this simple equation of right with might. But the best way to arrive at Freud's view, I think, is to consider various problems that would confront this simplistic version of it.

One problem is how the superego can credibly threaten the ego. What does the ego have to be afraid of?

What the child once feared from his parents is the loss of their love and of the protection that it afforded against their use of coercive force.[14] What the ego fears from the superego is less clear. Freud says, "The superego retain[s] essential features of the introjected persons – their strength, their severity, their inclination to supervise and to punish."[15] He says that the superego "observes the ego, gives it orders, judges it and threatens it with punishments."[16] Yet it is unclear what punishments the superego can actually inflict upon the ego, and so it is also unclear what punishments it can credibly threaten.

Although Freud refers repeatedly to the superego as aggressive, sadistic, and cruel, he never details its cruelties. At one point he says, "The super-ego torments the sinful ego with the same feeling of anxiety and is on the watch for opportunities of getting it punished by the external world."[17] Yet the feeling of anxiety mentioned here is just the ego's fear of harsh treatment, and so it cannot constitute the very harsh treatment that is feared.[18] And Freud never explains how the ego might foresee and hence fear the superego's ability to enlist the external world in administering punishments, since these machinations take place outside of the subject's consciousness.[19]

---

[14] *Civilization and Its Discontents*, S.E. 21:124 [71]; *New Introductory Lectures*, S.E. 22: 62 [77]; *An Outline of Psychoanalysis*, S.E. 23:141– 207, at 206 [95].

[15] "The Economic Problem of Masochism," *S.E.* 19:167.

[16] *Outline of Psychoanalysis S.E.* 23:205 [95]. See also *New Introductory Lectures, S.E.* 22:62 [77]: "the super-ego . . . observes, directs, and threatens the ego."

[17] *Civilization and Its Discontents, S.E.* 21:125 [72].

[18] For a similar problem, see *New Introductory Lectures, S.E.* 22:78 [97], where the superego is said to punish the ego with "tense feelings of inferiority and of guilt." How can the ego be punished with feelings of guilt, if feelings of guilt consist in the fear of this very punishment? (As for the feelings of inferiority, see the text at note 33.)

[19] One possible solution to the problem is suggested is this passage: "[W]e can tell what is hidden behind the ego's dread of the superego. The superior being, which turned into the ego ideal, once threatened castration, and this dread of castration is probably the nucleus around which the subsequent fear of conscience has gathered; it is this dread that persists as the fear of conscience" (*The Ego and the Id, S.E.* 19:57 [60]). Here the fear of conscience is described as a remnant of an earlier fear, felt by the child

A possible solution to the problem is contained in Richard Wollheim's account of introjection.[20] In Wollheim's account, the internalized parent is a figure of fantasy, whose aggression the child imagines both undergoing and watching himself undergo. Wollheim likens the fear of conscience to the fear felt by an audience when it empathizes with a character being victimized on the stage. The only difference is that victimization of the ego is enacted in the mind, with the subject imagining himself in the roles of victim and audience simultaneously. In his imagined capacity as empathetic audience to this scene, the subject experiences real fear.

Even if we concede the superego's ability to instill fear in the ego, a more serious problem remains, in that fear differs from guilt and cannot come to resemble it just by being internalized.[21] The merely "topographical" characteristics of fear – its being located in the ego and directed at the superego – seem insufficient to transform it into the emotion of guilt.[22]

There is no reason to think that an emotion originally felt by a person interacting with other people would give rise to an entirely new emotion just by being consigned to one part of his psyche interacting with other

---

(a boy, of course) who perceived his father as threatening castration. If *Gewissensangst* is castration anxiety redirected at the superego, then it is actually misdirected and cannot be explained by any real danger. The superego could nevertheless torment the ego by exacerbating its misdirected fear, like a mugger brandishing a toy knife. Elsewhere, however, Freud admits that tracing *Gewissensangst* to castration anxiety only deepens the mystery (*Inhibitions, Symptoms and Anxiety, S.E.* 20:139 [69]): "Castration anxiety develops into moral anxiety – social anxiety – and it is not so easy now to know what the anxiety is about." Freud therefore returns to his more general account of conscience anxiety: "[W]hat the ego regards as the danger and responds to with an anxiety-signal is that the super-ego should be angry with it or punish it or cease to love it." But why should the ego fear inciting the superego's anger or losing its love? In *Civilization and Its Discontents, S.E.* 21:124 [71], Freud says that the loss of love is feared because it opens the way to punishment; and surely the same should be said about the incitement of anger. So the explanation once again depends on the superego's power to punish the ego, which remains mysterious. In the *Outline* (*S.E.* 23:200 [87–88]), Freud says that the children fear "*loss of love* which would deliver them over helpless to the dangers of the external world," but this remark is once again inapplicable to the loss of love from the superego.

20 *The Thread of Life* (Cambridge: Harvard University Press, 1984), 121–29. Wollheim attributes this account to the work of Karl Abraham and Melanie Klein.

21 This point is the main thesis of David H. Jones, "Freud's Theory of Moral Conscience," *Philosophy* 41 (1966): 34–57. See also Scheffler, *Human Morality*, 87–88; Herbert Morris, "The Decline of Guilt," in *Ethics and Personality: Essays in Moral Psychology*, ed. John Deigh (Chicago: University of Chicago Press, 1992), 117–31, at 121–22.

22 Commentators on Freud tend to use the term 'topographical' to distinguish Freud's earlier model of unconscious, preconscious, and conscious minds from his later, "structural" model of id, ego, and superego. In their terminology, the location of fear with respect to ego and superego would be a matter of structure, not topography. But Freud himself used the term 'topographical' for the latter model as well as the former. See, for example, "Psycho-Analysis," *S.E.* 20:261–70, at 266.

parts.[23] Consider a child who is continually teased as ugly or stupid and who internalizes that teasing. We can expect that he will be unduly afraid of attracting attention, and that when he does attract it he will feel un-warranted embarrassment. That is, we can expect him to re-experience, in the face of his internal tormentors, the same emotions that he experienced in the face of their external models. To be sure, internal-ization will have altered the relevant interactions in some respects. For example, internal ridicule will greet his mere thought of saying some-thing in public, before he ever opens his mouth.[24] Although he never raises his hand in class, his teachers will be able to tell when he knows the answer, because he has blushed. But internalization won't alter the emotions themselves: internal teasing will arouse embarrassment just like real teasing.

Similarly, if a real threat inspires ordinary fear, then so should an intra-psychic threat. Why, then, does the ego's fear of the superego amount to the subject's feeling guilty rather than merely afraid?

This problem reflects back on the superego's authority, which was supposed to consist in the power to issue credible threats. Corresponding to the fact that this power might arouse only brute fear rather than guilt is the fact that it might constitute only brute muscle rather than authority. The power to threaten is the power of a bully.

Another way to pose this problem is to ask how the aggression of the parents or the superego comes to be conceived as punishment rather than some other form of coercion. Part of the answer ought to be that the parents' aggression is conceived as punishment because it is seen to be backed by authority. Yet what has been posited in back of this aggression, thus far, is merely the power to threaten it, which doesn't adequately differentiate it from any other form of aggression. The ques-tion therefore remains why the parents, and their internal surrogate, come to be conceived as authorities administering punishment rather than arm-twisting bullies.

---

[23] Here I am disagreeing with John Deigh, who argues that the occurrence of anxiety in the ego may well amount to the occurrence of some other emotion, such as guilt, in the person ("Remarks on Some Difficulties in Freud's Theory of Moral Development," 90ff.). In principle, Deigh is right to reject "the assumption . . . that for the purpose of ascribing emotions to someone that person and his ego are identical" (91). But I see no reason why the difference between a person and his ego should make the difference between guilt and anxiety.

[24] This point corresponds, of course, to Freud's point about the superego's punishing wishes as well as deeds (*Civilization and Its Discontents*, S.E. 21:125, 127 [72, 74]).

I doubt whether Freud thought that the authority of parents or the superego could be reduced to their power to issue credible threats. For that very reason, however, I doubt whether he thought that the superego inspired guilt simply by inspiring fear. I rather think that he sought to explain guilt as a particular species of fear, differentiated from other species by its intentional object.

Freud's Explanation of Guilt: Second Reading

The idea behind this explanation is that fear of being punished by an authority is a different emotion from fear of being coerced by a bully, because it has a different conceptual content. By "fear of the superego" Freud means, not fear of a figure that happens to be the superego, but fear of the superego so conceived – conceived, that is, as playing the superego's role, of an authority administering punishment. This "topographical variety of anxiety " differs from other varieties by being about a particular part of the psychic topography, functionally specified – namely, the part with the authority to punish.[25] Anxiety about this authority has moral content and therefore qualifies as intrinsically moral anxiety, which is equivalent to guilt.

This interpretation diminishes the explanatory importance of the subject's introjecting the object of his fear. Guilt does not arise, on this interpretation, whenever fear is redirected from outer to inner aggressors. Rather, guilt arises when the object of fear is conceived as a punishing authority. Hence the introjection of the parents to form the superego is not the crucial step in the development of guilt. The superego can inspire guilt only because it is formed out of figures already conceived as authorities administering punishment; and external authorities so conceived would already be capable of inspiring moral anxiety, and hence of inspiring guilt.[26]

[25] Freud himself says that his "topographical" method is in fact a way of expressing the interrelations of "*agencies* or *systems*" (*An Autobiographical Study, S.E.* 20:3–74, at 32 [34–35]). See also note 22.

[26] Note that Freud vacillates on precisely this point in *Civilization and Its Discontents*. In part 7 (*S.E.* 21:125 [71]) he suggests that the child's fear of external authority should not be described as a sense of guilt, because the phrase properly applies only to fear felt in the face of internal authority, or conscience. But in part 8 (*S.E.* 21:136 [83]), he says that the sense of guilt "is in existence before the super-ego, and therefore before conscience, too. At that time it is the immediate expression of fear of the external authority." Deigh resolves this inconsistency in the opposite direction. I discuss it further in note 35.

The crucial step in the development of guilt, according to this interpretation, is the recognition of aggressors as authorities, and of their
aggression as punishment. So interpreted, however, Freud appears to
have largely postponed his question rather than answered it.

The question was how some self-reproaches are recognized to have that
authority which inspires guilt. The answer initially attributed to Freud was
that they are recognized to have this authority when they are perceived
to be backed by a credible threat. That answer was inadequate because it
could explain only the production of generic anxiety rather than guilt,
which is specifically moral anxiety. The initial answer has therefore been
superseded by the claim that self-reproaches inspire moral anxiety when
they are recognized as the reproaches of an authority administering punishment; which is just to say that they are recognized to have the requisite
authority when they are seen to issue from a figure of authority; which is
not to say very much.

But it is to say more than nothing. The answer now attributed to Freud
gives some characterization of the authority that a self-reproach must be
seen to have if it is to occasion guilt: the requisite kind of authority is
the authority to punish. Even if Freud's answer to our question ended
here, it would not be entirely trivial. In fact, however, I think that Freud's
answer continues, with an explanation of how the authority to punish is
recognized. I therefore turn to this further explanation.

The Source of Moral Authority

In many passages, Freud describes the sense of guilt as something more
complex than fear of the superego. He describes it as "the expression
of the tension between the ego and the super-ego,"[27] making clear that
this tension reproduces a multiply ambivalent relation between child and
parent.

As we have seen, the child fears his parents in their capacity as disci-
plinarians, and he introjects them to form an agency of self-discipline.
But the child also loves and admires his parents, and he similarly gives
himself an inner object of love and admiration, the ego ideal. Although
Freud undergoes various changes of mind on this subject,[28] he generally

---

[27] *New Introductory Lectures*, *S.E.* 22:61 [76]. See also "The Economic Problem of
Masochism," *S.E.* 19:166–67; *The Ego and the Id*, *S.E.* 19:37, 51 [33, 51]; *Civilization and
Its Discontents*, *S.E.* 21:136 [83].

[28] As I shall explain later, Freud first hypothesized that the ego gave itself an ideal to receive
the narcissistic love that it could no longer invest in itself, in light of parental criticism; but

describes the feared disciplinarian and the admired ideal as coordinate functions of a single internal figure.²⁹ The disciplinarian criticizes and threatens to punish the ego for not living up to the example set by the ideal. The introjected parent, in which these functions are combined, is therefore the internal object of mixed feelings, which combine fear and admiration.³⁰

he later traced the ego ideal to the parents, on the hypothesis that the superego contained precipitates of them not only as objects of fear but also as objects of admiration. The vagaries of Freud's views on this subject are summarized in Joseph Sandler, Alex Holder, and Dale Meers, "The Ego Ideal and the Ideal Self," *The Psychoanalytic Study of the Child* 18 (1963): 139–58. See also Joseph Sandler, "On the Concept of the Superego," *The Psychoanalytic Study of the Child* 15 (1960): 128–62.

²⁹ An alternative interpretation holds that these two functions are independent: the disciplinary function enforces norms of conduct and inflicts feelings of guilt, drawing on the instinct of aggression; the ideal function holds out norms of personal excellence and inflicts feelings of inferiority, drawing on the erotic instincts. (See Deigh, "Freud, Naturalism, and Modern Moral Philosophy," in *The Sources of Moral Agency*, 111–32, at 126–28. See also Wollheim, *The Thread of Life*, 218–25; and Jeanne Lampl-de Groot, "Ego Ideal and Superego," *The Psychoanalytic Study of the Child* 17 [1962]: 94–106.) At best, I think, this interpretation reconstructs a view toward which Freud might have been gravitating in his later works: it is certainly not a view at which he ever arrived. There is no question but that the superego first entered Freud's thought as the critical faculty that compares the ego with its ideal (in "On Narcissism"). Here disciplinarian and ideal work together, the former taking the ego to task for violating the norms embodied in the latter. This alliance continues in subsequent works, such as *The Ego and the Id*, where the terms 'super-ego' and 'ego ideal' are used interchangeably. The alternative interpretation relies on the *New Introductory Lectures*, where Freud distinguishes a sense of inferiority from a sense of guilt, saying that "[i]t would perhaps be right to regard the former as the erotic complement to the moral sense of inferiority" (*S.E.* 22:66 [82]). Note that even here, Freud fails to draw a sharp distinction between inferiority and guilt, since he refers to the latter as "the moral sense of inferiority," to be distinguished from an erotic sense of inferiority that is found in the "inferiority complex" of neurotics. (See also *The Ego and the Id, S.E.* 19:51 [51–52].) Hence no general distinction between inferiority and guilt is intended. Nor is there any textual evidence, to my knowledge, for a division of labor between ego ideal and superego in producing these feelings. Freud goes on in the same passage, for example, to say that the superego "punishes [the ego] with tense feelings of inferiority and of guilt" (*S.E.* 22:78 [97]). (I discuss this statement in note 18 and in the text, later. See also *Group Psychology, S.E.* 18:131 [81].) The notion of an alliance between the disciplinary and ideal functions of the superego is supported not only by the weight of textual evidence but also by the philosophical considerations that I shall adduce. The alliance helps Freud to account for the moral content that differentiates guilt from other forms of anxiety.

³⁰ See, for example, *The Ego and the Id, S.E.* 19:36 [32]: "When we were little children we knew these higher natures, we admired them and feared them; and later we took them into ourselves." In *Totem and Taboo*, Freud asserts that conscience "arose, on a basis of emotional ambivalence, from quite specific human relations to which this ambivalence was attached" (*S.E.* 13:68). Freud's account of conscience in this work is rather different from the theory that he subsequently developed, beginning with the paper

The ego ideal provides the normative background against which the superego can be conceived as having authority. The superego's aggression is seen as premised on a normative judgment, to the effect that the ego has fallen short of the ideal. This judgment is what justifies the superego's aggression, insofar as it is justified. The question of moral authority thus comes down to the question why the ego recognizes this normative judgment as justifying aggression against itself.

Part of the answer is that the norm applied in this judgment is the ego's own ideal, "by which the ego measures itself, which it emulates, and whose demand for ever greater perfection it strives to fulfil."[31] The ego thinks that it is being criticized and punished for a failure to meet its own standards, the standards that it accepted as applicable to itself when it adopted an ideal.

Yet the ego's having accepted these standards as applicable to itself doesn't necessarily entail having acknowledged a particular figure as authorized to enforce them. Where does the superego get the authority to demand that the ego fulfil its own standards, and to punish it when it fails?

"On Narcissism," which appeared in the following year. Nevertheless, *Totem and Taboo* contains several references to the form of ambivalence that I am currently discussing – namely, the combination of admiration and fear. See, for example, p. 50 ("distrust of the father is intimately linked with admiration for him") and p. 130 (Little Hans "admired his father as possessing a big penis and feared him as threatening his own"). This particular combination of emotions is only one of many cited in this work as accounting for taboo, "the earliest form in which the phenomenon of conscience is met with" (*S.E.* 13:67). In a later work, however, it is singled out as carrying the entire explanation. Here (*Group Psychology*, S.E. 18: 135 [86–87]) Freud says that the father of the primal horde was "at once feared and honoured, a fact which led later to the idea of taboo." My interpretation of Freud preserves the connection between conscience and taboo, as objects of admiration and fear combined.

[31] *New Introductory Lectures*, *S.E.* 22:64–65 [81]. The idea that the ego's admiration for the ideal constitutes its acceptance of norms is supported by the following passage, with which the concept of the ideal is first introduced: "We have learnt that libidinal instinctual impulses undergo the vicissitude of pathogenic repression if they come into conflict with the subject's cultural and ethical ideas. By this we never mean that the individual in question has a merely intellectual knowledge of the existence of such ideas; we always mean that he recognizes them as a standard for himself and submits to the claims they make on him. Repression, we have said, proceeds from the ego; we might say with greater precision that it proceeds from the self-respect of the ego" ("On Narcissism," *S.E.* 14:93). Freud then introduces the ego ideal as the vehicle of the ego's self-respect. He thereby suggests that the ego ideal represents the subject's acceptance of ethical norms "as a standard for himself." See also this passage from the *Outline*, S.E. 23:206: "[I]f the ego has successfully resisted a temptation to do something which would be objectionable to the super-ego, it feels raised in its self-esteem and strengthened in its pride, as though it had made some precious acquisition."

The authority for the demand comes, I think, from the superego's being an aspect of one and the same figure as the ideal. This figure, in its capacity as ego ideal, sets an example for the ego; in its capacity as superego, it demands that the ego live up to the example. The demands that it makes in the latter capacity merely articulate the requirements that it mutely establishes in the former. The superego's authority to make demands on the ego was thus granted by the ego itself, as part and parcel of the ideal's authority to set requirements. The one authority is just the verbal correlative of the other.[32]

But what about the authority to punish? What gives the superego the authority to make the ego suffer for falling short of its own ideal?

At one point Freud describes the superego as punishing the ego with "feelings of inferiority."[33] This lash was placed in the superego's hands by the ego as well. Insofar as the ego can be punished with feelings of inferiority, it exposed itself to this punishment by idealizing the figure to which it can now be made to feel inferior.

Unfortunately, this subtle, psychological form of suffering is not one with which the ego can feel threatened when criticized by the superego. For as soon as the ego has been criticized, it already experiences this suffering and is no longer in a position to fear it. And if there is nothing further for the ego to fear, beyond the sense of inferiority that it already feels under the superego's criticism, then it will not feel any anxiety, without which there can be no sense of guilt. In order for the superego's reproaches to inspire moral anxiety in the ego, they must threaten something other than the feelings of inferiority that they have already inflicted.

But the child will have been punished by his actual parents, and unless he has been abused, their punishment will have inflicted more insult than injury. He will therefore have come to associate parental criticism with punishment, as if punishment were another form of criticism, expressed in actions rather than words. When the child's ego hears criticism from the introjected parent, it will expect punishment to follow, but it is unlikely to distinguish between them with respect to their legitimacy. It will regard the anticipated punishment as the practical aspect of criticism, which it has authorized the superego to make, as the voice of the ego ideal.

These psychic materials strike me as sufficient to constitute a rudimentary conception of the superego's authority to punish. It is not, in

---

[32] Also relevant here is Freud's suggestion that idealizing a person entails deferring to his judgment. See the passage from "Three Essays" quoted in note 42.

[33] *New Introductory Lectures,* S.E. 22:78 [97], discussed in notes 18 and 29.

my view, an adequate conception of such authority, but it comes as close as Freudian theory can come, pending revision. I shall therefore return to this topic briefly at the end of the essay, after I have proposed a philosophical revision to the theory.

The Importance of Idealization

If this reading of Freud is correct, then his explanation for the sense of guilt depends crucially on admiration as well as fear of the parents or their internal representative. The ego's idealization of these figures is what cloaks their aggression in the authority that inspires moral anxiety rather than brute fear. Because the ego has set these figures on a pedestal, it now fears their aggression *from above* – as aggression before which it bows as well as cowers – and this concessive form of anxiety constitutes the emotion of guilt.

Under this interpretation, however, a child internalizes his parents' discipline in two distinct senses.[34] On the one hand, he introjects his parents to form an inner agency of criticism and aggression. On the other hand, his admiration for these figures, both real and introjected, entails that his ego accepts and applies to itself the values that they express. So the child not only *takes in* the demanding figures of his parents but also *buys in* to their demands.[35]

---

[34] On the different modes of internalization, see Roy Schafer, *Aspects of Internalization* (New York: International Universities Press, 1968); and Drew Westen, "The Superego: A Revised Developmental Model," *Journal of the American Academy of Psychoanalysis* 14 (1986): 181–202, pp. 190ff.

[35] At times, Freud seems to assume that the former internalization necessarily entails the latter, perhaps because a figure that is introjected, or taken in, becomes "a differentiating grade in the ego," whose demands upon the subject also qualify as *his* demands upon himself. But when a subject issues himself demands in the guise of an internalized other, he still *receives* those demands *in propria persona*, as represented by the undifferentiated remainder of his ego. And in this capacity as recipient, he – or, rather, his ego – may or may not accept the demands as applicable to him. He may instead take a dismissive or defiant attitude toward them, despite their issuing from a part of himself. His accepting them as applicable to him is what would constitute the second internalization – the "buying in," as I have called it. I believe that Freud is confused, or at least undecided, about the relation between *taking in* a demanding figure and *buying in* to his demands. As I have said, Freud sometimes seems to think that the former entails and hence explains the latter; but he also provides the latter with an independent explanation – as if the former doesn't explain it, after all. The independent explanation is that a child buys in to the demands represented by his parents insofar as he loves and admires them. I have made this explanation central to the view that I attribute to Freud because I believe that it is indeed necessary to account for the sense of guilt. But I acknowledge that Freud himself seems uncertain as to its necessity. [Note continues on p. 143.]

Both operations are necessary to produce a sense of moral authority, and hence a sense of guilt. An introjected parent might not carry the authority needed for inspiring guilt rather than brute fear if it were not an object of admiration, expressing standards that the ego applies to itself. The voice of conscience is partly in the ear of the beholder, so to speak: it's the voice of an inner critic as heard by an admiring ego. And what lends this voice the authority that's distinctive of morality is precisely the admiration with which it is heard.

Freud's theory of moral authority thus requires an account of idealization, the process by which people, real and introjected, come to be admired as ideals. Freud offers two distinct accounts, both of which attribute idealization to the effects of love.

Before I discuss the relation between idealization and love in detail, I should say that I am favorably inclined toward the theory that I have attributed to Freud thus far – up to the relation between idealization and love, but not including the details of that relation. Experience and introspection lead me to believe that we do indeed give ourselves moral direction and criticism in identification with other people whom we have loved, idealized, and imaginatively incorporated into ourselves. Like Scheffler and Deigh, I think that these leading elements of Freud's theory help us to understand the motivational force of moral authority; I would add that they also help us to understand the morally formative role of love.

But Freud's overall outline of this role is separable from his specific conception of love, and of how it leads to idealization. I shall argue that Freud's conception of love actually undermines his attempt to cast it as a morally formative emotion.

Freud on Idealization

Freud initially describes the ego's establishment of an ideal as independent of – and, presumably, prior to – idealization of the parents. He says

---

I suggest that this uncertainty is what led Freud to vacillate on the question whether a child can experience guilt before having introjected his parents. (See note 26.) *Taking in* one's parents is not, in fact, necessary for guilt, since one can feel guilty in the face of one's actual parents, acknowledged as external authorities. But *buying in* to the demands of one's parents, or of other authority figures, is indeed necessary if fear of their punishment is to be transformed into moral anxiety, or guilt. Because Freud couldn't decide whether *taking in* parental authority entailed *buying in* to it, he vacillated on whether guilt without introjection was possible.

Note, by the way, that Freud claimed introjection to be necessary for the opposite of guilt as well – that is, for the feeling of pride in one's self-restraint (*Moses and Monotheism*, S.E. 23: 3–137, at 117). I suspect that the same confusion is at work in this passage as well.

that the ego ideal is conjured up by the maturing subject as a means of recapturing the narcissism of infancy:

> As always where the libido is concerned, man has here again shown himself incapable of giving up a satisfaction he had once enjoyed. He is not willing to forgo the narcissistic perfection of his childhood; and when, as he grows up, he is disturbed by the admonitions of others and by the awakening of his own critical judgement, so that he can no longer retain that perfection, he seeks to recover it in the new form of an ego ideal. What he projects before him as his ideal is the substitute for the lost narcissism of his childhood in which he was his own ideal.[36]

Here Freud may seem to have presupposed much of what he is trying to explain. He's trying to explain how the ego establishes standards of perfection for itself, in the form of an ego ideal. But his first step is to assume that the infantile ego already regards itself as perfect, and hence that it already possesses rudimentary standards of self-evaluation, however self-serving. At most, then, his story would seem to trace the evolution of these standards, not their inception.

Clearly, however, Freud thinks that he is also explaining the inception of self-evaluation, by explaining where the very idea of perfection comes from. He thinks that it comes from the experience of primary narcissism, which is a primordial pooling of libido within the ego.[37] During this period of development, the subject's ego, bathed in the positive energy of libido, is presented to him as a first instance of perfection – his first ideal, after which all subsequent ideals are fashioned.

Unfortunately, the details of this explanation reveal it to be fallacious. As we have seen, the subject is said to project the ego ideal because he is "incapable of giving up a satisfaction he had once enjoyed" or of "forgo[ing] the narcissistic perfection of his childhood."[38] He conjures up a new ideal "with the intention of re-establishing the self-satisfaction which was attached to primary infantile narcissism but which since then has suffered so many disturbances and mortifications."[39] The problem is that these passages describe the idealizing effects of the narcissistic libido in equivocal terms.

Since libido is an instinct, according to Freudian theory, it operates by means of an inner irritant that the subject is motivated to allay with

---

[36] "On Narcissism," *S.E.* 14:94.

[37] "Three Essays," *S.E.* 7:218; "On Narcissism," *S.E.* 14:75–76; *Introductory Lectures, S.E.* 15–16, at 16:416 [517–18].

[38] "On Narcissism," quoted at note 36.

[39] *Introductory Lectures, S.E.* 16:429 [533]. Freud also describes the narcissism of children as "self-contentment" ("On Narcissism," *S.E.* 14:89).

the help of an object, from which he thereby attains a temporary satisfaction.[40] The subject of primary narcissism can be described as self-satisfied, then, because he finds relief from instinctual tension within himself, without the need for an external object. And libido theory would indeed predict his unwillingness to give up such an immediate fulfillment of his needs – which might be described either as "a satisfaction he had once enjoyed" or as "the narcissistic perfection of his childhood."

But Freud then takes these phrases to denote a flattering self-image, such as would initially make the child "his own ideal" and would subsequently be undermined by "critical judgment." Freud thereby implies that the child initially satisfies himself, not only in the sense of fulfilling his own needs, but also in the sense of meeting with his own approval. The young narcissist is portrayed, not just as perfectly satisfied, but as satisfied *that* he's perfect. He isn't just inwardly sated; he's smug.

The term 'satisfaction' has now been used in two different senses. In libido theory proper, the term denotes the experienced fulfillment of instinctual need; when the theory is applied to primary narcissism, however, the term denotes a favorable value judgment.[41] By eliding the gap between these senses, Freud gives libido theory the semblance of explaining why a child would begin life with a favorable self-assessment, whose loss to external criticism would then oblige him to project an ego ideal. In fact, libido theory has no resources to explain why the child would initially approve of himself, much less why he would want to continue approving of himself or receiving his own approval.[42]

---

[40] "Instincts and their Vicissitudes," *S.E.* 14:111–140, at 118–23.

[41] For a particularly clear instance of this equivocation, see *Group Psychology*, 18:110 [52–53]: "We have said that [the ego ideal] is the heir to the original narcissism in which the childish ego enjoyed self-sufficiency [sich selbst genügte]; it gradually gathers up from the influences of the environment the demands which that environment makes upon the ego and which the ego cannot always rise to; so that a man, when he cannot be satisfied with his ego itself [mit seinem Ich selbst nicht zufrieden sein kann], may nevertheless be able to find satisfaction [Befriedigung] in the ego ideal which has been differentiated out of the ego."

[42] Freud sometimes attempts to provide an explanatory connection between libido and value judgment, but without success. In one passage, he explains that libidinal objects are idealized so that they can replace "some unattained ego ideal... as a means of satisfying our narcissism" (*Group Psychology*, S.E. 18:112–13 [56]). Of course, this explanation implicitly assumes the idealizing effect of libido in the case of narcissism, which is just another instance of what needs to be explained. Freud's other attempts at explanation are no more successful. For example: "It is only in the rarest instances that the psychical valuation that is set on the sexual object, as being the goal of the sexual instinct, stops short at its genitals. The appreciation extends to the whole body of the sexual object and tends to involve every sensation derived from it. The same over-valuation spreads

Freud's early account of the ego ideal therefore lacks the very element that's needed to complete his explanation of moral authority. What's needed is an explanation of how the ego comes to elevate someone or something to the status of an ideal, which can become the object of moral anxiety. In his first attempt at this explanation, however, Freud offers only an equivocation instead.

Freud later attributes the ego ideal to introjection of the parents as objects of admiration.[43] The ego ideal is now thought to preserve the idealized parents rather than replace the idealized self. As before, however, the question is how the prior idealization comes about – in this case, the idealization of the parents.

The answer in this case is that the parents are idealized through the mechanism of primary identification:

A little boy will exhibit a special interest in his father; he would like to grow like him and be like him, and take his place everywhere. We may say simply that he takes his father as his ideal.[44]

This primary identification antedates the boy's introjection of his father into his superego; indeed, it antedates the Oedipus complex, which will be resolved by that later, more consequential identification.[45]

over into the psychological sphere: the subject becomes, as it were, intellectually infatuated (that is, his powers of judgement are weakened) by the mental achievements and perfections of the sexual object and he submits to the latter's judgements with credulity. Thus, the credulity of love becomes an important, if not the most fundamental, source of *authority*" ("Three Essays," *S.E.* 7:150). At the beginning of this passage, Freud equates taking an object as "the goal of the sexual instinct" with setting a "valuation" on it, or having an "appreciation" for it. But the goal of the sexual instinct, according to libido theory, is either relief from sexual tension or an object sought as a source of that relief. And how does an object's being sought for sexual purposes amount to its being valued or appreciated? Freud then says that the subject expands his valuation of the object because of being "infatuated," in the sense that "his powers of judgement are weakened." This explanation would make no sense if the latter phrase meant that the subject loses his capacity to make evaluative judgments: the phrase must mean that the subject becomes less demanding or critical in his evaluations. The explanation therefore presupposes the existence of an evaluative faculty whose standards can be corrupted by the libido. And this evaluative faculty must then be the "fundamental source of authority," since it provides the capacity of judging another person to have "achievements" and "perfections" that justify deferring to him. The libido appears to be responsible only for the misapplication of these judgments – and hence the misattribution of authority – to undeserving objects.

43 For example, *New Introductory Lectures*, *S.E.* 22:65 [81]: "There is no doubt that this ego ideal is the precipitate of the old picture of the parents, the expression of admiration for the perfection which the child then attributed to them." See also note 28.

44 *Group Psychology*, *S.E.* 18:105 [46].

45 *The Ego and the Id*, *S.E.* 19:31ff. [26ff.]; *Group Psychology*, chapter 7; *New Introductory Lectures*, *S.E.* 22:64 [80].

In primary identification, the child idealizes his parents in the sense that he wants to be like them, and he wants to be like his parents because he wants to ingest them. The child is in his oral phase, when "sexual activity has not yet been separated from the ingestion of food" and so "the sexual *aim* consists in the incorporation of the object."[46] The child's love therefore takes the form of a desire for "the oral, cannibalistic incorporation of the other person."[47] And because of an imaginative association between incorporating and embodying, as it were, the desire to incorporate the other turns into a desire to *be* the other, or at least to resemble him.[48]

Now, idealizing someone does entail wanting to be like him, or even wishing that one were he; and this entailment lends some plausibility to Freud's account of identification. Strictly speaking, however, the account requires an entailment in the other direction, since it seeks to explain idealization of the father in terms of the desire to resemble or be him. This explanation will work only if wanting to resemble or be another person is sufficient for idealizing him.

We can imagine why this latter entailment might be thought to hold. Assume, for the sake of argument, that whatever is desired, is desired *sub specie boni*, as good.[49] This assumption implies that if a child wants to be like his father, then he regards being like him as good. And placing value on resembling someone comes very close to idealizing him.

But not close enough. In order to idealize a person, one must not just regard being like him as *a valuable way to be*; one must regard it as *a way of being valuable*. The idealizing thought is not just "It would be better if I resembled him" but "*I* would be better if I resembled him." Insofar as one places value on the state of resembling the other person, one must do so because of value placed on that person, or on the person one would be in that state.

Suppose that resembling another person appeals to you merely as fun. In that case, you value the resemblance without necessarily valuing who it would make you; and so a lack of resemblance would make you feel

[46] *Three Essays*, S.E. 7:198.

[47] *New Introductory Lectures*, S.E. 22:63 [79].

[48] If we say that the child's desire to be like his parents is, at bottom, a desire to incorporate them, then shouldn't we say that his desire to be like his ego ideal is, at bottom, a desire to incorporate *it*? Hasn't he already incorporated it? The answer, I suppose, is that in establishing his ego ideal, the child has incorporated his parents only incompletely, so that the incorporative desire persists. See the discussion in *Group Psychology*, chapter 11, of the ego's ongoing desire to "coincide" with the ego ideal.

[49] I believe that this assumption is false. See my paper, "The Guise of the Good," *Noûs* 26 (1992): 3–26.

frustrated without making you feel diminished – disappointed with the outcome but not disappointed in yourself.

The same goes for the boy who wants to embody his father. The boy has this desire only because he doesn't yet distinguish between loving a person and hungering for a meal. Loving his father, he hungers for him.[50] The resulting desire to incorporate his father should hardly lead him to like or dislike himself according to whether he succeeds. The desire to fill his belly isn't an aspiration to be a full-bellied person. Similarly, the desire to incorporate father, if formed on the model of hunger, wouldn't constitute an aspiration to be father-ful.[51]

More significantly, wanting to incorporate one's father would not entail conceding his authority to punish one's failure to incorporate him. Idealization brings a sense of exposure to punishment only because it places a value on the ideal, as worthy of governing one's life. As I put it before: when someone has been placed on a pedestal, his aggression can be feared as coming from above, as aggression before which to bow as well as cower. But he cannot inspire such moral anxiety by virtue of being placed on a serving dish instead. His aggression, in that case, is more likely to be perceived as a defense against being consumed than as punishment for one's failure to consume him.

Materials for an Alternative Account

I have now argued that Freud encounters two dead-ends in attempting to explain the authority of the superego. He attributes this authority to the love that was felt in infancy for one or another precursor of the superego – either narcissistic love for the self or identificatory love for a parent. In neither case can Freud explain how love endows its object with the sort of authority that, when inherited by the superego, would make it an object of moral anxiety.

I think that Freud makes various gestures toward a third and more successful account of idealization. These gestures point to a capacity in the ego to conduct evaluative reasoning about ideals that it has adopted or

---

[50] Freud contrasts object love with identification by saying that the former is a desire *to have* while the latter is a desire *to be* (*Group Psychology*, S.E. 18:106 [47]). But the desire to be, when traced to its origins in the oral phase, turns out to consist in a desire to incorporate. A more accurate contrast would be that between a desire *to have* and a desire *to have for dinner.* For an interesting discussion of this contrast, see Mikkel Borch-Jacobsen, *The Freudian Subject*, trans. Catherine Porter (Stanford: Stanford University Press, 1988), 28ff.
[51] Similar points are made by Schafer, *Aspects of Internalization*, 18–22.

might adopt. Freud never follows up these gestures: the rational capacities of the ego seem not to engage his interest. Pursuing this third account of idealization therefore entails a fair amount of extrapolation from the Freudian texts.

I want to attempt this extrapolation because I believe that it reveals, first, why the superego as Freud conceived it cannot play the role of moral authority; but, second, how Freud's conception of the superego can be revised so as to play that role. We can locate moral authority in figures who were loved and consequently internalized, I shall argue, provided that we expand on Freud's understanding of what gets internalized from the objects of love.

The third, implicit account of idealization is that it is the work of an independent faculty of normative judgment, located in the ego. This faculty is hinted at in both stories that Freud tells about the development of the ego ideal.

In Freud's first story, the ego ideal is created to receive the approval that the ego can no longer bestow on itself. The ideal is therefore fashioned out of those virtues which the ego has found itself to lack. It "gathers up from the influences of the environment the demands which that environment makes upon the ego and which the ego cannot always rise to."[52] The child's failure to meet these demands is reflected back to him in the "admonitions" that render his primary narcissism untenable.[53] And the ego now envisions its ideal as meeting those particular demands, and hence as an improvement upon its discredited self.

Yet the child must fail to meet a vast miscellany of demands, whose collective embodiment would yield a motley and rather banal ideal. The ego ideal that survives into adulthood cannot simply be the agglomeration of whichever demands the ego has not managed to satisfy in childhood. Of the demands that my father made on me as a child, the ones to which I was most notoriously unequal were to switch off the lights when I left a room, to wash my hands before coming to the table, and to lower my piercing voice. But I have never harbored an idealized image of myself as a well-manicured baritone conservationist.

Even if the raw materials of the ego ideal are derived from demands made on a child by others, he must somehow select among them, rank them, and organize them into a coherent image of a better self. He must

---

52 *Group Psychology*, S.E. 18:100 [52]. See also p. 131 [81]: "The ego ideal comprises the sum of all the limitations in which the ego has had to acquiesce."
53 "On Narcissim," S.E. 14:94 (quoted at note 36).

figure out how to extrapolate from the finite corpus of past demands to the indefinite series of novel situations that he will encounter in the future. Here is one point at which he must engage in evaluative reasoning.[54] Freud himself appears to acknowledge the child's use of such reasoning, for example, when he refers to "the awakening of his own critical judgement."[55]

This acknowledgement becomes clearer when Freud subsequently attributes the ideal to introjection of the admired parents. In telling this version of the story, Freud often points out that the child gradually transfers his admiration from his parents to other figures, who are often of his own choosing.

Freud describes this shift of allegiance as occurring in two phases. Initially, adults outside the family come to share the parental role, including that of shaping the superego:

The parental influence of course includes in its operation not only the personalities of the actual parents but also the family, racial and national traditions handed on through them, as well as the demands of the immediate social *milieu* which they represent. In the same way, the super-ego, in the course of an individual's development, receives contributions from later successors and substitutes of his parents, such as teachers and models in public life of admired social ideals.[56]

Subsequently the child becomes disillusioned with parental figures altogether and replaces them with other adults as objects of his admiration. But these replacements are not introjected:

The course of childhood development leads to an ever-increasing detachment from parents, and their personal significance for the super-ego recedes into the background. To the imagos they leave behind there are then linked the influences of teachers and authorities, self-chosen models and publicly recognized heroes,

---

54 One might argue that the parents select and organize their demands for the child, by offering general principles of conduct. This suggestion would be in keeping with a famous remark of Freud's: "[A] child's super-ego is in fact constructed on the model not of its parents but of its parents' super-ego; the contents which fill it are the same and it becomes the vehicle of tradition and of all the time-resisting judgements of value which have propagated themselves in this manner from generation to generation" (*New Introductory Lectures*, S.E. 22:67 [84]). Yet this remark suggests a mechanism for propagating principles of conduct, not a mechanism for formulating them in the first place. If the child's ancestors were, like him, passive receptacles of demands made upon them, then they would no more have organized and generalized their ideals than he.

55 "On Narcissism," quoted at note 36.

56 *Outline of Psychoanalysis*, S.E. 23:146 [16]. See also *The Ego and the Id*, S.E. 19:37 [33]; *Group Psychology*, S.E. 18:129 [78].

whose figures need no longer be introjected by an ego which has become more resistant.[57]

When these two phases are conjoined, the process looks like this:

In the course of development the super-ego also takes on the influences of those who have stepped into the place of parents – educators, teachers, people chosen as ideal models. Normally it departs more and more from the original parental figures; it becomes, so to say, more impersonal. Nor must it be forgotten that a child has a different estimate of its parents at different periods of its life. At the time at which the Oedipus complex gives place to the super-ego they are something quite magnificent; but later they lose much of this. Identifications then come about with these later parents as well, and indeed they regularly make important contributions to the formation of character; but in that case they only affect the ego, they no longer influence the super-ego, which has been determined by the earliest parental imagos.[58]

First the personal stamp of the actual parents is eroded from the superego by the imprints of other parental figures. Then the superego becomes fixed, and subsequent ideals make their impression upon the ego instead.

These descriptions indirectly credit the child with evaluative judgment in his attachment to adults other than his parents. Although the new objects of attachment usually occupy socially defined positions of authority, they do not include everyone occupying such positions. Not every caretaker, teacher, or cultural hero wins the child's admiration. In the passages just quoted, Freud twice describes the child as exercising a choice among the models available to him, and this capacity for choice would seem to require a capacity for evaluative reasoning.

Evaluative judgment plays an even clearer role in the child's detachment from his parents. Although this detachment is motivated in part by emotional conflict within the family, it is also guided by the child's growing appreciation for real differences in value:

For a small child his parents are at first the only authority and the source of all belief. The child's most intense and most momentous wish during these early years is to be like his parents (that is, the parent of his own sex) and to be big like his father and mother. But as intellectual growth increases, the child cannot help discovering by degrees the category to which his parents belong. He gets to know other parents and compares them with his own, and so acquires the right to doubt the incomparable and unique quality which he had attributed to them. Small events in the child's life which make him feel dissatisfied afford him provocation for beginning to criticize his parents, and for using, in order

---

[57] "The Economic Problem of Masochism," *S.E.* 19:168.
[58] *New Introductory Lectures, S.E.* 22:64 [80].

to support his critical attitude, the knowledge which he has acquired that other parents are in some respects preferable to them.[59]

Later the child will long for "the happy, vanished days when his father seemed to him the noblest and strongest of men and his mother the dearest and loveliest of women."[60]

Freud doesn't explain how the child acquires the knowledge that other parents are in some respects preferable to his own. If the child's standards of what is noble or lovely are in fact images of his own father and mother, then he won't discover anyone who meets those standards better than father and mother themselves. How, then, does he discover that other adults are nobler or lovelier than the figures who epitomize these qualities for him?

The answer must be that the "intellectual growth" and "critical attitude" to which Freud alludes somehow enable the child to apply evaluative concepts autonomously, even to the extent of reevaluating the instances from which he first learned them. This answer implies that the child possesses an evaluative faculty that is independent of the received values preserved in his superego.

This faculty is probably one and the same as that which Freud repeatedly cites as instrumental to the therapeutic efficacy of psychoanalysis. The benefit of revealing previously repressed impulses in psychoanalysis, Freud explains, is that they can then be submitted to "acts of judgment," by which they will be accepted or rejected rather than merely repressed.[61] In such acts of judgment "the compass of the ego [is] extended,"[62] and repression is thereby replaced by "the highest of the human mental functions."[63]

What now begins to emerge is that the superego is not a final or ultimate authority in the Freudian psyche. The superego wields authority only in the eyes of an admiring ego, and the ego possesses an independent faculty of judgment as to whom or what to admire. This evaluative

[59] "Family Romances," *S.E.* 9:236–41, at 237.
[60] Ibid., 241.
[61] *Autobiographical Study*, *S.E.* 20:30 [32]. See "Five Lectures on Psycho-Analysis," *S.E.* 11:3–55, at 28, 53; "Analysis of a Phobia in a Five-Year-Old Boy," *S.E.* 10:3–149, at 145; "Repression," *S.E.* 14:143–58, at 146; *Outline of Psycho-Analysis*, *S.E.* 23:179 [58]. See also *Introductory Lectures*, *S.E* 16:294 [364]; "A Disturbance of Memory on the Acropolis," *S.E.* 21:238–48, at 309–10.
[62] *Outline of Psycho-Analysis*, *S.E.* 23:179 [58].
[63] "Five Lectures," 11:28. See also "Analysis of a Phobia in a Five-Year-Old Boy," *S.E.* 10:145.

faculty lends authority to the superego but can also call that authority into doubt.

The Locus of Authority

The secondary position of the superego in the order of normative authority raises a question about Freud's account of morality. If Freud doesn't think that the superego holds ultimate authority for the subject, why does he make it the seat of conscience?

The answer, I suspect, is that Freud doesn't think of conscience or morality as holding ultimate authority, either. For Freud, "morality" means so-called morality – what society defines as morality – not the abstract, true morality of moral philosophers. By the same token, "conscience" means the psychic agent of so-called morality, the inner representative of a social force, rather than a faculty of moral perception or reasoning. Freud is deeply ambivalent about the social force called morality, and he consequently places its inner representative under the ultimate authority of the ego, whose evaluative capacities he would never have accused of being "moral."

To those who do not share Freud's moral skepticism, the superego's lack of ultimate normative authority is a reason for denying that it plays the role of moral authority. That role may appear to have fallen instead to the ego, which has the final say. Moral philosophers may therefore be tempted, if not to discard Freudian theory, then at least to revise it by relocating the seat of conscience.[64] But I favor an alternative approach. What Freud's account of the conscience needs, I think, is not so much revision as supplementation, at precisely that point where Freud loses interest – namely, the ego's capacity for evaluative judgment.

Freud describes the ego as the seat of "reason and good sense."[65] But how can the ego exercise reason and good sense if there are no standards of rationality to which it aspires? The rational function that Freud has assigned to the ego would seem to require that it have a more extensive ideal than he has provided.

The only ideal that Freud has provided for the ego embodies minor and essentially contestable virtues. It is modeled upon contingent features of people whose contingent relations to the subject placed them in the way of his instincts early in life. The standards set by this ideal are simply

[64] This appears to be the revision favored by Deigh (see the material at note 4).
[65] *New Introductory Lectures, S.E.* 22:76 [95].

the standards that happened to be set by the first people he happened to love. Indeed, they are standards set by the halo in which such people appeared to the child through the haze of his libido.

The Freudian superego lacks ultimate authority, then, because it reflects the child's infatuation with his parents, which is superseded in maturity by evaluative reasoning undertaken by the ego under norms of rationality. But how does a child acquire the latter norms? How does he learn to exercise reason and good sense, if not by observing and emulating the example of his parents?

To be sure, a child's love for his parents causes him to glamorize them, and the glamour is bound to fade. But the child's love is also, and fundamentally, his response to a value that the parents genuinely possess.

Out of their love for the child, the parents care for him with a wise good will, to which he responds with love. What the child experiences in being loved by his parents, and what he responds to in loving them, is their capacity to anticipate and provide for his needs, often at the expense of their own interests. And this capacity of the parents is nothing other than their practical reason, or practical good sense, by which their immediate self-gratification is subordinated to rational requirements embodied in another person. It's their capacity to take another person as an end. Hence the child's love for his parents doesn't merely project a superficial glow onto them; it registers the genuine value of their reason and good sense – what Kant would call their rational nature, or humanity – as manifested in their loving care.

Although the child may overvalue his parents as the noblest and loveliest specimens of humanity, he does not err in loving them, to begin with, as specimens of humanity, in the Kantian sense of the word. And when he later internalizes their tin nobility and paper loveliness, he must also internalize their humanity, which is pure gold – a standard not to be superseded by other ideals.

Thus, the parents' loving care of the child demonstrates their capacity to take him as an end in himself, and this capacity provides an object for his love, to begin with, and later an object for his reverence, as an ideal to be emulated. When he internalizes this ideal, in the image of his loving parents, he internalizes the Categorical Imperative, which just *is* a description of the capacity to take persons as ends.

This ideal carries genuine moral authority, which underwrites the issuance and enforcement of more specific demands. In issuing and enforcing these demands, parents do not merely spell out for the child what is required of him by the ideal of taking persons as ends; they also instantiate the ideal itself, by treating him as a responsible person who can be held to rational requirements.[66]

Insofar as the child sees parental discipline as expounding respect for persons and as expressing respect for him, his fear of that discipline will be tempered by respect or reverence for its moral authority, thus being transformed into genuinely moral anxiety. Of course, respect for parental discipline as embodying the Categorical Imperative is a sophisticated attainment, which cannot be expected of a younger child. But a younger child can still idealize his parents in other ways and hence feel an approximation of what he will feel later, when he can look to them as instances of the moral ideal.

For this reason, I do not want to reject Freud's notion that the child's fear of his parents is initially transformed into guilt by his admiration for their nobility and loveliness, or even for their physical size and strength. This admiration, too, depends on the ego's capacity for evaluation rather than to the effects of libidinal drives; but it is an immature admiration, yielding an immature sense of the parents' authority. The initial account of parental authority that I attributed to Freud, and the present account that I have imposed upon him by way of revision, should thus be taken as describing different stages of development, the one serving as an early prototype of the other.

So perhaps the superego really can be the Categorical Imperative. All that would be required for a true marriage of Freudian and Kantian moral theory is this: on Freud's side, that the ideals incorporated into the superego include an ideal of practical reason; and on Kant's side, that the Categorical Imperative – which *is* an ideal of practical reason – take the form of an ego ideal.

I have argued elsewhere that Kant's contribution to this marriage is available in his own words.[67] I have not argued here that the same can be said of Freud. What I have argued instead is that Freudian theory has a place for his contribution – a blank space, where Freud neglected to provide the ego with norms to govern its practical reasoning. I have also suggested that a self-ideal to fill this space could indeed be acquired in the manner posited by Freud, through the internalization of that which a child values in his parents by reciprocating their love.[68]

---

[66] Here I have benefited from Tamar Schapiro's paper, "What Is a Child," *Ethics* 109 (1999): 715–38.

[67] See my "Voice of Conscience," (Chapter 5 in the present volume).

[68] This suggestion depends on arguments that I give in "Love as a Moral Emotion," (Chapter 4 in the present volume).

7

Don't Worry, Feel Guilty

Introduction: The Worry

One can feel guilty without thinking that one actually is guilty of moral wrongdoing. For example, one can feel guilty about eating an ice cream or skipping aerobics, even if one doesn't take a moralistic view of self-indulgence. And one can feel guilty about things that aren't one's doing at all, as in the case of survivor's guilt about being spared some catastrophe suffered by others. Guilt without perceived wrongdoing may of course be irrational, but I think it is sometimes rational, and I want to explore how it can be.

If guilt were essentially a feeling about having done something morally wrong, then feeling guilty about self-indulgence or survival would of course be irrational. The only reason why I can conceive of guilt's being rational in these cases is that I think the emotion need not involve any judgment or perception of immorality. But I also think that the emotion of guilt must involve a judgment or perception whose content is normative in a more general sense. In particular, I believe that guilt requires a sense of *normative vulnerability*, which I would define as follows.

At the bottom of normative vulnerability is the sense of being somehow unjustified, of having nothing to say for oneself. But feeling unjustified in some respect does not by itself amount to feeling guilty, since one doesn't feel guilty, for instance, about beliefs or assertions for which one

This chapter originally appeared in Hatzimoysis, Anthony (ed.), *Philosophy and the Emotions*, Royal Institute of Philosophy Supplement 52 (New York: Cambridge University Press, 2003), 235–48. It is reprinted by permission of Cambridge University Press. Thanks to Justin D'Arms, P. J. Ivanhoe, and Nancy Sherman for comments on an earlier draft.

is aware of having no justification. Guilt arises only when the sense of inde-fens*ibility* yields a sense of being defence*less* against negative responses of some kind, variously thought to include blame, resentment, retaliation, or punishment, though their precise nature remains to be specified by a philosophical account of the emotion. One feels defenceless against these responses in the sense of having no claim or entitlement to be spared from them, because they are warranted. One thus feels defence-less in a normative sense.

The concept of normative vulnerability helps to explain why guilt is a feeling of both anxiety and diminished self-worth. The anxiety comes from feeling oneself exposed to something untoward. The sense of dimin-ished self-worth comes from conceiving of that exposure as a matter of being stripped of a claim or entitlement.

Any attempt to analyze guilt as lacking at least this much normative content is bound to fail, in my opinion. The most promising attempt of this kind, to my knowledge, is Freud's analysis of guilt, which focuses on the element of anxiety at the expense of the normative element. Accord-ing to Freud, a guilty mind is anxious about the prospect of being pun-ished by an internalized figure of authority, the super-ego. Freud notably avoids saying that this punishment is viewed in normative terms, as war-ranted. As I have argued elsewhere, however, this omission threatens to leave a gap in Freud's analysis of guilt, since anxiety that was merely about harsh treatment from a controlling figure might amount to noth-ing more than fear of a bully.[1] Unlike brute fear, guilt has a concessive or self-deprecatory quality, by virtue of which it disposes one neither to flee nor to fight but merely to hang one's head or to cringe. And the only way to read this aspect of guilt into Freud's analysis, I have argued, is to imagine that his description of being punished by an authority is, in fact, the description under which the guilty mind itself grasps the object of its anxiety – namely, as punishment administered with proper authorization. When thus reinterpreted, Freud's analysis ends up cred-iting the subject of guilt with a sense that his punishment is somehow warranted.

The resulting analysis raises a worry about the rationality of guilt even in cases of admitted wrongdoing, since it implies that such guilt is rational only if there really is some justification for punishing wrongdoers. If there is no justification for punishment, then it cannot be warranted, and so

---

[1] I argue for this claim at length in 'A Rational Superego' (Chapter 6 in the present volume).

one would be irrational to feel vulnerable on that score. The worry is that punishment is difficult to justify. The most persuasive justifications apply to punishment carried out by a legitimate state for the violation of valid laws. But guilt is felt on the basis of wrongs that are not and could not reasonably be subject to legal punishment – the breaking of intimate promises, minor injuries to people's feelings, and so on. Feeling guilty about private wrongs could perhaps involve the mistake or the phantasy that they are crimes punishable by law, but then guilt would be ripe for debunking. If guilt about wrongdoing is to be vindicated as rational, then wrongdoing must genuinely warrant that to which guilt makes one feel normatively vulnerable; and I do not see how the private wrongs of adults can make one normatively vulnerable to punishment.

Freud thinks that the authority figure envisioned in guilt is an internalization of the parent who disciplined the subject when he was a child. But if an adult conceives of himself as having done something that would have warranted parental discipline when he was a child, then he will have no grounds for anxiety in the present; and if he conceives of himself as warranting parental discipline in the present, then he is simply confused. He may of course entertain the phantasy that he is back in childhood facing an angry parent, and this phantasy may even cause him real anxiety. But this anxiety would evaporate under reflection on the facts about who he really is and where he really stands. Unless he can rationally think of punishment as warranted, a sense of normative vulnerability to it will be irrational.

Freud is not worried about this possibility, because he is not interested in vindicating human emotions as rational. He is satisfied to show that they are intelligible in light of external circumstances as viewed through phantasies, misplaced memories, and other sources of distortion. But moral philosophers are inclined to worry about the rationality of an emotion such as guilt. And I have undertaken to consider the rationality of this emotion in cases involving no moral judgment, where feelings of normative vulnerability are even less likely to make sense.

I will approach these problematic cases by way of the less problematic case of guilt felt about perceived wrongdoing. I will propose an unfavourable response other than punishment to which perceived wrongdoing can make one *feel* normatively vulnerable by causing one to *be* vulnerable in that sense, so that the feeling is at least potentially rational. I will then turn to the cases in which guilt is felt about matters other than wrongdoing. One of these cases will lead me to consider yet a third response that may be the object of anxiety in guilt. The result will be a disjunctive analysis of the emotion, as a sense of normative vulnerability to any one of several unfavourable responses.

Guilt About Wrongdoing

Freud sometimes gives a slightly different analysis of guilt, saying that it is anxiety over having alienated the internalized parent's love.[2] Freud doesn't clearly distinguish between this analysis and the one based on punishment, since he suggests that the loss of parental love is anxiety-provoking because it will lead to harsh treatment of the sort that makes for punishment. But Freud's conception of love is hopelessly consequentialist, in my opinion, and should be discarded.[3] The result of discarding it will be, at least initially, to divide his conception of guilt into two independent conceptions, one tracing the constitutive anxiety to anticipated punishment and the other tracing it to the anticipated loss of love.

The latter analysis of guilt is plausible on phenomenological grounds. Typically, the only specific danger that alarms a guilty mind is the danger of discovery, which is alarming because it would lead to whatever contingency is the ultimate object of anxiety. Beyond discovery, however, the prospect looming before a guilty mind is extremely vague: no very specific contingency is clearly in view. Discovery must therefore be expected to yield something nebulously conceived, and this expectation must provoke a fairly unfocussed anxiety. The subject of guilt fears a generalized loss of security, as if discovery would leave him standing on shaky ground. Such insecurity is precisely what a child would fear at the prospect of losing his parents' love. Having done something that might alienate them, he would vividly fear their discovering it, but only because he would then expect banishment to a no-man's-land of which he has no more than vague apprehensions.

As before, however, we have to wonder whose love the guilty-minded adult is afraid of losing, and why he should be afraid of losing it. Surely, an adult doesn't think that his mother will stop loving him, after all these years, simply because he has cheated on his taxes. If, alternatively, his feeling of guilt is a revival of anxiety that he felt about his parents when he was a child, then it is simply misplaced. And he is unlikely to think

---

[2] *Civilization and Its Discontents*, in *The Standard Edition of the Complete Psychological Works of Sigmund Freud*, James Strachey *et al.* (eds.) (London: the Hogarth Press), vol. 21, 59–145, p. 124. See also *Outline of Psychoanalysis*, S. E. 23: 205.

[3] See my "Love as a Moral Emotion" (Chapter 4 in the present volume).

that there is any love to be lost from the tax-collector – or, if there is, that there would be much harm in losing it.

Forfeiting Trust

Something that the guilty-minded adult might realistically anticipate losing, however, is trust; and the loss of trust results in the kind of nebulous vulnerability that might arouse the anxiety constitutive of guilt. Losing trust is indeed a kind of banishment to a vaguely imagined no-man's-land – a status that would strike the subject as inherently dangerous without posing particular, specifiable dangers. Losing trust, like losing love, would leave him out in the cold.

Consider the familiar strategy for dealing with iterated prisoners' dilemmas.[4] The strategy is to co-operate with others until they fail to co-operate, and then to withhold co-operation from them until they have resumed co-operating. This strategy requires a player to classify his fellow players as co-operators or non-co-operators, on the basis of their most recent behaviour, and then to co-operate or not with them, accordingly. If most of the players adopt this strategy, then any player who makes an unco-operative move can expect to lose his reputation as a co-operator – which would be, in effect, to lose the trust of his fellow players, who would then stop co-operating with him. His anxiety about having warranted this response might then constitute a feeling of guilt for his own failure to co-operate.

This kind of anxiety might account for guilt about wrongdoing if the moral choices in life were one long series of prisoners' dilemmas, to which morality was the co-operative solution. In that case, being a co-operator would consist in treating others morally, and a reputation for being a co-operator would elicit moral treatment from others in return. Conversely,

---

[4] The prisoners' dilemma gets its name from the following philosophical fiction. Two prisoners are questioned separately, under suspicion of having committed a crime together. Each is offered the following plea bargain: if he gives testimony against the other, his sentence (whatever it otherwise would have been) will be reduced by one year; if he is convicted on the other's testimony, his sentence will be increased by two years. Each person will benefit from giving testimony against the other, no matter what the other does; but if both avail themselves of this benefit, each will be harmed by the other's testimony, and the harm will be greater than the benefit of testifying.

The discussion in the text refers to 'iterated' prisoners' dilemmas – that is, a series of decision problems of the same form, as would confront a pair of hapless recidivists who were repeatedly caught and offered the same bargain. This series of decision problems is often described as a game, in which the prisoners are "players" who make successive "moves." In the context of this discussion, 'co-operating' is defined in relation to the other prisoner, rather than the authorities – that is, as withholding one's testimony.

wrongdoing would jeopardize one's reputation for co-operating and justify others in retaliating with similar wrongs. Anxiety about thus having forfeited their trust would correspond to the feeling of guilt for
wrongdoing.

This account of guilt has its points, but it needs some adjustment. It
characterizes guilt as a feeling of normative vulnerability to retaliatory
wrongdoing, and so it vindicates this feeling as rational only if such vulnerability is real, because retaliatory wrongdoing is indeed warranted.
But retaliatory wrongdoing isn't warranted: morality is not a co-operative
scheme from which wrongdoers can justly be excluded. So if guilt is anxiety about having forfeited trust, the trust at stake cannot be represented
by inclusion in the moral scheme.

Forms of Trust
The trust that is forfeited by wrongdoing is expressed, not in moral treatment, which is owed to the trustworthy and untrustworthy alike, but in
morally optional transactions that depend on mutual assumptions of
good will. One is obligated not to lie even to a liar; what one doesn't
owe to a liar is credence.

Attitudinal trust. In verbal communication, one person utters a sentence with the intention of thereby giving others reason to believe it, via
their recognition of that very intention. This communicative intention
necessarily depends on being recognized as a good intention. Its being
recognized by the hearers as the intention to give them reason to believe
wouldn't actually give them reason to believe unless they assumed that it
was based on the speaker's own awareness of such a reason. If communication wasn't assumed by the hearers to be well-intended in this sense, it
wouldn't succeed; and so if the speaker didn't assume that it would meet
with that assumption, he wouldn't be in a position to intend it, in the
first place. These mutual assumptions of communicative good will are
the rational infrastructure of conversation.

Now consider why someone's telling a lie warrants others in refusing
to trust him on future occasions. One possibility would be that the lie
betrays his lack of some truth-telling disposition without which others
have no grounds for trusting his word. In that case, his consciousness
of having told a lie would make him feel that he had warranted others
in withdrawing their trust specifically from his word, and the resulting
anxiety would have a specific content that might earn it the name of liar's
guilt. But guilt about wrongdoing is not divisible into specific modes
for specific wrongs – liar's guilt, thief's guilt, and so on. If it were, then

there would be modes of guilt only for common, repeatable wrongs that betrayed the lack of dispositions essential to warranting trust for various common purposes.

In reality, however, moral guilt is a unitary emotion, whose quality and content remain constant across many different occasions. Whatever serves as the object of anxiety in moral guilt should therefore be the same across different occasions for the emotion. If the object of anxiety is a loss of trust, then the trust at stake must be such as any guilty-minded subject can think of himself as having forfeited, by means of any wrongdoing. So what's at stake for the morally guilty mind must be the prospect of being regarded as well- or ill-intentioned *tout court* – of being simply included or simply excluded from the company of those who are recognized as persons of good will. Wrongdoing must be regarded as warranting a loss of trust, not because of any specific disposition that it might betray, but because it simply betrays a failure to consider the wrongness of the act or to be deterred by that consideration. And what such a failure warrants from others is a refusal to engage in any dealings that require a reliance on the wrongdoer's moral sensibility or motivation. The vague insecurity with which the guilty mind feels threatened must then be a general exclusion from optional dealings that depend on an assumption of good will.

This conception of guilt would explain why guilt tends to motivate acts of contrition and apology. Such acts are explicit expressions of the emotion, whose tendency to motivate them is therefore a tendency to motivate its own expression. The explanation of this tendency is that guilt seeks expression as a means of restoring generic trust. If the wrongdoer wants to regain acceptance as a person of good will, he must somehow demonstrate that the moral quality of his acts is indeed a motivationally effective consideration for him. Expressing a sense of guilt demonstrates that he is even now considering the moral quality of an act as justifying a loss of trust, and that he is hereby motivated by that consideration – too late on this occasion, of course, but in time to repair his ways for the future.

To accept the wrongdoer's apology, according to this conception, is to restore him to his previous position of trust, in effect readmitting him to the company of the well-intentioned. To forgive is not literally to forget, but it is to forget for practical purposes, to erase the practical consequences of the act's being remembered.

Practical trust. The practical consequences of losing trust can sometimes be described, in themselves, as a loss of trust, because they amount to the loss of what might be called practical trust. What I mean by 'practical trust' can best be explained if trust is defined as reliance on someone's good will. Merely to assume that someone is well-intentioned is already to rely on his good will in an attitudinal sense; but one can also rely on his good will in a practical sense, by doing something that puts one at risk if his will is bad. What one does may be mental rather than physical, since it may consist in no more than believing another's communication, on the assumption that it is well-intentioned. The point is that assuming a communication to be well-intentioned is one step short of believing it, and the intervening step represents the difference between attitudinal and practical trust.

Practical trust often involves *en*trusting someone with something – one's credence, a task, a piece of property, a secret – on the assumption that it will be treated with good will. (That with which the trustee is entrusted can then be called a trust in yet a third sense of the term.) But that with which someone is entrusted, in receiving practical trust, may be quite intangible and hence difficult to identify.

Consider again the trust involved in communication, as expressed by the various senses of the verbs 'to listen' and 'to hear.' To listen is always to attend in a way that makes one susceptible to hearing. But there are many kinds of hearing: hearing that consists in merely detecting sounds; hearing that consists in understanding sounds as words uttered with communicative intent; hearing that consists in weighing a communication as a possible reason for belief; hearing that consists in believing on the basis of that reason; hearing that consists in taking the belief to heart, as a basis for action; and perhaps further, or intervening, levels of hearing. At each level one can listen without actually hearing, and one can hear at one level without listening at the next. (That's why it can make sense to say either 'He listened but he didn't hear' or 'He heard but he didn't listen.') Beginning at the third level, listening becomes a form of practical trust. Attending to a communication in a way that makes one susceptible to regarding it as reason to believe; attending to it as a reason in a way that makes one susceptible to believing; attending to the resulting belief in a way that makes one susceptible to taking it as reason for acting – all of these ways of listening entail practical reliance on the speaker's good will.

With what does one entrust a speaker by listening to him in one of these ways? What one entrusts him with, obviously, is one's susceptibility to hearing in the corresponding senses. (That's why listening is aptly called 'lending an ear.') And since one's susceptibility to hearing, in all of these senses, includes one's susceptibility to his words regarded as reasons for belief and action, listening to him can entail entrusting him with nothing less than one's mind, or indeed with oneself. One entrusts a speaker with oneself by placing one's beliefs and actions under the influence of his words in a way that puts one at risk if his will is bad.

Another example of entrusting oneself to others is the formation of shared intentions.[5] A shared intention is formed by the pooling of individual intentions each of which is conditional on the others.

Each agent has an individual intention of the form 'I'm willing if you are,' and the agents 'pool' these intentions by expressing them so that, as all can see, the stated conditions on the intentions have been satisfied and the agents are now jointly committed to acting. Contributing to the pool of intentions doesn't necessarily require saying 'I'm willing if you are' in so many words, since the requisite intention can be expressed tacitly – for example, by holding out a hand in readiness to shake. But even a tacit contribution entails entrusting oneself to others, first, because their decision whether to reciprocate will determine whether one's intention becomes a positive commitment to act; and second, because that commitment will then be a commitment to do something whose point depends on whether they abide by their reciprocal commitment.

Even without joining a shared intention, one can do things whose point depends on the actions of others, and these shared activities may barely differ from actions based on shared intentions. Whether an extended hand is a signal of a willingness to shake if the other is willing, or the beginning of an actual handshake whose consummation is left up to the other, depends on subtle differences of expectation, resolution, timing, eye contact, momentum, and so on; and in the end, its status may be indeterminate. Whether or not one expresses an antecedent intention, however, doing one's part in a shared activity puts one at the other's disposal, by leaving the success of one's activity up to him.

Losing Practical Trust: A Form of Punishment
Withdrawing practical trust from someone thus entails refusing to do anything with him, in the sense of 'with' that applies to shared rather than parallel activities. It also entails not listening to him and hence not

---

[5] See my 'How to Share an Intention,' in *The Possibility of Practical Reason* (Oxford: Oxford University Press, 2000), 200–220. My conception of shared intention is based on the theory of Margaret Gilbert (see Gilbert's *On Social Facts* [Princeton: Princeton University Press, 1992]).

conversing with him, either. In short, withdrawing practical trust from someone entails excluding him from social interaction.

To exclude someone from social interaction is to shun him, at least to some extent, and shunning is a form of punishment. As I have explained, Freud thinks that anxiety about being punished will develop out of a child's anxiety about losing his parents' love, because the child will expect unloving parents to deal out harsh treatment of the sort in which punishment is generally thought to consist. But anxiety about losing trust, rather than love, may already amount to anxiety about being punished, if the trust at stake is practical trust, the loss of which amounts to being shunned.

Shunning sounds like an archaic and perhaps barbaric form of punishment, but in fact it is practiced by liberal-minded parents of the post-Spockian era, in the form of the 'time-out.' When parents require a child to take a time-out, they exclude him from the conversation and shared activities of the family, precisely on the grounds that he cannot be trusted to participate. The rationale of the time-out is not that the child deserves the suffering that accompanies this punishment; it's that the child's misbehaviour warrants the withdrawal of trust in which the punishment consists. Enlightened parents will convey to the child that his exclusion from the family circle is not intended to make him suffer but only to put the family out of the reach of untrustworthy hands. Of course, they will also convey that he will be readmitted to the family circle as soon as he shows himself ready to be governed by a good will. And, finally, they will convey their confidence in the child's ability to be governed by a good will – a confidence that underlies their respect for the child and perhaps even their love.

For an adult, the loss of practical trust often entails no more than being met with fixed smiles and deaf ears, treatment that is outwardly nothing like being sent to one's room or made to sit in the corner. But a guilty-minded adult can still recognize that, in forfeiting trust, he has warranted treatment that would have been formalized as a punishment when he was a child, and this recognition is a rational counterpart to the phantasy attributed to him by Freud, that he is even now a child facing punishment from an internalized parent. Thus, the present analysis of guilt, as anxiety about having forfeited trust, can serve as a rationalist revision of Freud's analysis. According to this revision, guilt is anxiety about having warranted a kind of treatment that is sometimes formalized as punishment.

Guilt Without Wrongdoing

I now turn to a consideration of guilt that is not about perceived wrongdoing. My first example is the guilt that we sometimes feel about being
self-indulgent, by breaking a diet or shirking exercise. I'll call it self-
disciplinary guilt. My second example will be so-called survivor guilt,
which will lead me to consider a different analysis of the emotion.

Self-Disciplinary Guilt
I think that Kant has the right account of self-disciplinary guilt. For Kant,
actions fail to be well-intentioned when they are performed for reasons
that cannot be universalized; and reasons resist universalization because
they must be regarded as applying either just to ourselves or, as Kant
puts it, 'just for this once.'[6] I suspect that reasons regarded as applying
just for this once are the basis for failures of self-discipline, which involve
making one-time exceptions to some regimen to which we are otherwise
committed. These actions violate the Categorical Imperative and therefore count, in Kantian terms, as violations of duty – specifically, of duties
to ourselves. When we fail to be self-disciplined, we cheat ourselves in
some way.

But why do we feel guilty about cheating ourselves, if guilt is anxiety
about having forfeited trust? Whose trust do we forfeit by eating a second
dessert?

The answer, to begin with, is that we forfeit our own trust, by undermining our grounds for relying on the commitments we make to ourselves.
If we cannot count on ourselves to stick with a diet, then we cannot
accept the commitment we make to ourselves in starting one, and then
we cannot honestly claim to be on a diet, in the first place. Indeed, every
future-directed plan that we make entails a commitment on which we
ourselves must be able to rely in deliberating about related matters.[7] A
loss of self-trust can therefore undermine our ability to organize and coordinate our activities over time – a consequence that is certainly a proper
object of anxiety.

What's more, the violation of commitments warrants a loss of trust
from people other than those to whom the commitments were made. If
we break our word to one person, we provide grounds for distrust not

---

[6] *Groundwork of the Metaphysic of Morals*, trans. H. J. Paton (New York: Harper, 1964), 91
   (p. 424 in the Royal Prussian Academy edition).
[7] See Michael Bratman's *Intention, Plans, and Practical Reason* (Cambridge, MA: Harvard
   University Press, 1987).

only to him but to others who might consider relying on our good will. And grounds for distrust are similarly generalizable even from instances of breaking our word to ourselves. Insofar as we are un-self-disciplined, we are unreliable, and insofar as we are unreliable, we are untrustworthy. Self-disciplinary guilt can therefore be a genuine and rational form of the emotion.

Of course, this account of self-disciplinary guilt, if followed to its Kantian conclusion, implies that failures of self-discipline are moral wrongs, because they are violations of the Categorical Imperative. Strictly speaking, then, the account does not show the rationality of guilt in the absence of perceived wrongdoing. Yet the moral status of Kantian duties to oneself, and of the corresponding wrongs, is not taken seriously by many present-day readers of Kant. The region carved out by the Categorical Imperative is not what is currently regarded as the moral realm. What I have argued is that it is nevertheless a region in which guilt can be rational.

Survivor Guilt

Let me turn, then, to survivor guilt, which is felt by those who have survived catastrophes that others have not. There may be an argument for the rationality of survivor guilt, but it would require a different analysis of guilt altogether. I will therefore make a brief digression, to explore this alternative analysis.

Of course, survivors may feel guilty because they accuse themselves of wrongdoing – of having exerted too little effort to save others, or too much effort to save themselves. They may also accuse themselves of indulging in immoral thoughts and feelings – for example, relief that others died in their place. These instances of guilt on the part of survivors can be accounted for by the foregoing analysis of guilt. But I am using the term 'survivor guilt' to denote guilt experienced about the mere fact of having survived, which cannot be regarded as wrong or as warranting the loss of trust.

Survivor guilt would be rational, however, if guilt were anxiety about having warranted resentment rather than the withdrawal of trust. Just as the victim of wrongdoing feels resentment against the wrongdoer, so the victim of misfortune often feels resentment against those who are more fortunate. Hence a survivor, like a wrongdoer, can be anxious about the prospect of being resented. And if resentment were warranted against both, then both could rationally be anxious about having warranted resentment, and survivor guilt would be just as rational as guilt about wrongdoing.

A possible objection to this analysis would be that resentment about another's good fortune is a modification of envy, whereas the resentment about wrongdoing is a modification of anger. But I see no reason why survivor guilt and moral guilt could not be two distinct species of the same emotion, precisely by virtue of consisting in anxiety about having warranted two distinct species of resentment. Indeed, anger and envy rise to the level of resentment under similar conditions – namely, when tinged with the bitterness that accompanies a sense of injustice. One can be envied even if one's good fortune is acknowledged to be deserved; only if it is regarded as undeserved, however, will envy turn into resentment. One can incur anger by causing harms accidentally or through the vicissitudes of fair-play; anger will turn into resentment only if the harms one causes are thought to be unjust. Thus, envious resentment and angry resentment form a natural pair of emotions embittered by a sense of injustice.

Another objection to the proposed analysis would be that envy is never warranted at all, especially not when it rises to the level of resentment. But why shouldn't envy be warranted? I can imagine saying that envy is pointless, counter-productive, and even potentially vicious. But I cannot imagine claiming that the victims of misfortune have no grounds for envying those who are more fortunate, or for resenting those whose good fortune is undeserved; and so I have to admit that a beneficiary of good fortune may rationally feel anxiety about providing others with grounds for resentment.

Yet a third objection would be that if someone is literally a survivor, then the victims of the corresponding misfortune are dead and hence in no position to resent him. But third parties can feel resentment on behalf of the deceased, a resentment that can only be sharpened by the thought that its proper subjects are no longer alive to feel it. And a survivor can rationally feel anxiety about providing grounds for such vicarious or sympathetic resentment.

Conclusion: Don't Worry

So is guilt about distrust or is it about resentment? I don't know what would count as the right answer to this question. Surely, we feel anxiety about having warranted both of these reactions, and both are warranted by wrongdoing as well as by related matters, which include failures of self-discipline, in the case of distrust, and undeserved disparities of fortune, in the case of resentment. The term 'guilt' is applied to anxiety about all of these reactions, and there seem to be no grounds for ruling any of these applications incorrect.

I therefore conclude that guilt is a family of emotions, including anxiety about having warranted not only distrust but also angry or envious resentment and perhaps other, related reactions as well. This conclusion helps to explain the confusion we often feel about whether guilt is appropriate. We often criticize ourselves for feeling guilty when, as we say, we have nothing to feel guilty about. But we shouldn't criticize ourselves for having no grounds for distrust-anxiety or angry-resentment-anxiety, if what we're feeling is envious-resentment-anxiety instead. The fact that we haven't wronged anyone doesn't necessarily show that we have no grounds for feeling guilty; it may show only that we need to interpret our feelings more carefully, as anxiety about warranting envious resentment rather than anger or distrust.

Correctly interpreting our emotions can thus alleviate our worries about feeling guilty. What a relief.

8

Self to Self

Images of myself being Napoleon can scarcely merely be images of the physical figure of Napoleon. . . . They will rather be images of, for instance, the desolation at Austerlitz as viewed by me vaguely aware of my short stature and my cockaded hat, my hand in my tunic.[1]

At the end of "The Imagination and the Self," Bernard Williams uncovers a common confusion about the range of thoughts in which the metaphysics of personal identity is implicated. When I imagine being someone else, I can be described as imagining that I am the other person – which sounds as if I am imagining a relation of identity between that person and me, David Velleman. As Williams points out, however, this particular

[1] Bernard Williams, "The Imagination and the Self," in *Problems of the Self* (Cambridge: Cambridge University Press, 1973), 26–45, 43.

From *The Philosophical Review* 105 (1996), 39–76. Copyright © 1996 Cornell University. Reprinted by permission of the publisher. Throughout my work on this essay, I have benefited from numerous conversations with David Hills. I was also helped by a seminar on metaphysics that I taught with Stephen Yablo, and by Steve's comments on several drafts of the essay. Others who provided comments and suggestions include Paul Boghossian, Linda Wimer Brakel, John Broome, Mark Crimmins, Neil Delaney, Cody Gilmore, Sally Haslanger, Tomis Kapitan, Krista Lawlor, Eric Lormand, Thomas Nagel, Lucy O'Brien, Derek Parfit, Jim Pryor, Henry Richardson, Amélie Rorty, Gideon Rosen, Ian Rumfitt, Sydney Shoemaker, and Paul Torek. This essay was presented at the 1994 Chapel Hill Colloquium, with Michaelis Michael serving as commentator; and to the Philosophy Departments of Princeton and Georgetown Universities. It is dedicated to Claudia Kraus Piper.

way of imagining that I am another person is not really about me or my identity with anyone.[2]

If my approach to imagining that I am Napoleon, for example, is to imagine *being* Napoleon, then I simply imagine a particular situation as experienced *by* Napoleon. I imagine the landscape at Austerlitz as seen through Napoleon's eyes, the sounds of battle as heard through his ears, the nap of a tunic as felt by his hand. Although Napoleon doesn't appear in the resulting mental image, he does appear in the content of my imagining, since I am imagining Austerlitz specifically as experienced by him. But I, David Velleman, am absent both from the image and from the content of the imagining: I'm not imagining anything about the person who I actually am.

Since I'm not imagining anything about my actual self, in this case, I'm certainly not imagining a relation of identity between me and Napoleon. Hence this way of thinking that I am or might be a given person doesn't establish the conceivability – much less the possibility – of any identities between persons.

Unfortunately, metaphysical discussions of personal identity have tended to embrace almost any thoughts about who one is or might be,

---

[2] Some philosophers have debated whether I can in fact imagine a relation of identity between Napoleon and David Velleman. Bruce Aune argues that I can, provided that I disregard "illusion-shattering facts" about Napoleon and me, such as the fact that I am a twentieth-century philosopher and he a nineteenth-century general ("Speaking of Selves," *The Philosophical Quarterly* 44 [1994]: 279–93, 290 ff.). Zeno Vendler takes the opposite view: "In imagining, for instance, being Ronald Reagan, I cannot be imagining the identity of Z.V. with R.R., for it is patently impossible for these two men to be one and the same, and the patently impossible cannot be imagined" (*The Matter of Minds* [Oxford: Clarendon Press, 1984], 105). (For an answer to Vendler's argument, see John Mackie, "The Transcendental 'I'," in *Philosophical Subjects: Essays Presented to P. F. Strawson*, ed. Zak van Straaten [Oxford: Clarendon Press, 1980], 48–61.)

As Eric Lormand has pointed out to me, however, there are many ways to imagine that I am Napoleon, including not only the method described by Williams but also, for example, imagining that Napoleon has been reincarnated as David Velleman, or that he was cryogenically preserved at birth, thawed out in 1952, and handed by the maternity nurses to an unsuspecting Mrs. Velleman. The latter methods would indeed involve imagining the supposedly problematic relation of identity.

The question, then, is not whether I can imagine a relation of identity between Napoleon and David Velleman but whether I am necessarily doing so when I imagine that I am Napoleon. I interpret Williams as offering a negative answer to this question, by describing a way of imagining that I am Napoleon without imagining anything about David Velleman at all. For a discussion congruent with mine, see Simon Blackburn, "Has Kant Refuted Parfit?" in *Reading Parfit*, ed. Jonathan Dancy (Oxford: Blackwell, 1997), 180–202.

including thoughts similar to the imagining analyzed by Williams. For example, when philosophers want to know whether a person would survive a surgical rearrangement of his brain, they tend to ask whether he would antecedently be in a position to anticipate waking up afterwards. The person's anticipation of waking up after the operation could of course be described as the anticipation that he would survive, in the form of the wakening patient; but it might amount to no more than his picturing the recovery room as seen through the eyes of the wakening patient; and this way of expecting to be that patient is strikingly similar to Williams's method for imagining that one is Napoleon.[3]

If I can imagine that I am Napoleon without imagining a Napoleonic identity for my actual self, then maybe I can anticipate that I will wake up in the future without anticipating a future for my actual self, either. Of course, the anticipation that I will wake up in the future is a first-personal thought; but so is imagining that I am Napoleon; and in that instance, the thought's being first-personal doesn't guarantee that it is about me, the thinker. Imagining that I am Napoleon is first-personal, but it is, so to speak, *first-personal about Napoleon,* in the sense that it is framed from Napoleon's point of view. Perhaps the anticipation that I will wake up in the future can be similarly first-personal about a future subject who may or may not be identical with me. If so, then students of personal identity should probably give up their fascination with first-personal anticipation.

Then again, maybe they should give up their fascination with personal identity instead. The appeal of this topic depends largely on its promise to address our concern about what we can look forward to, or what we can anticipate first-personally. If the mode of anticipation that arouses our concern is first-personal in the sense of being framed from the perspective of a future person, rather than in representing the future existence of the anticipator, then that concern should move us to study the psychology of perspectives rather than the metaphysics of persons.[4]

---

[3] I believe that Williams himself has gone in for this mode of thinking about personal identity. See, for example, "The Self and the Future," in *Problems of the Self,* 46–63.

[4] At the end of *A Dialogue on Personal Identity and Immortality* (Indianapolis: Hackett Publishing Company, 1978), John Perry has one of the interlocutors conclude, "Perhaps we were wrong, after all, in focusing on identity as the necessary condition of anticipation" (49). This possibility is explored by Raymond Martin in "*Having* the Experience: The Next Best Thing to Being There," *Philosophical Studies* 70 (1993): 305–21. It also figures prominently in Paul Torek's *Something to Look Forward To: Personal Identity, Prudence, and Ethics* (Ph.D. dissertation, University of Michigan, 1995). The present essay is an attempt to find a necessary condition other than identity for the mode of anticipation that arouses our future-directed self-concern.

My aim is to argue for this reinterpretation of our self-regarding concern about the future. What matters most, I shall suggest, is not whether the person I now regard as self will survive into the future; it's whether there will be a future person whom I can now regard as self. And whether I can regard a future person as self, I shall argue, doesn't necessarily depend on whether he will be the same person as me; it depends instead on my access to his point of view.[5]

My first step will be to review the work of other philosophers on first-personal thoughts such as "I am David Velleman" (§1). Drawing on this work, I shall analyze the clause "I am Napoleon" as it is used to characterize what I'm imagining in the case described by Williams (§2). My analysis of this case will lead to some further reflections on the nature of first-personal thought (§3); and the resulting account of the first-person will then be applied to memories of what I've experienced in the past (§4) and anticipations of what I will experience in the future (§5). Our desire for a future to anticipate, I shall argue, is a desire for first-personal access to a future point of view. Why we might have this desire is a question that I'll postpone until the final section of the essay (§6).

1. Who I Am

The connection between identity and perspective has been explored suggestively by Thomas Nagel in his discussions of "the objective self."[6]

---

[5] In arguing that identity is not what matters about our survival, I am of course following Derek Parfit (*Reasons and Persons* [Oxford: Clarendon Press, 1984]). Let me explain briefly how my views are related to Parfit's.

I agree with Parfit that much of our concern about survival is focused on our psychological continuity with future persons rather than our metaphysical identity with them. But I disagree with Parfit about the kind of psychological continuity that matters to us in this regard. As Parfit conceives it, the relevant continuity comprises not only the psychological connections forged by memory, for example, but also connections forged by the mere persistence of a psychological state or trait (205). I shall argue for a narrower conception of the relevant continuity, as comprising only those psychological connections which function like memory in giving us first-personal access to other points of view. At the end of the chapter, I'll point out that my conception of psychological continuity yields different judgments from Parfit's about various cases in which it's questionable whether the subject survives in the sense that matters.

I think that Parfit himself has reason to prefer my conception of psychological continuity to his own. For as I shall argue, we report our access to other points of view by using the first-person pronoun in ways that would naturally cause this continuity to be mistaken for an identity between persons. My account therefore enables me to explain why that which matters in survival might seem to be identity even when it is not.

[6] "Subjective and Objective," in *Mortal Questions* (Cambridge: Cambridge University Press, 1979), 196–213; "The Limits of Objectivity," in *The Tanner Lectures on Human Values, Vol. I,*

One of Nagel's concerns in these discussions is to locate the fact of who he is:[7]

[H]ow can a particular person be me? Given a complete description of the world from no particular point of view, including all the people in it, one of whom is Thomas Nagel, it seems on the one hand that something has been left out, something absolutely essential remains to be specified, namely which of them I am. But on the other hand there seems no room in the centerless world for such a further fact: the world as it is from no point of view seems complete in a way that excludes such additions; it is just the world, and everything true of TN is already in it. So . . . how can it be true of a particular person, a particular individual, TN, who is just one of many persons in an objectively centerless world, that he is me?

Nagel is puzzled here by the fact that he cannot incorporate the thought "I am TN" into an objective description of the world. In an objective description, this thought would have to appear without personal pronouns; but without personal pronouns, the thought would simply disappear. So long as Nagel speaks or thinks of TN in strictly impersonal terms, he cannot frame the thought that TN is *him*.[8]

The impossibility of framing this thought impersonally leads Nagel to worry that a description of the world must remain incomplete so long as it remains impersonal. This worry is metaphysical, in that it envisions things for which "the world" might have "room" even though they cannot be described impersonally. Indeed, Nagel's worry cannot be understood other than metaphysically. Nagel never questions the possibility that an objective description of the world might be complete in the sense of containing all of the objectively statable truths; and its omitting some subjectively stated truths could hardly count against its claim to be a complete objective description. What Nagel envisions is that a description containing all of the objectively statable truths might still be incomplete in the sense of failing to describe all of the world, since the world might include features that cannot be described objectively.[9]

---

ed. S. McMurrin (Salt Lake City: University of Utah Press, 1980), 77–139; "The Objective Self," in *Knowledge and Mind*, ed. Carl Ginet and Sydney Shoemaker (New York: Oxford University Press, 1983), 211–32; *The View From Nowhere* (New York: Oxford University Press, 1986), Chapter IV.

[7] *The View From Nowhere*, 54–55. Note that this is only one of Nagel's concerns in his discussions of the "objective self."

[8] The classic discussion of this phenomenon is John Perry's paper "The Problem of the Essential Indexical," *Noûs* 13 (1979): 3–21.

[9] The belief in a subjective feature of the world constituting *who I am* is like the belief in a tensed feature constituting *when now is*. The analogy has been drawn explicitly by D. H. Mellor in "I and Now," *Proceedings of the Aristotelian Society* 89 (1988): 79–94. For an

Nagel's reason for thinking that an objective description might be incomplete in this sense is that it could never convey the information conveyed in the subjective statement "I am TN." Nagel's metaphysical worry therefore rests on an observation about the informativeness of an identity statement. And the informativeness of identity statements has been studied extensively by philosophers of language since Frege, including some who have focused especially on identity statements involving the first person.[10]

What the work of these philosophers suggests, however, is that "I am TN" can be informative for Nagel without describing any objectively indescribable feature of the world, and hence that its informativeness shouldn't lead to any metaphysical worries. Let me summarize this work briefly, with the help of David Lewis's suggestion that self-locating thoughts like "I am TN" resemble the cartographic legend "This map is here."[11]

Suppose that you visit the battlefield at Austerlitz and find, at the former site of Napoleon's headquarters, a map that bears the legend "This map is here," followed by an arrow pointing to a rectangle in the map's lower left-hand corner. This legend is certainly informative, but what information does it give you?

The informativeness of the legend depends on the fact that its two indexical terms, "this" and "here," pick out their referents in two different ways. The word "here" is assigned a referent by the arrow that connects it to a rectangle on the map. The word doesn't refer to the rectangle itself, of course; if it did, the legend would make the absurd assertion that the map occupies a small rectangle in its own lower left-hand corner. The word

author who believes in such features of the world, see Geoffrey Madell, "Personal Identity and the Idea of a Human Being," in *Human Beings*, ed. David Cockburn (Cambridge: Cambridge University Press, 1991), 127–42.

[10] I shall be drawing especially on John Perry's "Problem of the Essential Indexical" and his "Self-Notions," *Logos: Philosophic Issues in Christian Perspective* 11 (1990): 17–31. (Both papers have been reprinted in *The Problem of the Essential Indexical and Other Essays* [New York: Oxford University Press, 1993].) See also Stephen E. Boër and William G. Lycan, *Knowing Who* (Cambridge, MA: MIT Press, 1986), Chapter 6; and Lycan, *Consciousness* (Cambridge: MIT Press, 1987), 80. The general account of identity statements on which I rely is similar to that offered by P. F. Strawson in *Subject and Predicate in Logic and Grammar* (London: Methuen, 1974), 51–56.

[11] "Attitudes *De Dicto* and *De Se*," *The Philosophical Review* 88 (1979): 513–14, 528. The moral that I draw from this analogy is similar to one drawn from Kant's Paralogisms of Pure Reason, to the effect that "in identifying 'myself' I am identifying no *more* than a point of view upon the world, and not an entity within it" (Roger Scruton, *Sexual Desire: A Moral Philosophy of the Erotic* [New York: The Free Press, 1986], 114.)

"here" refers instead to the region of the battlefield that's represented by the rectangle, that being where the map is actually located.

The map could refer to this region as "here" without the help of an arrow. For example, it might also bear the words "This map was placed here by the Austerlitz Tourist Board." In this inscription, the word "here" would refer directly to the general vicinity of the inscription itself, and so no arrow would be needed to complete the reference. In "This map was placed here by the Austerlitz Tourist Board," however, the word "here" would roughly mean "where you now see it, before your eyes." And the legend "This map is here" doesn't refer to the relevant region as "here" in the same sense. If the legend "This map is here" was displayed with no arrow, and you had to interpret "here" as meaning "here before your eyes," then the legend would give you no new information. You already know that the map is here before your eyes; what you want to know is where that location lies in the representational scheme of the map. Hence the need for the arrow, which secures reference to the map's actual location via the map's representation of it.

Unlike the word "here," the phrase "this map" does pick out its referent as an object before your eyes. If "this map" referred to the map indirectly, via its representation in the map, then the legend would once again become uninformative. Imagine a second arrow, leading from the phrase "this map" to the same rectangle that's indicated by the arrow leading from "here." This second arrow would reduce the map's legend to the trivial statement that a map located in the region represented by the rectangle is indeed located in the region represented by the rectangle.

The legend on the actual map is informative because it refers to the same location in two different ways – once as the location of "this map [before your eyes]" and once as the location that's "here [according to the map]." The legend tells you where the map that you are seeing can be found on the battlefield as seen by the map.

The reason for referring to the same location twice, as seen by you and by the map, is to help you align the map with your self-centered conception of your surroundings. For until you work out this alignment, you can't use the map to find your way around the battlefield.

In touring the battlefield, you will have to be guided by your senses, which give you a representation of the field from your own point of view. Unfortunately, this self-centered representation of your surroundings is incomplete, in that it includes only what you can perceive or remember perceiving. You want to expand it to include regions that you haven't perceived, so that it represents what is over the hillock on your left or behind the trees up ahead. These regions are represented in the map, of course, but not from the perspective of the perceptual representation by which you must navigate. You therefore need to transfer information from the map's complete, centerless representation of the battlefield to your incomplete, self-centered representation.

In order to transfer information between these representations, you have to know which parts of them are co-referential – which marks on the map refer to which landmarks within your perceptual field. The legend "This map is here" enables you to coordinate these schemes of reference, by showing how both schemes pick out a single landmark, the map itself.[12]

The informativeness of "This map is here" is thus potentially misleading. "This map is here" adds to your knowledge of the battlefield, but not by giving you knowledge about additional features of the battlefield – features that aren't described in the representations that you already have.

All that the legend reports is the map's location, which is already reported twice in your existing representations of the battlefield, once in the map itself and again in your self-centered conception. Hence the legend doesn't inform you by revealing some aspect of the battlefield that's left out of these representations; rather, it informs you by conveying a rule of translation between these representations, thus enabling you to make better use of the information that they already contain. And the legend conveys this rule of translation by demonstrating it, not by stating it. It *shows* you how to translate between these schemes of representation, by using both of them to specify the map's location.

Many different statements could provide this demonstration. What's conveyed by the legend "This map is here" could equally well be conveyed by a different statement, such as "The hillock on your left is here" or "The trees up ahead are here" or – as maps often say – "You are here." All the legend needs to do is identify some location or other within both representational schemes, thus demonstrating how to translate between them.

In showing you how to translate between schemes of representation, the legend offers practical guidance, which you must follow within the self-centered perspective that you occupy as an agent. That's why the

---

[12] Gareth Evans took this point further, by suggesting that nothing could count as one's objective conception of the world unless one grasped the possibility of correlating it with one's self-centered conception (*The Varieties of Reference* [Oxford: Oxford University Press, 1982], 212).

legend refers indexically to "this map" and literally points to a region within it, picking out both items as they appear in your visual field. A legend that spoke impersonally about how to transfer information between such-and-such a map and so-and-so's visual field would not be helpful – not, that is, unless you could translate it into your personal terms, such as "this map" and "here." For if you are to follow the rule for translating between the perspectives at hand, that rule must be framed from your own perspective, as it is by the legend "This map is here."

Nagel's thought "I am TN" is informative in the same way: it demonstrates, within his conception of the world as centered on "me," how to correlate that conception with a centerless conception of the world, as containing someone named "TN."[13] "I am TN" is informative, then, because it shows how to transfer information between these two conceptions of the world, not because it describes some feature of the world that they have omitted.[14]

2. Who I Might Be

This account of Nagel's self-locating thought helps us to understand cases of projective imagination as well. My being Napoleon is not a feature of the world that's depicted in the mental image by which I imagine that I am Napoleon; it's rather a rule for translating between that image and an objective description of what it depicts. The image represents that I am Napoleon in the sense that it is framed in a self-centered scheme of reference that's centered on NB.

When I speak of a scheme of reference that's centered on NB, I don't just mean, for example, an image of Austerlitz as it looked from a place where NB stood.[15] Entertaining such an image might amount to no more

[13] Here I am considering, with Nagel, why this statement would constitute an informative addition to a complete objective description of the world. Of course, if Nagel's objective conception of the world is *incomplete*, then "I am TN" may be informative in other ways as well.

[14] Nagel explains that "I am TN" is informative because it reports "the fact that this impersonal conception of the world, though it accords no special position to TN, is attached to and developed from the perspective of TN" (*The View From Nowhere*, 64). For a critique of Nagel's explanation, see Christopher Peacocke, *Sense and Content: Experience, Thought, and their Relations* (Oxford: Clarendon Press, 1983), 168–69. A different explanation is offered by Zeno Vendler in Chapter VI of *The Matter of Minds*.

[15] For the sake of simplicity, I am going to confine my attention to the visual image involved in my imagining. Some aspects of visual imagery – for example, its perspectival geometry – are better understood than the corresponding aspects (if any) of tactual, auditory, olfactory, or kinaesthetic imagery.

than visualizing Austerlitz as it looked to NB, which is not the same as imagining that I am NB seeing it. An account of imagined seeing must distinguish it from the less ambitious project of mere visualization.[16] Both imaginative projects involve a mental image drawn from NB's perspective. The difference is that only imagined seeing involves, in addition, the thought of that perspective as occupied – and, indeed, as occupied by NB.[17]

A visual image has a perspective because objects are represented in it by regions whose size and placement depend on the angles subtended by those objects at some common point in space. The representational scheme of the image is governed by lines of sight converging at a single vantage point, whose location the image suggests but doesn't depict.

In ordinary vision, this vantage point is occupied by the eyes of the person experiencing the visual image, and the image is presented as the immediate product of this sensory encounter with the depicted scene.[18] Thus, the image has a *centered* scheme of reference because it represents objects as they are intercepted by lines of sight that converge at a single point; and it has a *self*-centered scheme of reference because the point of convergence is thought of as occupied by the image's subject.

Yet the imagination can frame a visual image without the thought that its vantage point is occupied. The result in that case is visualization rather than imagined seeing. The image represents objects as they would appear to a viewer, if one were present, but it doesn't represent them as so appearing to anyone.

Going beyond mere visualization to imagined seeing entails conjuring up, not just a visual image, but also the thought of such an image as being experienced by someone occupying its vantage point and confronting the objects it depicts. Imaginary seeing thus requires an imagined viewer, who is imagined simultaneously as the mind containing the image, so to speak, and as an unseen object located where its lines of sight converge.

---

[16] This problem is the one that Williams considers in "Imagination and the Self." The solution I offer here is largely his.

[17] Wollheim distinguishes these modes of imagination as "acentral" and "central" ("Imagination and Identification," in *On Art and the Mind* [Cambridge, MA: Harvard University Press, 1974], 54–83). Williams distinguished them by calling the latter "participatory imagery."

[18] I am being deliberately vague in speaking of how an image is "presented." The "presentation" of the image may consist in a preceding or accompanying thought about the image; or in some distinctive phenomenal qualities of the image itself, combined perhaps with beliefs or cognitive dispositions of the subject with respect to such qualities. I hope to remain neutral among these possibilities.

This viewer is posited by the imagination, but he is not pictured: he is simply thought of, as providing the mental environs of the image and the sensorium at its spatial and causal point of origin.[19]

When I think of the image as having a subject, it becomes a way of thinking about that person reflexively, as "self." And to think of a person reflexively, as "self," is also to think of him as "me." If I think of the image as having a particular subject, such as Napoleon, the image becomes a way of thinking about Napoleon as "me," and so it becomes a way of thinking that I am Napoleon.

Let me elaborate for a moment on this notion of a visual image as a way of thinking about someone else as "me." Elaboration is needed because a visual image rarely contains uses of the first-person pronoun: it isn't a way of thinking about the imagined viewer as "me" in so many words, or in any words at all.

In a case of imagined seeing, however, the image is framed to depict things as seen by someone, who is thus introduced in thought as the subject of the image. The image still doesn't present this viewer as one of the objects visible in it; but it does present the viewer invisibly, insofar as it now depicts things as seen by him; and it thereby presents him reflexively, as the subject, in the way that a spoken first-person pronoun presents its speaker.[20]

Although the reflexivity of a mental image doesn't consist in a use of the first-person pronoun, it would occasion a use of the pronoun in the corresponding verbal report. A report of what I'm imagining would of course describe the objects depicted in the image – the field, the smoke

---

[19] The relation between the subject's role as the bearer of consciousness and his role as owner of the operative sensorium is discussed by Sydney Shoemaker, "Embodiment and Behavior," in *The Identities of Persons*, ed. Amélie Rorty (Berkeley: University of California Press, 1976), 109–37. It is also the implicit topic of Daniel Dennett's "Where Am I?" in *Brainstorms: Philosophical Essays on Mind and Psychology* (Cambridge: MIT Press, 1981), 310–23. Both papers point out that these roles can come apart.

[20] Throughout the chapter, I assume that "first-personal" thought is not necessarily personal, in that it need not involve the concept of a person. Creatures who lack the concept of a person can nevertheless manifest behavior that is to be explained by their having egocentric representations of their surroundings – representations whose content cannot be expressed without the help of first-person pronouns. We cannot explain the stalking behavior of a cat, for example, except in terms of perceptions expressible as "There's a mouse in front of *me*," "*I'm* close enough to pounce on it," and so on. Yet the attribution of such first-personal thoughts to the cat does not imply that it thinks of itself, or of anything else, as a person. Here I am in pointed disagreement with John Campbell, who thinks that even proprioceptions such as "I am about to fall over" are essentially about a person ("The Reductionist View of the Self," in *Reduction, Explanation, and Realism*, ed. David Charles and Kathleen Lennon [Oxford: Clarendon Press, 1992], 380–419, 392 ff.).

of battle, and so on. Yet it would also have to make clear that these objects were being imagined, not merely as they would appear if someone saw them, but as being seen. How could a verbal report make clear that it was conveying the contents of an imagined seeing? The obvious way would be to include a prefatory "I see," in which "I" would refer to the person who does the seeing; and the person who does the seeing, in this context, is the imagined viewer. The verbal expression of an imagined seeing thus confirms that its scheme of representation casts the imagined viewer in the role of first person, as the referent of "me."

But who would be speaking here? Whose image is being put into words?

I have thus far neglected to distinguish between the image that's in the mind of the imaginer and the one that's in the mind of the imagined viewer. When I imagine that I am Napoleon viewing Austerlitz, I don't imagine, of the faint and incomplete image in my own mind, that this very image belongs to a visual experience in the mind of NB.[21] Rather, my image is a medium for imagining NB's visual experience.

My image is a medium for imagining NB's experience because it purports to be a secondary version of NB's visual image – a duplicate of his visual impression, or a prototype for it. And the image regarded as having NB for its subject would seem to be the primary or original image in NB's mind, not the secondary version of it in mine. The question therefore arises whether my image still qualifies as a way of thinking about NB as "me."

By and large, secondary versions of an image share its referential scheme. A reproduction of a picture of Austerlitz is itself an image of Austerlitz; an artist's design for a mural of Austerlitz is an image of Austerlitz, too. Both are copies – one modeled after the primary image, the other serving as a model for it – and both share the referential scheme of the picture to which they stand as copies.[22] Similarly, the image in my mind, regarded as a copy of NB's visual impression, is an image of whatever NB is supposed to be seeing.

But what about reflexive or first-personal reference? In the referential scheme of NB's visual impression, NB occupies first-person position, since he is the subject. Yet the copy occurs in my mind, where I am the subject. So shouldn't I, DV, be the person who is reflexively presented in this image?

[21] Here I disagree with John Mackie's suggestion that the imagined subject is imagined to be "the subject of my present experiences" ("The Transcendental 'I,'" 56).
[22] In speaking of mental images as "copies," I do not mean to imply anything about their degree of resolution, detail, or faithfulness to the original. I am also attempting to remain neutral on the direction-of-fit between these copies and their originals.

There isn't a simple answer to this question. A mental copy of a visual impression can have two subjects. The person entertaining a secondary image is certainly the subject of that image. But insofar as the image is regarded as a copy of a primary impression, it resembles that impression not merely in depicting the objects seen but also in depicting those objects *as seen by the primary viewer.* Allusion to the primary viewer is essential to the representational scheme of the secondary image, and he is alluded to specifically as the subject, since objects are represented specifically as seen by him.

Considerations such as these have led some philosophers to speak of secondary images as having an "internal" subject in addition to any "external" subject they might have.[23] I find the terms "internal" and "external" uninformative, however, and so I will speak instead of the notional and actual subjects. The notional subject of a secondary image is the person thought of as occupying the image's vantage point and undergoing the visual impression of which the image is a copy.

In the representational scheme of such an image, the notional subject tends to crowd out the actual subject as the target of reflexive reference. The notional subject has to get into the act somehow, or the image won't amount to a representation of things as seen by him. And he can't get into the act, in his capacity as the viewer, just by getting into the image; for as the viewer, he occupies a role over and above that of anything viewed. He therefore gets into the act by being thought of as the subject, as the person reflexively presented by the image, and hence as the target of self-reference within the visual scheme of representation.

Consider again how the referential scheme of my mental image would be expressed in words. To ask whom the image presents in the position of subject or self is to ask how the image's self-centered scheme of reference is oriented in the objective world.[24] And as we have seen, an image's orientation can be demonstrated within its scheme of reference by an identity statement of the form "I am so-and-so."

---

[23] The term "internal subject" was coined, I believe, by Richard Wollheim. Wollheim's clearest discussion of the issue is in Lecture III of *Painting as an Art* (Princeton: Princeton University Press, 1987). In the case of paintings, of course, there is no external subject, since the secondary image is on canvas rather than in a person's mind. See also Wollheim's "Imagination and Identification." For a recent discussion of the issue in application to perceptual experience, see Bill Brewer, "Self-Location and Agency," *Mind* 101 (1992): 17–34.

[24] The objective world involved here is the *imaginary* world, objectively described. After all, I can imagine that I am Napoleon at the battle of Narnia rather than Austerlitz.

If such a statement were framed within my image's scheme of reference, it would be framed from the point of view embodied in the image,
which is that of the imagined viewer. And a statement framed from the
viewer's point of view would be a statement made by the viewer – who has
to be Napoleon if my image is to represent things as seen by him. The
identity statement that would demonstrate the referential orientation of
my image is therefore the statement that would be made by NB: "I am
Napoleon."

In his capacity as the viewer, of course, NB is merely imaginary, and
his statement would be imaginary, too. But it would be easy enough to
imagine. In fact, I may already be putting imaginary words into the mouth
of NB, if my imagining includes what Williams calls a "narration":[25]

Consider now the *narration.* . . . It is going to be of the general form: 'I have conquered; the ideals of the Revolution in my hands are sweeping away the old world.
Poor Maria Walewska, I wonder where she is now' and so on and so on, according
to whatever knowledge or illusions I possess about Napoleon.

When I imagine saying "I have conquered," I conjure up an image of
this utterance from the speaker's point of view, and I superimpose this
point of view on that embodied in the imagined visual impression, in such
a way that both are centered on NB as the notional subject of speech and
vision together. If I replaced "I have conquered" with "I am Napoleon"
(or perhaps "I, Napoleon, have conquered"), I would thereby give myself
a demonstration, within the referential scheme of my imagining, of how
that scheme is coordinated with an objective description of the world.

To imagine saying "I am Napoleon" would therefore be a way for me
to spell out for myself that I'm imagining everything as seen (and said)
by NB.[26] I could even use this statement to spell out for others what I'm
imagining, provided that I enclosed it in quotation marks to indicate that
it was couched in the terms of the imagining. For I could say this: I am
imagining, "I am Napoleon."

My report of imagining *that* I am Napoleon simply transposes this
quoted identity statement into indirect discourse. In doing so, it replaces

---

[25] "Imagination and the Self," 43.

[26] The imagined statement itself is not what gives my imagining the content that I am
Napoleon. For I can imagine saying "I am Napoleon" without imagining that I am
Napoleon – for example, in the course of imagining that I am someone with Napoleonic
delusions. To imagine that I am Napoleon is to imagine that which this imagined statement would express – namely, Napoleon's occupying the center of a self-centered scheme
of reference.

the pronoun "I" with something like what Castañeda called a quasi-indicator.[27]

A quasi-indicator is an indexical used in *oratio obliqua* to mark the position that would be occupied in *oratio recta* by a reflexive term such as "me." John Perry has analyzed the workings of quasi-indicators as follows:[28]

I think that when we use quasi-indicators we combine a remark about what [someone] believes with a remark, or a hint, about *how* he believes it. In the case of "he," the second bit of information is roughly that he believes what he believes *in virtue of* accepting a sentence with "I" in it. That is, "Smith believes that *he* is α" tells us that Smith believes Smith to be α in virtue of accepting "I am α." More precisely, it tells us that he [believes] it in virtue of being in a certain belief state, which in English-speaking adults typically results in the utterance, in appropriate circumstances, of "I am α."

Suppose that Smith overhears a conversation in which some unnamed person is confidently said to be α. Smith may come to believe, of that unnamed person, that he is α. Now suppose that the person under discussion is in fact Smith. Smith has then come to believe *Smith* to be α. But Smith may or may not be aware of being the person in question, and so in believing Smith to be α, he may believe it in one of two ways, which Perry analyzes as follows. He may believe it either by accepting a sentence of the form "He is α" or by accepting the sentence "I am α," depending on which sentence would typically be uttered by an English speaker in his state of mind.

When we say "Smith believes that he is α," we normally mean that Smith holds his belief in the latter, first-personal way: our report would be misleading if Smith were unaware of being the person in question. According to Perry, then, we mean not only that Smith believes Smith to be α but also that he believes it in virtue of accepting the sentence "I am α" – that is, in virtue of occupying a state that typically results in an utterance of this first-personal sentence. We thus use "he" as a quasi-indicator, marking the presence of a first-person pronoun in the sentence whose utterance would typically express Smith's belief.

As it stands, Perry's analysis applies only to beliefs: it cannot cover cases of imagining, because imaginings don't typically give rise to utterances. But the materials for extending the analysis are already at hand.

---

[27] See "Indicators and Quasi-Indicators," *American Philosophical Quarterly* 4 (1967): 203–10. A discussion of the literature on this subject can be found in John Perry's "Castañeda on He and I," in *The Problem of the Essential Indexical*.

[28] "Belief and Acceptance," in *The Problem of the Essential Indexical*, 53–67, 60. Note that Perry's account is different from Castañeda's.

For when Smith imagines that he is Napoleon, we have found, he may do so by conjuring up secondary images with NB as their notional subject, thereby entering a state of imagination whose referential orientation would be spelled out by a further image, of the utterance "I am Napoleon." Just as there is an actual utterance by which the believer would typically express what he believes, so there is an utterance-image by which the imaginer would typically express what he imagines. So Perry's analysis can be extended from beliefs to imaginings if the utterances expressive of beliefs are replaced in the analysis by the utterance-images expressive of imaginings.

This extension of Perry's analysis crucially affects the role of the quasi-indicator. In "Smith believes that he is Napoleon," the quasi-indicator "he" marks the place of the first-person pronoun in "I am Napoleon" as it might actually be said by Smith. The quasi-indicator thus stands in for a pronoun referring to Smith. But in "Smith imagines that he is Napoleon," the quasi-indicator marks the place of the first-person pronoun in "I am Napoleon" as it might be *imagined* by Smith but as *said* in this imagining by Napoleon. And in "I am Napoleon" as said by NB, "I" would refer to NB.[29]

Thus, the 'he' in "Smith imagines that he is Napoleon" echoes an imagined use of "I" that would refer to Napoleon and not to Smith. So it does not pick out Smith as the object of Smith's imaginings; it merely introduces the self-concept, or "I," under which Smith imagines Napoleon, as he would express by going on to imagine saying, "I am Napoleon." The same goes for the second occurrence of "I" in "I'm imagining that I am Napoleon." This 'I' isn't a reference to me, David Velleman. It simply marks the place of the first-person pronoun in the utterance-image "I am

[29] Here is a complication. In Perry's example ("Smith believes that he is α"), the quasi-indicator borrows its reference by anaphora to indicate *what* is believed; whereas it invokes the associated utterance only for the purpose of specifying *how* this content is believed. Fortunately, the grammatical antecedent of "he" (namely, "Smith") has the same referent as the pronoun to which it corresponds in the associated utterance ("I"), so that the *what* and the *how* of the attributed belief coincide. Yet if both of these mechanisms were at work in "Smith imagines that he is Napoleon," then what Smith was said to imagine would be something that he couldn't imagine in the way that he was said to imagine it; since the grammatical antecedent of "he," in this attribution, doesn't have the same referent as the pronoun "I" in the utterance naturally associated with the attributed imagining. Thus, the normal mechanisms of quasi-indication no longer work together. What I am suggesting is that, in case of such a conflict, the mechanism peculiar to quasi-indication takes precedence, so that no anaphora occurs, and both the *what* and the *how* of Smith's imagining are determined by the associated utterance. (Thanks to Tomis Kapitan for raising this problem.)

Napoleon," which would demonstrate the orientation of my imagining from within.

Here at last we see why Williams's method for imagining that I am Napoleon does not involve imagining anything about my actual self, DV. It simply involves entertaining imaginary thoughts in the Napoleonic first-person, so to speak, an egocentric scheme of reference whose center – and hence whose *ego* – is NB.

3. What "I" Is

But how can I think about Napoleon in the first-person? The first-person is a reflexive mode of thought, and I am in no position to think about NB reflexively, since reflexive thoughts are about their own thinker, and I, the thinker, am not NB.

I am happy to grant that my thoughts in this case are not reflexive in the objective sense of referring to the person who is in fact thinking them. But as Perry's analysis illustrates, philosophers have had to recognize a distinction between a thought's being objectively reflexive in this sense and its being subjectively reflexive, by presenting the thinker in the distinctively first-personal way, under the guise of self.[30] Although my thoughts about NB aren't about their own thinker, they do present NB in first-personal guise.

I now seem to be suggesting that some modes of thought may be subjectively but not objectively reflexive, presenting first-personally someone who is not the person thinking them. This suggestion would be problematic, to say the least.

Even those philosophers who recognize the distinction between subjective and objective reflexivity assume that a subjectively reflexive mode of thought – though individuated, perhaps, by its subjective character – must nevertheless be guaranteed to refer to the thinker in fact.[31] Otherwise, I could think about someone first-personally and yet be uncertain of his relation to the thinker of this thought. I would then be in a position to

---

[30] This recognition can perhaps be traced to Elizabeth Anscombe's paper "The First Person," in which Anscombe invented a mode of reference that was objectively but not subjectively reflexive. The paper is reprinted in Anscombe's *Metaphysics and the Philosophy of Mind: Collected Papers* (Oxford: Blackwell, 1981), 21–36.

[31] I think that this assumption is operative, for example, in John Campbell's discussion of "Self-Reference and Self-Knowledge," in *Past, Space, and Self* (Cambridge, MA: MIT Press, 1994), Chapter 4; and in Lucy F. O'Brien, "Anscombe and the Self-Reference Rule," *Analysis* 54 (1994): 277–81.

doubt whether "I" exist, since the doubt itself would guarantee only the existence of the doubter, who might not be the person whose existence was being doubted, however first-personally.

Fortunately, I needn't go so far as to suggest a gap between subjective and objective reflexivity. My point all along has been that secondary mental images have two subjects, one actual and one notional. The possibility of thoughts with notional as well as actual subjects requires us to enlarge our understanding of what it is for a thought to be reflexive.

The distinction between actual and notional subjects already figures in the subjective character of secondary images. Even to the imaginer himself, the image presents an imagining subject and a viewing subject, both in ways that are recognizably subject-presenting, and hence first-personal. So even within the category of subjective reflexivity, we must distinguish between actual and notional reflexivity, to mark the difference between the ways in which someone can be presented as the subject of thought.

We can then say that my mental image of Austerlitz, in its subjective character, is a notionally reflexive thought about Napoleon: I am thinking about NB in the notional first-person. And the notional first-person needn't refer to the actual subject of thought.

To claim that I can think of Napoleon in the notional first-person is still to claim too much, however. The notional reflexivity of my thoughts about Napoleon is less than genuine.

In order to imagine that I am Napoleon, I frame an image of Austerlitz as seen by someone who might thereby be moved to say "I see . . . ," and then I stipulate that the image and the associated utterance are oriented in such a way that "I" refers to NB. Without this referential stipulation, my mental image would not be a way of thinking about Napoleon as "me," and so it wouldn't be a way of imagining that I am Napoleon. Yet stipulations of this sort are foreign to reflexive usage. I don't usually specify to whom my uses of "me" refer – not even uses of the notional "me."

Suppose, for example, that I have a visual memory of a desolate field just like the one surveyed by Napoleon at Austerlitz. This memory includes a visual image that's presented as reprising an earlier visual experience, whose subject stood at the image's vantage point in front of the remembered scene. The memory image is thus presented as a duplicate, representing the field as seen by an original subject on some date in the past. It therefore has a notional subject, who would be the referent of the first-person pronoun in an accompanying image of the utterance "I see . . . ," if such an utterance were remembered from the same point of view.

If the image is indeed a copy of a visual impression, as it purports to be, then there is already a fact of the matter as to the identity of its notional subject: he is the person from whose experience the image was copied.[32] The image's notional reflexivity with respect to that person is not the product of any semantic stipulation on my part. I do not center the memory image on someone in the past so as to make him the notional subject. The image is just presented to me as having been copied from a visual impression, and it consequently represents things as seen by the subject of the impression from which it was, in fact, copied. Who he was is then determined by the image's causal history.

This mechanism makes the reflexivity of my memory genuine, I think, in a way that the reflexivity of imaginings is not. In memory I really think of the notional subject as "me"; in imagination, I only pretend to.

What makes a thought subjectively reflexive, after all, is that it is indexical in a special way: it has a peculiar way of pointing. A reflexive thought picks out a person at its center by mentally pointing to him in a distinctively inward-directed fashion. My experiential memories pick out past subjects by pointing to them in this way, but my imaginings cannot really do the same with Napoleon.

Before I can frame an image that points to Napoleon at its center – even its notional center – I must first frame another thought that picks him out, so that I can center the image on him. When I subsequently use that image to think of him at its center, I can only pretend to be using a mode of thought that's sufficient to pick him out. In fact, I couldn't have picked out NB as "me" without first picking him out as "Napoleon," in order to stipulate that he was the notional subject of thought.

Hence the thought of NB as "me" is less than genuinely reflexive. Genuinely reflexive thoughts don't rely on an antecedent specification of their target: they just point to the subject, at the center of thought. They are – to put it somewhat paradoxically – unselfconscious about their reference, in that they require no other thought about whom they refer to. I can think of NB as notionally "me" only by deliberately placing him where he will intercept this inward-directed pointer, thus rendering

---

[32] I do not mean to imply that the original viewer is the notional subject of the image solely because of its psychological origins in his experience. If the image wasn't presented in thought as the copy of a visual impression, then it might not present anyone as the notional subject, even if it was in fact copied from someone's experience. Because the image is presented as a copy, however, it has a notional subject, whose identity is then determined by his being the subject of the original. See also note 45.

its reference to him self-conscious. So I can only pretend to think of him in the notional first-person.[33]

4. Who I Was

But what if I believe that my memory is a vestige of Napoleon's experiences at the battle of Austerlitz rather than any experiences of my own?[34] In that case, I will believe it to be an image of Austerlitz as seen by Napoleon, on whom the image is centered naturally, without any stipulation on my part. And I will believe that it has a content that would be expressed by an accompanying memory of the utterance "I see Austerlitz," as spoken – and spoken truly – by a real person seeing Austerlitz. I may then transpose this utterance into indirect discourse by claiming to remember that I saw the battle of Austerlitz.[35]

[33] Note that the same considerations may apply to cases in which I imagine that I am David Velleman. For example, if I re-center my image of Austerlitz so as to imagine that I, David Velleman, am fighting in Napoleon's place, my thoughts do not become genuinely first-personal simply because they are now about DV rather than NB. I am still stipulating who is the notional "me," and hence only pretending to pick him out just by pointing.

[34] Gareth Evans argued that one could not question whether apparent memories derived from one's own experiences (*Varieties of Reference*, 235–48). According to Evans, one cannot even have a self-concept unless one is disposed to assimilate the information in memories and perceptions in ways that already constitute taking oneself as their source. A subject who didn't already treat himself as the source of memories, Evans argued, couldn't go on to doubt whether he was the source, since he would lack a concept needed for framing this doubt.

Note, however, that Evans's argument yields no conclusions about apparent memories taken singly. What the argument shows, if anything, is that I could not question whether I was the source of my recovered images in general. If I treat recovered images in general as derived from own experiences, however, then even by Evans's lights I will have the self-concept with which to doubt, about any particular image, whether I was its source. Hence Evans's argument does not preclude the possibility of my thinking that I have particular images recovered from Napoleon's experiences rather than my own. (Other potential obstacles to my taking this view are discussed in the following note.)

[35] Of course, I will also think that the image's content would be expressed by an accompanying memory of the utterance "I, Napoleon, see Austerlitz." Will I consequently claim to remember that I, *Napoleon*, saw Austerlitz?

Compare Andy Hamilton's remarks on the difficulty of reporting an apparent memory derived from Derek Parfit's experience of arriving at Bournemouth station:

One could try 'I remember arriving at Bournemouth station – only the "I" then was Parfit!'. (It was the same 'I', only the person had changed his identity.) Or 'I remember arriving at Bournemouth, only it was not my body that arrived.' But these are desperate expedients. ["A New Look at Personal Identity," *The Philosophical Quarterly* 45: (1995), 332–49, 342.] [Note continues on p. 190.]

This report would be odd because the verb "to remember" is factive: the claim to remember something implies that it's true. If I speak the truth in claiming to remember that I saw Austerlitz, then what I claim to remember must be true as well; and what I claim to remember would seem to be that I saw Austerlitz. The merely bizarre belief that I have inherited one of NB's visual images seems to yield the truly absurd conclusion that I underwent one of his visual experiences.

One way to avoid such absurdities would be to qualify the description of my mental image. If I called it something other than a memory – say, an apparent memory or a quasi-memory[36] – then I wouldn't imply that it was veridical.

Yet my claim to remember that I saw Austerlitz wouldn't lead to absurd conclusions if it was properly understood. In saying "I remember that I saw Austerlitz," I am indeed claiming to occupy a mental state whose content is true. But I am not attributing to that state the content that would be conveyed by my saying "I saw Austerlitz" in *oratio recta*, where "I" would refer to the speaker, DV. Rather, I'm attributing to it the content that would be conveyed by an accompanying image of the utterance "I see Austerlitz," where "I" would refer to the original viewer. So I'm not reporting that I, DV, witnessed the battle of Austerlitz; I'm merely reporting memories of Austerlitz in which a witness of it is the notional "me."[37]

These are indeed desperate expedients, but only because they rely on an exchange of bodies or identities, which is quite unnecessary. What the subject of this transplanted memory should say is "I remember that I was Derek Parfit arriving at Bournemouth." This claim says nothing about an exchange between Parfit and the remembering subject, because – as I shall argue in the text – the second "I" is, not a reference to the rememberer, but a quasi-indicator echoing the first-personal conception under which Parfit's arrival at Bournemouth is being remembered. Similarly, my belief in having inherited Napoleon's visual image of Austerlitz should lead me to say, "I remember that I was Napoleon viewing the battle of Austerlitz." Again, the arguments required for a defense of this report are contained in the text, later.

[36] For the term "quasi-memory," see Sydney Shoemaker, "Persons and Their Pasts," *American Philosophical Quarterly* 7 (1970): 269–85. Actually, the mental states I am discussing would not be called quasi-memories by Shoemaker, because they are, as I put it, "recovered from" – and hence appropriately caused by – the original experiences.

[37] Thus, in "I remember that I saw Austerlitz," the second "I" is a quasi-indicator, which Castañeda would write with an asterisk, thus: "I remember that I* saw Austerlitz." So formulated, this statement begins to look like the formulations in Carol Rovane's "Branching Self-Consciousness" (*The Philosophical Review* 99 [1990]: 355–95, 368 ff.). According to Rovane, my image of Austerlitz would have to be reported as a quasi-memory of what "*I**" – rather than "I" – saw.

The resulting similarity between my view and Rovane's is potentially misleading, however. Rovane introduces "I*" as a "new pronoun" that is needed, she believes, because a

My mental image is indeed notionally reflexive with respect to such a person, if (as I believe) it was inherited from Napoleon. For in that case, the referential scheme of the image is not dependent on any prior specification of NB as the notional subject. Napoleon is the notional subject of my image because it is presented to me as derived from the visual experience of an original viewer, and that viewer was (so I believe) NB. His being the notional subject of the image is thus a matter of historical fact rather than stipulation; and so the image picks him out as "me" unselfconsciously, just by pointing to him in the center of its referential scheme.

Thus, if my mental image was inherited from Napoleon, then it represents Austerlitz as seen by a notional "me." I claim no more in saying "I remember that I saw Austerlitz." So why should I qualify my claim?

Some would answer that if I take myself to have an image of Austerlitz as it looked to Napoleon, then I shouldn't call it a memory, because a memory of how Austerlitz looked would have to be a memory of how it looked to me. In the view of these philosophers, experiential memory necessarily represents things as having been experienced by oneself, and it is "immune to error through misidentification" on this score.[38]

In my view, however, the nature of experiential memory can be fully explained by the fact that it represents things as experienced by a notional subject, whom it casts in the notional first-person, as "me." My memory of seeing something is necessarily a memory of *my* seeing it for the same reason that my image of being someone is necessarily an image of *my* being him – that is, simply because it is a first-personal way of thinking about the subject in question.[39]

---

report of what "I" experienced would pick out the subject of that experience as someone identical with me, the subject of memory. Since these subjects are not identical in this case, Rovane would have me replace the ordinary "I" with a different pronoun. In my view, however, the ordinary pronoun used in memory reports is the one that should be written as "I*," and it should be written this way precisely because it's a quasi-indicator that *doesn't* pick out the original subject as identical with me. I therefore deny that a new pronoun is needed: "I*" is just philosophical notation for the first-person pronoun as it is already used in memory reports. (For the same reasons, I shall also deny that there is any need for the notion of quasi-memory.)

[38] For these claims, see Shoemaker, "Persons and their Pasts," and Evans, *Varieties of Reference*, 235–48. More recent discussions include: John Campbell, "The Reductionist View of the Self"; and Andy Hamilton, "A New Look at Personal Identity."

[39] As P. F. Strawson put it: "[J]ust as nothing counts as an experience of a present state of consciousness which doesn't count as an experience of *being, oneself*, in that state of consciousness, so nothing counts ... as an apparent memory of a past state of consciousness which doesn't count as an apparent memory of *being, oneself*, in that state of

To be sure, such a memory cannot misidentify the viewer in represent-ing him as me. But it cannot thereby misidentify the viewer, I say, only because it doesn't thereby identify him at all. A visual memory represents the viewer as me only in the sense that it represents the viewer *as the viewer*, who occupies first-person position in the visual scheme of reference. The original viewer was "me" in this sense no matter who he was, just by virtue of being the notional subject of the image; and his having been "me" in this sense does not entail his having been DV. Memory can thus succeed in making someone "me" to me even if he was Napoleon – not, of course, by making him the same person as me, but rather by presenting him to me in the notional first-person.

The assertion that experiential memory can make Napoleon "me" to me sounds like Locke's assertion that memory makes a person "self to himself" across time. It therefore suggests a way of re-interpreting Locke's theory of personal identity, by suggesting a perspectival sense in which one can be "self to oneself."[40]

The word "self" has two related but ultimately distinct strands of mean-ing. It connotes both identity and reflexivity, and either of these connota-tions might dominate when the word serves as a noun. On the one hand, a past self of mine might be one and the same person as me, identified at some time in the past. On the other hand, a past self might be someone in the past whom I can think of reflexively, in the first-person. In the first sense, selfhood is a metaphysical relation that holds between per-sons at times, if they are the same person. In the second sense, selfhood

---

consciousness.... What we have here is an enriched version of Kant's repeated point about the 'I think' merely being the form of consciousness in general" ("Kant's Par-alogisms: Self-Consciousness and the 'Outside Observer'," in *Theorie der Subjectivität*, ed. Konrad Cramer et al. [Frankfurt:Suhrkamp, 1987], 203–19, 216–17).

[40] *An Essay Concerning Human Understanding*, ed. Peter H. Nidditch (Oxford: Oxford Uni-versity Press, 1975), Book II, Chapter xxvii. See also the following passage, in which Kant criticizes the notion that first-personal thought reveals the existence of a persisting mental substance:

Despite the logical identity of the 'I', such a change may have occurred in it as does not allow of the retention of its identity, and yet we may ascribe to it the same-sounding 'I', which in every different state, even in one involving change of the [thinking] sub-ject, might still retain the thought of the preceding subject and so hand it over to the subsequent subject. (*Critique of Pure Reason*, trans. Norman Kemp Smith [New York: St. Martin's Press, 1965], 342.)

This passage is related to Locke's argument purporting to show "that two thinking Sub-stances may make but one Person" at different times (*Essay*, 338). As Kant's version of the argument makes clear, however, what the argument really shows is that different thinking substances could be accessible to one another's first-personal thought – which, as I am about to suggest, makes them one and the same *self*.

is a psychological relation that holds between subjects who are on first-personal terms.

Memory really does make a person "self to himself" in the latter sense. When I entertain experiential memories, I have thoughts that present a past individual to me in the notional first-person. Memory thereby recruits past selves for me, by putting them within reach of subjectively reflexive thought.

Locke's memory theory is thus a correct account of perspectival self-hood. Of course, Locke clearly intended the theory to be a metaphysics of persons. But what if he confused the two?[41] Maybe Locke got perspectival selfhood right but then mistook it for personal identity.[42]

In order to minimize confusion, let me divide the available meanings between the terms "selfhood" and "personal identity." From now on, I'll use "selfhood" to denote the relation borne to me by those whom I can think of first-personally – my grammatical person-mates, so to speak, whom I shall call "selves." I'll use "personal identity" for the relation among those who are one and the same person, and I'll describe them as the same person rather than as selves.

If Locke had been clearer-headed, he might have offered a theory of selfhood and left it at that. This theory would have had nothing to say about whether Napoleon and I are the same person; but it would have had plenty to say about whether Napoleon was among my past selves. Napoleon was a past self of mine, the theory would have said, if I have memories derived from his experiences and can therefore think of him in the first-person, just by pointing to him unselfconsciously as "me."

Of course, Napoleon wasn't really a past self of mine. My memory of surveying a desolate field may make me think that he was, by making me think that he is the referent of the first-person in its referential scheme.

---

[41] This interpretation of Locke was suggested by Elizabeth Anscombe in "The First Person," 25–26. The present essay can in fact be read as an attempt to salvage something of interest from the confusion that Anscombe identified in Locke. For a different theory of selfhood as based on reflexivity rather than identity, see Robert Nozick, *Philosophical Explanations* (Cambridge, MA: Harvard University Press, 1981), 71–114.

[42] Here I do not mean to imply that Locke's metaphysics of persons is necessarily wrong. Indeed, one might argue that Locke ended up getting the metaphysics of persons right by thinking in perspectival terms. For under some conceptions of what persons are, their persistence through time might reasonably be thought to depend on relations of first-person accessibility between temporally disparate points of view, and hence on perspectival selfhood. Yet to say that persons are entities whose identity depends on perspectival selfhood is to make a substantive philosophical claim, which must not be obscured by a conflation of the metaphysical and perspectival notions. (In fact, however, I do not think that a theory of perspectival selfhood can serve as a theory of metaphysical identity without some modification, for reasons that are explained in note 53.)

But the referent of "me" in my memory image is the subject from whom the image has been inherited, and that person wasn't really NB.

In reality, let's suppose, my memory is derived from a visual experience received on Breed's Hill in 1976, during a 4th of July celebration reenacting a Revolutionary battle. The battlefield represented in my memory image must therefore be Breed's Hill rather than Austerlitz, and the referent of "me" in the image is the person who stood at its vantage point, undergoing the visual experience from which it is derived – DV, as it happens, rather than NB.[43]

Since NB is not the person whose encounter with the depicted scene produced this image, he is not the notional subject of the image, and the image doesn't recruit him as one of my former selves. He can of course be an imaginary self of mine, since I can pretend to have notionally reflexive thoughts about him. But these thoughts would not be genuinely reflexive with respect to NB, because they would have to be self-consciously centered on him before they could point to him, at their center, as "me." Because I am not really on first-personal terms with Napoleon, he is not really one of my former selves.

A clearer-headed Locke might have offered this theory of selfhood, but would we have had any use for it? Isn't personal identity what we really care about? If so, the Lockean theory of selfhood would have been true but pointless.

I now want to argue that this theory would not have been pointless, because selfhood is of independent philosophical interest. Indeed, I think that some of the deepest concerns expressed in terms of personal identity are actually perspectival concerns about the self.

In order to address these concerns, however, Locke would have had to extend his theory slightly. For they are primarily concerns, not about whose past we are remembering, but rather about whose future, if any, we are in a position to anticipate. And addressing these concerns would have required Locke to extend his theory from the past selves who are recruited by memory to the future selves who are recruited by anticipation.

5. Who I Will Be

What we most want to know about our survival, I believe, is how much of the future we are in a position to anticipate experiencing. We peer up

---

[43] On this point, see Hidé Ishiguro, "Imagination II," *Proceedings of the Aristotelian Society* Supp. Vol. 41 (1967): 37–56, 43, 52.

the stream of consciousness, so to speak, and wonder how far up there is still a stream to see.

To wonder how much of the future I can anticipate experiencing is just to wonder how far into the future there will be experiences that I am now in a position to prefigure first-personally. If this question truly expresses what I want to know about my survival, then what I want to know is a matter of perspective rather than metaphysics. My question is not how long there will be an individual identical with my present self, DV. My question is how long there will be someone to occupy the position that is the center of my self-centered projections – someone to serve as the referent of "me" as it occurs in my prospective thoughts. The future "me" whose existence matters here is picked out precisely by his owning a point of view into which I am attempting to project my representations of the future, just as a past "me" can be picked out by his having owned the point of view from which I have recovered representations of the past.

One complication is that in the context of anticipation, the reference of "me" may not be determined as it is in the context of memory. "I" refers to the notional subject in either case, but the notional subject may not be determined in quite the same way.

Suppose that while preparing for this year's 4th of July celebration, I anticipate my role in the annual reenactment of a Revolutionary battle. I conjure up a mental image of the climactic moment – the field, the tunic, and so on. In its intrinsic features, this mental image is no different from that in a memory or an imagining. What differentiates it from these images must be how it is presented.[44] Whereas the image in a memory is presented as the vestige of a past experience, for example, the image in anticipation must be presented – or intentionally framed – as prefiguring a future experience.

In the case of memory, we noted, the presentation of an image does not fully determine its references. Even when I think that I'm recalling Napoleon's experiences at Austerlitz, my memory is not an image of Austerlitz if it is actually derived from a glimpse of Breed's Hill.[45]

---

[44] On the question of how an image is "presented," see note 18.

[45] Of course, what places the references of an image under the control of its causal history may be its presentation as a recovered experience. After all, an image that was actually derived from a glimpse of Breed's Hill could subsequently be incorporated into an imagining of Austerlitz – in which case, its causal history would not prevent the imaginer's intention from making it refer to Austerlitz instead of Breed's Hill. But when an image is presented as reprising a past experience, its references are thereby hitched to its origins in experience, despite concomitant misjudgments as to what those origins might be. (Here I am indebted to Michaelis Michael for his objections to a purely causal analysis of a memory's references.)

But the reverse appears to be true of images framed in anticipation. My anticipatory image is of the forthcoming military maneuvers precisely because I think of it as prefiguring my experience of those maneuvers. The presentation of this image may even consist in an intention on my part, which places the image's references under my voluntary control. For I may conjure up the image with the express intention of thereby prefiguring the experience of playing my role in the reenacted battle – in which case, the image is of playing my role, as I intend.[46]

In this respect, anticipation appears to resemble imagination, whose references are similarly determined by an accompanying intention or stipulation. Unfortunately, this resemblance seems to prevent anticipation from providing a context in which I can think about future individuals unselfconsciously as "me." In framing a mental image with the intention of prefiguring a future experience, I have to specify the experience to be prefigured. And in order to specify the experience, don't I have to specify its subject?

If so, I will end up deliberately centering my image on someone, and then it won't be a genuinely first-personal thought about him, since I won't have picked him out simply by pointing to him at its center. He will be at most an imaginary self of mine. Perhaps, then, my future selves are all imaginary.

I think that there are indeed modes of anticipation in which I project myself into the perspective of the future DV in a manner no different from that in which I can project myself into just anyone's point of view. In these cases, anticipating my future amounts to no more than imagining the future life of DV. But there are other modes of anticipation, I think, which are quite unselfconscious about the future perspectives that they prefigure, and which consequently place me on genuinely first-personal terms with future subjects. I shall argue that these modes of anticipation ground a distinction between real and imaginary future selves.

One such mode of anticipation is that in which I frame an intention to do something in the future. Framing an intention entails projecting myself into a future perspective because it entails representing the intended action from the point of view of the agent who is to perform it.

Of course, the agent who is to perform any action that I intend must be me, since I can't intend the actions of others. But intentions of doing

---

[46] I may therefore enjoy infallibility with respect to the references of my anticipation. See Wittgenstein's remarks on this subject in *The Blue and Brown Books* (Oxford: Blackwell, 1972), 39.

something are always intentions of *my* doing it, I would argue, in the same sense as memories of seeing something are always memories of *my* seeing it – namely, in the sense that these attitudes always have a notional subject, whom they present as "me."

Intentions always have a notional subject because their function is to be acted on, and they can be acted on only if they are drawn from the agent's point of view. Intentions are consequently framed in a referential scheme centered on their potential executor, who is thereby thought of as "me," no matter who he will be.[47]

Intention resembles memory, furthermore, in that I do not have to stipulate who its notional subject shall be. For if my intention is going to be executed, its executor will have to be the person who finds himself in possession of the intention when the time for executing it arrives.

An intention must be framed on the assumption that it or its mental traces will persist until they can serve as a basis for action.[48] In framing an intention, then, I project my thoughts into the future in two distinct senses. On the one hand, I project my thoughts into the future in the sense that I represent the world from a specified future point of view. On the other hand, I project my thoughts into the future in the sense that I *send* them into the future, by depositing them in memory for future retrieval. And the point of view into which I mean to project my thoughts in the first sense is simply that point of view into which I shall have projected them in the second. That is, I mean to represent an action from that perspective at which this representation will, at the relevant moment, be available as a basis on which to act.[49]

47 This statement oversimplifies a very complicated story. In many cases, intentions cannot be framed from the executor's perspective, because his perspective cannot yet be fully envisioned. For example, I may intend to go north in the future because I cannot yet envision whether going north, at the relevant point in my travels, will entail going left or right, backwards or straight ahead. But if I intend to go north, my intention is incomplete, precisely because it will have to be translated into self-centered terms before I can act on it.

48 This assumption need not be distinct from the intention, since part of what is intended may be precisely that this very intention persist until it can be put into action. See, for example, Gilbert Harman's view that intentions refer to themselves as causes of the intended actions (*Change in View: Principles of Reasoning* [Cambridge, MA: Bradford Books, 1986], 85 ff.).

49 To speak of the perspective at which the representation itself will be available is of course to presuppose a theory of diachronic identity for mental representations – which may be too much of a presupposition in this context. But my references to the storage and retrieval of a single, persisting representation can be replaced with references to a momentary representation and its causal descendants at later times. The language of persisting representations is just an expository convenience.

Thus, I don't have to specify a person from whose point of view I am trying to frame my intention, because that point of view is fixed by the future causal history of the intention itself. I attempt to frame the intention, if you will, from the intention's own future perspective, the perspective in which the intention itself will turn up to be executed. Just as a memory purports to represent the past from the perspective at which it originated in experience, so an intention purports to represent the future from the perspective at which it will arrive to guide action. In either case, the relevant perspective is picked out by the natural history of the representation itself; and the referent of "me" in the context is simply whoever fills the role of subject within that perspective.

As it happens, of course, the perspective at which any intention of mine will turn up to be executed, and from which I have therefore tried to frame it, will belong to the future David Velleman. This older DV will turn out to occupy the position of notional subject in my intention, and so he will turn out to be the person of whom I was thinking first-personally in the context. Being accessible to unselfconscious first-personal thought on my part, he qualifies as my real future self.

The double projection that characterizes intentions is not confined to practical thought, however. Even when I am just picturing the future, without planning to do anything in it, I usually regard my mental image as entering into a future perspective both representationally and causally. I don't just anticipate experiencing the future; I anticipate experiencing it as the payoff of this anticipation, as the cadence resolving the present, anticipatory phrase of thought. Now, a musical phrase is resolved by its final notes only for a listener who is still mindful of how it began. So when I anticipate experiencing the future as resolving this anticipation, I picture it as experienced from a perspective in which this picture is recalled.

This mode of projective thought has a look and feel all its own. Within the frame of my anticipatory image, I glimpse a state of mind that will include a memory of its having been glimpsed through this frame – as if the image were a window through which to climb into the prefigured experience.[50] Anticipating the future in this manner, I once again look to future selves unselfconsciously. I don't specify the notional subject of my anticipatory image. He is simply the person who will confront the envisioned future with this image at his back, glimpsed in memory as the

---

[50] This "window" is unfortunately not a WYSIWYG environment: What You See looking through it Is not necessarily What You Get upon climbing through.

image through which his state was glimpsed in anticipation. And he is a real future self of mine because, as the one who will experience the imagined future from the other side of this image, he is picked out by the natural history of the image, as the person whom it presents in the notional first-person.

Finally, my allusions to future subjects can be unselfconscious without necessarily involving the thought that they themselves will be remembered. My prior image of an event may produce various other thoughts, emotions, or inclinations whose remnants will color a future experience of the event even if no memory of the image itself remains. I can then picture the event as experienced in the psychological wake of this picture, whether or not a memory of itself will be among the items that the picture leaves in its wake.

If the wake of an experiential image is expected to wash over the prefigured experience, the image may then be constrained in what it can justifiably portray. I'm hardly entitled to anticipate an event as being experienced with shock and disbelief from a perspective that will have been influenced even indirectly by this anticipation, since the event is unlikely to incite either shock or disbelief in a mind bearing the traces of its having been hereby anticipated. Conversely, there may be events that I'm entitled to anticipate as being met with equanimity only from a future perspective that will retain traces of this anticipation.

What will transpire in perspectives that intercommunicate with mine in this fashion matters more to me than what will transpire in other perspectives. Indeed, my epistemic relation to these perspectives may partly constitute their mattering to me. To imagine a future pain, for example, as it will feel in the psychological wake of my hereby imagining it is to do more than just imagine it. It's to imagine the pain as befalling a mind that has somehow been prepared by this very prospect of its occurrence. And to imagine a pain as experienced by a mind hereby so prepared for it is already to brace for the pain, to shrink from it, or to be otherwise caught up in it in some way. Anticipation that's cognizant of its effect on the prefigured experiences is thus a form of mental engagement with them that, to some degree, already constitutes their mattering.

This engagement with future experiences coincides, of course, with an ability to regard their subjects unselfconsciously as "me." When I frame an image prefiguring an experience that will follow in the image's wake, causally speaking, I needn't specify for whom the experience will follow: in the context of the image, the experience is simply "to follow" – to follow the image itself, that is. The image thus prefigures the experience simply as forthcoming, and so it provides a context for thinking about the subject of that experience unselfconsciously as "me."

6. Why "Me"?

In sum, anticipation that engages its object tends to be genuinely first-personal, and vice versa. This association may help to explain why I care about my future selves: they are the persons whose experiences I cannot prefigure without already being caught up in them, as lying in the wake of this anticipation.

But the association between selfhood and engaged anticipation is merely an association, which can sometimes fail, if not in reality, then at least in imaginary circumstances. The question therefore arises whether I care about my selves only in virtue of my psychological engagement with them. Or do I care about my selves as such?

The best way to approach this question will be to entertain an imaginary case in which selfhood and psychological engagement come apart. I will therefore conclude with a brief discussion of a familiar philosophical fiction.

Imagine that my brain will be divided and each half transplanted into a different body, with the result that two people will wake up tomorrow remembering my past and carrying on my anticipations and intentions for the future.[51] If I know what is in store for me, I can frame anticipations today that will have effects on, and perhaps be remembered in, two different perspectives tomorrow. Hence I can actively anticipate the future as experienced by two different people.

Even so, I cannot make either person the notional subject of my anticipations unselfconsciously. Suppose that I try to think ahead into some future moment at which I shall have two psychological successors. If I try to picture the moment as it will appear in an experience specified merely as forthcoming, or to follow, I won't succeed in picking out the perspective from which I'm trying to picture it, since my picture may be followed, in the relevant sense, by two different experiences of the moment in question, and I cannot be trying to draw it from both perspectives at once. Similarly, my anticipation may be remembered in two

---

[51] See David Wiggins, *Identity and Spatio-Temporal Continuity* (Oxford: Blackwell, 1967), 50; and Parfit, *Reasons and Persons*, 254 ff. Parfit says (fn. 40), "I decided to study philosophy almost entirely because I was enthralled by Wiggins's imagined case."

different perspectives, and so I cannot frame it from a perspective specified merely as that in which it will be remembered.

In order to specify the perspective from which I'm trying to picture the future, I'll have to identify it with one of my psychological successors or the other.[52] That is, I'll have to pick out the person whose perspective is the intended target and destination of my projective thoughts – whereupon I'll be doing exactly what I do when imagining that I am Napoleon. My anticipation of the future will be nothing more than an act of imagination.

By depriving me of unique future perspectives, fission would deprive me of real future selves.[53] It wouldn't prevent me from being fully engaged with both successors, however, since both lie in the causal path of my present thoughts. The question is whether anticipatory engagement with them would preserve all that matters about survival. Would I suffer a significant loss in having no subject with whom I was on genuinely first-personal terms?

My inclination is to say that I would indeed suffer a loss. I could no longer think just about how the future would look; I'd have to think about how it would look to particular, specified observers. I could no longer plan just to act; I'd have to plan actions to be performed by particular, specified agents. I could no longer imagine a future as existing simply on the other side of this image; I'd have to imagine it as existing on one or another of the image's "other sides," in the lives of one or another of my psychological successors.

Here I am tempted to borrow again from Bernard Williams, by saying that my relations with successors-by-fission would always involve "one thought too many." Williams coined this phrase to express the loss of intimacy that a Kantian moral agent would suffer in relations with others.[54]

---

[52] This point figures prominently in Rovane's "Branching Self-Consciousness."

[53] Note that first-person reference is asymmetrical in this case. Although I cannot refer first-personally to the products of my fission, they can refer first-personally to me, in the context of their experiential memories. This result strikes me as intuitively correct. When I imagine undergoing fission tomorrow, I don't seem to have much of a future; but when I imagine that I am the product of fission that occurred yesterday, I still seem to have a complete past. (This intuition is shared by Simon Blackburn, "Has Kant Refuted Parfit?") This result also demonstrates that selfhood, defined perspectivally, cannot coincide with the identity of a person, since selfhood turns out to be asymmetric whereas relations of identity cannot.

For the claim that "creatures involved in fission and fusion could have nothing like our ordinary use of the first person," see John Campbell, *Past, Space, and Self,* 97. Campbell bases this claim on very different grounds.

[54] "Persons, Character, and Morality," in *Moral Luck* (Cambridge: Cambridge University Press, 1981), 1–19.

I, too, am using the phrase to express a loss of intimacy, but the intimacy lost in this case would be in relation to my own psychological successors, and the excess thought would simply be the thought of who they were. In cases of fission, I would have to identify particular successors before I could enter their perspectives: there would be no future perspectives that I could enter without a second thought. And the second thought of whose perspective I was entering would be an alienating thought, one too many for the intimacy that holds among selves.

In some respects, of course, I would still be in a position to anticipate the lives of my successors "from the inside," as we sometimes say. In particular, I would be able to project my thoughts into their perspectives both causally and representationally, sending into their points of view images drawn from those points of view. But in another respect I would no longer be in a position to anticipate any future life from the inside, since there would be no life that I could anticipate without first picking it out for the purpose of projecting myself into it. Surely, a position from which I must deliberately project myself into a life is not a position on the inside of that life.

My sense, then, is that the ability to prefigure future experiences unselfconsciously is an important part of having a future at all. Not being just plain "me" to myself would be more than the loss of a pronoun; it would be the loss of a self-intimacy that is part of what matters about having future selves.

9

The Self as Narrator

Many philosophers have thought that human autonomy includes, or perhaps even consists in, a capacity for self-constitution – a capacity, that is, to define or invent or create oneself.[1] Unfortunately, self-constitution sounds not just magical but paradoxical, as if the rabbit could go solo and pull himself out of the hat. Suspicions about the very idea of this trick have sometimes been allayed by appeal to the political analogy implicit in the term "self-constitution": a person is claimed to constitute himself in the same way as a polity does, by writing, ratifying, and revising articles of constitution.[2] But a polity is constituted, in the first instance, by its

---

[1] A list of philosophers who have held this view would include Charles Taylor (*Sources of the Self: The Making of the Modern Identity* [Cambridge, MA: Harvard University Press, 1989]; *Human Agency and Language* [Cambridge: Cambridge University Press, 1985]); Harry Frankfurt (*The Importance of What We Care About* [Cambridge: Cambridge University Press, 1987]); Christine Korsgaard (*The Sources of Normativity* [Cambridge: Cambridge University Press, 1996]; "Self-Constitution in the Ethics of Plato and Kant," *Journal of Ethics* 3 [1999]: 1–29); Tamar Schapiro ("What Is a Child?" *Ethics* 109 [1999]: 715–38); and Michael Bratman ("Reflection, Planning, and Temporally Extended Agency," *Philosophical Review* 109 [2000]: 35–61).

[2] See, especially, Schapiro.

The material in this chapter was first presented to a seminar on the self, taught in the fall of 1999 at the University of Michigan. Versions of the chapter have been presented to the philosophy departments of the University of Pittsburgh, the University of Maryland, the University of Chicago, and the University of Göttingen; to a conference on Morality and the Arts at the University of California, Riverside, with John Martin Fischer serving as commentator; and as one of the Jerome Simon Lectures at the University of Toronto. I have received helpful comments from the audiences on these occasions as well as from Linda Brakel and Dan Dennett. The chapter first appeared in *Autonomy and the Challenges to Liberalism: New Essays*, edited by Joel Anderson and John Christman (Cambridge: Cambridge University Press, 2005), 56–57, and is reprinted here with the permission of the publisher.

constituent persons, who are constituted antecedently to it; and suspicions therefore remain about the idea of self-constitution at the level of the individual person.

One philosopher has tried to save personal self-constitution from suspicions of paradox by freely admitting that it is a trick. A real rabbit can't pull himself out of a hat, according to this philosopher, but an illusory rabbit can appear to do so: the secret of the trick is that the rabbit isn't real. We ask, "But if the rabbit isn't real – and there's no magician, either – then who is performing the trick?" He replies, "Why, of course: the hat." A rabbit can't pull himself out of a hat, but a hat can make it appear that a rabbit is pulling himself out of it.

Notwithstanding my frivolous analogy, I think that there is much to be learned from this view of self-constitution, and so I propose to examine it in detail and to offer my own variation on it. The philosopher in question is Daniel Dennett, and his view is that the autonomous person (the rabbit) is an illusion conjured up by the human organism (the hat).[3] In the end, I will adopt most of Dennett's view, except for the part about the rabbit's being unreal. In my view, the rabbit really does pull himself out of the hat, after all.

Dennett's metaphor for this process is not sleight-of-hand but fiction. In Dennett's metaphor, the self is the non-existent author of a merely fictional autobiography composed by the human organism, which neither is nor embodies a real self.[4] So understood, the self has the status of an *abstractum*, a fictional object that we "use as part of a theoretical apparatus to understand, and predict, and make sense of, the behavior of some very complicated things"[5] – namely, human beings, including ourselves.

Dennett compares the human's autobiography to the spider's web or the beaver's dam:

Our fundamental tactic of self-protection, self-control, and self-definition is not spinning webs or building dams, but telling stories, and more particularly

---

[3] "The Origins of Selves," *Cogito* 3 (1989): 163–73 [hereinafter OS]; "The Reality of Selves," in *Consciousness Explained* (Boston: Little, Brown and Company, 1991), Chapter 13 [RS]; "The Self as a Center of Narrative Gravity," in *Self and Consciousness: Multiple Perspectives*, eds., Frank S. Kessel, Pamela M. Cole, and Dale L. Johnson (Hillsdale, NJ: Erlbaum Associates, 1992), 103–115 [CNG]; with Nicholas Humphrey, "Speaking for Our Selves," reprinted in *Brainchildren: Essays on Designing Minds* (Cambridge, MA: MIT Press, 1998), 31–58 [SO].

[4] Dennett describes his view as a "middle-ground position" on the question "whether there really are selves" (RS, 413).

[5] CNG, 114–15.

concocting and controlling the story we tell others – and ourselves – about who we are. [...] These strings or streams of narrative issue forth *as if* from a single source – not just in the obvious physical sense of flowing from just one mouth, or one pencil or pen, but in a more subtle sense: their effect on any audience is to encourage them to (try to) posit a unified agent whose words they are, about whom they are: in short, to posit a *center of narrative gravity*. [RS, 418]

The point of this last phrase is that an object's physical center of gravity can figure in legitimate scientific explanations but mustn't be identified with any physical part of the object:

That would be a category mistake. A center of gravity is *just* an abstractum. It is just a fictional object. But when I say it is a fictional object, I do not mean to disparage it; it is a wonderful fictional object, and it has a perfectly legitimate place within serious, sober, *echt* physical science. [CNG, 104]

Similarly, the "unified agent" conjured up by our narrative is a theoretical abstraction, but it too has a legitimate place in a serious theory. Dennett concludes the analogy as follows:

[W]e are virtuoso novelists, who find ourselves engaged in all sorts of behavior, more or less unified, but sometimes disunified, and we always put the best "faces" on it we can. We try to make all of our material cohere into a single good story. And that story is our autobiography. The chief fictional character at the center of that autobiography is one's *self*. And if you still want to know what the self *really* is, you are making a category mistake. [CNG, 114]

What exactly is the category mistake that we make about the self, according to Dennett? I shall first attempt to identify the mistake, and then I'll consider whether it really is a mistake. Specifically, I'll ask whether Dennett himself can afford to call it a mistake, given the philosophical commitments he undertakes in the course of diagnosing it. I shall argue that in at least some respects, the conception of the self that Dennett calls mistaken is in fact likely to be correct.

In arguing against Dennett's diagnosis of this mistake, I shall not be arguing against his positive conception of the self as the fictive protagonist of a person's autobiography.[6] On the contrary, I'll argue that Dennett's positive conception of the self is largely right. My only disagreement with

---

[6] I use the term "fictive" because, to my ear, it shares with "fictional" the sense of "invented" or "made up," but not the sense of "untrue." Those who do not already share these linguistic intuitions should take them as stipulated hereby.

Dennett will be that, whereas he regards an autobiography as fictive and consequently false in characterizing its protagonist, I regard it as both fictive and true. We invent ourselves, I shall argue, but we really are the characters whom we invent.

Dennett describes our mistaken conception as "the myth of selves as brain-pearls, particular concrete, countable things rather than abstractions."[7] Sometimes he suggests that this myth mistakenly credits the self with physical existence, as "a proper physical part of an organism or a brain."[8] But he also considers a version of the myth in which the self resides in software rather than hardware, as "a supervisory brain program, a central controller, or whatever."[9] Mostly, Dennett relies on metaphors that can be read as alluding either to hardware or software: the "Oval Office in the brain, housing a Highest Authority"[10] or "the Cartesian Theater with its Witness or Central Meaner"[11] or "the central headquarters responsible for organizing and directing all the subsidiary bureaucracies that keep life and limb together."[12]

Dennett cannot be faulted for describing the self in metaphorical terms. His thesis, after all, is that the self is like one of those mythical beasts that incorporate parts from different creatures and straddle boundaries between different realms, in a way that defies literal description. Yet unless we understand what Dennett thinks is wrong with our conception of the self, we cannot understand what he thinks is right about his own, alternative conception. So we must look behind Dennett's metaphors for the error that they purport to reveal.

In Dennett's view, our error about the self is to assume that the protagonist of a human being's autobiography is identical with the author. Dennett imagines that his own autobiography opens in the manner of *Moby Dick* – "Call me Dan" – and he claims that this opening sentence would prompt us to apply that name to "the theorists' fiction created by . . . well, not by me but by my brain [. . .]."[13] In Dennett's view, then, the author of his autobiography is his brain, whereas the "me" whom we call Dan is a purely fictional narrator, who is no more the real author

[7] RS, 424. See p. 423: "independently existing soul-pearls."
[8] RS, 420.
[9] RS, 420.
[10] RS, 428.
[11] RS, 422.
[12] OS, 163.
[13] RS, 429.

of the story than Ishmael is the author of the story that begins "Call me Ishmael." Dennett concludes:

Our tales are spun, but for the most part we don't spin them; they spin us. Our human consciousness, and our narrative selfhood, is their product, not their source. [RS, 418]

But in what respect does the real source of Dennett's autobiography differ from the fictional source that it conjures up for itself? Why should Dan be compared to Ishmael rather than the author of a veridical auto-biography, who really is identical with the protagonist of his story?

This question is especially pressing in light of the sophistication with which Dennett is obliged to credit his real autobiographer. The brain that composes Dennett's autobiography has to be so clever as to approximate the powers of its supposedly fictional protagonist. We may therefore sus-pect that Dennett, now in his capacity as philosopher, has tacitly posited the existence of a real self to serve as the inventor of the supposedly fictional one. Dennett anticipates and counters this suspicion:

Now, how can I make the claim that a self – your own real self, for instance – is rather like a fictional character? Aren't all *fictional* selves dependent for their very creation on the existence of *real* selves? It may seem so, but I will argue that this is an illusion. Let us go back to Ishmael. Ishmael is a fictional character [...]. But, one thinks, Ishmael was created by Melville, and Melville is a real character – was a real character – a real self. Doesn't this show that it takes a real self to create a fictional self? I think not, but if I am to convince you, I must push you through an exercise of the imagination. [CNG, 107]

The exercise mentioned here is to imagine a robot that emits a running narration of its life, as the story of a character named Gilbert:

"Call me Gilbert," it says. What follows is the apparent autobiography of this fictional Gilbert. Now Gilbert is a fictional, created self but its creator is no self. Of course there were human designers who designed the machine, but they did not design Gilbert. Gilbert is the product of a process in which there are no selves at all. [*Ibid.*]

Dennett insists that he is not committed to crediting the robot with selfhood:

That is, I am *stipulating* that this is not a conscious machine, not a "thinker." It is a dumb machine, but it does have the power to write a passable novel. [*Ibid.*]

[T]he robot's *brain*, the robot's computer, really knows nothing about the world; *it* is not a self. It's just a clanky computer. It doesn't know what it's doing. It doesn't even know that it's creating this fictional character. (The same is just as true of your brain: *it* doesn't know what it's doing either.) [CNG, 108]

One might challenge this stipulation as self-contradictory. Stipulating a "dumb machine" that writes a "passable novel," one might think, is like stipulating a blind man who sees. If someone sees, then he isn't really blind; and if something writes a passable novel, then it can't be all that dumb, no matter how loudly it may clank.[14] How, then, can Dennett claim that the computer generating Gilbert's story doesn't know what it's doing?

Part of the answer is that, according to Dennett, the computer isn't conscious; but I want to set aside the concept of consciousness, which is only one aspect of selfhood. To be sure, Gilbert's autobiographer portrays him as conscious, while Dennett denies that he really is. But the robot's claim to be conscious is not quite the same as his claim to be a self. For as we have seen, claiming to be a self entails claiming not only the status of "Witness," who is the subject of experience, but also that of "Central Meaner," "central controller," or "Highest Authority."[15] Indeed, Dennett defines a center of narrative gravity as a fictional "unified agent."[16] Leaving aside the question whether Gilbert's autobiographer is conscious, then, we can ask whether he really is a unified agent in the sense that would satisfy the terms of this fiction.

Here again, one might think that Dennett's stipulation is incoherent, on the grounds that describing something as the author of a novel already entails describing it as a unified agent. Yet I am willing to grant, for the sake of argument, that a passable novel could be authored by a machine endowed with no "Highest Authority," "Central Meaner," or other ironically capitalized locus of agency. What I suggest, however, is that Dennett has equipped Gilbert's and Dan's autobiographers with more than the mere capacity to produce passable novels, and that in doing so, he has implicitly equipped them with enough of a self to be agents.

Dennett denies agency to the inventors of Gilbert and Dan primarily by denying them agential unity. He defends this denial by citing the example

---

[14] If the objection here is merely that writing a passable novel is an activity that is most perspicuously interpreted as the product of a conscious thinker, then Dennett can of course agree, since he believes that positing a conscious thinker, Gilbert, is the most perspicuous way of interpreting the novel-writing robot. What he denies is that writing a novel requires a real, conscious thinker of the sort that would be postulated by such an interpretation.

[15] Quoted at notes 9–11.

[16] RS, 418, quoted after note 13.

of a termite colony:

> The revisionist case is that there really is no proper-self: none of the fictive-selves –
> including one's own firsthand version – corresponds to anything that actually
> exists in one's head.
>
> At first sight this might not seem reasonable. Granted that whatever *is* inside
> the head might be difficult to observe, and granted that it might also be a mistake
> to talk about a "ghostly supervisor," nonetheless there surely has to be some kind
> of a supervisor in there: a supervisory brain program, a central controller, or
> whatever. How else could anybody function – as most people clearly do function –
> as a purposeful and relatively well-integrated agent?
>
> The answer that is emerging from both biology and Artificial Intelligence is
> that complex systems can in fact function in what seems to be a thoroughly "pur-
> poseful and integrated" way simply by having *lots of subsystems doing their own thing*
> without any central supervision. Indeed most systems on earth that appear to
> have central controllers (and are usefully described as having them) do not. The
> behavior of a termite colony provides a wonderful example of it. The colony as
> a whole builds elaborate mounds, gets to know its territory, organizes foraging
> expeditions, sends out raiding parties against other colonies, and so on. [. . .] Yet,
> in fact, all this group wisdom results from nothing other than myriads of individ-
> ual termites, specialized as several different castes, going about their individual
> business – influenced by each other, but quite uninfluenced by any master-plan.
> [SO, 39–40][17]

Dennett illustrates the unreality of central supervision in humans with
the phenomenon of Multiple Personality Disorder (MPD). Writing with a
collaborator, Nicholas Humphrey, he hypothesizes that a child subjected
to severe abuse may be forced to invent more than one fictional self,
whereupon the child is obliged to elect one of these fictional characters as
"Head of Mind," who can then be occasionally deposed by competitors.[18]
The currently active personality purports to be in control, but we who
observe the succession of pretended controllers know that, in reality,
nobody is home.

There is no doubt but that Dennett's fictionalism about the self provides an attractive explanation for the phenomenon diagnosed as MPD.
According to Dennett, the self is like an imaginary friend from our
childhood – an especially close imaginary friend who became not merely
our *alter* ego but, so to speak, our *auto* ego. Just as some of us may have
developed more than one imaginary friend, if we had unusual emotional

---

[17] See also OS, 167–68, and RS, 416, where Dennett remarks, "There is [. . .] no Oval Office
in the anthill," just as he subsequently remarks that "there is no Oval Office in the brain"
[RS, 429].

[18] SO, 41. For another narrative-based analysis of MPD, see Valerie Gray Hardcastle and
Owen Flanagan, "Multiplex vs. Multiple Selves: Distinguishing Dissociative Disorders,"
The Monist 82 (1999): 645–57.

needs, so others may have developed more than one self, in response to unusual circumstances, such as sexual abuse. What could be easier for a child already engaged in populating an imaginary world? And just as our imaginary playmates vied for the status of being our "best friend," so our imaginary selves may vie for the status of being our "true self." If so, then we suffer from MPD. Different selves take control at different times, but only in the same way as different imaginary friends succeed one another as favorite.

At this point, however, there is a gap in Dennett and Humphrey's account. When one imaginary friend supplants another as favorite, nothing much changes in the real world. But when one self supplants another in a patient diagnosed with MPD, the patient's behavior changes dramatically: he walks a different walk, talks a different talk, and expresses different states of mind. Surely, something has changed in the processes controlling his behavior.

Here is how Dennett and Humphrey explain changes of personality:

> The language-producing systems of the brain have to get their instructions from somewhere, and the very demands of pragmatics and grammar would conspire to confer something like Head of Mind authority on whatever subsystem currently controls their input. [...] Suppose, at different times, different subsystems within the brain produce "clusters" of speech that simply cannot easily be interpreted as the output of a single self. Then – as a Bible scholar may discover when working on the authorship of what is putatively a single-authored text – it may turn out that the cluster makes *best sense* when attributed to different selves. [SO, 42–43]

According to this explanation, different modules in the brain take control of the language-producing systems, yielding output whose interpretation calls for postulation of different Heads of Mind. Different selves thus correspond to different actual centers of control, but the selves are still fictional personifications of those centers, different *abstracta* postulated for the sake of interpreting a narrative containing severe discontinuities.

The problem with this explanation is that it accounts only for changes in the patient's verbal behavior, whereas multiples are reported to change their posture, gait, handwriting, and their projects and pursuits as well. Why should discontinuities in the patient's autobiography be accompanied by corresponding changes in the patient's course and manner of action? If a human being just contains "lots of subsystems doing their own thing," then why can't one of them do its thing with his feet even as another does its thing with his mouth, so that he walks the walk of one personality while telling the story of the other?

An answer to this question is implicit in some of Dennett's descriptions of self-narration, but it attributes more sophistication to the self-inventor than Dennett acknowledges. The answer is that an autobiography and the behavior that it narrates are mutually determining.

In the case of the self-narrating robot, Dennett imagines a strict order of determination in one direction. He observes that "[t]he adventures of Gilbert, the fictional character, [. . .] bear a striking and presumably non-coincidental relationship to the adventures of this robot rolling around in the world."[19] And he explains this relationship between story and life by suggesting that the one is determined by the other: "If you hit the robot with a baseball bat, very shortly thereafter the story of Gilbert includes being hit by a baseball bat by somebody who looks like you." Presumably, the robot is designed to tell a story that corresponds to the life of that very robot.

What Dennett doesn't seem to imagine, in the case of this robot, is that he might also be designed to make his life correspond to his story. As Dennett tells it, the robot gets locked in a closet, calls out "Help me," and later sends us a thank-you note for letting him out. But surely a robot smart enough to thank us for letting him out of the closet would also be smart enough to tell us before he went back in. "I'm going into the closet" he would say, "Don't lock the door." And then he'd go into the closet, just as he had said he would. (If he didn't do what he had said, he might get stuck somewhere else and have to wait for help while we went looking for him in the closet.) A robot that can maintain correspondence in one direction, by saying that he's locked in the closet when he is, should be able to maintain correspondence in the other direction, by going into the closet when he has said that he will. Thus, whereas the robot will sometimes update his story to reflect recent events in his career, at other times he will narrate ahead of himself and then follow a career that reflects his story.

Although Dennett doesn't attribute this sort of sophistication to the robot, he does implicitly attribute it to a patient with MPD:

Consider the putatively true case histories recorded in *The Three Faces of Eve* (Thigpen & Cleckley, 1957) and *Sybil* (Schreiber, 1973). Eve's three faces were

---

[19] CNG, 108. Note, then, that Dennett does not conceive of autobiographies as "entirely confabulated" narratives in which "anything goes" (Hardcastle and Flanagan, 650, 653).

the faces of three distinct personalities, it seems, and the woman portrayed in Sybil had many different selves, or so it seems. How can we make sense of this? Here is one way, a solemn, skeptical way favored by the psychotherapists with whom I have talked about the case: When Sybil went in to see her therapist for the first time, she was not several different people rolled into one body. Sybil was a novel-writing machine that fell in with a very ingenious questioner, a very eager reader. And together they collaborated to write many, many chapters of a new novel. And, of course, since Sybil was a sort of living novel, she went out and engaged the world with these new selves, more or less created on demand, under the eager suggestion of a therapist. [CNG, 111]

What does Dennett mean when he says that Sybil "engaged the world with these new selves"? Surely, he means that Sybil *acted out* the stories that she and her therapist had composed. She was a "living novel" in the sense that she not only narrated the roles she played but also played the roles that she narrated.

That's why Sybil's behavior always manifested the personality whose story she was telling at the moment. Her life shaped her story, and her story shaped her life, all because she was designed to maintain correspondence between the two. Hence the control of her speech and the control of her movements were not entirely independent. They were in fact *inter*dependent, since the controller of her speech must have been responsive to her movements, and the controller of her movements must have been responsive to her speech.

Yet if a self-narrator works in both directions, then the self he invents is not just an idle fiction, a useful abstraction for interpreting his behavior. It – or, more precisely, his representation of it – is a determinant of the very behavior that it's useful for interpreting.[20] Indeed, the reason why the narrator's representation of a centrally controlling self is so useful for interpreting his behavior is that it, the representation, really does control his behavior to some extent.

Of course, the central controller he has may not be much like the one he represents himself as having. After all, a self-narrator doesn't represent himself as being centrally controlled by his own story.

---

[20] Flanagan says, "[T]he self as represented has motivational bearing and behavioral effects. Often this motivational bearing is congruent with motivational tendencies that the entire system already has. In such cases, placing one's conception of the self into the motivational circuits enables certain gains in ongoing conscious control and in the fine-tuning of action" ("Multiple Identity, Character Transformation, and Self-Reclamation," in G. Graham and Lynn Stephens, eds., *Philosophical Psychopathology* [Cambridge, MA: MIT Press, 1994], p. 140).

Or does he?

In order to answer this question, we must consider some prior questions that Dennett overlooks. First, consider whether the behaviors attributed to Gilbert by the robot's novel-writing computer include the behavior of writing the novel. When the robot gets locked in a closet, he tells about Gilbert's being locked in a closet; but when he tells the story of Gilbert, does he also tell about Gilbert's telling that story? He says "Call me Gilbert"; but does he ever say, "I'm Gilbert and this is my story"? He writes a note that says "Thank you," but can he also write a note that says "I'm writing to say thanks"? I can't imagine why not.

Nor can I imagine how the robot would tell the story of Gilbert without including information about the causes and effects of the events therein. When he calls for help, he might well elaborate, "I've gotten myself locked in the closet," thus attributing his current predicament to what he did a moment ago. And when he writes his thank-you note, he might well begin, "I'm writing because you let me out of the closet," thereby attributing his present behavior to an earlier cause. A story that merely described one event after another, without mentioning any causal connections, would hardly qualify as a narrative.

Thus, the features of himself that the robot can ascribe to Gilbert ought to include this very activity of self-description; and he should also be able to describe the causes and effects of his activities, including this one. Hence in ascribing his activities to Gilbert, the robot should be able to describe the causes and effects of his doing so.

Now, what causal role might the robot attribute to his own remark, "I'm going into the closet"? He might say, "I'm telling you this because I'm on my way into the closet," thereby casting his speech as an effect of his movements. But this remark would be strictly accurate only if the robot was going into the closet anyway and was merely reporting on his current trajectory. What I have imagined, however, is that the robot goes into the closet partly because of having said so, in order to maintain correspondence between his story and his life. Insofar as the robot can report on the causes and effects of his behavior, then, he ought to say, "I'm going into the closet partly because I've just said so" – or, perhaps, "I'm hereby heading for the closet," a remark that implicitly ascribes this causal role to itself.

I think that human self-narrators make such remarks frequently, whenever they make promises or other verbal commitments, which may be as trivial as "I'm heading for the closet." As you putter around the office at the end of the day, you finally say, "I'm going home," not because you were already about to leave, but because saying so will prompt you to leave. As your hand hovers indecisively over the candy dish, you say, "No, I won't," not because you weren't about to take a candy, but because saying so may stop you from taking one.[21] These utterances are issued *as* commitments, in the understanding that they will feed back into your behavior. Hence you do understand that your running autobiography not only reflects but is also reflected in what you do.

These observations suggest that the "central controller" of a person may indeed be a fiction, not in the sense that it is a fictional character in the person's autobiography, but in the sense that it *is* the person's autobiography – the reflective representation that feeds back into the person's behavior.[22] This central controller is in fact what social psychologists call the self. In the social-psychology literature, the word "self" denotes a person's self-conception rather than the entity, real or imagined, that this conception represents. And the same literature reports evidence for the feedback loop I have posited.

Researchers have found, for example, that subjects tend to predict that they will vote in the next election at a far higher rate than the average turnout; but that the turnout among those who have predicted that they will vote is also higher than the average.[23] Many who wouldn't otherwise have voted, it seems, end up voting because of having predicted that

---

[21] I discuss cases like these in "How to Share an Intention," *Philosophy and Phenomenological Research* 57 (1997): 29–50; reprinted in *The Possibility of Practical Reason* (Oxford: Oxford University Press, 2000).

[22] Dennett almost strays into this second conception of the self. For example:

> A self, according to my theory, is not any old mathematical point, but an abstraction defined by the myriads of attributions and interpretations (including self-attributions and self-interpretations) that have composed the biography of the living body whose Center of Narrative Gravity it is. As such, it plays a singularly important role in the ongoing cognitive economy of that living body, because, of all the things in the environment an active body must make mental models of, none is more crucial than the model the agent has of itself. [RS 426–27]

> Dennett begins this passage by speaking of the self as an abstract object posited by the host's autobiography. But then he speaks of the self as playing "a singularly important role in the ongoing cognitive economy" of the host, and finally he describes it as "the model that the agent has of itself." At this point, it is unclear whether he is speaking of an abstract object or of the host's representation of it, which is a real element in the host's psychology, positioned to play a causal role in his mental economy.

[23] Greenwald, A.G., Carnot, C.G., Beach, R., and Young, B., "Increasing Voting Behavior by Asking People if They Expect to Vote," *Journal of Applied Psychology* 72 (1987): 315–18.

they would, thus conforming their lives to their stories.[24] Like Sybil, who "lived out" the novels that she composed with her therapist, these subjects lived out the predictions that they were prompted to make by the experimenters.

Similar research has documented a slightly different phenomenon, known as the attribution effect. Subjects can be led to act annoyed or euphoric depending on whether they are led to believe, of artificially induced feelings of arousal, that they are symptoms of annoyance or euphoria.[25] Subjects can be prevented from acting shyly in unfamiliar company by being led to attribute their feelings of anxiety to something other than shyness.[26] And researchers can modify the degree of retaliation that a subject carries out against putative aggressors by modifying the degree of anger that he believes himself to be feeling toward them.[27] All of these experiments suggest that people tend to manifest not just what they're feeling but also what they represent themselves as feeling. Whether they behave angrily depends, not just on whether they are angry, but on whether they interpret their feelings by updating their autobiographies with the attribution "I'm angry." Whether they behave shyly depends on whether the current episode of their autobiography says "I'm feeling shy."

Here the subjects are "living out" their self-conceptions in a more holistic sense. Unlike the self-predicting voters, they aren't doing things that they have described themselves as doing. Rather, they are doing things that would accord with what they have described themselves as feeling. But this process, too, is implicit in Dennett's account of self-narration.

[24] I explore this literature in "From Self Psychology to Moral Philosophy" (Chapter 10 in the present volume). For a more recent philosophical discussion of this phenomenon, see Richard Moran, *Authority and Estrangement: An Essay on Self-Knowledge* (Princeton: Princeton University Press, 2001), pp. 38 ff.

[25] Schachter, S., and Singer, J.E., "Cognitive, Social and Physiological Determinants of Emotional State," *Psychological Review* 69 (1962): 379–99.

[26] Brodt, S.E., and Zimbardo, P., "Modifying Shyness-Related Social Behavior Through Symptom Misattribution," *Journal of Personality and Social Psychology* 41 (1981): 437–49.

[27] Berkowitz, L., and Turner, C., "Perceived Anger Level, Instigating Agent, and Aggression," in *Cognitive Alteration of Feeling States,* eds. H. London and R.E. Nisbett (Chicago: Aldine, 1972), 174–89; Zillman, E., Johnson, R.C., and Day, K.D., "Attribution of apparent arousal and proficiency of recovery for sympathetic activation affecting excitation transfer to aggressive behavior," *Journal of Experimental Social Psychology* 10 (1974): 503–15; Zillman, D., "Attribution and Misattribution of Excitatory Reactions," *New Directions in Attribution Research,* vol. 2, eds. John H. Harvey, William Ickes, and Robert F. Kidd (Hillsdale, NJ: Erlbaum, 1978), 335–68.

For as we have seen, Dennett says that "[w]e try to make all of our material cohere into a single good story."[28] And acting in accordance with our self-ascribed emotions is a way of ensuring that our story-material will cohere.

Consider how this process might be implemented in the robot who calls himself Gilbert. If the robot is locked in the closet, his internal state may include the initiation of a subroutine that searches for avenues of escape from danger and quickly selects the one most readily available. This subroutine will have a name – say, "fear" – and so the robot will report "I'm locked in the closet and I'm starting to get frightened." And now two different modules in the robot will dispose him to take action. One is the fear module, which may recommend breaking down the door as one of several preferred alternative avenues of escape; the other is the narrative module, which will recommend "I'm breaking down the door" as one of several preferred continuations of the story. If after he said "I'm getting frightened," the robot continued his story with "I think I'll back up my hard disk," then he would no longer be writing a passable novel, since his "material" wouldn't cohere. His narrative module will therefore favor "I'm breaking down the door" as a more coherent way to continue the story. And the narrative module can go ahead with this continuation of the story, confident of being borne out by the robot's behavior, since the robot is sure to break down the door once his preexisting fear is reinforced, in motivating that behavior, by his disposition to maintain correspondence between his story and his life.

Thus, having attributed an internal state to himself ("I'm getting frightened"), the robot is influenced to act in accordance with that attribution. Like a human being, he tends to manifest fear not only because he's "feeling" it but also because he "thinks" it's what he's feeling.

I have now introduced the idea of the robot's having a "narrative module" that produces Gilbert's autobiography. This module must incorporate, first, the function of ensuring that the robot's story corresponds to its life and, second, the function of maintaining the internal coherence of the story itself. The module must be designed to produce a text that is both consonant with the facts and sufficiently consonant with itself to qualify as a story.

---

[28] CNG, 114, quoted on p. 205.

Moreover, I have suggested that the robot can maintain correspondence between its story and its life in either direction, by narrating its actions or by acting out its narrative. Hence in pursuit of narrative coherence, the module can sometimes choose, among possible turns in its story, the one that would best fit the story thus far, precisely because it can then influence the robot's life to take the corresponding turn. The narrative module needn't always depend on the robot's career to provide material for a coherent story; it can sometimes tell a coherent story and induce the robot's career to follow.

In previous work, I have argued that a creature equipped with such a module would amount to an autonomous agent.[29] I won't repeat those arguments here, but let me briefly illustrate some of them with the help of Dennett's self-narrating robot.

As Gilbert rolls down the hall, he may autobiographically announce where he is going. But he needn't just report where he is already programmed to go, since his disposition to maintain correspondence between story and life will dispose him to go wherever he says he's going. Suppose that he is in the middle of his Fetch New Batteries subroutine, which sends him to the supply closet (where he sometimes gets locked in). The fact remains that if he said "I'm on my way to the library," his disposition to maintain correspondence would dispose him to head for the library instead. So if another, concurrently running subroutine can get Gilbert's speech-producing module to emit "I'm on my way to the library," then it may be able to bring about a change of course.

Now, Gilbert's disposition to maintain correspondence wouldn't be sufficient to make him head for the library if no other subroutines inclined him in that direction. Even if he said "I'm on my way to the library," his Fetch New Batteries routine would still favor heading for the supply closet, and his disposition to bear out his story would be unlikely to override a routine for obtaining essential resources. But I imagine his inner workings to be in the following, rather complicated state. Various task-specific subroutines are running concurrently, and some of them are making bids for control of his locomotive unit, to propel him toward one destination or another. His Fetch New Batteries subroutine is bidding for a trip to the supply closet, while his Departmental Service subroutine may be bidding for a trip to the library, in order to fill a faculty member's

[29] See *Practical Reflection* (Princeton: Princeton University Press, 1989); and *The Possibility of Practical Reason* (Oxford: Oxford University Press, 2000).

request for a book. Meanwhile, the narrative-composing module is busy updating the story of Gilbert's most recent adventures and the ongoing evolution of his inner states, including which task-specific subroutines are running and where they are bidding him to go. And the disposition of this module to maintain correspondence between his story and his life, though not sufficient by itself to override other demands for loco-motion, is sufficient to tip the balance in favor of one or another of those demands. So if Gilbert says "I'm heading for the supply closet," his disposition to bear out his story will reinforce the battery-fetching demands, and he'll head for the supply closet; whereas if he says "I'm heading for the library," his disposition to bear out his story will rein-force the demands of departmental service, and he'll head for the library instead. As long as the competition among those subroutines is not too lopsided, the narrative module is in a position to decide where Gilbert goes.

When I say that the narrative module can "decide" where Gilbert goes, I mean it can literally *decide*. For as we have seen, this module is in a position to have Gilbert speak the truth in naming any one of several destinations, each of which he would thereby head for, if he said so. The novelist in Gilbert can therefore *make up* where Gilbert is headed, choosing among different available turns in his story, none of which is privileged as the turn that the story must take in order to be true. As a self-narrator, then, Gilbert faces an epistemically open future – which gives him, in my view, as much free will as a human being.[30]

On what basis will the narrative-composing module make its decision? It can declare a winner in the contest among demands for locomo-tion, but on what basis will it adjudicate among those demands? The answer, already implicit in Dennett's theory, is that it will adjudicate on the basis of how best to continue the story – how to "make [its] material cohere."[31]

In many cases, acting on one demand will already make more nar-rative sense than acting on another, and the narrative-composing mod-ule will therefore declare a winner simply by telling the more coherent continuation of the story. But if neither continuation would make more narrative sense at this point, then the module can fill in more detail

---

[30] For a detailed defense of this claim, see my "Epistemic Freedom," *Pacific Philosophical Quarterly* 70 (1989): 73–97; reprinted in *The Possibility of Practical Reason*.
[31] CNG 114.

about its current situation, by recording which demand is stronger than the other or by recording more of the circumstances – which may arouse more internal states, which can in turn be recorded. At some point, the story will *become* more amenable to one continuation or other, and the narrative module can go ahead with the better continuation, thereby making its decision.

In this way, I believe, the module will decide on the basis of considerations that serve as reasons for acting. In canvassing Gilbert's outer circumstances and inner states, it will weigh them as considerations in light of which various possible actions would make sense. It will thus weigh Gilbert's circumstances and states as providing a potential *rationale* for his next action – that is, an account that would make the action intelligible, a coherent development in his story. When the novelist in Gilbert writes in the action with the best rationale, he will in effect be deciding for reasons.

Note that this claim places significant constraints on the conception of narrative coherence on which I can rely. One might have thought that whether an action would make for a coherent continuation of Gilbert's story ultimately depends on whether he has reason for taking it. My claim, however, is that whether Gilbert has reason for taking an action ultimately depends on whether it would make for a coherent continuation of his story. Because I make the latter claim, I cannot adopt the former in order to explicate narrative coherence, since my account would then become viciously circular: narrative coherence cannot ultimately depend on rational justification if rational justification ultimately depends on narrative coherence.

Of course, *we* can tell a story about Gilbert that makes sense because it portrays him as taking actions for which he has reasons; for we can portray him as taking actions because they cohere with *his* story. Indeed, I have already claimed that self-narration takes account of its own effect on the subject's behavior, by portraying him as *hereby* heading for the supply closet or the library. To this extent, self-narration already relies for some of its coherence on the fact that the subject is doing what coheres with this very story – hence on the fact that he is doing something for which he has reasons, as I conceive them. But this fact cannot be the sole basis for the narrative coherence involved. There must be some prior basis on which the subject's action makes sense in light of his story before it can also make sense in light of his tendency to do what makes sense.

The nature of narrative coherence is a topic that lies beyond the scope of this chapter.[32] But I have already indicated one basis on which Gilbert can regard actions as cohering with his story independently of his having reasons for taking them. I have supposed that Gilbert understands his own inner workings, in the form of the various subroutines that are vying to control his behavior. Gilbert understands that whatever he does will be controlled by one of these subroutines and will consequently make sense by virtue of having a causal explanation, which cites the relevant subroutine as the controlling cause. In considering which action would make for a coherent continuation of his story, Gilbert can look for an action that would have the most satisfying causal explanation in light of the subroutines vying for control.

Of course, where Gilbert has subroutines vying for control, human beings have conflicting motives, which serve as controlling causes of their behavior. Where Gilbert looks for an action that would best be explained by his subroutines, humans look for an action that would best be explained by their motives. That's why humans look to their motives – that is, to their desires and beliefs – as reasons for acting.

In deciding for reasons, the inner novelist plays the role that is ordinarily attributed to the self. A third conception of the self has therefore emerged. According to Dennett's conception of the self, with which I began, the self is the merely fictional protagonist of a self-narrator's autobiography. According to the second conception, the self is the autobiographer's reflective representation, which guides his actions as well as his speech. What has now emerged, however, is that control rests with the narrative module – the inner novelist, recording the subject's last step and declaring his next step, in a way that amounts to deciding for reasons. According to the third conception, then, the self is the narrator.

This third conception of the self no longer supports the skepticism of Dennett's initial conception. The protagonist of Gilbert's autobiography is no longer, as Dennett believes, a merely fictional character whose shoes cannot be filled by the actual author. Now that the robot has a central controller that makes decisions for reasons, he has a self, and so his story has come true.

Note that what fills the shoes of the protagonist in the story of Gilbert is the robot, not the robot's self. "Gilbert" is not the name of a self; it's the

---

[32] But see my "Narrative Explanation," *The Philosophical Review* 112 (2003): 1–25.

name of a unified agent who *has* a self, in the form of an inner locus of agential control. My current claim is that the self-narrating robot really is endowed with a self in this sense and can therefore live up to the portrait of the protagonist in his autobiography. He is endowed with a self because his inner narrator is a locus of control that unifies him as an agent by making decisions on the basis of reasons.

The self-narrating agent is a bit like an improvisational actor, enacting a role that he invents as he goes. The difference is that an improvisational actor usually invents and enacts a role that he is not playing in fact. His actions represent what they are not – actions other than themselves, performed out of motives other than his. By contrast, the self-narrator is an ingenuous improviser, inventing a role that expresses his actual motives in response to real events. He can improvise his actual role in these events because his motives take shape and produce behavior under the influence of his self-descriptions, which are therefore underdetermined by antecedent facts, so that he partly invents what he enacts.

Yet how can an agent act out invented self-descriptions without somehow falsifying them, by being or doing something other than is therein described? How can enacting a role fail to involve fakery or bad faith?

The answer is that when the agent invents descriptions to be enacted, he describes himself as the inventor-enactor of those descriptions. He describes himself as *hereby* heading for the supply closet or the library, thus describing his actions as flowing from these descriptions, as realizations thereof. The protagonist in his autobiography is therefore both fictive and factual – fictive, because his role is invented by the one who enacts it; factual, because it is the role of one inventing and enacting that role.

To be sure, a self-narrator can go beyond what is factual, if he applies self-descriptions whose autobiographical application won't make them true. Although he can sometimes tip the balance of his antecedent motives in favor of leaving the office by saying "I'm leaving," at other times he can't, and then a declaration of departure would be ineffectual – an instance of weakness of will. Alternatively, his motives for going home may already be sufficient to make him go home no matter what he says – in which case, "I'm leaving" is the only true thing for him to say. Within these constraints, however, the self-narrator retains considerable latitude for invention. Even if he is already determined to leave the office, he is probably capable of going home or going out for a drink, or perhaps just taking a walk, depending on what he writes into his story.

To this extent, I can endorse Dennett's claim that the self is a fictive character. Where I disagree with Dennett is over the claim that being fictive, this character doesn't exist in fact. Dennett thinks the real-life author of an autobiography is significantly different from the character portrayed as the protagonist. I think that the author of an autobiography is just like the protagonist, since the protagonist is portrayed as a self-improvising character, the inventor-enactor of his own story – or, as I prefer to say, an autonomous agent.

My disagreement with Dennett over the truth-value of a human being's autobiography results from two subsidiary disagreements. On the one hand, Dennett believes that a human being has no central controller, whereas I believe that Dennett himself is committed to crediting a human being with a central controller, in the form of a narrative intelligence. On the other hand, Dennett believes that a human being's autobiography portrays his central controller as a "brain pearl" or Cartesian ego, whereas I believe that this autobiography portrays the central controller as the narrative intelligence that it is. We live up to our aspirations with respect to selfhood, then, partly because we have more of a self than Dennett expressly allows, and partly because we aspire to less than he thinks.

I have overlooked another disagreement with Dennett, which I should mention before closing. Although Dennett tries to deny the unity of the self-narrating agent, he commits himself expressly to the unity of the narrative – to the proposition that "We try to make all of our material cohere into a *single* good story."[33] Indeed, the unity of this narrative seems to account for the temporal unity of the purely fictional self in which Dennett believes. This fictional character remains one and the same self because he is the protagonist in one and the same continuing story.[34]

In my view, however, we tell many small, disconnected stories about ourselves – short episodes that do not get incorporated into our life-stories. The process of self-narration shapes our day-to-day lives in units as small as the eating of a meal, the answering of a phone, or even the scratching of an itch; but our life stories do not record every meal eaten,

---

[33] CNG 114 (quoted on p. 205), emphasis added.

[34] This view is endorsed by Flanagan, "Multiple Identity," p. 136: "Augustine's *Confessions* is an autobiography. It is the story of a single self. This is established in part because Augustine is able to produce an account that narratively links up the multifarious episodes of his life from the first-person point of view."

every phone answered, or every itch scratched. Because the narratives of these minor episodes are never unified into a single story, their protagonist cannot derive his unity from theirs. The agent who types this letter 'a' is the same person who cut his forefinger with that pocketknife in the summer of 1959, but not because there is any single narrative in which he figures as the protagonist of both episodes.

So when I describe the inner narrator as a unified self, I am not speaking of the temporal unity that joins a person to his past and future selves; I am speaking of agential unity, in virtue of which a person is self-governed, or autonomous. In my view, autonomy is not related to personal identity in such a way that a single entity plays the role of self in both phenomena: that which makes us self-governed is not that which makes us self-same through time.[35]

---

[35] I argue for this view in "Identification and Identity" (Chapter 14 in the present volume).

10

From Self Psychology to Moral Philosophy

Prescott Lecky's *Self-Consistency* was published in 1945, four years after the author's death, at the age of 48.[1] Subtitled *A Theory of Personality*, the book defended a simple but startling thesis:[2]

We propose to apprehend all psychological phenomena as illustrations of the single principle of unity or self-consistency. We conceive of the personality as an organization of values which are felt to be consistent with one another. Behavior expresses the effort to maintain the integrity and unity of the organization.

Lecky regarded self-consistency as the object of a cognitive or epistemic motive from which all other motives are derived.[3] "The subject must feel that he lives in a stable and intelligible environment," Lecky wrote: "In a

[1] See the "Biographical Sketch" in the 1961 edition of Lecky's book. At the time of his death, Lecky was employed as an instructor in the Extension Division of Columbia University, having been fired seven years earlier from a faculty position at Columbia College for failing to complete his Ph.D. dissertation.

[2] Lecky (1945), 82.

[3] "One source of motivation only, the necessity to maintain the unity of the system, must serve as the universal dynamic principle" (81). "By interpreting all behavior as motivated by the need for unity, we understand particular motives or tendencies simply as expressions of the main motive, pursuing different immediate goals as necessary means to that end" (82).

This chapter originally appeared in *Philosophical Perspectives* 14, Action and Freedom (October 2000), pp. 349–77. It is reprinted by permission of Blackwell Publishing. Work on this chapter was supported by a fellowship from the John Simon Guggenheim Memorial Foundation and by a matching leave funded by the Philosophy Department and the College of Literature, Science, and the Arts, University of Michigan. For comments on an earlier draft of the chapter, I am grateful to Elizabeth Anderson, Elliot Aronson, Don Herzog, Richard Nisbett, Bill Swann, and Dan Wegner.

world which is incomprehensible, no one can feel secure."[4] The subject therefore constructs an organized conception of his world – an "organization of experience into an integrated whole" – and this organization just *is* his personality, because the effort to maintain its consistency is what gives shape to his thought and behavior.[5]

Central to the personality, so conceived, is the subject's conception of himself. "The most constant factor in the individual's experience," according to Lecky, "is himself and the interpretation of his own meaning; the kind of person he is, the place which he occupies in the world, appear to represent the center or nucleus of the personality."[6] Because the subject's world-view is thus centered on his self-view, his efforts to maintain coherence in the one are centered on maintaining coherence in the other. "Any idea entering the system which is inconsistent with the individual's conception of himself cannot be assimilated but instead gives rise to an inconsistency which must be removed as promptly as possible."[7]

If a person is to maintain consistency in his self-conception, he has to *be* consistent – to think and behave in ways that lend themselves to a coherent representation. That's why the person's conception of his world, and especially of himself, can play the functional role of his personality: it organizes his thought and behavior into a unified whole. Lecky offered the following illustration of how this process works.[8]

Let us take the case of an intelligent student who is deficient, say, in spelling. In almost every instance poor spellers have been tutored and practiced in spelling over long periods without improvement. For some reason such a student has a special handicap in learning how to spell, though not in learning the other subjects which are usually considered more difficult. This deficiency is not due to a lack of ability, but rather to an active resistance which prevents him from learning how to spell in spite of the extra instruction. The resistance arises from the fact that at some time in the past the suggestion that he is a poor speller was accepted and incorporated into his definition of himself, and is now an integral part of his total personality. . . . His difficulty is thus explained as a special instance of the general principle that a person can only be true to himself. If he defines himself as a poor speller, the misspelling of a certain proportion of the words which he uses becomes for him a moral issue. He misspells words for the same reason that he refuses to be a thief. That is, he must endeavor to behave in a manner consistent with his conception of himself.

[4] *Ibid.,* 50.
[5] *Ibid.,* 85. See also 90.
[6] *Ibid.,* 86.
[7] *Ibid.,* 136.
[8] *Ibid.,* 103–04.

I regard this as one of the most remarkable passages in twentieth-century moral psychology. On the one hand, it offers an explanation for a pathology that has become especially significant to us – the pathology of being defeated by a negative self-conception. We now look for this particular form of self-defeat not only in children's failure to learn spelling but also, for example, in the perpetuation of racial and sexual stereotypes that are internalized by their victims.[9] On the other hand, this passage also offers, in capsule form, a theory of moral motivation. It says that a person refrains from stealing because he cannot assimilate stealing into his self-conception.

What's remarkable about the passage is that it attributes self-defeat and moral behavior to one and the same motive. A child fails to learn as if on principle, while thieving is, as it were, against his stereotype; or, rather, acting on principle and acting to type are both manifestations of one and the same drive, to maintain a coherent self-conception. Could the question *Why be moral* be so closely related to *Why Johnny can't spell*?

Clearly, Lecky overstated his hypothesis in the passage just quoted. Many psychological factors may go into causing a particular person to spell badly or to refrain from stealing: a self-consistency motive is unlikely to be the only cause or even the primary cause of such behavior. But I would like to believe that this motive can figure among the causes, in roughly the manner described by Lecky; and so I would like to believe that the quoted passage is merely exaggerated rather than false.

My reasons for *wanting* to believe this don't amount to reasons for *believing* it, because they are philosophical rather than empirical. I have presented these reasons elsewhere, in arguing that various philosophical problems about agency can be resolved by the assumption that agents have a motive for doing what makes sense to them.[10] People's having such a motive, I claim, would account for their being autonomous, acting for reasons, having an open future, and thus satisfying our concept of an agent. As a philosopher of action, then, I hope that Lecky is right.

I think that my arguments may be of philosophical interest even if Lecky is wrong, since they show our concept of agency to be realizable, whether or not it is realized in human beings.[11] But experience has taught me that philosophers aren't interested in an account of purely possible agents, and that they tend to regard my account as no more than that,

---

[9] For recent research on this topic, see Jussim, Eccles, & Madon (1996).

[10] Velleman (1989), (1993), and the Introduction to Velleman (2000c).

[11] See the Introduction to Velleman (1989).

because they find its motivational assumption implausible. Philosophers are generally unwilling to believe that people have a motive for doing what they understand.

I have therefore decided to venture out of the philosophical armchair in order to examine the empirical evidence, as gathered by psychologists aiming to prove or disprove motivational conjectures like mine. By and large, this evidence is indirect in relation to my account of agency, since it is drawn from cases in which the relevant motive has been forced into the open by the manipulations of an experimenter. The resulting evidence doesn't tend to show the mechanism of agency humming along in accordance with my specifications; it tends to show the knocks and shudders that such a mechanism emits when put under stress. But we often learn about the normal workings of things by subjecting them to abnormal conditions; and viewed in this light, various programs of psychological research offer indirect support to my account of agency. I'll begin by reviewing the relevant research, leaving its relevance to my account of agency for the final section of the chapter.

Cognitive Dissonance

The largest and most well-known program of research on cognitive motivation is the theory of cognitive dissonance. In the classic demonstration of dissonance, by Festinger and Carlsmith (1959), subjects performed an extremely tedious task and then were asked to tell the next subject that the task was enjoyable. Some were offered \$1 by the experimenter for performing this service; others were offered \$20. Those who received only \$1 for saying the task was enjoyable subsequently came to believe that it *was* enjoyable, whereas those who had received \$20 continued to believe that it was tedious. Festinger and Carlsmith hypothesized that the subjects who received only \$1 experienced greater "dissonance" between their attitudes and their behavior, and altered their opinion in order to reduce this dissonance.

The effect reported by Festinger and Carlsmith has been replicated hundreds if not thousands of times, but its interpretation remains controversial. Festinger and Carlsmith did not clearly explain their dissonance hypothesis, and others have proposed alternative hypotheses to account for their results.[12]

---

[12] For recent contributions to the dissonance debate, see Harmon-Jones & Mills (1999).

Aronson's Version of the Dissonance Hypothesis

The clearest version of the dissonance hypothesis was proposed by Elliot Aronson (1968).[13] Aronson argued that the subjects' cognition of their behavior was at odds with what they would expect themselves to have done under the circumstances. What they would expect themselves to have done, having found the task boring, is to say that it was boring; but they found it boring and said that it was interesting. Their cognition of what they had done therefore clashed with the expectation that would naturally follow from their cognition of the circumstances. The subjects changed their opinion of the task, according to Aronson, so that they could change their cognition of the circumstances, rendering it consistent with their cognition of what they had done.

The hypothesis that Aronson thus framed in terms of expectations can also be framed in terms of explanations. Just as the subjects' cognition of having found the task boring would lead to an expectation at odds with their having said that it was interesting, so it would leave them at a loss to explain why they had said that it was interesting. Finding their behavior inexplicable and finding it contrary to expectation would be two aspects of the same cognitive predicament. And changing their opinion of the task would resolve the predicament under either description, by rendering their behavior both explicable and predictable under the circumstances as re-conceived.

This hypothesis relies on two assumptions that are not explicitly stated either by Aronson or by Festinger and Carlsmith. The first assumption, pointed out by Kelley (1967), is that *none* of the subjects knew the full explanation of their behavior.[14]

The pressure that induced these subjects to lie was covert: it was the pressure exerted by the experimental setting and the authority conferred by that setting on the experimenter. People are notoriously unaware of how powerful such pressure can be.[15] Hence the subjects in Festinger and Carlsmith's experiment didn't know why they lied. One group of subjects were offered an explanation designed to seem adequate to them, while the others were offered an explanation designed to seem inadequate. In all probability, $20 would not have been sufficient to induce most of the subjects to lie if it had been offered by a stranger with no authority; but

---

[13] See also Aronson (1969); Thibodeau & Aronson (1992).

[14] On this point, see also Nisbett & Valins (1972).

[15] See Sherman (1980), in which subjects greatly under-predicted their compliance with a typical dissonance protocol.

$20 was sufficient for the subjects *to believe* that it had been a sufficient inducement for them, whereas $1 was not. Hence some of the subjects but not others were supplied with what seemed like an adequate explanation of their behavior, or an adequate basis on which to expect it.

The second assumption required by the dissonance hypothesis is that the subjects who changed their opinion also deceived themselves about having changed it. The awareness of having retroactively come to believe what they had already said would not have provided them with an explanation of why they had said it, or with a basis on which their saying it could have been expected. The premise required to explain or predict their behavior was that they had believed what they were saying at the time, as they said it. In retroactively coming to believe what they had said, then, they must also have come to believe, falsely, that they had believed it all along.

As supplemented by these assumptions, the dissonance hypothesis says that when people cannot identify the forces that have shaped their behavior, they conjure up forces to make it seem intelligible and predictable – if necessary, by retroactively forming a motivationally relevant attitude and projecting it back in time.[16] This maneuver would appear to be motivated by the subjects' desire for explanatory and predictive coherence in their self-conceptions, a motive of the sort postulated by Lecky. Hence the results of forced-compliance experiments, as explained by the dissonance hypothesis, appear to support Lecky's theory of self-consistency.

A Rival Explanation: Self-Perception
Daryl Bem (1972) has argued that subjects who seem to be motivated by cognitive dissonance are merely interpreting their own behavior as if they were external observers:

Just as an outside observer might ask himself, "What must this man's attitude be if he is willing to behave in this fashion in this situation?" so too, the subject implicitly asks himself, "What must my attitude be if I am willing to behave in this fashion in this situation?" Thus the subject who receives $1 discards the monetary inducement as the major motivating factor for his behavior and infers that it must reflect his actual attitude; he infers that he must have actually enjoyed the tasks. The subject who receives $20 notes that his behavior is adequately accounted for by the monetary inducement, and hence he cannot extract from the behavior any information relevant to his actual opinions; he is in the same situation as a control subject insofar as information about his attitude is concerned. (pp. 16–17)

---

[16] See also Nisbett & Wilson (1977).

In this "self-perception explanation," Bem says, "there is no aversive motivational pressure postulated." As described by Nisbett and Valins (1972),
"Bem's reinterpretation of dissonance phenomena avoids the use of any
motivational concept," and so "the two positions appear to be at a logical
impasse": dissonance theory attributes the subjects' change of attitude to
"a motivated process" whereas Bem attributes it to "a passive, inferential
process."[17]

Subsequent research has shown that the correct explanation for
dissonance phenomena is indeed motivational.[18] But I do not want to
interpret this research as discrediting Bem's explanation in terms of self-
perception. Bem's only mistake, I believe, is in claiming that his self-
perception explanation doesn't depend on any motivational postulate.
In fact, his self-perception theory postulates the same motive as cognitive-
dissonance theory; and so the two theories give coordinate explanations
that are mutually reinforcing.[19]

Bem's thesis is that a person often comes to know about his own attitudes in much the same way as we do when observing him from the
outside. Bem's formulation of the thesis suggests that a person receives
his self-knowledge passively, as if by a process of sensory perception. But
this suggestion is superfluous to the thesis – and, indeed, incompatible
with Bem's defense of it.

To be sure, our knowledge of a person's attitudes is often obtained by a
process that is quasi-perceptual. That is, hearing a person's vocalizations
is often inseparable from hearing them as the assertion of a particular
proposition, and seeing his bodily movements is often inseparable from
seeing them as an effort to attain a particular end. On other occasions,
however, we hear a person's voice without hearing what he's saying, or we
see his movements without seeing what he's doing; and what he is saying
or doing are then matters that we have to figure out.

On the latter occasions, detecting the attitudes behind a person's
behavior requires a process that is not passive and perceptual but active
and intellectual: it requires a process of interpretive inquiry. We will not
undertake that process unless we have the requisite motives. If the meaning of someone's vocalizations or movements doesn't impress itself upon
us immediately, we won't bother to figure it out unless we want to – that is,

---

[17] *Ibid.*, p. 68.
[18] Zanna & Cooper (1974); Zanna, Higgins, & Taves (1976); Cooper, Zanna, & Taves
(1978); Higgins, Rhodewalt, & Zanna (1979); Elliott & Devine (1994).
[19] See Fazio, Zanna, & Cooper (1977).

unless we want to understand what he is saying or doing, or to anticipate what he's likely to say and do next. On such occasions, interpretation is an activity that must be motivated.

Unfortunately, social psychologists tend to speak of all interpretation as perceptual, as in the phrases "self-perception," "interpersonal perception," "social perception," and the like. This usage highlights the cases in which interpretation is passive and receptive rather than active and motivated. Even though Bem denies that one is automatically given a knowledge of one's attitudes, he calls the process of acquiring such knowledge "self-perception," and so he is naturally interpreted as describing a process that is passive. The possibility that self-perception might be a motivated activity therefore goes unnoticed.

Yet Bem himself implicitly concedes this possibility, when he says that an observer "might ask himself, 'What must this man's attitude be if he is willing to behave in this fashion in this situation?'" This question expresses the observer's desire to understand and anticipate, a desire without which he wouldn't ask the question or, having asked it, would let it go unanswered. Bem's thesis is that the subject "implicitly asks himself" the same question about himself, because a knowledge of his attitudes is not automatically given to him any more than it is to an observer. To portray the subject as asking this question is to acknowledge that he doesn't passively perceive his own attitudes but must sometimes actively inquire into them. It is therefore to acknowledge a motive for self-inquiry.

Now, an interest in explanation and prediction is the basis of all consistency motivation, according to Lecky. Consistency isn't desired for its own sake; it's desired as the form of the predictable and the intelligible, by a creature who "must feel that he lives in a stable and intelligible environment." Inconsistency isn't intrinsically disturbing; it's disturbing because it stymies comprehension, and "[i]n a world which is incomprehensible, no one can feel secure."[20] A desire for consistency in one's self-conception thus arises, according to Lecky, from the desire to understand and be able to anticipate oneself – the very desire expressed by the question that Bem attributes to the self-interpreting subject.

Hence the motive implicitly conceded by Bem is the same motive that is explicitly postulated by Lecky, the desire for self-knowledge. Bem should not deny the existence of this cognitive motive, since his own theory presupposes it.

---

[20] These phrases are drawn from the quotations on pp. 224–5.

Lecky's insight was that the desire for self-knowledge can drive either of two coordinate processes. If we want to understand what we do, we can either figure out why we've done things, after we've done them, or we can make sure that we don't do things unless we already know why. The latter process entails doing only what we are aware of having motives or other dispositions to do; and so it amounts to the process of being true to ourselves by acting in accordance with our self-conceptions, the self-consistency process described by Lecky. The former process entails interpreting our behavior after the fact: it is the self-perception process described by Bem. Self-consistency and self-perception are thus two phases of a single activity – the practical and intellectual phases of self-interpretation.

Note that dissonance-reduction lies on the intellectual side of this contrast. When a subject experiences cognitive dissonance, it's too late for him to make his behavior consistent with his self-conception; he has to adjust his self-conception to fit his behavior, which is in the past. Bem and Aronson are thus describing one and the same process, of fitting an interpretive hypothesis to past behavior.

In Aronson's story, the subject begins with an interpretation that doesn't fit – namely, that he believed the experimental task to be tedious – and the resulting discomfort moves him to frame a new hypothesis, that he believed the task to be fun. In Bem's story, the subject appears to have no initial interpretation, and so he isn't motivated by any discomfort. But he is still motivated by a desire for an interpretation that fits his behavior, the desire whose frustration caused the initial discomfort in Aronson's version. The only point of disagreement between Aronson and Bem is whether the subject was dissatisfied with one interpretation before being moved to frame an interpretation that satisfied him.[21]

---

[21] There may be one other point of disagreement, but it is too small to worry about. Aronson tends to describe the subject as changing his belief about the experimental task; Bem tends to describe him as attributing such a belief to his earlier self. As I have explained, Aronson's version requires the assumption that the subject not only forms the belief in the present but also projects it back into the past, thus arriving at the same attribution as in Bem's version. But Bem's version says only that the subject attributes the belief to his earlier self – which, in principle, he could do without forming the belief in the present. Bem doesn't say that the subject now believes the task to have been enjoyable; what Bem says is that the subject believes himself to have believed what he was saying when he said that the task was enjoyable.

But this in-principle difference between Bem and Aronson makes no difference in practice. Surely, if someone believes that shortly after finishing a task, he believed it to have been enjoyable, then he is likely to believe, in the present, that the task was enjoyable, unless he has some reason for doubting the truth of his earlier belief. In

Thus, the dissonance theorist and the self-perception theorist aren't at a "logical impasse": they are in fact comrades in arms. Both are describing a process of self-interpretation, motivated by a desire for self-knowledge.[22]

If the differences between dissonance theory and self-perception theory are so small, why do their proponents believe that they yield different predictions, and that they are consequently supported by different experimental results?[23] The answer, I think, is that each theory isolates and simplifies one aspect of a large and complicated reality. The reality behind both theories is the holistic process of fitting an interpretation to behavior – a process that is complicated, in the first-personal case, by the possibility of working in the opposite direction, by fitting one's behavior to an interpretation. Each theory treats a single aspect of this process as if it were the whole, thus obscuring the fact that they are, as it were, different ends of the same elephant.[24]

I have already explained how self-perception theorists focus on the case of automatic, passive self-understanding, neglecting cases in which self-understanding is attained through active self-inquiry, motivated partly by the discomforts of reflective ignorance and incomprehension. The

the absence of such a reason, he will probably be unable to attribute the belief to his former self without adopting it. Bem and Aronson agree that what the subject wants is to attribute the belief to his former self, so as to account for his behavior. Bem doesn't mention that the subject will probably have to adopt the belief in order to attribute it to his former self, in the absence of reasons for doubting it. But this omission hardly constitutes an important difference of opinion with Aronson.

[22] In a paper presented to the 1967 Nebraska Symposium on Motivation, Harold Kelley connected dissonance theory and self-perception theory by way of attribution theory, which he presented as containing a "broad motivational assumption," to the effect that attributional processes "operate *as if* the individual were motivated to attain a cognitive mastery of the causal structure of his environment." Commenting on the passage in which this statement occurred, Bem says: "It is an admirable attempt, but the strongest motivation to emerge from this quotation appears to be Kelley's need to understand why he was there" (Bem [1972], p. 45).

This remark is wonderfully self-refuting. Bem claims that the processes discussed by Kelley involve no motivation, despite Kelley's assertions to the contrary. Yet Bem's attempt to discredit the latter assertions ends up confirming them instead. Bem suggests that we shouldn't credit Kelley's assertions about motivation because he made them only in order to satisfy his need to understand why he was addressing a symposium on motivation. The psychological process to which Bem thus attributes Kelley's assertions is one of the very processes whose existence Kelley was asserting – a process driven by the need for self-understanding. What better reason could we have for accepting Kelley's assertions as true than his having made them out of a need to understand himself?

[23] See Bem (1972); Nisbett & Valins (1972).

[24] This view of the debate is suggested by Aronson (1992).

corresponding fault among dissonance theorists is a tendency to focus on individual inconsistencies of particular kinds, neglecting the overall cognitive goals in relation to which inconsistency is undesirable, in the first place. The narrow focus of either theory allows its proponents to state specific algorithms – an algorithm for attributing attitudes, in the one case, and an algorithm for computing total dissonance, in the other. These algorithms do yield conflicting predictions, which would be confirmed by different experimental outcomes. But the algorithms are radically underdetermined by the theories to which they have been attached, and in both cases they are implausible. Attributing attitudes and eliminating inconsistencies are two aspects of the overall process of making sense of the world, a process that has not been and probably cannot be reduced to an algorithm.

Consider an experiment by Snyder and Ebbesen (1972), billed as "a test of dissonance theory versus self-perception theory."[25] This experiment modified a standard dissonance protocol by making salient to the subject either his initial attitude, or the behavior inconsistent with that attitude, or both. Snyder and Ebbesen claimed that making the subject's attitude salient to him ought to increase his awareness of dissonance between it and his behavior, thereby increasing his tendency to alter the attitude, if dissonance theory were correct; whereas if self-perception theory were correct, making the subject's attitude salient ought to discourage him from attributing a different attitude to himself. Snyder and Ebbesen reported that their results favored self-perception theory in this respect.

But the "prediction" that Snyder and Ebbesen derived from dissonance theory depends on a very narrow view of the circumstances. To be sure, if the subject's belief that a task was tedious is made salient to him, then he will be more aware of its inconsistency with his statement that the task was interesting.[26] But his initial belief would also be inconsistent with a subsequent *belief* that the task was interesting, and this potential inconsistency will also be impressed on him by the salience of the former belief. Once he is made aware of believing that the task was tedious, he cannot come to believe that it was interesting without acknowledging that he has changed his mind, for no apparent reason. Thus, even as the discomfort associated with his initial belief is intensified, so is the discomfort to be expected from the alternative.

---

[25] Discussed by Bem (1972), 31–33.

[26] For ease of exposition, I speak here as if Snyder & Ebbesen applied their modifications to the dissonance experiment of Festinger & Carlsmith (1959). In fact, they modified a different dissonance experiment, but the differences aren't relevant in this context.

What, then, does dissonance theory predict that the subject will do? Surely, the theory cannot make a definite prediction in a case so under-described. What the subject will do depends on circumstances that will vary from one subject to another, since he will seek the most coherent view of the situation *all things considered.* Among the things he'll have to consider will be such questions as what the task was, specifically, and how offensive to his personal tastes; whether he is the sort of person to lie, or the sort of person to be unsure of what he likes; whether he identifies with the experimenter or with his fellow subjects; and so on. If dissonance theorists think that they have an algorithm for predicting how such questions will be resolved, they are mistaken. But their critics are also mistaken if they think that the failure of some particular algorithm entails the failure of the theory.

Another Rival Explanation: Self-Enhancement
I have now argued that self-perception theory tacitly presupposes the same cognitive motive that is explicitly postulated by dissonance theory, and that these theories can appear to yield conflicting predictions only if formulated with more precision than their shared theoretical basis can support. But self-perception theory is not the only attempt to re-interpret the evidence gathered in dissonance research. Others have explained that evidence by postulating motives that clearly aren't cognitive.

According to dissonance theory, the Festinger-Carlsmith subjects came to believe what they had said in order to escape a specifically cognitive predicament, of being unable to explain their behavior, or of finding it contrary to expectation. But they might instead have come to believe what they had said in order to escape the appearance of having been irra-tional, in having said it for no good reason. In that case, their change of mind would have aimed to rationalize their past behavior rather than to remedy their current state of reflective ignorance or incomprehension; and it would thus have aimed at removing not a cognitive problem but a threat to their self-esteem as rational agents. The effects of forced com-pliance have therefore been taken by other psychologists to indicate a motive for attaining a favorable view of oneself rather than for maintain-ing consistency with one's actual self-view – a motive of self-enhancement rather than self-consistency.[27]

---

[27] See, e.g., Steele & Liu (1983). Aronson (1968) rightly points out that this self-enhancement hypothesis can be subsumed under the hypothesis of cognitive disso-nance. People tend to conceive of themselves as rational agents, and their perception of having acted with insufficient justification will be inconsistent with this self-conception,

Of course, dissonance theory is not committed to denying the influence of the former motive. Everyone prefers not to look foolish, and this preference may well be implicated in the forced-compliance phenomena. Dissonance theory is merely committed to asserting the influence of an additional motive, a motive to avoid that which is inexplicable or contrary to expectation. But if the phenomena cited in support of dissonance theory can be completely explained by a desire not to look foolish, then the theory will have lost most of its empirical support.

Attribution Effects

A number of experimenters claim to have found dissonance effects that cannot be explained as instances of self-enhancement.[28] But I am less interested in dissonance *per se* than in the cognitive motive for reducing it – a motive that, as we have seen, can drive not only dissonance-reduction but self-perception and other attributional processes as well. I therefore prefer to draw further evidence from phenomena that don't clearly involve dissonance but turn out to involve the same cognitive motive.

Self-Verification
One such phenomenon has been explored by William B. Swann, Jr., under the label "self-verification."[29] Swann has shown that people tend to seek, credit, and retain feedback that confirms their actual self-conception, even if that conception is negative. Thus, for example, people tend to choose and feel committed to partners who view them as they view themselves, for better or worse.[30] When interacting with someone who appears to view them differently, they tend to behave in ways designed to bring him around to their view, even if it is unflattering.[31] They also lend more credence to his feedback about them, and are more likely to

<hr>

producing a higher-order dissonance that is cognitive. Yet there is a difference between a desire to avoid seeming irrational and a desire to avoid the inconsistency of believing that one is rational while also believing that one has behaved irrationally.

[28] See, e.g., Prislin & Pool (1996); Stone, Cooper, Wiegand, & Aronson (1997).

[29] For reviews of Swann's research, see: Swann (1983); Swann (1985); Swann and Brown (1990); McNulty and Swann (1991); Swann (1996).

[30] Swann, De La Ronde, and Hixon (1992); Swann, De La Ronde, and Hixon, (1994); Swann, Pelham, and Krull (1989), Study 3. See also Swann and Predmore (1985) and the research by Swann and B.W. Pelham reported in Swann (1986), pp. 419–20.

[31] Swann and Read (1981b), Investigation II; Swann and Hill (1982).

remember that feedback, if it confirms their conception of themselves, favorable or unfavorable.[32]

Because these tendencies are associated with negative as well as positive self-conceptions, they cannot be explained by a desire for self-enhancement.[33] Yet they don't exactly confirm the Leckian hypothesis. What Swann and his colleagues have found are biases in people's collection and interpretation of feedback from others. These biases may well be motivated by a self-consistency motive such as Lecky postulated. But Lecky hypothesized that this motive would lead people to confirm their self-conceptions directly, by behaving in ways that verified those conceptions. Lecky's hypothesis was that people who think of themselves as poor spellers would not just choose friends who think of them as poor spellers, too, but would actually tend to spell poorly in order to be true to themselves. Swann's research does not demonstrate a tendency toward such direct, behavioral self-verification.

There is ample evidence for behavioral self-verification of positive self-views, especially in children. This evidence is less than conclusive, because it can be explained, at least in part, by a motive for self-enhancement; but it is nevertheless worth reviewing, since it coincides in interesting respects with Lecky's views.

Miller, Brickman, and Bolen (1975) compared attribution and persuasion as means of modifying the behavior of elementary school pupils. In one experiment, they compared the littering behavior of children who had repeatedly been told that they *ought to be* tidy (persuasion) with that of children who had repeatedly been told that they *were* tidy (attribution). Both groups decreased their rate of littering, in comparison with both their own prior rate and that of a control group that was offered no messages on the subject. But the effects of attribution were significantly greater and lasted significantly longer than those of persuasion. Children who had been told that they were tidy showed a sharp and lasting decrease in their rate of littering, whereas children who had been told that they ought to be tidy showed only a moderate decrease in littering and then returned to littering at the same rate as the control group. In another experiment, the same researchers found a similar difference in the effect of attribution and persuasion on children's performance in arithmetic.

---

[32] Swann and Read (1981b), Investigation III.

[33] See Swann (1986); Swann, Pelham, and Krull (1989); Swann, Hixon, Stein-Seroussi, and Gilbert (1990); Swann, Stein-Seroussi, and Giesler (1992); Jussim, Yen, and Aiello (1995).

Children told that they *were* skillful and highly motivated in arithmetic showed a greater and more long-lasting improvement than children told that they *ought to be* skillful or motivated.

These experiments compared favorable attributions with injunctions, which did not have a similarly favorable tone and might even have been interpreted by the children as presupposing an unfavorable attribution instead. (Why would teacher exhort us to be tidy if we weren't in fact untidy?) Perhaps, then, the experiments demonstrated, not an interesting motivational difference between attributions and injunctions, but an utterly unsurprising difference between positive and negative reinforcement. Grusec and Redler (1980) sought to rule out this alternative explanation by comparing favorable attributions with equally reinforcing praise offered for the same behavior. Children who had won marbles in a game were induced to deposit some of them in a collection bowl for poor children, whereupon they were either praised for doing so (reinforcement), told that their doing so showed that they liked to help others (attribution), or given no feedback at all (control). The children were then left to play the marble game on their own, while an experimenter observed through a one-way mirror to record how many marbles they placed in the collection bowl. Finally, the children were given colored pencils as a reward for their participation in the experiment and told that they could deposit some of them in a box for classmates who had not participated. Among 8-year-olds, the treatments were equally effective in increasing donations of marbles, but only attribution increased the donation of pencils. The 8-year-olds generalized their increased helpfulness to a new situation only if they had heard themselves described as helpful. These results were confirmed in subsequent sessions with the same children.[34]

Grusec and Redler gathered additional, developmental evidence by repeating the marble-and-pencil experiment with older and younger children. Neither treatment had any effect on 5- and 6-year-olds, while they

[34] On a later occasion, the 8-year-olds were induced to help a different experimenter prepare materials for building toy houses, and they were again given praise, an attribution of helpfulness, or no feedback. They were then left alone and allowed to choose between playing with a toy or continuing with the helpful task, while an experimenter observed through a one-way mirror. Only attribution showed an effect on their tendency to help. One or two weeks later, these children were given an opportunity to donate drawings and craft materials to hospitalized children. Although total donations were too few for a full statistical analysis, more donations were received from the attribution group than from either of the others.

were equally effective on the 10-year-olds. Grusec and Redler hypothesized that the former subjects were too young to understand the implications of trait attributions, whereas the latter were sufficiently mature to extend the attributions on their own, without hearing them from the experimenters.

This developmental hypothesis was subsequently bolstered by research applying Freedman and Fraser's (1966) "foot-in-the-door" technique to children in the same range of ages. Eisenberg *et al.* (1987, 1989) rewarded children with prize coupons for participating in an experiment, and then induced some of them to donate part of their winnings to the poor. By eliciting this first donation, the experimenters had gotten a "foot in the door," designed to help them elicit further sharing behavior. Eisenberg *et al.* found that children were susceptible to this technique only if they were old enough to demonstrate an understanding of trait stability; and then their susceptibility was correlated with an independent measurement of their motivation toward self-consistency. These results suggest that the technique depended on the children's motivation to behave in accordance with self-attributions of helpfulness or generosity induced by their first donation.[35]

All of these experiments seem to show subjects being true to themselves by behaving in ways that verify self-attributions. Indeed, some of the experiments seem to confirm Lecky's claim that such behavioral self-verification accounts for moral behavior, while others seem to confirm his corresponding claim about academic performance. Hence attribution research with children is at least consistent with Lecky's views on the connection between being a bad speller and not being a thief.

Unfortunately, these findings involve the attribution of positive traits, and so they can in principle be explained by a motive of self-enhancement.[36] The children who heard themselves described as tidy or helpful may have come to regard tidy or helpful behavior as a way of earning that favorable description rather than as a way of making sense to themselves in light of it. Of course, a self-enhancement motive would not necessarily account for the difference in effectiveness between

---

35 For research connecting the foot-in-the-door effect to self-consistency motivation in adults, see Kraut (1973) and Goldman, Seever, & Seever (1982). For contrary findings, see Gorassini & Olson (1995). For other experiments in which children show a tendency to verify attributions, see Jensen & Moore (1977), Toner, Moore, & Emmons (1980), Biddle *et al.* (1985), and McGrath, Wilson, & Frassetto (1995).

36 The same is true of Jensen and Moore (1977); Toner, Moore, & Emmons (1980); Goldman, Seever, & Seever (1982); and Kraut (1973).

attribution and praise, or for the observed correlations with the development of trait-based self-understanding or with independently measured levels of motivation for self-consistency. But these phenomena may be too subtle to determine a choice between rival explanations.

What would confirm the existence of a cognitive motive is evidence that people tend to verify self-conceptions that don't enhance their self-esteem. Some researchers have therefore attempted to demonstrate a tendency to confirm negative self-conceptions.

In the classic experiment of this type, Aronson and Carlsmith (1962) asked subjects to identify the pictures of schizophrenics from among pictures that had in fact been randomly cut from a Harvard yearbook. Since subjects had no grounds for questioning the feedback they received about their rate of success, that feedback could be manipulated by the experimenters. Some subjects were led to believe that they were being consistently successful or unsuccessful; others were led to believe that they were scoring a long string of failures followed by a short string of successes, or a long string of successes followed by a short string of failures. All subjects were then given an opportunity to re-do the last set of items, on which some of them had seemed to take a turn for the better or the worse. Those who had seemed to take such a turn changed more of their answers, even if the turn they had taken was for the better. They thus appeared to prefer scoring consistently poorly to scoring inconsistently – as if trying to confirm the self-conception that they had formed during their initial string of failures.

Unfortunately, efforts to duplicate this result have met with only intermittent success.[37] One possible explanation, proposed by Swann (1986), is that most of the attempts at duplication have tested the effects of artificially induced self-conceptions about one's ability at a previously unfamiliar task. Yet the tendency to verify a self-conception appears to depend on the degree of certainty with which that conception is held.[38] Hence these experiments may not have induced self-conceptions with the degree of certainty required to produce an observable effect. And, indeed, the most persuasive replication of Aronson and Carlsmith's result was in subjects who had been found to hold negative overall self-views with relative certainty.[39] For these subjects, success was inconsistent

[37] See the review in Dipboye (1977).
[38] Swann & Ely (1984); Maracek & Mettee (1972); see also Setterlund & Niedenthal (1993).
[39] Maracek & Mettee (1972).

not only with an immediately prior series of failures but with a well-entrenched conception of themselves. Even so, this line of research cannot be regarded as clearly demonstrating the presence of self-consistency motivation.

Self-Attribution of Emotion

The research summarized in the previous section is inconclusive partly because it focuses on self-conceptions of personal traits. These traits are often conceived in evaluative terms, and so attributing them to oneself often yields a self-conception that is clearly favorable or clearly unfavorable. A tendency to verify favorable self-conceptions can always be explained by a motive of self-enhancement; and whatever cognitive motive there is to verify self-conceptions may not be sufficiently strong to prevail reliably over the desire to falsify them when they are unfavorable. Hence the self-attribution of personal traits is unlikely to produce clear evidence of self-consistency motivation. A more likely source of such evidence is the self-attribution of motives or emotions, which – unlike traits of character – are often evaluatively neutral.

In the classic experiment on such attributions, Schachter and Singer (1962) recruited subjects for an experiment billed as testing the effects of a vitamin on vision. Two thirds of the subjects were injected with adrenaline, labeled as the vitamin; one third were injected with a saline solution but told it was the vitamin as well. One of the adrenaline-injected groups was informed that the drug would cause symptoms of arousal – trembling hands, racing heart, and so on. The others were not warned of any side effects.

Each of the subjects then moved on to the next activity, at which he was ostensibly joined by a fellow subject, who was in fact a confederate of the experimenters. For half of each group, the confederate became increasingly angry at the next activity; for the other half, the confederate became giddy and playful. The experimenters then observed the extent to which the subjects were influenced by the confederates' behavior. Those who had received a placebo, and those who had received adrenaline and been warned of its side effects, were influenced significantly less than those who had received adrenaline without being warned. The latter group showed a marked tendency to behave as if they were angry or giddy, depending on how their fellow subjects were behaving.

Schachter and Singer hypothesized that the subjects in this group interpreted their arousal as anger or euphoria, according to the suggestion provided by their fellow subjects, and then enacted the emotion that they had attributed to themselves. So interpreted, the experiment showed that people have a tendency to behave in accordance with the motives that they *believe* themselves to have – which would be a tendency toward self-consistency.[40]

The Schachter-Singer results have repeatedly been called into question on methodological grounds.[41] But the underlying hypothesis has been confirmed in experiments of a significantly different design.

Zillman, Johnson, and Day (1974) arranged for subjects to be angered by someone and then to engage in vigorous exercise. Some of the subjects were given an opportunity to retaliate against their provoker shortly after exercising; others were given the same opportunity after a longer interval. The latter group retaliated more intensely than the former. Zillman and his colleagues hypothesized that the subjects' retaliation expressed the degree of anger that they perceived themselves as having; and that the excitatory effects of exercise were correctly interpreted by the first group but misinterpreted by the second as heightened anger.

This hypothesis was subsequently tested by Cantor, Zillman, and Bryant (1975), who asked subjects to report, at intervals following exercise, whether they still felt its excitatory effects. By measuring the subjects' levels of excitation at the same intervals, these experimenters detected an initial phase during which the effects of exercise continued and were perceived as continuing; a second phase during which the effects of exercise continued but were not perceived as such; and a third phase during which these effects had disappeared both objectively and subjectively. During each of these phases, erotic materials were shown to one third of the subjects, who were asked to report their degree of sexual arousal. Subjects exposed to erotica during the first phase reported no greater arousal than those exposed during the third phase; but those exposed during the second phase reported greater arousal than the others. Thus, arousal that was not attributed to exercise appears to have been misattributed to the erotica, supporting the hypothesis of a similar misattribution in the previous experiment.

---

[40] Actually, Schachter's (1964) theory of emotion implies that people actually *have* the emotions that they believe themselves to have, provided that they are in fact aroused or excited. This feature of Schachter's theory is philosophically problematic, but I won't discuss it here.

[41] Most recently by Messacappa, Katkin, & Palmer (1999).

Zillman (1978) therefore concludes that what led the previous subjects to behave angrily was a self-attribution of anger.[42] These experiments suggest that people tend to manifest not only what they're feeling but also what they think they're feeling. Note that there is no competing explanation of this tendency in terms of self-enhancement, since people are unlikely to regard anger as a self-enhancing attribute. The most likely explanation is that people tend to behave consistently with their self-attributions, being true to themselves in precisely the manner envisioned by Lecky.

Summary

This review of dissonance and attribution research has yielded two tentative conclusions. The research appears to show, first, that we tend to act in accordance with the motives and traits of character that we conceive of ourselves as having. The research is also consistent with a second

---

[42] For related experiments, see Brodt & Zimbardo (1981); Olson (1990); and the research of Berkowitz, discussed later.

Bem (1972) points out that experiments of this form often show more effect on the subjects' behavior than on their reported attitudes. In the Schachter-Singer study, for example, the misattribution condition was more strongly correlated with a tendency to join in the angry or giddy behavior of a fellow subject than with a tendency to report anger or giddiness. Bem argues that if the behavior were caused, as hypothesized, by the subjects' self-attributions, then the self-attributions ought to have been more strongly correlated with the experimental manipulations, not less. Bem therefore concludes that such experiments support self-perception theory, according to which the subjects' self-attributions were based on their behavior rather than vice versa.

Yet there are many ways of accounting for the weaker effect on attitudes than on behavior, even under the hypothesis that the attitudes came first in the order of causation. After all, the problematic correlations were observed, not with the attitudes themselves, but rather with the subjects' reports of those attitudes. Any gaps in the process of articulating self-attributions could therefore account for the results. Suppose, for example, that the subjects attributed anger or euphoria to themselves but not in so many words, or not in words at all. Perhaps they had mental images of those emotions (say, images of facial expressions or bodily postures), which they immediately associated with particular kinds of behavior, but to which they were not equally quick to attach names. Their self-attributions would then have been less reliable in prompting self-reports than in prompting behavior.

Even if we grant that Bem is right about the order of causation, his interpretation of the results would still support the hypothesis of cognitive motivation. A plausible explanation of the results, even as interpreted by Bem, is that the subjects behaved emotionally in order to facilitate the emotional attributions that would render their feelings intelligible. Feeling aroused, they sought a self-conception that would explain why, and they consequently behaved in ways that would make such a self-conception applicable to them. If their behavior was thus designed to facilitate the attribution, then it preceded the attribution in the order of causation; but it would still have been motivated by a cognitive interest in the self-understanding that the attribution would provide.

conclusion, that this tendency is due to a cognitive motive, to find ourselves explicable and predictable.

In the past I have argued that creatures endowed with such a motive would satisfy our ordinary concept of an agent in the respects that often seem to make that concept seem unsatisfiable. Creatures so motivated would have futures that were open in a sense sufficient to afford them choices or decisions;[43] they would be the causes rather than the mere vehicles of behavior;[44] they would be guided by the normative force of reasons for acting;[45] and they would find such force in principles requiring them to be moral.[46]

I will not repeat these arguments here. What I'll attempt instead is to highlight pieces of the psychological literature that already point the way toward the philosophy of action. This work by psychologists tends to support a philosophical theory like mine.

Philosophical Implications

Some psychologists have gestured toward the philosophy of action in the course of discussing self-consistency motivation. Zillman, for example, having concluded that self-attributions of emotion can influence behavior, goes on to speculate that their influence makes for the difference between automatic manifestations of emotion and emotional actions that are under voluntary control. In Zillman's view, an emotion involves some basic motor responses, which can be reinforced, suppressed, or redirected by the subject's interpretation of them. The basic motor responses belong to "the primitive heritage of man," which we share with the lower animals, and they are not under voluntary control; their modulation by the subject's self-interpretation manifests his "rational capabilities," by which he controls his behavioral response.[47]

Berkowitz draws a similar distinction between impulsive and purposive aggression. In collaboration with Turner (1974), he manipulated the degree of anger that subjects attributed to themselves toward a particular person, thereby modifying the intensity of the "punishment" that they inflicted on that person, though not their aggression toward a third party. Berkowitz emphasizes that the attribution-governed aggression observed

---

[43] Velleman (1989a).
[44] Velleman (1992b) and Introduction to 2000c.
[45] Velleman (1996) and Introduction to 2000c.
[46] Velleman (1989b), Part Four.
[47] Zillman (1978), pp. 356–57. See also Cross & Markus (1990); Wegner & Bargh (1998).

in this experiment was purposive rather than impulsive. "[I]mpulsive acts," he says, "are automatic, stimulus-elicited responses to the external situation governed primarily by associative factors and relatively unaffected by cognitive processes."[48] By contrast, purposive aggression is subject to cognitive governance:[49]

The present results generally support [my] cognitive analysis of purposive aggression. Emotionally aroused people seek to attack a particular target when (a) they interpret their internal sensations as "anger," and (b) they believe this specific target had been the cause of their feelings. As indicated in this study, the intensity of the subjects' desire to hurt a particular person, reflected in the intensity of the punishment given him, arose from their perceptions of the strength of their anger and their belief that this person had been the one who had provoked them.

Berkowitz goes on to explain this mechanism in terms of a cognitive motive toward self-consistency:[50]

Looked at from a larger perspective, the findings also provide yet another demonstration of the search for cognitive consistency. We want our actions to be in accord with our emotions, as we understand them, and apparently we are also disturbed if these feelings do not seem to be warranted by the causal incident. The emotion as well as the behavior must be consistent with our other cognitions.

The idea that behavior becomes purposive or intentional when it is regulated for self-consistency can be traced back to the early days of self-consistency theory. Six years after the publication of Lecky's treatise, Carl Rogers published "A Theory of Personality and Behavior" offering a similar postulate:[51]

Most of the ways of behaving which are adopted by the organism are those which are consistent with the concept of self.... As the organism strives to meet its needs in the world as it is experienced, the form which the striving takes must be a form consistent with the concept of self.... The person who regards himself as having no aggressive feelings cannot satisfy a need for aggression in any direct fashion. The only channels by which needs may be satisfied are those which are consistent with the organized concept of self.

[48] *Ibid.*, p. 176.
[49] *Ibid.*, pp. 186–87. See also Berkowitz (1987).
[50] *Ibid.* See also Berkowitz (1987).
[51] *Client-Centered Therapy: Its Current Practice, Implications, and Theory* (Boston: Houghton Mifflin, 1951), Chapter 11, 507–08. For other theories in the Leckian tradition, see Snygg & Combs (1959); Kelley (1967); Korman (1970); Epstein (1973), (1981); Andrews (1991); Nuttin (1984).

To this Leckian postulate, Rogers added the following piece of action theory:[52]

Behavior may, in some instances, be brought about by organic experiences and needs which have not been symbolized. Such behavior may be inconsistent with the structure of the self, but in such instances the behavior is not "owned" by the individual. . . . In such instances the individual feels "I didn't know what I was doing," "I really wasn't responsible for what I was doing." The conscious self feels no degree of government over the actions which took place.

According to Rogers, then, only behavior that is regulated for self-consistency is experienced as intentional action, for which the subject takes responsibility. Hence the difference between mere behavior and intentional action – the difference, as Wittgenstein put it, between my arm's rising and my raising it – may be due to the intervention of a self-consistency motive.

Carrying Out an Intention

Other psychologists have filled in the self-verification process with steps that correspond to steps in the production of intentional action, as it is ordinarily understood. They have pointed out that people must have not only a conception of their motives but also a conception of what they are doing out of those motives – for example, that they are "retaliating" against someone, or that they are "donating" to the poor. There is evidence that the latter conception also tends to influence their behavior, thereby playing the role of an intention to act.

Wegner, Vallacher, and colleagues (1986) led subjects through a sham experiment involving a clerical task, and then asked them to complete a questionnaire about the degree to which various descriptions applied to the activity in which they had just participated. Some of the suggested descriptions were designed to test whether the subjects conceived of the activity in low-level, mechanical terms, such as "making marks on paper," or high-level, explanatory terms, such as "participating in an experiment."

---

[52] *Ibid.*, p. 509. In this quotation, philosophers of action will detect a resemblance to Harry Frankfurt's theory of autonomy (1988c, 1999c). Like Frankfurt, Rogers believed that whether behavior amounts to an autonomous action depends on its relation to the self. But if Rogers had expressed his view in these terms, he would have been using the psychologist's sense of 'self', which refers to the self-conception; whereas Frankfurt uses the term in a philosophical sense referring to the core or essence of the person. Rogers thus resembles Frankfurt partly by courtesy of ambiguity. (For psychologists who prefer a Frankfurtian conception of the self, see Deci & Ryan [1991].)

The last seven items were designed to suggest either altruistic descriptions ("helping people study psychology," "aiding the experimenter") or egoistic descriptions ("getting a better grade in psychology," "earning extra credit"). The experimenters then left the room, to allow the subject-pool coordinator to distribute a questionnaire about the subjects' preferences among future opportunities to participate in research. Among the opportunities offered, one was described in altruistic terms, and another in egoistic terms.

The experimenters found that subjects who initially conceived of the prior activity in low-level terms were more likely to adopt the suggested high-level descriptions and also expressed a higher preference for future opportunities described in similar terms. In other words, subjects who could be induced to think of their current participation as "helping" were more inclined to "help" in the future, whereas subjects who could be induced to think of their current participation as "getting ahead" were more inclined toward future opportunities to "get ahead."

This experiment can be interpreted as demonstrating a "foot-in-the-door" effect; but in this case the effect appears to be mediated by act-descriptions rather that trait- or motive-attributions. The experimenters got their foot in the door by enlisting a subject's participation in one experiment, and they were then able to elicit his willingness to participate in another, but only by getting him to conceive of the second under the same description as the first.[53] This dependence was the same for egoistic as for altruistic actions. Vallacher and Wegner (1985) therefore remark, "although egoism and altruism can represent opposing forces in everyday life, they arise from similar action identification processes."[54]

On the basis of this and related experiments, Wegner and Vallacher have proposed a theory of action identification. The first principle of their theory is "that people do what they think they are doing," by selecting a "prepotent act identity," or act description, and then instantiating it in their behavior.[55] The result, according to Wegner and Vallacher, is that

---

[53] Kraut (1973) links the foot-in-the-door effect to the attribution of traits, such as "charitable" and "uncharitable," rather than to act-descriptions. But my view is that attributions of traits, motives, and acts are themselves linked, under the principle of self-consistency. That is, someone who conceives of himself as angry finds it consistent to conceive of himself as retaliating; someone who conceives of himself as uncharitable finds it inconsistent to conceive of himself as donating to charity; and so on.

[54] Vallacher & Wegner (1985), p. 143.

[55] Wegner & Vallacher (1986), p. 552.

people usually *know* what they're doing, because they are doing what they think.[56]

This principle can readily be interpreted as describing an intermediate step in the self-verification process described here.[57] We can imagine, first, that the cognitively motivated agent selects a "prepotent act identity" consistent with the motives and other dispositions that he conceives himself to have. Conceiving of himself as angry, he thinks of doing something consistent with anger, such as retaliating; conceiving of himself as generous, he thinks of doing something consistent with generosity, such as making a donation. He thereby maintains the coherence of his self-conception. When he goes on to do what he is thinking, we can regard him as taking the next step in the same process. For we can imagine that he does what he's thinking *in order to* know what he's doing, given that whatever he thinks he's about to do is the thing that he would consequently know about, if he did it. The agent thinks of doing something that fits his self-attributed motive, and then he does what fits this self-attribution of action, so that his self-conception is consistent with itself and with his actual behavior.

Wegner and Vallacher suggest that the agent's "prepotent act identity" is in fact an intention to act: in doing what he thinks, the agent is carrying out an intention.[58] This suggestion enables us to map the self-verification process, as now elaborated, onto the process of intentional action as ordinarily understood. Described in theoretical terms, the process goes like this: first, something arouses the agent's anger, which already involves some behavioral dispositions; then the agent interprets his arousal *as* anger and thinks of what, in light of it, would make sense for him to do; finally, the agent's anger and his thought of behaving angrily jointly cause the corresponding behavior – the behavioral impetus of the one being regulated for consistency with the other by the agent's motive for making sense. But now we can redescribe the same process in ordinary language, by attaching the term 'motive' to the agent's anger and the term 'intention' to his thought of behaving angrily. Thus redescribed, the process goes like this: the agent forms an intention that's consistent with his motive; and then he acts, under the impetus of his motive, as regulated for consistency with his intention. The theory of self-verification can thus be seen to coincide with our ordinary understanding of intentional action.

---

[56] Ibid., p. 568. See also Velleman (1989), Chapters 1 and 2.
[57] See also Aronson, 1992, p. 307.
[58] Vallacher & Wegner (1985), pp. 6–11.

Acting for Reasons

If the agent's doing what he is thinking constitutes the carrying out of an intention, then what about the preceding step, in which he thinks of doing what would make the most sense? To which phase or aspect of an action, as ordinarily understood, does that earlier part of the self-consistency process correspond?

Wegner and Vallacher allude to this step in a further principle, which says that people ordinarily seek to identify their behavior at a "high" or "comprehensive" level, representing their underlying motives and ultimate goals. Wegner and Vallacher describe this tendency as a "search for meaning in action"[59] or "a human inclination to be informed of what we are doing in the most integrative and general way available."[60] An act-description will be "integrative," of course, insofar as it incorporates the motives and traits that the act expresses and in light of which it will make sense. Hence the "search for meaning" posited by Wegner and Vallacher coincides with the agent's search for an act-description that makes sense in light of his self-conception.

The process of adopting and then instantiating integrative act-descriptions resembles – or, in fact, may just *be* – a process of enacting a coherent narrative.[61] Consider Trzebinski's (1995) discussion of self-narratives, which makes them sound like Wegner and Vallacher's act identities:

Constructing self-narratives is the mode of searching for a meaning.... To find meaning, and more often just to maintain meaning and avoid disruption of the ordered world, an individual has to move in a specified way within the narrated events. In this way the active schema...not only directs the individual's interpretations of on-going and foreseen events, but also pushes him toward specific aspirations, decisions, and actions. By particular moves within the events an individual elaborates, fulfils, and closes important episodes in the developing self-narrative. Personal decisions and actions are inspired by, and take strength from self-narratives – devices for meaning searching.

A self-narrative can thus provide the meaningful act-descriptions that enable the agent to understand what he's doing. When he instantiates one of these narrative act descriptions, he performs an action that "elaborates, fulfils, and closes" an episode in his self-narrative, so that his behavior is intelligible as part of the story.

---

[59] Wegner & Vallacher (1986), pp. 555–56.
[60] Vallacher & Wegner (1985), p. 26.
[61] See Velleman (1993).

I suggest that the narrative background on which the agent draws, in order to fashion an integrative act description, is material that would ordinarily be called his reasons for acting – the circumstances, motives, and other considerations that make one action rather than another the sensible thing to do. I therefore suggest that adopting an integrative act description amounts to forming an intention on the basis of a reason, and that enacting such a description amounts to acting for the reason on which the intention was based.

Philosophers have long noted a distinction between doing something that one has reason to do, on the one hand, and doing it *for* that reason, on the other.[62] One can do something that one has reason to do without necessarily doing it *for* that reason, because one can fail to be appropriately influenced by the reason that one has. Philosophers have therefore sought to analyze the influence that a reason exerts when one acts for that reason.

The traditional assumption among philosophers is that a reason for acting must include the expectation of a desired outcome, and that this expectation influences the agent by appealing to his desire for the outcome expected. Elsewhere I have argued that the influence exerted by an agent's expectation of a desired outcome does not satisfy our concept of the influence exerted by a reason.[63] Indeed, the assumption that expectations of desire- or preference-satisfaction have the normative force of reasons is itself in need of justification.[64]

In my view, an agent is influenced by a reason, and his action is consequently performed *for* that reason, when he is influenced by a representation of the action that makes it intelligible to him. Naturally, this representation may make the action intelligible precisely by setting it in the context of his desires and expectations, but his reason for the action consists in this cognitively attractive representation of it rather than in the desires and expectations to which it alludes. A reason is a *rationale*, in light of which an action makes sense to the agent, and promoting a desired outcome is one such rationale.

If I am right, then the search for an integrative act description to instantiate, or a meaningful story to enact, is in fact a search for an action supported by reasons. And an act identity has "pre-potency" insofar as it

---

[62] E.g., Davidson (1980).

[63] Velleman (1992a), (1992b), (1996); "Introduction" to Velleman (2000c).

[64] Velleman (1993); Korsgaard (1997).

satisfies this search, by serving as a rationale. When the agent does what he is thinking under an integrative act description, or "fulfills and closes" an episode in his self-narrative, he is doing what philosophers call acting for reasons. The upshot is that the steps of finding and acting for reasons correspond to successive steps in the self-verification process, the process of being true to oneself.

Conclusion

Nuttin has illustrated the resulting theory of practical reasoning as follows:[65]

Consider a son who is tempted to lie to his parents in order to be able to accompany his friends on a vacation despite the anticipated opposition of his father. The son must evaluate and determine the extent to which he is able to integrate within one structure the two conflicting components: his image of himself and the lie to his parents as he perceives it in the present behavioral context. Is he able to take up, subsume, or accept that concrete type of lying within his dynamic self-concept? The strength of the tendency to accompany his friends will be one of the factors determining the degree of distortion of the self-image that can be tolerated by the personality. The degree of inner consistency within the subject's personality will be another factor. In some people, there will be no difficulty at all in subsuming the lying behavior in the self-concept; in other people, accepting such a lie within their own personality functioning will not be possible. In the latter case, the subject is not "willing" to lie in the present behavioral context.

In my view, the conflict between the boy's desire to accompany his friends, on the one hand, and his need for a coherent self-conception, on the other, is a conflict between inclination and practical reason. If the boy finds a way to reconcile the lie with his self-conception – a story to tell himself about telling the lie, which would amount to a rationale for telling it – then his practical reason condones telling the lie, and he is consequently "willing" to tell it. But if he cannot reconcile telling a lie with his self-conception, then his need for self-understanding opposes his telling it, and this opposition embodies the restraint that practical reason places on his inclination to lie.

As Vallacher and Wegner point out,[66] this same process can lead to immoral as well as moral behavior. Or, as Lecky suggested, it can lead to bad spelling. What a Leckian moral philosophy will need, then, is an

---

[65] Nuttin (1984), p. 187.
[66] Quoted at note 54.

account of why a conception of oneself as honest is more rational than a conception of oneself as dishonest; or, for that matter, why a conception of oneself as a good speller is more rational than a conception of oneself as a poor one, given that one will do as one conceives. I have attempted such an account elsewhere.[67] Here I have tried to connect the underlying moral philosophy to an empirical basis in the psychological research that Lecky inspired.

[67] See Velleman (1989a), Part III.

11

The Centered Self

In that demand he was obeying the voice of his rigid conscience, which
had never left him perfectly at rest under his one act of deception – the
concealment from Esther that he was not her natural father, the assertion
of a false claim upon her. 'Let my path be henceforth simple,' he had said
to himself in the anguish of that night; 'let me seek to know what is, and if
possible to declare it.'

– George Eliot, *Felix Holt*

We have many expressions to describe a person who is trustworthy and
true – a *rock*, a *brick*, a *Mensch*. In a more analytical mood, we describe
such a person as *grounded* or *centered*. I want to consider what it is to

An ancestor of this chapter, entitled "A Sense of Self," was presented as one of the Jerome
Simon lectures at the University of Toronto; to a conference on personal identity and
practical reason at the University of Illinois, Chicago; to the Moral Philosophy Seminar at
Oxford University; and to the philosophy departments at the University of Virginia, NYU,
and Tufts University. "A Sense of Self" was the target of a paper delivered by Maik Tåndler to
the Göttinger Philosophisches Kolloquium in January 2003, where much helpful discussion
ensued; and it was the topic of discussion at a September 2003 meeting of the Ohio Reading
Group in Ethics. Thanks are due to Ted Hinchman, Jim Joyce, Dick Moran, and Thomas
Schmidt for extensive comments on drafts of that essay.

The present chapter was delivered at the University of Michigan; to the philosophy
departments of the University of Saskatchewan, the University of California at Riverside, the
University of Dundee, the University of Stirling; the University of Edinburgh, the University
of St. Andrews, and the University of Bristol; at a conference on Values, Rational Choice, and
the Will at the University of Wisconsin, Stevens Point; and at the 2004 Oberlin Colloquium,
where the commentator was Tom Hill. This chapter contains material from the "Precis" and
"Replies" that I contributed to a symposium on my book *The Possibility of Practical Reason*
(Oxford: Oxford University Press, 2000). The symposium, with commentaries by Jonathan
Dancy, Alfred Mele, and Nadeem Hussain, was published in *Philosophical Studies* 121 (2004).

be grounded or centered, and then to explain what being grounded or centered has to do with being trustworthy and true.

My account begins with a quality generally regarded as distinctive of persons – namely, self-awareness.[1] Of course, a brick or a rock isn't self-aware; but a person can be a brick or a rock in the figurative sense only through the utmost development of that which differentiates him as a person from bricks and rocks literally so called. If we want to identify the relevant differences, however, we do better to contrast a person with something that comes a bit closer to personhood – say, a cat.

Now, a cat is conscious, I assume, and it has the sort of consciousness whose content can be put into words only with the help of the first-person pronoun. A cat could never catch a mouse if it couldn't have thoughts representing the world from its own egocentric perspective, thoughts with English-language equivalents such as "I'm gaining on it" or "I've got it." There is a sense, then, in which a cat has first-personal awareness. A cat can even have a reflexive awareness of a sort, as when it realizes that the tail it has been chasing is its own.

---

[1] This section is heavily indebted to Thomas Nagel's work on "the objective self" and John Perry's work on self-knowledge. I include a discussion of Perry in Appendix A. In the remainder of this note I'll briefly summarize my debt to Nagel.

Nagel has argued that the self is that part or aspect of a person that harbors his objective conception of the world. This conception provides the mental context for the question "Who am I?" When a person asks himself "Who am I?" he is in effect asking "Which person am I?" while surveying the possible candidates from an impartial distance. "Who am I?" must therefore be understood as spoken from a standpoint that's objective in the sense that it views all persons from the outside as possible referents for the pronoun 'who'. And the 'I' in this question must emanate from that part or aspect of a person which occupies this stance, surveying people from a distance and seeking to identify with one of them.

This conception of oneself, as a person among others, figured in Nagel's first book, *The Possibility of Altruism*, as the starting point of moral thought. There, Nagel argued that the conception of oneself as a person among others constrains one's practical reasoning in the manner of Kant's Categorical Imperative. If this argument is combined with the premise of Nagel's argument about the self, the result is a conclusion about the source of morality. The conclusion is that moral constraints on practical reasoning are imposed by nothing other than one's sense of identity. My aim in this chapter can be described in the same terms.

See Nagel, "Subjective and Objective," in *Mortal Questions* (Cambridge: Cambridge University Press, 1979), 196–213; 'The Limits of Objectivity," in *The Tanner Lectures on Human Values*, Vol. I, ed. S. McMurrin (Salt Lake City: University of Utah Press, 1980), 77–139; "The Objective Self," in *Knowledge and Mind*, ed. Carl Ginet and Sydney Shoemaker (New York: Oxford University Press, 1983), 211–32; *The View From Nowhere* (New York: Oxford University Press, 1986), Chapter IV. *The View From Nowhere* is perhaps the most widely read of these works, but its chapter on the "objective self" is, in my view, considerably watered down. I recommend the essay entitled "The Objective Self" in the volume edited by Ginet and Shoemaker.

What a cat lacks, however, is a conception of a creature that it is. A cat is aware of the mouse that it is chasing, but it is not aware of there being a creature by whom the mouse is hereby being chased. When a cat recognizes its own tail, it merely forges a mental association between an object seen to its rear and a locus of sensation or motion at its rear end. It has no conception of being a creature chasing its own tail.

By contrast, when a person realizes that he's stepping on his own shoelaces, he attains more than a mental association between the sensation of treading on something with one foot and the sensation of being tripped up in the other. He has the concept of a particular person bearing the name to which he answers, sporting the face that looks back at him from the mirror, and doing the things that he is aware of doing – including, at the moment, stepping on his own shoelaces. Unlike a cat, a person is aware of being somebody, and he usually knows a fair amount about the somebody who he is.

A person's conception of who he is constitutes the axis on which he can potentially be centered, or the anchor by which he can potentially be grounded. Here I hope to be saying nothing new. I take it to be part of the ordinary concept of being grounded or centered that these qualities depend on a person's sense of identity. Less obvious, perhaps, is that a person's sense of identity involves an objective conception of someone in the world who he is – a particular, persisting member of the objective order to whom he can pin the unseen point at the center of his point-of-view. What is not at all obvious, and what I hope to explain, is how pinning his point-of-view to that person can make him a rock or a brick or a *Mensch*, trustworthy and true.

In order to explore this question, I'll need an example of a situation that (you should pardon the expression) separates the *Menschen* from the boys and girls. I'm going to use the most familiar example that I know of – the prisoners' dilemma. My goal is to show how our understanding of this tired example can be refreshed by reflection on the nature of human self-awareness. I'll start with a quick review of how the dilemma comes about.

Suppose that you and I find ourselves in circumstances where each would lose something by cooperating with the other, no matter what the other does, but would lose even more from the other's failure to cooperate. The cooperation at issue might be helping to harvest one another's fields or, to invoke the relevant cliché, merely scratching one another's backs. In these circumstances, neither of us has anything to gain from helping the other, whether or not the other helps us, and both of us therefore face the prospect of the other's refusing to help. We might wish that we could escape the dilemma through an exchange of mutually dependent offers of the form "I will cooperate if you will."[2] As is well known, however, the resulting agreement would generate a second-order dilemma, since each of us would lose by following through on the agreement, though he would lose even more from the other's refusal to follow through.

Assume that none of the usual devices for resolving our dilemma is available – no past experience with one another, no external sanctions against cheating, no future opportunities for retaliation or repayment. Assume, in other words, that ours is a classic, one-time prisoners' dilemma, in which the parties have knowledge of nothing but the payoffs and one another's rationality. The point of this assumption, for my purposes, is to deprive us of any social, emotional, or indeed moral resources for coping with our dilemma, not because such resources are absent from dilemmas in real life but because their absence from this imagined dilemma will force us to rely on resources of the solitary, even solipsistic kind to which centeredness and groundedness belong. My exclusive

---

[2] I will discuss a version of the dilemma in which the parties are given the opportunity to make a cooperative agreement, if they can; and my resolution of the dilemma will ultimately depend on the rationality of making and then abiding by such an agreement. Hence my discussion of the prisoners' dilemma is not about the rationality of cooperation *per se*; it's about the rationality of truth-telling and constancy in agreements. I do not try to show that acting cooperatively is rational in itself; I try to show only that it can be made rational by the exchange of commitments that are in turn rational for the parties to exchange and then to carry out.

This distinction is essential to coordinating the present discussion with the discussions of Kantian ethics elsewhere in this volume. As I explain in "A Brief Introduction to Kantian Ethics" (Chapter 2 in the present volume), a moral requirement to cooperate in the prisoners' dilemma must be derived, in Kantian theory, from a contradiction in the will. A universal law of non-cooperation is not impossible in itself, and so Kantianism must find a rational obstacle to our willing there to be such a law. (See also "Willing the Law" [Chapter 12 in the present volume].) But as I also explain in the "Brief Introduction," moral strictures against breaking commitments and lying are derived from contradictions in conception – that is, from the impossibility of there being universal laws for these practices rather than from our inability to will such laws. Since my resolution of the prisoners' dilemma in this chapter depends on the rationality of truth-telling and constancy in cooperative agreements, rather than the rationality of cooperative action in itself, my argument will correspond to the Kantian derivation of a contradiction in conception rather than a contradiction in the will. My remarks in the "Brief Introduction" to the effect that prisoners' dilemmas generate contradictions in the will are about the morality of acting cooperatively in such dilemmas, not the morality of making and keeping agreements to do so.

focus on these resources should not be taken to imply that they are the only resources available for coping with prisoners' dilemmas.

The idea of offering to cooperate in these circumstances is not entirely daft. Mutually beneficial cooperation would be possible if only we had, and knew that we had, two crucial abilities. First, each of us would need the ability to form an effective conditional intention, to cooperate if the other formed a reciprocal and equally effective intention.[3] By "an effective intention" I mean an intention that would determine the course of the subject's future behavior – in this case, by determining the subject to cooperate if he knew that the other party intended likewise. Second, each would need the ability to let the other know his state of mind. By "to let the other know his state of mind" I mean making his state of mind evident to the other so as to instill in him a true and reliably justified belief as to whether the condition on his own intention had been fulfilled. If we had these two abilities, and our having them was common knowledge between us, then each of us would have good reason to form the conditional intention to cooperate if the other intended likewise, and then to let the other know of that intention, by saying "I'll cooperate if you will."[4] Each party's intention would lead him to bear the cost of actually cooperating only if its condition were fulfilled by the other's intention, in which case it would fulfill the condition of the other's intention, thereby leading to the greater benefit of the other's cooperation. The costs of committing himself to cooperate would therefore be appropriately linked to overriding benefits, which would accrue from triggering the other's commitment.

This calculation is what gives rise to the idea of saying "I'll cooperate if you will." Unfortunately, the calculation reckons on our having abilities that can seem impossible for us to have. How can I determine my future behavior by means of a present intention? And how can I give you reliable grounds for believing that I have such an intention? In any cooperative agreement, the benefit to me flows from your believing in my effectively

---

[3] Note that each commitment is conditional on the other speaker's commitment rather than his action. That is, each says "I will cooperate if you will," not ". . . if you do." Hence the condition on each commitment is satisfied as soon as the other commitment is issued. I discuss such commitments at length in the Appendix to "Deciding How to Decide," reprinted in *The Possibility of Practical Reason*, 242–43.

[4] Here I am assuming that, although we have the ability to make our intentions known to one another, we do *not* have the ability to lead one another to believe in intentions that we do not actually have. The latter ability would enable us to skip the step of forming a cooperative intention before expressing it.

intending to cooperate, not from my actually intending to cooperate, and certainly not from my so intending effectively. Even if I formed an intention to cooperate, I would have no reason to let it take effect in my future behavior, and I have no reason to form a cooperative intention if I can convincingly feign one instead. It therefore seems that I cannot commit my future self to cooperate, and that, even if I could, I cannot give credible evidence of having done so. A classic, one-time prisoners' dilemma thus generates two problems – a problem of commitment and a problem of credibility – neither of which appears to be soluble in the circumstances.

What makes these problems seem insoluble, however, is the instrumental conception of practical reasoning as a calculation of costs and benefits, a conception that narrows the range of considerations available to us as participants in the dilemma. We are in fact capable of making rationally effective commitments and of giving one another rational grounds for believing in them. Not surprisingly, our capacity to be credibly committed depends on our capacity to be centered or grounded, which in turn depends on the sense of identity made available to us by our distinctively human form of self-awareness. The problem with the instrumental conception of practical reasoning is that it affords no role for our sense of identity to play, and hence no role for our capacity to be centered or grounded. No wonder, then, that it makes credible commitments seem impossible. What's needed is a conception of practical reasoning that has a role for our sense of identity, which might in turn explain our capacity for credible commitments. So let's examine the connection between practical reasoning and self-awareness.

As we have seen, self-awareness gives me an objective conception of the person who I am. That conception bears on practical reasoning, to begin with, by giving me access to objective knowledge of what I am doing.

Of course, a cat is also aware of doing things, such as hissing at someone by whom it feels threatened. But a cat's awareness of its own doings never extends to the knowledge that they are being done by a creature in the world. It represents them from the perspective of the one doing them, without representing the creature occupying that perspective. Thus, even when a cat is aware of hissing at you, and even if it is hissing with the thought of scaring you away, it cannot be thinking that you will be scared of this hissing creature – scared, that is, of its hissing self – because it has no conception of being one of the world's creatures, and hence no sense of self. By contrast, if I tried to scare you away, I would be aware of confronting you with a person saying "Scram!" as would be manifest in that very utterance, since a person saying "Scram!" is intimidating precisely by virtue of manifesting the intention to be an intimidating person.

In performing a communicative action of this kind, I must be able to understand what I am doing as I intend it to be understood by you. In order to tell whether my behavior might be understood as my trying to scare you away, I must find it potentially understandable in those terms, vicariously sharing the understanding that I intend to elicit. This shared understanding requires me to conceive of what I'm doing as done by the creature who I am, a creature who might potentially scare you away by saying "Scram!" – which is different from conceiving merely of doing it, from the perspective of the unrepresented do-er.

Along with the ability to understand what I'm doing as done by the creature who I am comes the possibility of finding it unintelligible in those terms. A cat can round on its own tail and wonder, "What is that thing up to?" But I can round on my entire self and wonder, "What is this creature up to?" As soon as a cat associates the waving motion that it sees to its rear with the motion that it is aware of making from its rear end, its puzzlement is over. It knows why the tail is waving, since it is now aware of waving it. It cannot go on with "Yes, but why am I waving my tail?" That question would be about the behavior of a tail-waving creature, which it has no cognizance of being. Self-puzzlement of this latter kind is possible only for a creature whose awareness of doing things results in an awareness of their being done by the creature who he is.

I think that the state of mind variously described as puzzlement, mystification, confusion, perplexity, or bewilderment deserves more philosophical attention than it ordinarily receives. This state is aversive: we try to avoid it, and when we have gotten into it, we try to get out. The aversiveness of this state is a reminder that we have intellectual drives. We do not passively receive knowledge; we gain it through cognitive activity, driven by intellectual impulses. And the frustration of these impulses is aversive, like the frustration of any fundamental drive.

A human being's intellectual impulses are sometimes directed at the person who he is. The creature with whom he is aware of being identical naturally has a special salience for him – as the creature walking in his shoes, sleeping in his bed, eating his meals – and the doings of that creature therefore become the object of his intellectual drives. But the person's awareness of being identical with that creature opens up an obvious shortcut to knowledge about its doings. He must realize that doing things – that is, behaviors conceived from his perspective as the unrepresented agent – constitutes their being done by that creature, the same behavior conceived objectively. And he must realize that seeking to know what it is doing – an intellectual activity conceived from his perspective as the unrepresented inquirer – constitutes that creature's striving for self-knowledge. Finally, then, he must realize that he can know what that creature is doing simply by doing what he conceives of it as doing, or as being about to do, since his conception will then turn out to be not only true but also justified, on the grounds of the creature's having this very intellectual incentive to bear it out. He tends to behave as he conceives of that creature as behaving because he will then have, embodied in that conception, a knowledge of what that creature is doing; and that conception will have the reliability of knowledge because it is about a creature for whom the prospect of having knowledge embodied in it is an incentive to behave accordingly.

Strange as this psychological mechanism may sound, it has been copiously documented by social psychologists working in the area that is sometimes labeled "self-consistency," an area encompassing the topics of cognitive dissonance and attribution. Research in this area has shown that people have a broad tendency to behave in ways that cohere with their own conceptions of themselves – of how they behave in general and of their motives on a particular occasion. Potential voters are more likely to vote in an election if they have antecedently predicted that they are going to. Children are more likely to be tidy if told that they *are* tidy than if told that they ought to be. People behave angrily if they are led to believe that they are angry – the more angrily, the more angry they are led to believe they are. Shy people don't behave shyly if they are led to attribute the symptoms of their social anxiety to other causes. And so on.[5]

One team of researchers has observed that subjects' behavior can be influenced by the act-descriptions that they are antecedently prompted to frame, as if they have a tendency to fulfill antecedently framed descriptions of their forthcoming actions.[6] This tendency is cited by the researchers to explain how people know what they are doing – which is the very explanation that I have just offered: people know what they're doing because they tend to do what they have just now thought that they

---

[5] I discuss these and other empirical results in "From Self Psychology to Moral Philosophy" (Chapter 10 in the present volume).

[6] See the publications of Wegner, Vallacher, and colleagues cited at notes 59 and 60 of "From Self Psychology to Moral Philosophy" (Chapter 10 of the present volume).

are just about to do. The psychologists give this mechanism the label "act identification." And they invoke this mechanism, not only to explain how people generally know what they are doing, but also as a model for the process of acting on an intention: to frame an act-description and then fulfill it, they suggest, is just to form an intention and act on it.

With this reference to acting on an intention, we begin to see the true relevance of self-awareness to practical reasoning. Because I have an objective conception of the creature who I am, I can be puzzled by the behavior of that creature, but I can also avoid such puzzlement by first framing an idea of the creature's next action and then enacting that idea, a process that social psychologists have observed and have identified with the process of forming and acting on an intention. And acting on an intention is the consummation of practical reasoning.

This model of intention illustrates a central thesis of the book entitled *Intention*, by Elizabeth Anscombe. In that book, Anscombe analyzes the difference between what we do and what merely happens to us, or in us. The difference, she argues, is that our doings are the object of a special kind of knowledge, which Anscombe calls "knowledge without observation."

Anscombe uses the notion of knowledge without observation to explain the difference between two kinds of indicative statements about the future: expressions of belief, such as "I'm going to be sick," and expressions of intention, such as "I am going to take a walk" (p. 1). If someone responds to the statement "I am going to be sick" by asking "Why would you do a thing like that?" he has misinterpreted the speech act, by failing to recognize it as an expression of belief rather than intention. Conversely, if someone responds to "I am going to take a walk" with "How can you tell?" he has failed to recognize it as an expression of intention rather than belief. Now, the difference between these statements cannot lie in the former's being informative and hence potentially knowledge-conveying, since the latter is also informative and hence potentially knowledge-conveying. As Anscombe puts it, "the indicative (descriptive, informatory) character is not the distinctive mark of 'predictions' *as opposed to* 'expressions of intention', as we might at first sight have been tempted to think" (§2, p. 3).

In Anscombe's view, the difference between "I am going to take a walk" and "I am going to be sick," given that both can convey knowledge possessed by the speaker, is that the knowledge conveyed by the latter is speculative, whereas the knowledge conveyed by the former is practical, in the sense that it causes the facts that make it true (§48, p. 87). "I am going to be sick" expresses a belief that is caused by evidence of the speaker's becoming sick, whereas "I am going to take a walk" expresses an intention that causes the speaker to take a walk. In expressing this intention, however, the speaker is also expressing his knowledge of what he is going to do, which must therefore be "known by the being the content of [his] intention" (§30, p. 53). Hence the speaker has knowledge embodied in a mental state that causes – rather than being caused by, or causally concomitant to – the facts that make it true (§48, p. 87).[7] Knowledge that is thus productive rather than receptive of what is known is what Anscombe has in mind when speaking of "knowledge without observation."

Why might one be tempted to think of agency in this way? Anscombe attributes her use of the phrase "practical knowledge" to Aquinas, for whom the phrase described God's knowledge of His creation. God knows what the world is like, but not by dint of having found out; He knows what the world is like because it is just as He means it to be. And His meaning it to be that way already constitutes knowledge on His part of how it is. This epistemological relation that God bears to the world – knowing how it is just by meaning it to be that way – is constitutive of His role as the world's designer. The designer of something is the one whose conception of the thing determines how it is, rather than vice versa, and determines this by a mechanism reliable enough to justify his confidence in that conception as an accurate representation. To be the designer of something is just to be the one whose conception of it has epistemic authority by virtue of being its cause rather than its concomitant or effect.

Anscombe's nod to medieval theology as her source for the term "practical knowledge" suggests that she conceives of intentional action as a realm in which human beings exercise a minor share of divinity. We create our intentional actions, just as God creates the world, and our creating them consists in our framing a conception of them that has epistemic authority by virtue of being determinative of them.

What I have sometimes presumed to call my theory of agency is little more than a variation on this theme of Anscombe's. My main departure from Anscombe has been to introduce a story about the dynamics of practical

---

[7] It is important not to confuse practical knowledge, in Anscombe's sense of the term, with practical wisdom, or *phronesis*, as discussed by Aristotle. Practical knowledge, also called maker's knowledge, is distinguished not by its subject matter but by its causal relation to its object. When judged by this causal relation, Aristotelian practical wisdom is actually theoretical rather than practical, since it is receptive rather than productive of the facts known.

knowledge – the story that I have just now been telling, of how our actions are guided by our conceptions of them because of our intellectual drives toward the knowledge that is consequently embodied therein.

The same researchers who claim to have observed this process in action also claim to have shown that we ordinarily seek to identify our behavior at a "high" or "comprehensive" level, representing our underlying motives and ultimate goals. They describe this further tendency as a "search for meaning in action"[8] or "a human inclination to be informed of what we are doing in the most integrative and general way available."[9] Here the empirical findings harmonize with my dynamic version of Anscombe's theory in a further respect.

With a now famous example, Anscombe points out that an agent often knows what he is doing under a series of descriptions each of which incorporates the answer to the question "Why?" directed at the same action under the previous description in the series. Why is he moving his arm? Because he is pumping water. Why is he pumping water? Because he is replenishing the water supply. Why is he replenishing the water supply? Because he is poisoning the inhabitants of the building. Why is he poisoning the inhabitants? Because he is assassinating enemy agents. And so on. With the exception of the first, purely physical description, all of the descriptions under which this person knows what he's doing are answers to the question why he is doing it as previously described.[10]

The sequence from "moving his arm" to "killing enemy agents" displays a progression toward increasingly "high-level" or "comprehensive" act-descriptions. So if there is empirical evidence of "a human inclination to be informed of what we are doing in the most integrative and general way available," as the act-identification theorists claim, then it is evidence of an inclination to progress from rudimentary descriptions like the former toward comprehensive descriptions like the latter.

I believe that the existence of such an inclination follows directly from our having intellectual impulses directed at the behavior of the person

---

[8] Wegner & Vallacher, "Action Identification," in *Handbook of Motivation and Cognition*, ed. Richard M. Sorrentino and E. Tory Higgins (New York: Guilford Press, 1986), pp. 555–56.

[9] Vallacher & Wegner, *The Theory of Action Identification* (Hillsdale, NJ: Erlbaum, 1985), p. 26.

[10] Mere act descriptions do not amount to explanations, of course. The successive descriptions in Anscombe's example are descriptions under which the agent's action is intentional, and it is the corresponding intentions on his part that explain his action. When the act-descriptions are spoken in the first person – "I am pumping water," and so on – they express the relevant intentions, but a complete explanation would have to cite those intentions rather than merely express them.

who we are. The object of our intellectual drives must be, not merely the recording of rudimentary, observable facts, but also the development of "integrative and general" ways of formulating them. When directed at our own behavior, these drives must demand a knowledge of what we are doing in the sort of comprehensive terms that also explain why we are doing it. And the previously described shortcut to self-knowledge – the shortcut of doing what we think we are doing, or are about to do – is also a route to this "high level" self-knowledge. For we can attain integrative knowledge of what we are doing simply by framing and fulfilling integrative conceptions of our behavior, conceptions formulated in terms of the dispositions and circumstances that help to explain it.

In order to frame and fulfill integrative conceptions of our behavior, of course, we must be aware of relevant factors with which to integrate it – desires by which it might be motivated, emotions that it might express, customs and policies that it might implement, traits of character that it might manifest. These other aspects of our self-conception – motives, emotions, customs, policies, traits of character – can fill out an integrative knowledge of what we are doing, provided that we do things appropriately integrated with them. The drive toward a more comprehensive knowledge of what we are doing therefore favors doing things that can be understood as motivated by our desires, expressing our emotions, implementing our policies, manifesting our characters, and so on.

Aspects of ourselves and our circumstances that could fill out an integrative conception of doing something turn out to coincide with what we ordinarily count as reasons for doing it. Examples of desire-based reasons are well known, but reasons can also be based on other considerations that would help to explain an action, as illustrated by these examples:

Why are you whistling?
Because I'm happy.

Why aren't you having any wine?
Because I don't drink.

Why worry about his problems?
Because I'm his friend.

Why are you shaking your head?
Because I think you're wrong.

Why do you have her picture on your wall?
Because I admire her.

Here already?
I'm punctual.

I believe that reasons for doing something are facts that would inform an integrative knowledge of what we were doing, if we did that thing. Our intellectual drives favor framing and fulfilling a conception of ourselves as doing that thing, understood in the light of those facts, rather than other things for which we lack an equally integrative conception. Reasons for doing something are facts in light of which doing it would make sense.[11]

This concludes my account of how human self-awareness structures practical reasoning. Being driven to know what I am doing, and to know it in terms that explain why, I frame an explanatory conception of doing something and then I do it. My antecedent conception of doing something is my intention to act, and the explanatory facts on which it draws are my reasons for the intended action.

I now want to argue that this account provides the resources for resolving or at least mitigating the prisoners' dilemma. Specifically, this account of practical reason provides resources for attacking the problems of commitment and credibility, which stand in the way of our reaching a cooperative agreement. I will begin with the problem of credibility, assuming for the moment that the problem of commitment can be solved; I will then turn to the latter problem.

According to the traditional understanding of the prisoners' dilemma, neither of us has any reason to take the first step of saying "I will cooperate if you will." If I made this offer, you would know that I stood to lose by following through, and so you would suspect that rationality would lead me to default. Indeed, you would know that I must already intend or at least expect to default, since the costs of following through must be as obvious to me as they are to you. My offer would thus be transparently insincere, and so it would elicit nothing from you in return, except perhaps an offer of equally transparent insincerity. The whole exchange would therefore be pointless, as would be common knowledge between us.

But suppose that I nevertheless proceeded to say "I will cooperate if you will." How might you understand my utterance?

You might consider the possibility that I was doing something superficially pointless, by offering to cooperate, for the deeper purpose of signaling a genuine intention to do something outright irrational, by following through on that offer. But any thought you might entertain of attributing cooperative intent to my utterance is a thought that I should have foreseen and thought of exploiting to my advantage. The thought

[11] Since the main purpose of this chapter is to apply this conception of reasons for acting, not to defend it, I have relegated objections and replies to Appendix B.

of attributing cooperative intent to my utterance would therefore lead
you to the opposite hypothesis, that I hoped to elicit that very attribution
in order to take advantage of you – a train of thought that I should have
foreseen, thereby foreseeing that my utterance would be fundamentally
pointless, after all.

Knowing that my offer was pointless, you might well ask yourself, "What
on earth is he doing?" But you would also know that the pointlessness of
my offer was known to me – knowledge that should have left me, as it left
you, at a loss to understand what I was doing. The question that you pose
to yourself might therefore be not just "What on earth is he doing?" but
"What on earth does he *think* he is doing?"

Now, there is a significant difference between the questions "What are
you doing?" and "What do you think you are doing?" The former is a
straightforward request for information, but the latter is often an expression of protest or surprise. This question expresses protest or surprise
because a rational agent is normally expected to do things that he can
understand. If someone's action makes no sense to us, we are prepared to
believe that the failure is ours and can be remedied by more information,
which is usually available from him; but if we cannot see how his action
could make sense to him, then we believe that the failure is his, and that
it is a failure not merely of intellect but of action, a failure not just to
understand what he's doing but also to do what he can understand. We
are surprised to find him doing something that he himself cannot understand, and our asking "What do you think you are doing?" expresses our
surprise at his doing it.

According to the theory outlined here, having an answer to this question is the cognitive goal to which there is an irresistible shortcut that is
constitutive of practical reasoning. Hence the assumption that I should
be able to answer the question follows from the assumption that I am
rational in a sense derived from the foregoing account of practical reasoning. And as parties to a classic prisoners' dilemma, you and I are
allowed to assume one another's rationality. These mutual assumptions
of rationality can now be reinterpreted, as assumptions of one another's
tendency to act so as to understand what he's doing, by doing what he has
the resources to understand. When our mutual assumptions of rationality
are reinterpreted in this way, our dilemma takes on a new complexion.

Thus far, the discussion of whether a cooperative offer would be intelligible has proceeded on a familiar assumption about how behavior can be
understood. The assumption has been that in order to understand what

I'm doing, in offering to cooperate, you and I must find desired consequences to which I might regard the offer as instrumental. Since I can't
expect my offer of cooperation to be taken seriously, I can't regard it as
instrumental to anything I want, and so I have seemed unequipped to
understand it. Yet the conception of practical reasoning as the shortcut
to self-understanding does not presuppose that behavior must be understood instrumentally; it can accommodate the fact that behavior is often
understood in other ways.

For present purposes, the relevant alternative is to understand behavior expressively. For example, my belief that there's leftover chili in the
fridge involves a motivational disposition to go to the fridge if I want some
chili; but it also involves an expressive disposition to think or say "It's in
the fridge" if a question arises about the availability of chili. The expressive disposition associated with belief is what causes us on occasion to say
what we think even though we have no desire to communicate it – indeed,
to blurt out what we think despite a positive desire to keep it to ourselves.
As the latter case suggests, this expressive disposition is antecedent to
any practical reasoning. This expressive disposition may actually conflict
with the motivational disposition associated with the very same belief. For
example, suppose that there's only one serving of chili left, and I want to
eat it. If asked "Is there any chili left?" in that case, I can act instrumentally
and say "No" while sidling toward the fridge, or I can act expressively and
say "It's in the fridge." The disposition toward the latter, expressive behavior is what I might have to restrain by (as we say) biting my tongue in order
to take the former, instrumental course. Either course of action will be
intelligible, the one as motivated by my belief, the other as expressive of it.

If reasons for acting are considerations in light of which an action
would make sense, then a belief can provide either instrumental or
expressive reasons for acting, by rendering an action intelligible either
as motivated by the belief or as expressive of it.[12] Asked whether there is
any chili left, I may find expressive reason to say "It's in the fridge," if I
believe there to be chili in the fridge, and I may find instrumental reason
to say "No," if I also want the chili for myself. Which reason is stronger
depends, in my view, on which action would allow for the best overall
self-understanding.

In the case of our prisoner's dilemma, saying "I'll cooperate if you
will" would make no sense when considered as motivated by desire and

[12] For a somewhat different view of expressive reasons for acting, see Robert Nozick, *The
Nature of Rationality* (Princeton: Princeton University Press, 1993), 26–35.

belief, because it cannot rationally be expected to promote anything that I want; but it could easily be understood as the natural expression of an intention – specifically, an intention to cooperate if you should express a corresponding intention.[13] If I had such an intention, then my saying "I'll cooperate if you will" would be perfectly intelligible, as expressing my state of mind. The hypothesis that I have such an intention would therefore enable you to understand what I was doing. What's more, this hypothesis would enable you to understand how *I* could understand what I was doing; to understand how I could expect to be understood; and so on.

In short, it is common knowledge between us that my offer to cooperate would make sense if it expressed an intention to cooperate but not if conceived in purely instrumental terms, as a means to desired ends. And we have assumed it to be common knowledge that I am rational and therefore unlikely to do things that I don't understand. Since I could understand what I was doing, in offering to cooperate, only if I had the cooperative intention that my offer would express, you would have reason to assume that I had the intention and understood myself as expressing it. You would therefore have grounds for interpreting my offer as sincere, and I would have grounds for expecting it to be so interpreted. A solution to the problem of credibility appears to be at hand.

Unfortunately, this solution can be suspected of reviving the problem. For as soon as I have an expectation of being believed, I can have instrumental motives for offering to cooperate, and so I can understand making such an offer insincerely, without cooperative intent. If you might figure that I wouldn't offer to cooperate unless I had the intention that I could understand such an offer as expressing, then I can hope to gain the benefit of your cooperation by making the offer, and I can consequently understand it as motivated by that hope, even in the absence of any cooperative intention for it to express. Any nascent possibility of trust, or hope of being trusted, would thus appear to nip itself in the bud.

---

[13] Here I assume that the expressive disposition attached to beliefs is also attached to intentions. I base this assumption partly on my view that intention is a cognitive state that is similar to belief in taking its propositional content to be true, with the aim of so taking it only if it really is true. See my *The Possibility of Practical Reason*, esp. Chapters 1, 2, and 9. My conception of intention is borrowed from Anscombe, who bases it precisely on the observation that the natural way to express an intention is to assert that one is going to act.

Yet my revived instrumental understanding of an insincere offer would once again be unstable, precisely because its availability to me would be evident to you, as would in turn be evident to me, thus rendering the offer instrumentally pointless in my eyes. As soon as I begin to think instrumentally in this case, I enter a dizzying spiral of anticipating that my instrumental calculations have been anticipated, that their validity has thus been compromised, that their being so compromised has also been anticipated, with the result that they gain new validity, which has of course been anticipated, and so on. Hence the best instrumental understanding that I can achieve of what I am doing, if I offer to cooperate in these circumstances, is that I am taking a shot at being trusted, a shot whose prospects of success are obscured by endless complications. It is indeed a tangled web we weave, not only when we practice to deceive, but even when we practice honesty on instrumental grounds.

If I understand myself expressively, as intending to reciprocate your cooperation and saying what I intend, my self-understanding will be far simpler and more stable than any instrumental understanding I can achieve in these circumstances. Unlike an instrumental understanding of my behavior in this case, an expressive understanding will not undermine itself, suspicions to the contrary notwithstanding. The thought that instrumental calculations are revived at the prospect that I might be interpreted as thinking expressively and hence as sincere – *that* thought occurred to me just now, not in my imagined capacity as an agent thinking expressively about his behavior in a prisoners' dilemma, but rather in my capacity as a philosopher accommodating his reader's bias in favor of instrumental thinking. As an agent thinking expressively about his behavior in a prisoners' dilemma, I would find a perfectly stable self-understanding in the conception of myself as intending to cooperate and expressing my intention. Expressive thinking would not itself lead back to instrumental calculations, and if it did, those calculations would be unstable, as we have seen.

In short, I face a choice antecedent to the choice between sincerity and insincerity – namely, the choice between thinking instrumentally and thinking expressively about that subsequent choice.[14] Thinking

---

[14] Here my argument is similar in form to David Gauthier's argument about the choice between straightforward and constrained maximization. But there is a crucial difference between us. According to Gauthier, an agent chooses between straightforward and constrained maximization as the fundamental principle of his practical reasoning, and so he

instrumentally leads to an endlessly vacillating calculation, whereas thinking expressively leads to a clear and consistent self-understanding. Whether honesty or dishonesty is the best policy, in the sense of yielding the best consequences, is a vexed question whose answer defies deduction. But honesty is certainly the clearest, most perspicuous policy, the policy that affords me the clearest sense of what I am about. I think that many of us adopt the policy of honesty on precisely these grounds.

I do not claim to have shown that the rational pressure in favor of sincerity always prevails. In particular, there are extreme losses that it makes sense to take a shot at avoiding, and extreme gains that it makes sense to take a shot at obtaining, no matter how wild or how blind a shot. But there are many gains and losses that it makes more sense to ignore, given the more intelligible alternative of speaking our minds. And what's more intelligible is, on my view of practical reason, the more rational course to take.

Thus far I have addressed only the problem of credibility – of how one agent might give another valid grounds to believe that he has formed an intention to cooperate. I haven't yet addressed the problem of commitment. How can an agent form a cooperative intention that will take effect in his future behavior, given the incentives for his future self to change his mind?

In discussing Anscombe's theory of intention, I confined myself to immediate intentions to act. This discussion is not immediately relevant to the intentions required by cooperative agreements of the sort that would offer an escape from the prisoners' dilemma. The latter must be long-range intentions, to do something in the future, when the relevant conditions have been fulfilled and the opportunity arises. Such long-range intentions do not appear to offer any shortcut to the cognitive aim of knowing what I am doing here and now.

---

can choose only on the basis of whichever one of these principles he last chose. There is no prior, unchosen principle with which to reason about his choice. In my view, however, the agent chooses between instrumental and expressive thinking, not as fundamental modes of practical reasoning, but as different versions of the one mode of thinking that constitutes practical reasoning, antecedently to his choice – namely, making sense of what he does, by doing what makes sense. What shows that this practical pursuit of self-knowledge constitutes practical reasoning is, not that a rational agent would choose it, but that it helps us to explain many of the phenomena of rational agency, including the nature of intention, an agent's non-observational self-knowledge, and so on.

What long-range intentions do, of course, is enable me to coordinate my behavior at different times – to take present steps in preparation for future steps that I am going to take, to postpone steps until later so that I needn't take them now, to think through at leisure a sequence of steps that I will have to execute when there's no time to think.[15] Yet this instrumental function of long-range intentions rests, at bottom, on the cognitive function of letting me know what I am going to do in the future. In order to take a trip next month, I must buy a plane ticket in advance, but I can see no reason for buying the ticket until I know that I would indeed use it to take the trip. The intention to take the trip gives me access to a reason for buying the ticket, by ruling out the possibility of its going to waste. Similarly, intending to buy the ticket this evening can cancel my reason for taking out my cell phone and buying it right now – a reason that conflicts with my reasons for finishing this essay. My reason for buying the ticket now is cancelled by the knowledge that I needn't do so, because I am going to buy it later.

Furthermore, the ability to know what I am going to do in the future enables me to know what I am doing now in terms that are even more comprehensive or integrative than before. I am not just writing an essay and postponing the purchase of a ticket; I am postponing the purchase of a ticket so as to finish the essay that I am due to present at the conference to which I will buy a ticket later this evening. My present action can therefore be understood as one step in a temporally coherent course of action, but only because I can expect to take the future steps with which it will cohere.

The knowledge embodied in my long-range plans bears several points of resemblance to that embodied in my immediate intentions. For one thing, it depends for its possibility on my having an objective conception of myself as one of the world's creatures, toward whom I occupy an epistemic position somewhat similar to yours. The question what I am going to do in the future simply wouldn't arise for me if I couldn't conceive of a future person who would be me.

What's more, my epistemic position with respect to this future person affords me a shortcut to knowledge about him. In order to take my present intentions for the future as predictive of future action, I must

---

[15] This sentence summarizes many of the points made by Michael Bratman in *Intention, Plans, and Practical Reason* (Cambridge, MA: Harvard University Press, 1987). I discuss Bratman's view at greater length in "What Good Is a Will?" (MS).

have grounds for expecting them to be fulfilled, but I am fortunately in a position to give myself those grounds, by fulfilling my past intentions for the present and thereby demonstrating my tendency to fulfill long-range intentions. My intellectual drives therefore favor fulfilling my past intentions and can be expected later to favor fulfilling my present ones. When those drives are directed toward my objectively conceived self, they motivate me, not only to be intelligible to myself, but also to give myself evidence of my own reliability.[16]

What generates this rational pressure toward fulfilling commitments is that, although the present dilemma is the first and last one that I will ever share with you, it is not the only one that I share with myself. I have no incentive to convince you that I tend to reciprocate cooperation, because I will have no opportunity to realize the benefit of that conviction on your part; but I do have an incentive to convince myself that I tend to carry out my long-range intentions, because my ability to settle what I will do in the future depends on my grounds for that conviction.[17]

---

[16] I am not imagining here that constancy, as I call it, is a distinct disposition – a disposition specifically to carry out intentions – on which I must rely when forming intentions. If it were, then carrying out intentions for the purpose of giving myself evidence of that disposition would be self-deceptive, since it would manifest my desire for that evidence rather than the distinct disposition of constancy. As I imagine it, however, constancy can consist in any psychological state or mechanism that makes me reliable in fulfilling intentions. My constancy can even consist in my desire for the ability to tell what I am going to do in the future, if that desire motivates me to fulfill my intentions. What I want, after all, is some grounds or other on which I can regard my future course of action as determined, even if those grounds consist in the fact that this very desire will determine me to do what I have regarded in that way. And there is nothing self-deceptive about being motivated by this desire to carry out intentions for the sake of giving myself evidence that I am so motivated. The thought of fulfilling an intention in order to maintain my grounds for relying on my own intentions is not undermined by the realization that I would be fulfilling the intention for that purpose, since that purpose is one I can rely on myself to have. I discuss this mechanism in greater detail in Chapter 8 of *Practical Reflection* (Princeton: Princeton University Press, 1989).

[17] Another way of making this point is to note that Gregory Kavka's famous toxin puzzle can be solved by iteration. (See Kavka, "The Toxin Puzzle," *Analysis* 43 (1983), 33–36.) The puzzle is this: A mind-reader offers to give you a million dollars if you form the intention to drink a toxin that will make you painfully ill, without causing any lasting injury. The mind-reader will pay you the money as soon as he detects your intention, leaving you with an intention that you have every reason not to fulfill. Can you form the intention, and if you do form it, should you fulfill it?

In my view, an intention to drink the toxin would entail a cognitive commitment to the truth of the proposition that you are going to drink it – a commitment of the sort that would constitute knowledge if it were true and appropriately justified. Because of being an intention rather than a mere prediction, however, this commitment would have to be justified in part by its own power to bring about the facts that would make it true. Thus, you must form the intention to drink the toxin by committing yourself to

Finally, my access to this epistemic shortcut is known to you and can give you grounds on which to reason about my behavior. Just as you realize that I share your interest in finding me intelligible, so you realize that I share your interest in finding me reliable, because I conceive of myself as if from your perspective, as a creature from whom either unintelligibility or unreliability would be problematic. Knowing of my need to understand my behavior, you are entitled to interpret my offer of cooperation as the genuine expression of an intention, which would be intelligible, rather than a strategic gambit, which would not. Knowing of my need to project my future behavior, you are entitled to expect me to carry out my cooperative intention, in order to preserve my grounds for such projections.[18]

---

the truth of the proposition that you will drink it; and you cannot commit yourself to the truth of the proposition unless you can expect thereby to cause the proposition to come true.

Now suppose that Kavka's mind-reader offers to play the toxin game with you many times, and suppose that you succeed in forming the crucial intention on the first play. In that case, you will realize that fulfilling your intention, by drinking the toxin, is essential to maintaining your ability to form similar intentions on future plays. For if on the second play you knew that, in the only relevant prior instance, you formed the intention but then failed to fulfill it, then you would not be in a position to commit yourself to the truth of the relevant proposition in this present instance, because you would not be in a position to expect thereby to cause the proposition to come true; and so you would be unable to form the second intention and claim the second prize. So when you have formed the intention and collected the prize on the first play, you will see that fulfilling your intention is essential to preserving your ability to form the intention and claim the prize on subsequent plays. Rationality will therefore favor drinking the toxin.

The only reason why the toxin puzzle is puzzling to begin with is that the situation is described so as to seem overwhelmingly unlikely to recur. If the situation were described in terms that highlighted its similarity to everyday situations that call for resoluteness, it wouldn't seem so puzzling, since the importance of retaining grounds for planning would be clearer.

[18] According to this conception of the reasons generated by an intention, their strength can vary with the circumstances. In circumstances of some kinds, the agent doesn't especially want or need the ability to settle the question what he is going to do on some future occasion. If he does settle the question in some particular instance of such circumstances, by forming an intention, he will feel especially free to unsettle it again, by reconsidering or changing his mind, since a record of inconstancy is of little consequence in circumstances of that kind. In circumstances of other kinds, however, the agent really does need to know and be able to say what he is going to do on some future occasion, and a record of inconstancy in those circumstances would be seriously problematic. An agent has greater motivation for vindicating his own self-trust when circumstances are of the kind in which the ability to tell what he is going to do is especially important. For that very reason, however, he has better grounds for self-trust in circumstances of this latter kind, knowing that he will have motives for rising to the occasion. And circumstances of this kind surely include the opportunity to escape a prisoners' dilemma through a cooperative agreement.

Conclusion

A person who gives himself no grounds for credence in his long-range intentions, or who gets tangled up in instrumental reasoning about the truth, sacrifices a considerable degree of self-knowledge. The objectively conceived personality to which this person has pinned his subjective point-of-view is less intelligible and less predictable than it otherwise might be.[19] In this respect, the axis on which he is centered, or the anchor by which he is grounded, is less sure. A person who says what he thinks and does what he says has a better grasp on the person who he is. He can therefore be described as better centered or better grounded.

I have now arrived at the explanation that I set out to find, of the relation between being centered and being trustworthy. The relation is that the trustworthy person has a surer sense of self than the person who strategizes with the truth or defaults on his commitments.

As I mentioned earlier, I have purposely developed this explanation in abstraction from the social, emotional, and moral considerations that bear on prisoners' dilemmas in real life. My reason for adopting this idealization has been to isolate rational pressures toward trustworthiness within the individual perspective of a rational agent considered merely as such. I do not believe that these pressures are sufficient in themselves to resolve actual dilemmas. Rather, I believe that they subtly favor the gradual accretion of social, emotional, and moral resources that jointly provide a resolution. Explaining this process is more than I can do in this essay, but let me offer an idea of how that explanation would go.

The process of practical reasoning, as I conceive it, extends beyond the immediate step of doing what makes sense here and now. I have already mentioned one further step, in which one fulfills intentions from the past in order to preserve the credibility of one's intentions for the future. In my view, there are many other ways by which one can cultivate intelligibility in oneself. For example, one can try to resolve conflicts among one's ends, so as to avoid situations in which one would have trouble explaining the pursuit of either end given one's commitment to the other. One can also adopt policies of behavior that generalize about how one deals with situations of repeatable kinds. A particularly fruitful

---

[19] Note that the predictability at issue here is not of the boring sort that characterizes a person set in his ways. The predictability at issue is that of a person who is in a position to know what he will do in the future precisely because he is in a position to make it up, by making up his mind.

kind of policy – fruitful, that is, for self-understanding – is a norm of the sort described by Allan Gibbard.[20] Accepting such a norm involves adopting a disposition to favor or oppose the relevant kind of behavior, by adopting or eschewing it oneself and approving or disapproving of it in others – a broad pattern of conduct that can be understood in terms of a single attitude. Finally, one's conception of oneself will gain in generality and explanatory power insofar as it can be subsumed under one's conception of people in general – who are, of course, similarly striving to understand themselves under self-conceptions subsumable insofar as possible under a conception of people in general, including oneself. People are therefore jointly encouraged to converge on a conception of what "we" are like, or how "we" live, so that they can understand themselves individually, to some extent, by conceiving of themselves as one of "us."

In pursuing these long-range strategies of practical reasoning, one is influenced by the cognitive attractions of saying what one thinks and doing what one says. For example, cultivating ends and norms compatible with truth-telling, and weeding out ends and norms incompatible with it, will enable one to avail oneself of expressive self-understanding without any confusing motivational conflict. That's how the fairly subtle pressures that I have identified in the perspective of the bare rational agent can lead to the gradual accretion of additional resources for coping with prisoners' dilemmas in real life. I believe that a fuller exploration of this process would yield a detailed explanation of why it is rational to be a *Mensch.*

Appendix A: Perry's Theory of Self-Knowledge

My opening remarks about the differences between humans and cats were based in part on Thomas Nagel's theory of the "objective self" and

---

[20] *Wise Choices, Apt Feelings: A Theory of Normative Judgment* (Cambridge, MA: Harvard University Press, 1990). Note that my use of Gibbard's idea differs from his in one crucial respect. According to Gibbard, different consistent sets of norms can be comparatively assessed only in light of some higher-order norm, which itself is evaluable only in light of some yet higher-order norm, and so on. In my view, however, practical reasoning has a substantive criterion of success – self-understanding – in light of which alternative sets of norms can be assessed. The foundation for this criterion of rationality lies, not in our adoption of some norm, but rather in the nature of autonomous action, as revealed by moral psychology. On this last point, see my paper "Deciding How to Decide," in *Ethics and Practical Reason*, ed. Garrett Cullity and Berys Gaut (Oxford: Clarendon Press, 1997), 29–52.

John Perry's theory of self-knowledge.[21] In this Appendix, I summarize Perry's theory and expand upon my application of it.

Perry begins with a form of self-knowledge that he calls "agent-relative," which characterizes the world in terms that are implicitly relative to the subject. For example, my belief that there's an accident blocking the road up ahead is true if and only if the accident is situated ahead of David Velleman, and in that sense the belief is about myself. Yet this aspect of its truth-condition is not explicit, either in my verbal expression of the belief or in the mental representation that is a constituent of the belief itself. That is, I do not refer to myself as the person ahead of whom the accident is situated, nor do I exercise an idea of myself in mentally representing the accident as up ahead. In this respect, my verbal expression of the belief and the belief itself are elliptical.[22]

What implicitly fills the ellipsis is indicated by the point-of-origin in my perspective. A visual image, for example, is organized along sight-lines that converge on a point presumably occupied by the unseen subject of vision; and things are represented in the image as "up ahead" by being implicitly represented as ahead of that point and its presumed occupant. Similarly, an utterance presumably issues from the mouth of a speaker, and what is represented as "up ahead" in the utterance is implicitly represented as ahead of the presumed speaker.[23] When I believe that there is an accident up ahead, the content of my belief must likewise be framed from a perspective, and the origin of that perspective must be the point to which I implicitly believe the accident to bear the relation "up ahead."

---

[21] See John Perry, "Self-Notions," *Logos*, 1990: 17–31; and "Myself and 'I'," in *Philosophie in Synthetischer Absicht* (A Festschrift for Dieter Heinrich), ed. Marcelo Stamm (Stuttgart: Klett-Cotta, 1998), pp. 83–103. See also "The Problem of the Essential Indexical," *Noûs* 13 (1979): 3–21.

[22] On egocentric thought that is elliptically first-personal, see also D. H. Mellor, "I and Now," *Proceedings of the Aristotelian Society* 89: 79–94 (1989), reprinted in *Matters of Metaphysics* (Cambridge: Cambridge University Press, 1991); and the discussion of Mellor in José Luis Bermúdez, *The Paradox of Self-Consciousness* (Cambridge, MA: MIT Press, 1998), Chapter 2, section 2.1. Bermúdez believes that the notion of elliptically first-personal thought must be defended against "the classical theory of content," according to which a subject cannot have thoughts without having concepts sufficient to compose complete propositions to serve as their contents. While I agree with Bermúdez in rejecting this theory of content, I do not think that we need independent grounds for rejecting it – grounds independent, that is, of the obvious counterexample consisting in elliptically first-personal thought. (Nor do I agree with Bermúdez's view that, once we reject the classical theory of content, we must fashion a positive theory of nonconceptual content in order to account for first-personal thought.)

[23] Of course, if a different point-of-view is more salient in the context than the speaker's, then the words "up ahead" are interpreted in relation to that point-of-view. My point here is merely that the speaker's perspective is the default.

Perry replaces the notion of a perspective with that of an "epistemic/pragmatic relation" – that is, a relation that structures ways of detecting things and ways of dealing with them, which Perry describes, in turn, as epistemic and pragmatic methods. To represent a traffic accident as "up ahead" is to represent it in a manner that's structured like the output of epistemic methods for detecting what's up ahead, and like the input to pragmatic methods for dealing with what's up ahead. The former methods include looking into the middle distance in the direction I am traveling and switching on my headlights; the latter include honking my horn to alert people blocking the road; and these methods can be combined, as when I take a second look to see whether a second honk is needed. The "up ahead" relation determines how my representations of the world are structured when obtained by the former, epistemic method and how they must be structured in order to guide the latter, pragmatic method.

Some epistemic/pragmatic relations are reflexive: they necessarily structure information that is received from, and relevant to dealing with, the agent's own body or mind. My proprioceptions and tactual sensations arrive as if from particular locations, which I recognize by their orientation in tactual or proprioceptive space; and I direct muscular control at locations similarly oriented in kinaesthetic space. These orientations can be expressed by phrases such as "my right hand" or "my left foot," but the fact that they pick out a hand or a foot is not evident in the orientations themselves. That is, sensations felt "in my left foot" are not felt as originating in a particular anatomical structure; they are simply felt as "there," in tactual space, under an epistemic/pragmatic relation that is ultimately ineffable. Similarly, I wiggle my left toes by wiggling "there," a location conceived under the same ineffable relation.

What's accessible under reflexive epistemic/pragmatic relations is often accessible under relations that are not reflexive. The source of sensations felt "there" (in my right hand), which also moves when I move "there" (with my right hand), is an object that is seen as "to my right," under a relation that isn't reflexive, because it can be occupied by many things that aren't part of my body, if they come to occupy that region of my visual field. My dual relation to such objects allows for a rudimentary kind of self-knowledge that can be formulated entirely within agent-relative thought. If I see a tangle of arms to my right, then making a movement with my right hand may reveal an important fact – namely, which of the visually perceived arms is mine.

This sort of self-knowledge is even available to my cat Snowflake – for example, when she recognizes that the tail she is chasing is her own.

When Snowflake sees her tail, she sees it "to the rear," a relation that also governs epistemic methods of hearing as well as pragmatic methods of fleeing and chasing. "To the rear" is a very different relation from "my rear end," which governs epistemic methods of tactual sensation as well as pragmatic methods of flicking and licking. When Snowflake sees her tail merely "to the rear," she may end up chasing it; she finally stops chasing it when she connects what she is seeing rearward with what she is feeling and doing rear-endward. She can then be said to have recognized that the tail she is chasing is her own.

But in what sense does Snowflake recognize the tail as her own? All she does is forge a mental association between an object seen "back there" in visual space and the locus of sensations felt "there" in tactual space, or of movements made "there" in kinaesthetic space, so that she can now think of causing the thing "back there" to wave by waving "there," or of causing a sharp sensation "there" by nipping the thing "back there." To be sure, her sensory-motor relation to "there" is reflexive, because it picks out a location within her own body; and its being reflexive in this sense is our grounds for crediting her with the discovery that the tail is her own. But Snowflake remains unaware that "there" is a location within her body, because she does not conceive of herself as an embodied subject. She is unaware that sensations felt "there" and movements executed "there" are the perceptions and actions by which the conscious life of a particular creature extends to a part of its body; and so in recognizing the object seen to her rear as the locus of those sensations and movements, she does not conceive of it as belonging to herself in the way that a tail belongs to its owner. She has no conception of a self to whom the object seen rearward might belong – of a creature who she is and who feels sensations and executes movements with that object.

The theoretical tools presented thus far will therefore have to be supplemented if they are to account for the self-knowledge that separates man from cat. Perry supplements them with the notion of "self-attached knowledge."

Compare two different ways in which I can recognize my reflection in a store window. First, I can associate the movements made by a figure reflected in the window with the movements that I am aware of making; second, I can recognize the same reflected figure, by his looks, as me. The first recognition is of the sort that the cat attains when she recognizes her own tail: it involves no more than making a connection between non-reflexive and reflexive perceptions, all of which are still agent-relative.

But the second recognition requires me to have standing non-reflexive knowledge about myself: I have to recognize a particular appearance as mine.

Now, my knowledge that a particular appearance is mine cannot depend on its being structured in a way that's distinctive of reflexive methods, since the relevant appearance is structured by a perspective other than my own. It's the appearance I have when seen as another person. How do I remember that this appearance as of another person is mine?

Perry's answer is that I establish a more lasting association between reflexive and non-reflexive information about myself. I frame a standing idea of a human body, and I use it to store, as attributable to that body, information about what I reflexively feel "in my body" and do "with my body," and as a source of information to guide such reflexive methods. Because it is thus associated with my reflexive methods, the idea comes to represent the particular human body that is mine; yet because it is framed from no particular perspective, it can serve as my repository for non-egocentrically structured information about my body, such as information about how it looks from perspectives other than my own. This information will be marked as pertaining to my own body, not by virtue of the structure of its representation, but by virtue of being stored in an idea that is permanently associated with my own-body–oriented methods.[24] That's how non-egocentric knowledge about the person I happen to be can become, as Perry puts it, self-attached.

Perry describes this idea as my conception of "the person identical," explaining that the one to whom the person is therein represented as identical is the unrepresented subject. "The person identical" is elliptical, because it doesn't specify to whom the person is identical; but in that respect, Perry argues, it is on a par with "up ahead," which doesn't specify the anchor of that relation, either.[25]

I would add one final note to Perry's analysis, which seems to end prematurely. To conceive of a person as the one whose left foot is the locus of what I feel "there" (in my left foot) or do "there" (with my left

---

[24] In order to become my idea of myself as a whole person, this idea would have to be associated with my reflexive methods of introspection and thought-control, so that it incorporated information about my mental states as well.

[25] As Perry points out, specifying the anchor of the relation "the person identical" would lead to a vicious regress. Indeed, avoiding this regress is the purpose of positing elliptically first-personal thoughts, in the first place. See also Mellor, "I and Now," and Bermúdez, *The Paradox of Self-Consciousness*, loc. cit.

foot) is not yet to conceive of that person as the "I" feeling and doing those things. The latter conception would have to represent the person not only as the target but also as the subject of my reflexive epistemic/pragmatic methods, and so it would have to be associated with my reflexive methods more closely, as follows. What I feel "in my body" or do "with my body" must be represented in this idea of a person, not just as being felt or done in that person's body, but also as being felt or done by that person. Hence this idea of a person must represent him as using reflexive methods to detect and cause the events that I detect and cause "there," in and with my body. So conceived, that person will fully occupy the role of the person identical, and my conception of him will be a conception of who I am – or, as it is often called, a sense of identify or self.

Appendix B: Reasons for Acting

My conception of reasons for doing something is that they are considerations in light of which one's doing that thing would make sense, because they would help to explain one's doing it. This conception of reasons raises various objections, to which I have offered replies in my first book, *Practical Reflection*, and in a symposium on my second book, *The Possibility of Practical Reason*.[26] In this Appendix, I summarize a few of those objections and replies.

The most obvious objection is that reasons for acting are not about oneself and one's attitudes, as I claim, but rather about those aspects of the world at which one's attitudes are directed. This objection depends, I believe, on a confusion between the logic of practical reasoning and the explicit content of practical thought.

If you look up from reading *Felix Holt* and say to yourself, "What a genius she was!" your thought is explicitly about the author George Eliot; but in articulating this thought, you express an attitude that lends intelligibility to various further thoughts and actions on your part. Suppose that your next thought is "I wonder what else she wrote" (or perhaps just "What else did she write?"). The rational connection between your thoughts is that admiration of the sort expressed in the first naturally leads to curiosity about its object, as reported (or expressed) in the second. This connection cannot be discerned in the explicit content of your thoughts. There is no rule of inference leading from the premise that George Eliot was a genius to the conclusion that you wonder what she wrote in addition

[26] *Philosophical Studies* 121 (2004): 225–38, 277–98.

to *Felix Holt*. Unless the first of these thoughts is understood as expressing an attitude held by the thinker of the second, they amount to a *non sequitur*.

The only way to make the logic of these thoughts explicit would be with further, reflective information – "I admire the author of *Felix Holt* as a genius, and so I am moved to wonder what else she wrote" – which describes a psychologically intelligible transition of thought. Yet to articulate this reflective information to yourself would be to shift the focus of attention, from the author whom you admire to your own attitude of admiration. And this shift would make your admiration less rather than more evident, because admiring someone entails attending to her rather than yourself. "I admire the author of *Felix Holt*" would be a less admiring thought, a thought less expressive of your attitude, than "She was a genius." Articulating your awareness of admiring Eliot would therefore leave you less vividly aware of admiring her than articulating thoughts expressive of that admiration, which would be thoughts about Eliot.

Thus, explicit reflection is often self-defeating. Reflective reasoning is best left implicit, in the background, so that the attitudes that are its objects can be revealed more clearly in explicit thoughts about other things. Hence the fact that your thoughts prior to acting are not explicitly about yourself is no evidence that their logic is not reflective. Thoughts that are explicitly about other things may yet be structured by what they reveal about yourself – as in "What a genius she was! I wonder what else she wrote."

Note that this response to the present objection points to a flaw in the traditional philosophical method of studying practical reason. The traditional method is to construct an argument-schema that will both represent the explicit content of, and illustrate the rational connections among, the thoughts leading up to an action performed for reasons. Aristotle's practical syllogism was the first attempt to construct such an argument-schema, and many other attempts have followed. In my view, however, the rational connections in an agent's deliberations are connections of reflective intelligibility, and such connections tend to hold, not between the contents of the agent's explicit thoughts, but rather between the self-attributions that remain in the background, implicitly registering the attitudes that his explicit thoughts express. Because these unarticulated self-attributions provide the logical structure of the agent's thinking, they contain the agent's reasons for acting, in my view; but because they remain unarticulated, they cannot be represented by the same argument-schema that represents the agent's explicit thinking.

In sum, an agent's reasons for acting are not the things that he says to himself before acting. That he doesn't say anything about himself to himself before acting doesn't prove that his reasons for acting are not considerations conducive to self-understanding.

Another objection to my view of reasons for acting is that an agent may understand his behavior in terms of unfortunate traits that do not provide reasons for their behavioral manifestations. Someone who knows himself to be lazy, for example, may find his avoidance of work intelligible in that light without thereby finding it supported by reasons. My answer to this objection is that the conception of himself as lazy, rather than as easygoing or laid back, expresses disapproval, which would have to be included in a complete conception of himself. And manifesting laziness while condemning it as such is not altogether intelligible, after all.

A deeper objection is that although my account explains the influence of reasons, it fails to explain their normative force.[27] My answer to this objection has two parts. First, the intellectual drive that reasons for acting engage, in exerting their influence, carries a kind of authority by virtue of being inextricably identified with the agent himself. The agent cannot stand back from his drive toward self-understanding and regard it as an alien influence on him, because regarding it as an influence at all is an exercise of self-understanding, animated by the self-same drive, which consequently has not been banished to the realm of the alien, after all.[28]

The second part of my reply to the present objection is that the normative force of reasons for acting may be supplied to some extent by a norm in favor of doing what makes sense – a norm that we adopt in the course of pursuing self-knowledge, precisely because it helps us to make sense of that very pursuit. Practical reasoning, as I conceive it, favors the adoption of norms that ratify and regularize aspects of our behavior. When norms are accepted consciously, they provide generalizations that guide our behavior by offering us the means to understand the behavior so guided. In adopting the posture of being "for" some things and "against" others, we thereby adopt a comprehensive description for some

[27] This objection has been pressed independently by Nishi Shah, Kieran Setiya, Nadeem Hussain, and Matthew Silverstein. See Hussain's contribution to the *Philosophical Studies* symposium on *The Possibility of Practical Reason* and Shah's paper "How Truth Governs Belief," *The Philosophical Review* 112 (2003): 447–82.

[28] This point is developed further in "What Happens When Someone Acts?" in *The Possibility of Practical Reason* (Oxford: Oxford University Press, 2000), 123–43; and in "Identification and Identity" (Chapter 14 in the present volume).

region of our conduct, which subsequently tends to follow suit, so as to be comprehensible under that description. We adopt the norm of doing what makes sense in order to regiment and make sense of a process by which our actions are already regulated – in this case, the very process of making sense of what we do by doing what makes sense. Hence the natural process of attaining practical knowledge affirms itself, by leading to the adoption of a norm that ratifies and regularizes it as the process of practical reasoning.[29]

---

[29] This paragraph borrows significantly from unpublished work by Nishi Shah.

12

Willing the Law

Kant believes that we must come up against practical conflicts in order to feel the normative force of morality, because that force consists in our own unwillingness to live with practical conflicts of two kinds: contradictions in conception and contradictions in the will. Every instance of immorality is, according to Kant, an instance of one or the other conflict; and only by recognizing and recoiling from these conflicts do we come under the guidance of morality. Because these conflicts are contradictions, they are conflicts of reason, and their instances are irrational as well as immoral. We come under moral guidance, then, in recognizing and recoiling from conflicts of practical reason.

I am going to argue against Kant's account of contradictions in the will, and in favor of an alternative account, which I shall call "concessive." My arguments will imply that Kant is wrong about one of the ways in which wrongdoing is irrational, and hence about one of the ways in which we are guided by morality.

This chapter originally appeared in Baumann, Peter, and Betzler, Monika (eds.), *Practical Conflicts: New Philosophical Essays* (Cambridge: Cambridge University Press, 2004), 27–56. It is reprinted by permission of Cambridge University Press. The chapter develops a suggestion that I make at the end of "The Self as Narrator," a paper on Dan Dennett's conception of the self (Chapter 9 in the present volume). Audiences to which I presented that paper have helped me to write this one; they include the philosophy departments at the University of Pittsburgh, the University of Maryland (College Park), and the University of Chicago. This paper was the target of a critique by Jürgen Müller, delivered to the Göttinger Philosophisches Kolloquium in January 2003, where much helpful discussion ensued. I am also grateful to Jerry Cohen, Tamar Schapiro, Nishiten Shah, and Ralph Wedgwood for comments on earlier drafts.

Kant is committed to the proposition (i) that wrongdoing entails irrationality in the agent, since a perfectly rational agent always does the right thing. He is also committed to the more specific proposition (ii) that wrongdoing entails irrationality in the action, since the balance of valid reasons for acting always favors doing the right thing. The latter, more specific proposition has often been the target of criticism.[1] The reasons there are for an agent to act seem to depend on aspects of his circumstances and psychological makeup that cannot be guaranteed to harmonize with what's right. A particular agent can therefore be a "hard case" in the sense that the right act is one that he has no reason to perform.[2] A proposition to which Kant is committed thus appears to be false.

In the debate over this proposition, Kantians have pointed out that a person can indeed be a hard case in the sense that he is not moved by reasons for him to do right; but in that instance, he is not exempt from those reasons but rather irrationally insensitive to them.[3] What depends on the agent's psychological makeup, then, is whether he is rational in responding to reasons for doing right, not whether such reasons apply to him.

Although I have in the past seconded this response to the critics of Kantianism,[4] I am also tempted to make a more concessive response. I am tempted to concede that an agent may do something wrong, not because he is insensitive to reasons for doing right, but because he has no such reasons. Yet having conceded that an agent can lack sufficient reason for doing the right thing, I would insist that such an agent is nevertheless irrational. I am therefore inclined to assert proposition (i) but deny (ii). The resulting view is what I shall call "concessive Kantianism."

My goal in this chapter is not so much to defend concessive Kantianism as to explain it and to show that it may in fact be implicit in a prominent reconstruction of Kantian ethics. I'll begin by explaining how an immoral act can be rational in itself while being the act of an irrational agent. The explanation will be that an agent can be irrational by virtue of having a problematic set of reasons for acting, even though he proceeds to take the course of action favored by the balance of those reasons. The result is a rational act performed by an irrational agent.[5]

---

[1] See, e.g., Foot 1978a, 1978b; Williams 1981a, 1995.

[2] The phrase "hard case" comes from Williams 1995: 39.

[3] See Korsgaard 1986.

[4] See Velleman 1996.

[5] A similar thesis is defended by Michelle Mason in her doctoral dissertation, "Moral Virtue and Reasons for Action" (2001); see esp. ch. 2.

This explanation commits me to evaluating an agent as rational or irrational on the basis of the reasons that he has for acting. It therefore commits me to holding an agent responsible for the reasons available to him. After offering a rather breezy defense of this commitment, I'll point out that it originates in the moral psychology of Kant's *Groundwork*. Indeed, Kant himself is committed to holding an agent responsible for his reasons in an especially rigorous way, and here is where my version of Kantianism makes its characteristic concession. I'll try to explain why my concessive way of holding an agent responsible for his reasons should be preferred to Kant's. Finally, I'll argue that this concessive version of Kantianism is implicit in the reconstruction of Kantian ethics recently offered by Christine Korsgaard in the symposium on her Tanner Lectures (1996d).

The upshot will be a novel account of contradictions in the will – the second and, I think, less obvious kind of practical conflict that we are enjoined to avoid in Kantian ethics. I call the account novel not to boast but to concede that it is historically inaccurate. Then again, maybe Kantian ethics could do with a little less historical accuracy.

An Irrational Sort of Person

Let me turn, then, to my exposition of the view that I call concessive Kantianism. And let me begin by illustrating the view with an example borrowed from Bernard Williams:[6]

Suppose, for example, I think someone . . . ought to be nicer to his wife. I say, "You have a reason to be nicer to her." He says, "What reason?" I say, "Because she is your wife." He says – and he is a very hard case – "I don't care. Don't you understand. I really do not care." I try various things on him, and try to involve him in this business; and I find that he really is a hard case: there is *nothing* in his motivational set that gives him a reason to be nicer to his wife as things are.

Here an orthodox Kantian may insist that the man doesn't need his "motivational set" to give him a reason for being nicer: he already has plenty of reasons. What his motivational set must give him is a motive responsive to those reasons, a motive in the absence of which the agent counts as irrational. The possibility that I am now entertaining, however, is that the agent may not have any reason for being nicer to his wife, and

---

[6] 1995: 39. I have omitted a parenthetical remark that the "ought" in this passage is used "in an unspecific way" – which means, I take it, a way that isn't specifically moral. I have followed Williams in this respect by speaking of actions as "right" and "wrong" in senses that aren't necessarily moral.

this because of his motivational profile. Given the sort of man he is, he may in fact have no reason to be nicer. But the sort of man who has no reason to be nice to his wife, I want to say, is an irrational sort of man to be.

How can someone be irrational when he is nevertheless acting on the balance of reasons that apply to him? How can he be irrational for failing to have the right reasons? The answer is that there is more than one way to be irrational.

On the one hand, a person is irrational if he lacks some capacities or dispositions that are essential to the activity of practical reasoning. If someone lacks the ability to recognize which considerations are the stronger reasons for him to act, or a disposition to be guided by such considerations, then he is deficient as a practical reasoner and hence irrational. On the other hand, a person can be irrational because his situation or personality presents him with reasons that hinder practical reasoning, without necessarily undermining his capacities as a reasoner.

Consider a person who is torn between two conflicting projects. He aspires to great wealth and success, for example, while also seeking a simple life of reflection and self-cultivation. He may be perfectly capable of weighing the reasons that issue from these ideals, and perfectly responsive to the force of those reasons. Indeed, long experience with difficult choices may have made him unusually adept at the art of deliberation. Yet there is something irrational about being so conflicted, about holding on to goals that cannot be jointly attained.

This example, underdescribed though it is, suggests that Williams's hard case has been described even less adequately. Not even the most demanding Kantian would balk at the idea of two people's having no reason to be nice to one another, even if they happen to be married. The Categorical Imperative doesn't require that everyone be nice to everyone else, and marriage is a context in which people can lose their reasons for being nice. But in such cases, people have usually lost their reasons for being married, or for living together in circumstances that provide opportunities for being nice or the reverse. What Williams's example invites us to imagine, I think, is a case in which a man isn't as nice to a woman as he should be in light of their remaining together as husband and wife. For some reason – and we imagine that the man has a reason – he stays in the marriage while treating his wife as would be appropriate only for a stranger or even an enemy. And now we have imagined an agent who is, in some way that remains to be described, committed to conflicting projects. Something in his life gives him reason to be married to a woman to whom he is unsympathetic or even hostile, and so there must be an underlying practical conflict of some sort.

One might argue that the man is failing to act on the reasons that apply to him, because each of his conflicting projects gives him reason to abandon the other. But reasons for abandoning a project tend to undermine the reasons that issue from it, and so the agent's reasons for abandoning either project are undermined by his reasons for abandoning the other. The man's problem is not that he's inappropriately hostile in light of his commitment to the relationship, since he has reason to give up the relationship in light of his hostility; nor is the problem that he's inappropriately committed to the relationship in light of his hostility, since he has reason to give up the hostility in light of the commitment. His problem is that he has gotten himself into a bind, which is a problem merely in light of his being an agent.

We can thus describe this agent's problem in terms that abstract from the particulars of his case: He is irrationally conflicted. This description specifies the form of the agent's motivational set but not its content.

One might insist that the irrationality of being conflicted does too depend on the content of the agent's motivational set. Being conflicted is irrational, one might say, only because it frustrates the pursuit of a higher-order end that any agent must have, the end of attaining his lower-order ends. This end gives any agent reason to avoid having lower-order ends that cannot be jointly attained, and hence to avoid conflicts. But this way of stating the problem is misleading and consequently unpersuasive. Can't an agent's motivational set fail to include the higher-order motive that would give him the requisite end? What if an agent cares about his several ends but not about the master end of their joint attainment?

What's misleading about this statement of the problem is that, in mandating a higher-order end, it seems to be mandating a motive, as an element of the agent's motivational set; whereas an agent's motivational set is supposed to represent the contingent, individually variable input to his practical reasoning. This statement of the problem therefore invites the question why an agent must have a motive toward attaining his lower-order ends.

Yet if ends are conceived as variable between agents, because of arising from their individual motivational sets, then each agent must have something else – a project, it might be called – that isn't an end in this sense. An agent must have the project of coping with, or doing justice to, the reasons that issue from his motivational set (or from anywhere else, for that matter). The reasons there are for him to act define a practical problem for him, and he must have the project of solving such problems, if he is to be a rational agent. This project isn't an end because it isn't just given to the rational agent by the contingent elements of his motivational set; it's a prerequisite for his being a rational agent, who can regard his motivational set (or anything else) as a source of reasons.

So even if we start from the assumption that reasons for acting must issue from the projects represented in the agent's motivational set, we end up at the realization that an agent must have at least one additional project, simply by virtue of being an agent – namely, the project of coping with the reasons that issue from his motivational set, a project that requires a motivational set that issues in reasons with which he can cope. Since the reasons that issue from deeply conflicting projects are extremely difficult to cope with, being conflicted is a hindrance to the project of practical reasoning itself.

I want to say that this hindrance to the project of practical reasoning renders the conflicted agent irrational. In so saying, however, I seem to be blaming a difficult situation on its victim. How can an agent be irrational for facing a difficult practical problem?

At this point, a contrast with theoretical reasoning might be helpful. In theoretical reasoning, we must cope with the various reasons for belief that confront us – the evidence, the arguments, our prior assumptions, and so on. Our task is to arrive at a belief that accommodates these reasons as well as possible, as if it were the solution to a set of simultaneous equations. Some sets of equations admit of an obvious solution and are therefore easy to solve; but other sets admit of no solutions, in which case we are obliged to discount some of our evidence, discard some of our assumptions, or otherwise adjust the set of reasons to be accommodated.

In theoretical reasoning, our task is to cope as best we can with whatever reasons the world serves up to us. A difficult theoretical problem is an inscrutability in the world, not an irrationality in ourselves. But in practical reasoning, the reasons with which we must cope, the simultaneous equations that we must solve, are served up by our personalities and circumstances, which are partly our own responsibility. The man in Williams's example didn't just wake up in a bind: he probably got himself into a bind by ignoring signs of trouble, shirking crucial choices, and making fateful compromises over time. More importantly, he can and ought to get himself out of his bind, though doing so will also take time. For he can and ought to resolve the conflicts in himself, by altering his motives or his circumstances, or both. So whereas a theorist with deeply conflicting evidence is merely unfortunate, an agent with deeply

conflicting projects may be rationally criticizable, insofar as he is responsible for getting into, and is in any case responsible for getting out of, his
own deliberative difficulties.

One might object that the epistemic agent can also avoid deliberative
difficulties, simply by closing his eyes to recalcitrant evidence or closing his ears to distracting hypotheses. But such maneuvers would defeat
the purpose of theoretical reasoning, which is to arrive at the truth, or
at least at the hypothesis that best accounts for the phenomena, where
the truth and the phenomena are fixed by the way the world is. By contrast, the purpose of practical reasoning is not just to cope with reasons
that are fixed by the agent's current motives and circumstances, since
changing his motives or circumstances often remains one of the agent's
options, a possible outcome of his practical reasoning. The epistemic
agent's predicament is defined by what the world is like, and he must
cope with that predicament, because he cannot change it. But the practical agent's predicament is defined by what his life is like, and one of
the resolutions available to him is to change his life. The practical agent
can therefore be held rationally responsible for getting himself into, or
not getting himself out of, the wrong predicaments, predicaments that
are wrong in the sense that they confront him with a problematic set of
reasons.

How to Hold an Agent Responsible for His Reasons

Kant is committed to holding an agent responsible for the reasons that
apply to him. This commitment appears in Kant's doctrine of willing
the law.

An agent wills the law, according to Kant, when he wills his maxim in
the form of a law for all rational agents; and his maxim is a principle of
practical reason, specifying a proposed course of action and his reasons
for taking it.[7] The agent wills that the principle of taking that course for
those reasons be valid for any rational agent, as it would have to be in
order to be rationally valid at all, even for him.[8] Thus, when the agent

---

[7] For this conception of maxims see, e.g., Korsgaard 1996a: 13: "Your maxim must contain
your reason for action: it must say what you are going to do, and why."

[8] In many formulations, the Categorical Imperative appears to require only that the agent
be *able* to will that his maxim become a universal law. But the best justification for requiring
that he be able to will the universalization of his maxim is that he must actually will it,
or at least regard himself as willing it. And this necessity is indeed asserted in Kant's
Formula of Autonomy: "The principle of autonomy is . . . : to choose only in such a way

acts for reasons, he acts on the basis of considerations that he has willed to be valid as reasons, for himself or anyone else.

In the form enunciated by Kant and adopted by contemporary Kantians, the doctrine of willing the law does not fit the process that I have imagined as making an agent responsible for the reasons that apply to him. But that orthodox form of the doctrine is also flawed, in my opinion; and its flaws turn out to coincide with its differences from the process that I have imagined. In my opinion, my concessions to the critics of Kant turn out to be an improvement over the orthodoxy.

In the process that I imagined here, an agent is responsible for the reasons that apply to him insofar as he is responsible for his personality and his circumstances, which at any particular time determine the set of applicable reasons. But the agent's responsibility for his reasons, in my conception, does not involve the capacity to decide, at a particular moment, which reasons apply to him. His personality and his circumstances determine the set of applicable reasons in a systematic way that is not up to him;[9] and because he cannot change his personality or his circumstances on the spot, he cannot immediately change the reasons that apply to him, either. He is responsible for the reasons that apply to him only because his choices over time have shaped, and will continue to shape, the attitudes, traits, and circumstances that determine the set of applicable reasons.

By contrast, Kant's doctrine of willing the law seems to imply that an agent is in a position simply to will that particular considerations have validity as reasons – as if their rational force were up to him. This implication follows from a combination of passages, as follows. First, Kant defines the will as "the capacity to act *in accordance with the representation* of laws, that is, in accordance with principles"; he adds that "[s]ince *reason* is required for the derivation of actions from laws, the will is nothing other

that the maxims of your choice are also included as universal law in the same volition" (*Groundwork of the Metaphysics of Morals*, 47 [4: 440]). See also 45 [4: 437–8], "the basic principle, act on a maxim that at the same time contains in itself its own universal validity for every rational being," and 46 [4: 438–9], "act in accordance with the maxims of a member giving universal laws for a merely possible kingdom of ends." (Note that in the last quotation, what is qualified as merely possible is, not the agent's willing of his maxim as a law, but the kingdom of ends that would exist if the law were universally obeyed.)

9 I haven't specified how the agent's motivational set determines the set of applicable reasons, because I disagree with Williams and other so-called internalists on this question. In particular, I don't believe that reasons applicable to an agent are dependent on his motivational set, as conceived by Williams, for their capacity to influence the agent's behavior.

than practical reason."[10] Kant subsequently asserts that "every rational being having a will" must exercise that will under the idea of freedom, because the will consists in practical reason and "[r]eason must regard itself as the author of its principles."[11] Thus, in any being with a will, practical reason must derive actions from laws of which it regards itself as the author; and those laws, as we have seen, are universalized principles of acting in particular ways for particular reasons. Any rational being must therefore purport to originate the principles expressing the validity of his own reasons for acting.

As I have said, I think that the orthodox Kantian doctrine of willing the law is flawed. I think that practical reason need not – indeed, cannot – regard itself as the author of its principles, because an agent cannot regard himself as originating the validity of his reasons for acting. I will now try to explain this flaw in the Kantian view and how it can be corrected.

The flaw in this conception of practical reason is that it cannot explain how an agent is guided by reasons for acting. The volition in which the agent wills the universal validity of his reasons is the same as the volition in which he wills his action, since his decision to act for those reasons "contains in itself its own universal validity for every rational being"[12] or is "also included as universal law in the same volition."[13] Because the agent's decision to act for reasons contains or includes his willing the validity of those reasons, it cannot be guided by any prior recognition of their validity. All that guides the agent's decision, according to Kant, is his recognition that he is not precluded from willing the universal validity of his reasons for acting. In framing his decision, the agent is not bound by any antecedently valid principles of practical reasoning other than the principle of framing his decisions as principles whose universal validity he can simultaneously will.[14]

Critics of Kant have long complained that when the Categorical Imperative is so understood, it does not constrain the agent's choices in the determinate way that morality constrains them, because it constrains their form but not their substance. I am not sympathetic to this complaint when it is directed against Kantianism as a moral theory, since I think that an important part of morality is precisely a constraint on the

---

[10] *Groundwork*, 24 [4: 412]; see also 36 [4: 427].

[11] *Groundwork*, 54 [4: 448].

[12] *Groundwork*, 46 [4: 438–9].

[13] *Groundwork*, 47 [4: 440].

[14] See *Groundwork*, 40 [4: 442]: "[T]he human being . . . is subject *only to laws given by himself but still universal* and . . . he is bound only to act in conformity with his own will, which, however, in accordance with nature's end is a will giving universal law."

form rather than the content of the will. But I am sympathetic to the complaint when it is directed against Kantianism as a theory of practical reason. In this capacity, the Categorical Imperative implies that the reasons for an agent's decision must be reasons whose validity is willed in that very decision. And a decision that wills the validity of its own reasons cannot be guided by a recognition of their validity.

The only guidance available for such a decision is the guidance of the Categorical Imperative itself, which rules out deciding to act for reasons whose universal validity cannot simultaneously be willed. Within this purely formal constraint, the agent can decide to act for any reasons that he thereby wills to be universally valid. But how can the agent regard his decision as being guided by reasons whose validity he regards as being conferred on them by that very decision? How can he actually *be* guided by reasons so regarded?

A deeper aspect of this problem is that the validity of reasons is not the sort of thing that we ordinarily conceive as being subject to the will at all. A reason for acting is a consideration that purports to justify acting, and a valid reason is a consideration that, if true, really does justify what it purports to. But to justify something is to show (at least prima facie) that it is just, in the archaic sense of being in accordance with a *jus*, or rule of correctness. Hence a consideration justifies an action by tending to show that it would be a correct thing to do. How can the agent decide whether a consideration tends to show that a particular action would be correct?

If Kant were to acquiesce in this manner of speaking, he would point out that we are puzzled by the notion of an agent's deciding the justificatory force of reasons only because we assume that they must exert that force in relation to antecedently fixed rules of correctness for action. Perhaps we are improperly assimilating the case of action to that of belief, in which reasons must exert their justificatory force in relation to the antecedently fixed rule that a belief is correct only if true. A believer is in no position to decide which considerations shall have validity as reasons for belief, because he cannot decide which considerations show a belief to be correct in relation to the rule of truth. But in the practical case, the agent can decide the validity of reasons, Kant would argue, because he decides the rules of correctness as well: the autonomous agent adopts his own rules of correctness for action, subject only to the proviso that he adopt them in universal form, avoiding any rules that he cannot thus universalize.

Thus, Kant would say, we were puzzled about willing the law only because we had too narrow a conception of this process, as a process of willing merely that particular considerations should count as showing an action to be correct. That conception left us wondering how an agent could possibly decide the import that particular considerations would have for the correctness of an action. The answer is that we need a broader conception of willing the law, as a process of willing the rules of correctness themselves, and only thereby willing the validity of the associated reasons. The agent wills that actions of a particular kind shall be correct in circumstances of a particular kind – which amounts to willing that consideration of the circumstances shall tend to justify the actions.

Unfortunately, this clarification doesn't solve the problem. If one's actions are subject to no fixed rules of correctness other than a rule for willing what those rules of correctness shall be, then one cannot really place one's actions under rules of correctness after all, since one's latitude in willing those rules reveals that, when it comes to actions, anything goes. How can one make an action correct in the circumstances by willing it to be correct, given that one could equally have conferred such correctness on a different action? Willing the law now looks like an empty exercise in self-congratulation – a matter of ruling one's choice to be correct so that one can pat oneself on the back for choosing correctly.

Of course, Kant will respond that not *quite* anything goes when it comes to actions, because in willing rules under which his actions are correct, the agent is restricted to rules that he can will in universal form. Perhaps the rules that he adopts can be rules of correctness because they have been constrained by the master rule of universalization – that is, by the Categorical Imperative. Yet this response brings us back to the problem of empty formalism, regarded again as a problem in the Kantian conception of practical reason. When the agent doesn't know what to do, he looks for reasons to guide him; but all he finds, according to Kant, is a set of actions that (under some description) he could will to be universally correct in circumstances that (under some description) are similar to his. Even if we believe that this set would exclude any morally impermissible actions, we must doubt whether the agent can will distinctions of correctness among the remaining, permissible alternatives. Within the constraints of the Categorical Imperative, the agent appears to face an arbitrary choice among various universal rules, which would specify various actions as correct in light of the circumstances, variously considered, thereby constituting different considerations as reasons for taking different actions. Having decided to act under one of these rules, how can the agent regard it as conferring correctness on his action, or normative force on his reasons, given that he has simply adopted it from among various rules that would have constituted other permissible actions as correct, and other considerations as reasons?

Let me repeat that this problem is more difficult for a Kantian conception of practical reason than it is for Kantian ethics. The availability of many act descriptions that the agent could consistently incorporate into a universal law is not necessarily a problem for the Categorical Imperative in its capacity as a test of morality. The test of the Categorical Imperative applies to any description under which the agent proposes to act, and it yields an up-or-down verdict on the permissibility of acting under that description. Once the agent has discovered which of the available acts would be permissible, and which would not, he has completed the moral reflections required of him, according to Kant. But having sorted the available acts into the permissible and the impermissible, the agent has not yet completed his practical reasoning about which of the permissible acts to perform. He must still choose one of the permissible acts rather than the others, and he must choose it for reasons. (If he didn't have to choose on the basis of reasons, then his choice wouldn't have been constrained by the Categorical Imperative, since the necessity of choosing for reasons is what generates the need to universalize.) The problem is that the reasons favoring one permissible act or the other are reasons that the agent himself must will into validity as he chooses between them. So how can he look to the validity of these reasons as a basis on which to choose?

One might think that the problem is solved by the additional constraint of hypothetical imperatives, which require the agent to will adequate means to his ends. Yet hypothetical imperatives, too, are merely formal constraints that provide only minimal guidance. They require only that an agent either abandon an end or adopt adequate means to it; and in the latter case, only that he adopt some adequate means or other. Of course, many philosophers believe that such formal constraints exhaust the guidance available from practical reason, which does no more, in their view, than enforce consistency on an agent's choices. But this solution is not available to Kant, precisely because he regards every rational choice as adopting not just a particular action but a corresponding rule of correctness, which is more specific than the purely formal imperatives that constrain it. In choosing among the actions conducive to his ends, the agent must will a law conferring correctness on actions like his in circumstances like his, so that his choice is derived from a law of which he can regard himself as the author. (Otherwise, he wouldn't qualify as choosing at all, and unchosen behavior, not purporting to embody a rule, would not have to be universalizable.)[15]

---

[15] See the quotation from pp. 231–2 of Korsgaard's Tanner lectures (1996d), on p. 299.

Thus, the agent still appears to be engaged in an empty form of self-congratulation. The rule of correctness that ought to be the basis for a choice is only willed into force as the choice is being made. The problem is how the basis of a choice can be willed into being by the same volition as the choice itself.[16]

Korsgaard's Concessive Version of Kant

Christine Korsgaard grapples with these problems in her Tanner Lectures, where she offers her own model of willing the law.[17] I am going to argue that Korsgaard comes close to adopting what I call concessive Kantianism; but first I'll need to explain how the relevant criticisms bear on Korsgaard's version of Kantian ethics.

---

[16] I think that there are cases in which practical reasoning takes this puzzling form, but they aren't cases that support the Kantian conception. For they are clearly unsuited to be a model of practical reasoning in general.

   When you are tempted to eat or drink too much, to work or exercise too little, to shirk a social obligation or make an undue imposition – in short, to indulge yourself in some way – you tend to look for aspects of the occasion that make it unusual, precisely so that you can endorse such self-indulgence only on similarly unusual occasions, while continuing to condemn it more generally. These circumstances needn't be ones that you antecedently regard as positive reasons for self-indulgence: they may be as trivial as the fact that it's Tuesday. Yet if you allow yourself, say, to overeat in light of the fact that it's Tuesday, then you seem to make its being Tuesday a reason for allowing yourself to overeat. You thus seem able to choose what shall count as a reason for your action on this occasion and others like it.

   I think that when you preemptively excuse or rationalize an action by finding an acceptable principle for it, you may indeed be in the position of willing the law; and your principle may indeed have justifying force insofar as you accept it under the constraint of having to accept it in universal form. Not just anything goes when it comes to self-indulgence, only those things which you're willing to accept as going in general – including, perhaps, overeating on Tuesdays, but not overeating every day. And because you've confined yourself to what you're willing to accept as going in general, you seem to be justified in letting it go today. So you seem to have willed your action into being correct, and your circumstances into being reasons for it.

   Although such cases exemplify the Kantian conception of willing the law, they don't lend that conception much support. For they are cases not so much of adopting reasons as of adopting excuses or pretexts – cases in which your principles at best permit you to do something but don't positively guide you to do it. Again, your reasoning in these cases may be an adequate model of moral reasoning, insofar as moral reasoning is just a matter of asking, "May I?" But practical reasoning is not in general permissive, not just a matter of asking, "May I?" It's a matter of asking what you should do from among the many things that you may. Practical reasoning must give you a positive basis for choosing among the many morally permissible actions, and cases in which you adopt principles for permitting or excusing self-indulgence cannot be a model for such reasoning.

[17] Korsgaard 1996d.

In Korsgaard's version of Kantian ethics, willing the law is a matter of adopting a self-conception, or "practical identity." Korsgaard derives the notion of practical identities from the phenomenology of reflective agency:[18]

When you deliberate, it is as if there were something over and above all of your desires, something which is *you*, and which *chooses* which desire to act on. This means that the principle or law by which you determine your actions is one that you regard as being expressive of *yourself*. To identify with such a principle or way of choosing is to be, in St. Paul's famous phrase, a law to yourself.

Because an agent identifies with the principle that dictates his choice, the principle can actually be expressed as a self-conception:

An agent might think of herself as a Citizen of the Kingdom of Ends. Or she might think of herself as someone's friend or lover, or as a member of a family or an ethnic group or a nation. She might think of herself as the steward of her own interests, and then she will be an egoist. Or she might think of herself as the slave of her passions, and then she will be a wanton. And how she thinks of herself will determine whether it is the law of the Kingdom of Ends, or the law of some smaller group, or the law of egoism, or the law of the wanton that will be the law that she is to herself. (101)

As we have seen, the law with which the agent identifies, by adopting one of these self-conceptions, is in fact a principle of choosing to act in particular ways under particular circumstances – circumstances that the law constitutes as reasons for acting in those ways. Thus:

That you desire something is a reason for doing it from the perspective of the principle of self-love. . . . That Susan is in trouble is a reason for action from the perspective of Susan's friend; that the law requires it is a reason for action from the perspective of a citizen, and so forth. (243)

In sum, an agent adopts a principle that determines what counts as a reason, but he adopts that principle in the form of a conception of himself as someone's friend, or as a citizen of a nation, or whatever.

Korsgaard's lectures seem to equate practical identities with principles of choice. She appears to say that adopting the identity of Susan's friend just consists in identifying with particular principles of choice, such as the principle of helping Susan when she's in trouble. This view implies that insofar as the reason-giving import of Susan's troubles depends on whether the agent is her friend, it depends on whether the agent adopts

---

[18] Korsgaard 1996d: 100. All parenthetical references from here on are to that volume.

particular principles of choice, including the principle that explicitly specifies her troubles as reasons. The view therefore implies that the agent can decide whether Susan's troubles have reason-giving force for him, simply by deciding whether to adopt a principle conferring such force upon them.

Cohen's Objection and the Beginning of Korsgaard's Reply

In the symposium on Korsgaard's lectures, G. A. Cohen objects that a law adopted at will by the agent can just as easily be repealed by the agent and therefore fails to bind him in any meaningful way: "[A]lthough you may be bound by a law that you can change, the fact that you can change it diminishes the significance of the fact that you are bound by it. There's not much 'must' in a 'must' that you can readily get rid of."[19] To say that "there's not much 'must'" is to say that almost anything goes, and so Cohen's objection to Korsgaard resembles the one that I raised earlier against Kant. In either case, the objection is that being adopted at will would drain rules or laws of any significant normative force.

Korsgaard's answer to this objection shows that her conception of willing the law already differs from the conception that I have attributed to Kant. Her answer begins with a point that Cohen himself has acknowledged, "that even if I can change the law that I make for myself, I remain bound by it until I can change it" (234). What this point reveals is that in Korsgaard's model, an agent's decision is constrained, not only by the principle of choice that he wills in making that very decision, but also by principles that he has willed on previous occasions. And the latter principles are antecedently available to guide the agent's present decision, unlike the principle that he wills in making the decision itself.

An agent can thus be guided, in making his present decision, by reasons whose validity he has willed in the past. Each time he has made a choice in the past, he has willed and thus committed himself to a principle dictating similar choices in similar cases, including cases that he might encounter in the future. If he now encounters such a case, he will be bound by his former commitment to that principle of choice. In time, the agent will find himself encumbered with commitments to many principles, of which it is likely that some will apply to any particular case he may encounter; and he remains encumbered by those commitments until he revokes

---

[19] Cohen 1996: 170.

them. On any particular occasion, the relevant principles will constitute various considerations as reasons for him to act.

With this background in place, Korsgaard is now in a position to answer Cohen's objection. The objection, remember, was that even if a principle adopted by the agent is binding until revoked, it does not significantly bind him given that he is empowered to revoke it. Korsgaard's answer to the objection is this: "[I]f I am to be an agent, I cannot change my law without changing my mind, and I cannot change my mind without a reason." Hence "we cannot change our minds about just anything" (234). Korsgaard derives this answer from the results of an earlier discussion, in which she put the point as follows:

> If I am to regard *this* act, the one I do now, as the act of my *will*, I must at least make a claim to universality, a claim that the reason for which I act now will be valid on other occasions, or on occasions of this type.... Again, the form of the act of the will is general. The claim to generality, to universality, is essential to an act's being an act of the will.
>
> A couple of paragraphs ago I put into the objector's mouth the claim that when I make a decision I need not refer to any past or future acts of my will. But now we see that this turns out to be false, for according to the above argument it is the claim to universality that *gives* me a will, that makes my will distinguishable from the operation of desires and impulses in me. If I change my mind and my will every time I have a new impulse, then I don't really have an active mind or a will at all – I am just a kind of location where these impulses are at play. And that means that to *make up my mind* even now – to give myself a reason – I must conceive of my reason as an instance of some general type. Of course this is not to say that I cannot ever change my mind, but only to say that I must do it for a reason, and not at random. (231–2)

We'll need to spend a moment analyzing this passage in order to understand Korsgaard's conception of willing the law.

In this passage, Korsgaard observes that making up one's mind requires one to adopt some stable or settled practical stance, which must consist in more than an occurrent impulse. From this observation, she infers that making up one's mind requires one to have a general principle, which will embody one's made-up mind. The conclusion of this inference has both subjective and objective aspects. The subjective aspect is that in order to *view* oneself as making up one's mind, one must view oneself as instituting a stable practical stance; and one must attain this view by framing one's decision in the form of a general principle that purports to cover occasions beyond the present. But one can thus purport to make up one's mind without actually succeeding, since the purportedly stable stance that one has instituted may consist in a general principle that one might instantly revoke at any time. Objectively speaking, then, making up one's mind requires not only that one's practical stance purport to cover future occasions but also that it really have some stability across the occasions that it purports to cover.

Korsgaard's argument continues from the latter, objective condition on making up one's mind. Before one can change one's mind, one must have succeeded in making it up one way or another, so that there is something for one to change; and in order to have made up one's mind one way or another, one must have arrived at a stance with some real stability. Hence one cannot change one's mind if it is unduly changeable, since what is unduly changeable does not amount to a made-up mind, to begin with. Changing one's mind entails becoming differently *minded*, which requires being antecedently minded in some determinate way, which in turn requires being resistant to undue change.

According to Korsgaard, this restriction on undue changes of mind restricts one to changes of mind for which one has a reason. What she says is that one must change one's mind "for a reason, not at random." Her thought appears to be that change at random is undue change, which made-up minds tend to resist, and that the opposite of change at random is change for a reason. If one changes one's mind at random, then it will not really have been made up, in the first place, and to that extent won't amount to a mind to be changed. But if one changes one's mind only for a reason, then one's mind, though proving to have been changeable, will not have been unduly so, and hence will really have been made up, after all. The requirement to have a reason for changing one's mind ensures that a change will amount to a transition between determinate ways of being minded rather than a dissolution of determinate mindedness altogether.

But now the problem of empty formalism reemerges. For if one's change of mind is not an undue change so long as it is based on a reason, then the ready availability of reasons will take the bite out of any restriction on changes of mind. In order to change his mind for a reason, the agent need only make the change under cover of a relevant principle, which will constitute some considerations as the requisite reasons. Of course, the agent may already be committed to principles about how and when to change his mind; but those principles will themselves be subject to reconsideration and revision, provided only that their revision be adopted under a yet further principle.

Let me clarify the problem by summarizing how it has arisen. Kant says that when an agent decides to take an action, he must will not just the action but also a relevant principle of correctness, which constitutes particular considerations as reasons for taking the action. We worried that giving the agent this much latitude to bless his own actions as correct, and thus to constitute considerations as reasons for taking it, would undermine the very possibility of correctness in actions, or of normative force in reasons for acting. When Cohen expressed this worry, in response to Korsgaard's reconstruction of Kant, her answer was that the agent's latitude is significantly restricted by the blessings he has conferred on actions in the past, whereby he committed himself to principles of correctness, and hence to reasons for acting, to which he remains committed.

What worries us now is that the agent's latitude cannot be restricted by past commitments, precisely because it undermines those commitments as well. No rational commitment is so binding that it cannot be revoked for good reasons – that is, on the basis of considerations tending to show that revoking it would be correct. Hence the agent's latitude to confer correctness on actions, and thus to constitute considerations as reasons, cannot be restricted by past commitments, because it includes latitude to confer correctness on the act of revoking those commitments, and thus to constitute reasons for revoking them. Although the agent has committed himself by blessing his actions in the past, he can always revoke those commitments under cover of a new blessing. *The problem is that reasons are too easy for the agent to conjure up, and so the solution cannot be that once having conjured them up, he needs a reason for conjuring them away.*[20]

---

[20] The problem of empty formalism runs even deeper than Korsgaard's conception of practical reason: it runs all the way down to the agent's conception of his own agency. For in Korsgaard's version of Kant, principles of choice are constitutive not only of practical reasoning but of the agent himself. Korsgaard puts the point most clearly in a recent article:

To conceive yourself as the cause of your actions is to identify with the principle of choice on which you act. A rational will is a self-conscious causality, and a self-conscious causality is aware of itself as a cause. To be aware of yourself as a cause is to identify yourself with something in the scenario that gives rise to the action, and this must be the principle of choice. . . . You regard the choice as yours, as the product of your own activity, because you regard the principle of choice as expressive, or representative, of yourself. . . . Self-conscious or rational agency, then, requires identification with the principle of choice on which you act. (1999: 26)

Yet if the person casts himself as author of his actions by identifying with the principles that generate those actions, then how does he cast himself as the author of his principles, as Kant says he must? The answer would seem to be that he generates the principles of his actions from antecedent principles with which he also identifies. Yet this regress of principles cannot go on forever; and where it ultimately stops is at the Categorical Imperative, which is the principle simply of deriving things from principles – a purely formal principle, from which no particular substantive principles can be derived. [Note continues on p. 302.]

The Rest of Korsgaard's Reply

Korsgaard's version of Kantian theory has various additional resources for addressing this problem. After I describe those resources, I will argue that they add up to what I call the concessive response to critics of Kant – the response that accepts the proposition designated (i) in my introduction, while rejecting the proposition designated (ii). (I do not claim that Korsgaard herself would add things up in the same way.)

The first of these resources is the claim that, with one important exception, the principles willed by an agent must be endorsements of his antecedent impulses toward acting:[21]

[T]he contrast between being motivated by reason and being motivated by affection . . . is, on my view, incoherent. To be motivated "by reason" is normally to be motivated by one's reflective endorsement of incentives and impulses, including affections, which arise in a natural way. (127)

The exception to this generalization is the case in which action is required or forbidden by the Categorical Imperative:[22]

It is only in cases of reflective rejection that the impulse to act or refrain has to "come from reason." For example, when I discover that my impulse to break a burdensome promise must be reflectively rejected, that discovery itself must be the source of a new impulse, an impulse to keep the promise. This second impulse is strictly speaking what Kant called "respect for law." But respect for law

---

So here is the problem: somewhere between the agent's commitment to the Categorical Imperative and his authorship of a particular action, he must acquire substantive principles without having prior principles sufficiently substantive to generate them. And those substantive principles, to which his action will be ultimately attributable, will not be attributable to him as their author. The empty formalism of the Categorical Imperative thus seems to have emptied human action of a responsible agent. (Readers of Harry Frankfurt may recognize this problem as the infinite regress of higher-order identifications.)

[21] Korsgaard bases this claim on her interpretation of Kantian ethics as a "reflective endorsement" theory. "That after all is the whole point of using the reflective endorsement method to justify morality: We are supposing that when we reflect on the things which we find ourselves inclined to do, we can then accept or reject the authority those inclinations claim over our conduct and act accordingly" (1996d: 89).

[22] The passage quoted here expresses Kant's view. Korsgaard's view is that the impulse that Kant attributed to the Categorical Imperative can also be generated by the agent's other, contingent practical identities:

In some cases our conception of a contingent practical identity will give rise to new motives in a way that parallels the generation of the motive of duty by the thought of the categorical imperative. You may be tempted to do something but find that it is inconsistent with your identity as a teacher or a mother or a friend, and the thought that it is inconsistent may give rise to a new incentive, an incentive not to do this thing. (239–40)

more generally is expressed by the standing commitment to act only on morally endorsable impulses. (127, n. 41)

Korsgaard thus arrives at what she calls a "double-aspect" theory of reasons for acting. Except in cases of acting purely out of respect for law, acting for a reason involves acting on the conjunction of an impulse and an endorsement of that impulse, which consists in a principle of acting on impulses of its kind. Although Korsgaard sometimes says, "A reason is an endorsement of an impulse" (154), her considered view is that a reason consists in the conjunction of the two: "Neither the incentive nor the principle of choice is, by itself 'the reason' for the action; rather, the reason is the incentive as seen from the perspective of the principle of choice" (243).

The upshot is that Korsgaard believes reasons for acting are to be determined by the agent's motivational set, after all. The vast majority of reasons for acting are impulses as endorsed by principles of choice. The only exceptions are reasons that consist in laws that require the rejection of particular impulses as reasons. Thus, all reasons involve the endorsement or rejection of impulses, and to that extent, all reasons are impulse-based.[23]

Furthermore, Korsgaard believes that the impulses in an agent's motivational set are under his control to some small extent:

Our contingent practical identities are, to some extent, given to us – by our cultures, by our societies and their role structures, by the accidents of birth, and by our natural abilities – but it is also clear that we enter into their constitution. And this means that desires and impulses associated with them do not just *arise* in us. When we adopt (or come to wholeheartedly inhabit) a conception of practical identity, we also adopt a way of life and a set of projects, and the new desires which this brings in its wake. . . . The motives and desires that spring from our contingent practical identities are . . . in part the result of our own activity. (239–40)

Insofar as an agent is responsible for adopting identities and the motives that they entail, he is also responsible for the range of reasons that will be available to him. But his ability to alter the range of available reasons

---

[23] Why must the will operate on the agent's antecedent impulses? In a recent paper, Korsgaard answers as follows: "According to Kant you must always act on some incentive or other, for every action, even action from duty, involves a decision on a proposal: something must suggest the action to you" (1999: 26). Yet in the Tanner Lectures, Korsgaard points out that an action can be suggested, not just by the agent's impulses, but by other agents (1996d: 139–40). And we might wonder, more generally, why a faculty that can be the author of its own principles cannot be the author its own suggestions, too. This aspect of Kantian moral psychology seems undermotivated, to say the least.

is limited. He can alter the range of available reasons only by adopting, shedding, or somehow modifying his practical identities, and this process takes time. Hence he cannot alter the available reasons on the spot: "Although I have just been suggesting that we do make an active contribution to our practical identities and the impulses that arise from them, it remains true that *at the moment of action these impulses are the incentives, the passively confronted material upon which the active will operates*" (240–1, emphasis added).

Finally, Korsgaard believes that the motives and principles associated with an agent's contingent practical identities can be genuinely normative even if they are ultimately in conflict with the Categorical Imperative. Discussing the case (introduced by Cohen) of a man whose practical identities include that of a Mafioso, Korsgaard says:

> It would be intellectually tidy, and no doubt spare me trouble from critics, if I . . . said that only those obligations consistent with morality are "real" or in Cohen's phrase "genuine." Then I could say that it seems to the Mafioso as if he had an obligation to be strong and in his sense honour-bound, but actually he does not. I could say that there's no obligation here, only the sense of obligation: no normativity, only the psychic appearance of it. . . . But I am not comfortable with this easy way out, for a reason related to one of Cohen's own points – that there is a real sense in which you are bound by a law you make for yourself until you make another. . . . There is a sense in which these obligations are real – not just psychologically but normatively. And this is because it is the endorsement . . . that does the normative work. (257)

The endorsement that "does the normative work" of obligating the mobster to his mob is embodied in the principles that make up his identity as a Mafioso – principles of perfect loyalty to the mob and perfect ruthlessness to outsiders. And these principles underlie not only the mobster's obligations, when he is tempted to be less than completely loyal or completely ruthless, but also his reasons for being loyal or ruthless on occasions when he isn't tempted to be otherwise. If these principles can lend normative force to the obligations, then they must also be able to lend normative force to the associated reasons.[24]

---

[24] Korsgaard describes the relation between obligations and reasons as follows:

> To make a law for yourself . . . is at the same time to give expression to a practical conception of your identity. Practical conceptions of our identity determine which of our impulses will count as reasons. And to the extent that we cannot act against them without losing our sense that our lives are worth living and our actions are worth undertaking, they can obligate us. (129)

Korsgaard believes that the normative force of these reasons, like that of the associated obligations, can ultimately be undermined by the mobster's more fundamental identity as a human being who must act for reasons, the identity that consists in his commitment to the Categorical Imperative: "If Cohen's Mafioso attempted to answer the question why it matters that he should be strong and in his sense honour-bound even when he was tempted not to, he would find that its mattering depends on the value of his humanity, and if my other arguments go through, he would find that that commits him to the value of humanity in general, and so to giving up his role as a Mafioso" (256). But Korsgaard does not say that the existence of this latent conflict between the mobster's commitment to humanity and his commitment to the role of a mobster already undermines the normative force of the latter commitment, even before the conflict is discovered and the latter commitment revoked. On the contrary, she says that the latter commitment gives rise to genuinely normative obligations.

The resulting view severely constrains an agent's latitude in constituting and reconstituting reasons for acting. Reasons for him to act must consist in impulses endorsed by principles; his impulses are "passively confronted material" that he cannot change at the moment of action; and his principles can be revised only on the basis of reasons, which themselves require passively confronted impulses and/or conflicting principles to dictate the revision. Hence the agent cannot simply conjure up reasons for acting, or reasons for revising his principles, since he is confined in both instances to reasons based either on impulses already available in his motivational set or principles already available among his practical identities. Changing the set of available reasons therefore requires substantive psychological change, which the agent cannot effect at will.

In sum, we can no longer object that anything goes for a rational agent. His psychological makeup now provides substantive constraints on his practical reasoning, and so his practical reasoning is no longer an empty form. At the same time, however, the agent's practical reasoning is no longer guaranteed to encounter a set of reasons that weighs in favor of moral action. That's why I think that Korsgaard's view has become concessive.

Why Korsgaard's Version of Kantianism Is Concessive

Consider again the mobster introduced by Cohen. This man may have inherited the practical identity of a mobster from his family, or adopted that identity on his own, or acquired it through some combination of these processes. In any case, his acquisition of that identity will have entailed the acquisition of associated desires and impulses, such as the desire to kill anyone who threatens the interests of the mob. When anyone threatens those interests, the desire to kill him will unavoidably arise as "passively confronted material on which [the mobster's] will operates." And his identity as a mobster will include principles endorsing such desires as reasons for acting. As endorsed by those principles, his murderous desires will have genuine normative force as reasons for the mobster to act. He will therefore have genuine reasons for committing murder.

To be sure, the mobster also has countervailing reasons, based in his fundamental identity as a human being, as expressed in the Categorical Imperative. But these reasons weigh against acts of murder only indirectly, by committing him to "giving up his role as a Mafioso." They are reasons for him to revoke his commitment to that more particular identity, which turns out to conflict with his underlying identity as a human being, and so they are reasons for him to become someone who no longer has reasons for committing murder. The mobster is irrational to commit murder, not because he doesn't have reasons for committing such an act, but rather because he has reasons against being the sort of person who has those reasons.

One might think that the mobster's fundamental commitment to his humanity, as expressed in the Categorical Imperative, militates directly against acts of murder, thus overriding the reasons generated by his identity as a mobster. The Categorical Imperative does militate directly against particular immoral acts in Kant's own version of the theory. Unfortunately, Korsgaard's version of the theory has eliminated the mechanism by which it militates against those acts.

In Kant's theory, the Categorical Imperative rules out particular acts only by ruling out the volitions behind them; and it rules out those volitions by requiring every volition to include not just the description of an action but also a universalized maxim of acting under that description – what Korsgaard calls a principle of choice. In order to commit a murder, the agent must will not just the particular killing but, at the same time, a principle of killing. And willing such a principle turns out to involve a contradiction. Because Kant's theory requires the agent to will the particular act only in conjunction with a principle, the contradiction involved in willing such a principle stands in the way of willing the act.

In Korsgaard's version of the theory, however, the agent may already be committed to the relevant principle by virtue of having adopted it earlier and not repealed it since. In that case, there would seem to be no need for him to will the principle afresh in acting on it again. Indeed, he would seem to be in no position to will the principle any more, given that he is already committed to it: He can no longer will it to be a law for him, because it already is one, whether he likes it or not. And if his volition to act need not encompass his principle as well, then the contradiction involved in willing the principle cannot pose any rational obstacle to the act.

Imagine that Kant himself wrote in Korsgaard's language of self-constitution. In that case, Kant would say that the Categorical Imperative requires that, in choosing to kill, the agent adopt the identity of a killer, by adopting a general principle of killing. Kant would add that adopting the identity of a killer entails a contradiction that consequently stands in the way of choosing to kill. But Korsgaard's view is that the agent may already *have* the identity of a killer, and so the contradiction that would be involved in adopting that identity no longer stands in his way.

The result of retroactively imposing Korsgaard's terminology on Kant himself is a theory of radical self-constitution: with every act, the agent re-adopts the relevant identities all over again, reconstituting himself as a killer with every killing, as a friend with every act of friendship, and so on. This theory raises the problem of empty formalism precisely because it has the agent reinventing himself from the ground up with every choice. Because the agent can reinvent himself, he can rewrite the set of available reasons, and so almost anything goes. Korsgaard solves the problem of empty formalism by restricting the scope of the self-constitution that accompanies a particular choice: the agent approaches each choice with antecedently fixed identities, which he can revise only within constraints fixed, in part, by those identities themselves. Unfortunately, this solution to the problem of empty formalism removes the mechanism by which the Categorical Imperative militates against individual actions, since the Imperative militates against actions only by requiring them to include bits of radical self-constitution that would be contradictory. I therefore suspect that Korsgaard cannot avoid the concessive version of Kantian theory, in which moral considerations do not necessarily provide sufficient reasons against immoral acts.

Conclusion

This concessive version of Kantian theory has the strength of entailing weaker consequences than the orthodox version. It doesn't imply that every agent, on every occasion, has reasons for acting that on balance forbid committing murder. It concedes that the first-order reasons available to a particular agent on a particular occasion – the reasons for choosing one action over another – may on balance favor his committing murder. It merely adds that someone who finds himself with such a set of first-order reasons will also have higher-order reasons for changing the reasons available to him, by changing himself. And then it adds the further concession that changing himself will take time.

Korsgaard puts the point like this:

I am certainly not suggesting that the *rest of us* should encourage the Mafioso to stick to his code of strength and honour and manfully resist any wanton urges to tenderness or forgiveness that threaten to trip him up. The rest of us should be trying to get him to the place where he can see that he can't see his way to this kind of life anymore. (257)

In order to maneuver the Mafioso out from under the force of reasons for committing murder, then, we would have to "get him to a place" from which he could see something that he can't currently see from the place he's in, at the moment of pulling the trigger. Indeed, we'd have to get him to a place where he could turn around and see that he couldn't find his way back, a place that would therefore have to be far removed, in the space of reasons, from the place he currently occupies. Such changes of perspective cannot be brought about on the spot, when push has already come to shove, or shove to shoot.

Because this concessive Kantianism entails weaker consequences than the orthodoxy, it is harder to attack and easier to defend. Although Korsgaard suggests that it will evoke "trouble from critics," it will in fact disarm the traditional critics of Kant, who can no longer adduce the usual "hard cases" as counterexamples. The existence of hardened immoralists, who have no first-order reasons for doing the moral thing on some occasions, is perfectly compatible with the concessive version of Kantian theory. Critics will therefore have to go further afield for their counterexamples.

Here is a problem, though. If Korsgaard's version of the theory doesn't bring the Categorical Imperative to bear on particular murders, but only against being a person who has reason to commit them, then maybe it doesn't condemn murders as immoral; maybe all that it condemns as immoral is a willingness to acquire, or an unwillingness to shed, the identity of a murderer. This leniency may be implicit in Korsgaard's description of how "the rest of us" should regard the Mafioso. When she says that we "should be trying to get him to the place where he can see that he can't see his way to this kind of life anymore," perhaps she means that we should blame him for going astray in life but not for pulling the trigger here and now.

Note that *this* moral theory wouldn't fit my model of concessive Kantianism, since it would preserve the equivalence between morality and rationality in action. The mobster would have sufficient reason to commit murders, but the murders that he committed would not in themselves be immoral; what's immoral would be his acquiring or failing to shed the identity that provides his reason for murdering, and this act or omission would indeed be contrary to the balance of reasons for him to act. So the fact would remain, as stated in proposition (ii), that wrongdoing entails irrationality in action; the extension of the term "wrongdoing" would merely have shrunk, to include primarily acts of self-constitution rather than garden-variety, first-order acts.

But surely Korsgaard's concession to the normativity of the Mafioso's commitments is not meant to imply that they are normative in the moral sense. I assume that Korsgaard believes the mobster's killings to be morally wrong, even though he has normatively potent reasons, and perhaps even obligations, to commit them. I assume that when she recommends coaxing the Mafioso into a different "place," she doesn't mean that this therapeutic approach should preempt moral condemnation of his actions. The therapeutic approach is the only way to reason with the mobster, given that his existing identities support only a defective set of reasons; but gently reasoning him out of his identity as a mobster is meant to be compatible, I assume, with uncompromising condemnation of what that identity leads him to do.

I have no idea whether these suggestions capture Korsgaard's intentions, but I think that they capture what is plausible in her treatment of the case. And they imply that Korsgaard has brought us to a version of Kantian ethics in which morality and rationality really do come apart. In this version of Kantianism, which really is concessive, what rationality recommends on a particular occasion is that an agent do what he has the strongest reasons for doing, even if those reasons arise from an identity that's irrational for him to have. But morality requires an agent *not* to do things for reasons that arise from irrational identities: morality requires him to act only on reasons that he could rationally have.

If this theory is right, then what becomes of reasons for being moral?

The theory insists that every agent has reasons for being a sort of person who has reasons for acting morally. In this sense, it insists on reasons for *being* moral. And the reasons for being moral, in this sense, are the ones defined by Korsgaard's version of contradictions in the will: they are reasons that arise from underlying conflicts between immoral identities and the Categorical Imperative, which expresses the fundamental identity of a person. Because of these conflicts, being an immoral person is an irrational way of being a person, and so it isn't a way that any person could rationally choose to be, or to continue being. Therein lies the contradiction in the will of an immoral person, according to concessive Kantianism.

But concessive Kantianism doesn't insist on reasons for *acting* morally – not, at least, for agents who have failed to heed their reasons for *being* moral. If an agent has overlooked or tolerated the contradictions involved in having an immoral identity, he may then have insufficient reason for acting morally, according to this theory. This much the theory concedes, not only to the critic of Kant, but also to the immoralist.

Even so, the theory has one remaining resource for softening this concession. It can point out that acting morally represents, as it were, a higher rationality – a rationality of acting on the reasons of one's ideally rational self rather than one's actual selves. What morality requires one to do may not be what one actually has reason for doing, but it is what one could have reason for doing if one had a rational set of reasons.[25] And the same cannot be said for immoral actions. To be sure, it's rational to act on the reasons one actually has, even if they favor acting immorally. But to act instead on reasons that it would be rational to have is not exactly irrational: it is rather extrarational, above and beyond the call of practical reason.[26]

Consider again how the Mafioso might find his way out of the bind created by his immoral identity. As Korsgaard points out, he might reason his way out, but only by way of a long and subtle train of reasoning, which is unavailable in the heat of the moment. Yet even in the heat of the moment, the mobster might simply step out of his bind: The scales might fall from his eyes, and he might drop his gun and walk away, never to return to his life of crime. (Of course, this sudden change of practical identities might not be accepted by his former associates without help

---

[25] Why do I say "what one *could* have reason for doing. . . ."? The reason is that if one has an irrational set of reasons, then there is no particular set of reasons that one would necessarily have if one had a rational set instead. There is no particular identity that the Mafioso would necessarily adopt instead of his identity as a mobster. There are many ways for him to be moral, and morality requires only that he adopt one of them.

[26] What I'm suggesting, then, is that although the moral act is not always rationally required, under concessive Kantianism, it is at least rationally supererogatory.

from the Witness Protection Program.) In the latter case, I would say, the mobster would not be acting on the balance of reasons that were currently available to him. Rather, he would be rejecting some of the reasons available to him, thereby reconstituting his current set of reasons.

As I have said, the act of reconstituting his current set of reasons is not supported by the overall balance of reasons in that set. Shedding his identity as a mobster would be a betrayal of the mob and hence of the commitments fundamental to that identity. Hence it is not a rational step for the agent to take, all things considered. But the act of reconstituting his set of reasons is indeed supported by a crucial subset thereof – namely, the reasons arising from his underlying identity as a rational human being. And the agent can act on that subset of reasons while holding the others in abeyance; for he can think of himself merely as a human being, reflecting with critical detachment on his more specific identities. Thus, he can tentatively suspend his identity as a mobster for the sake of considering whether to reject it altogether.

Even this tentative suspension of an identity would not be rational for the agent, all things considered. His commitments to the mob strongly militate against even toying with the idea of betrayal. But he can still toy with the idea, albeit irrationally. Indeed, he can *literally* toy with it, by playing or pretending for a moment that he isn't committed to the mob. He can imagine himself to be only a part or aspect of everything that he is, so as to make believe that he is deciding from scratch what to be.[27]

Let me repeat that toying with an idea in this fashion would be an irrational process, since it would require the agent to pretend that he didn't have commitments and reasons that he actually has. But this irrational process would enable the agent to become a more rational person, who wasn't caught in a bind of conflicting reasons. The process would therefore constitute an irrational leap to a greater rationality – a leap of faith in the possibility of being more rational. Kant might call it a leap of faith in oneself as a person.

---

[27] For further discussion of this process, see Chapter 13 in the present volume. I discuss another instance of the same process in Chapter 14 in the present volume.

13

Motivation by Ideal

When philosophers discuss our motive for acting morally, they tend to assume that it serves as one contributor to the broad conflux of motives that jointly determine most of our behavior. Although philosophers recognize the possibility of our being divided into mutually isolated motivational currents of the sort posited, at the extreme, to explain phenomena such as multiple personality, they assume that our moral motive must not be thus divided from our other motives, lest its manifestations in our behavior turn out to be irrational and, at the extreme, insane. Their assumption is that the actions flowing from our moral motive must in fact flow from a unified stream of all our motives, augmented by a moral tributary.

This chapter originally appeared in *Philosophical Explorations*, 5 (May 2002): 89–104. It is reprinted by permission of Taylor & Francis Ltd. This is the third in a series of four essays on narrative self-conceptions and their role in moral motivation. In the first essay, "The Self as Narrator" (Chapter 9 in the present volume), I explore the motivational role of narrative self-conceptions, drawing on Daniel Dennett's notion of the self as a "center of narrative gravity." In the second essay, "Willing the Law" (Chapter 12 in the present volume), I explore the role of self-conceptions in Kantian "conflicts in the will," drawing on Christine Korsgaard's notion of "practical identities." In a fourth essay, "The Centered Self" (Chapter 11 in the present volume), I explore the role of narrative self-conceptions in Kantian "conflicts in conception," drawing on the work of Thomas Nagel and John Perry on the self.

For initial conversations on the topic of the current essay, I am grateful to Nishi Shah. For comments on an earlier draft, I am indebted to the departments of philosophy at the University of Illinois at Chicago, the University of Pittsburgh, and Syracuse University; to members of ORGiE (the Ohio Reading Group in Ethics), including Justin D'Arms, Dan Farrell, Don Hubin, Janice Dowell, David Sobel, Sigrun Svavarsdottir, and special guest Doug Lavin; and to an anonymous referee for *Philosophical Explorations*.

This assumption influences which questions are asked about moral motivation and which answers are considered plausible. The assumption encourages philosophers to ask, for example, how to identify our moral motive among the impulses that pass under the eye of ordinary deliberative reflection, and how that motive can possibly prevail against the impulses that so conspicuously favor immorality.

I am going to argue that the motive behind moral actions can become isolated from our other motives, generating behavior that is irrational in some respects though rational in others. In my view, moral action performed from moral motives can be less than fully rational precisely because of the division in its motivation. The reason why moral motivation can become isolated from our other motives, I shall argue, is that it often depends on the force of an ideal; an ideal gains motivational force when we identify with it; and acting out of identification with an ideal is like a game of make-believe, in which we pretend to be that with which we identify. My argument will begin, then, with a consideration of adult make-believe.

For many years, I regularly kicked my wife in the head. We were studying Tae Kwon Do, and we often found ourselves paired together in drills or sparring. There we stood, high-school sweethearts from the sixties, each apparently trying to knock the other's block off.

What is the motivational explanation for such behavior? The motives most obviously actuating me in the circumstances were my desires to enhance my cardiovascular fitness and to have some fun in the process. But surely there would be something odd about saying that I kicked my wife in the head in order to lower my cholesterol or just for fun. Of course, I knew – or, at least, hoped – that my wife would suffer no harm. She was wearing a foam helmet, I was wearing padded footgear, and I didn't strike with all of my strength. You might think, in fact, that I didn't so much kick her in the head as do something else that was only superficially similar, such as tap her on the temple with my toe. Such a tap could indeed have been produced by many motives of mine, including affection. Yet to say that I was trying to deliver a tap would misrepresent the encounter: a pulled punch or kick may feel like a tap to the recipient, but it is in fact quite dissimilar, since it is thrown with full force and "pulled" only in the sense of being aimed to fall short.

What calls for further explanation is not so much the fact that I kicked my wife on these occasions as the spirit in which I did so. For one thing, the effort behind my kicks was disproportionate to the motives that led me to the activity of sparring. The desires and beliefs that militated for kicking my wife may well have been stronger than the desires and beliefs that militated against, but not by enough of a margin to account for the zeal with which I went at her. Shouldn't effort be proportionate to motivation?

Then there is the manner of my kicks, which also seems to require further explanation. One and the same gross movement can evince different motives through subtle differences of posture, timing, muscle tension, and body english. The kicks that I aimed at my wife did not have the inflection of calisthenics or soccer or dance; they had the inflection of combat.

The key to explaining these aspects of my behavior, I think, is that Tae Kwon Do had helped me to solve a familiar motivational problem. The effort that one must expend in order to stay fit tends to require more motivation than can be supplied by one's desire for fitness: that's why so many exercise programs fail. If one wants to stay fit, one needs to find some additional source of motivation to draw on. Some forms of exercise give one access to competitiveness as an additional motive, others to team spirit, a love of nature, or musical inspiration. My additional source of motivation in Tae Kwon Do was aggression, and aggression is what accounted for the energy and inflection of my kicks.

Reflection on this case convinces me that there must be some truth in Freud's theory of the drives. What's true in that theory, I think, is the postulation of highly labile psychic energies, which have only a vague direction in themselves but can be invested in specific activities.[1]

In studying Tae Kwon Do, I discovered that I had a fund of aggression to spend on kicks and punches, whether they were aimed at a leather bag, a handheld target, or a person's head. This aggression is not best characterized in terms of desire and belief. I did not enter the *do jang* wanting to smash something and looking for something to smash: rough contact with medium-sized objects was not something I desired at all. But it was something for which I found a considerable reserve of energy, in the form of aggression; and that aggression could be turned on virtually

---

[1] Let me emphasize that I am borrowing only some elements of Freudian drive theory. I am not borrowing the model of stimulus reduction, for example, but only the notion of indeterminate motivational forces. Indeed, my conception of their indeterminacy is different from Freud's. Freud described drives as having determinate aims but being readily redirected toward different objects. I prefer to think of drives as having only inchoate aims.

any solid object, including any person who happened to be my assigned opponent.

I am similarly inclined to believe in a drive corresponding roughly to the Freudian libido. We sometimes describe a person as having a lot of love to give but nowhere to give it. Such a person has a fund of tenderness that could potentially be spent on a lover, a child, a cat, even a garden or a scrapbook. In this case, unspent energy may be experienced as frustration, and so the person may develop a desire for someone or something to love. But such a desire need not develop; and even when it does, it remains distinct from the fund of energy whose disbursement it seeks. The person's desire for someone or something to love is a contingent reaction to his unspent tenderness, not an essential constituent of it.

I realize that talk of psychic energies will strike philosophical readers as intolerably metaphorical. In principle, the metaphor can be eliminated in favor of concepts drawn from propositional-attitude psychology: we can conceive of aggression as a conative attitude whose object is picked out by a mental representation of some kind. But we shall then be forced to conceive of this representation either as radically indeterminate in content or as playing a non-standard role;[2] and the resulting conception of aggression will not lend itself to the kind of formalization that has so endeared propositional-attitude psychology to philosophers ever since Aristotle discovered the practical syllogism.

On the one hand, if we think of aggression as motivating the pursuit of, and being temporarily quelled by, the literal truth of the associated representation, then we shall have to say that the representation is far too vague to be expressed in the concepts with which we consciously reason, or the terms in which we write and speak. There is no finite "that" clause of ordinary language that will suffice to specify the pursuits or satisfactions in which aggression can eventuate. If, on the other hand, we insist on framing a written or spoken "that" clause to express the content of aggression, we shall have to concede that what the attitude can motivate someone towards, or be satisfied by, includes not only the literal truth of the clause but also indefinitely many other outcomes related only by analogy, by metaphorical similarity, or by other mental associations of an open-ended variety. Either way, propositional-attitude psychology will not afford the same computational advantages in this case as it does in

---

[2] The substance of this paragraph is borrowed from Linda Brakel's work on primary process. See Brakel (2002).

the case of ordinary beliefs and desires, whose tendencies to motivate and to be satisfied can be summed up in sentences of ordinary language.

Thus, we can accommodate drives within the basic principles of propositional attitude psychology, but only by allowing for a level of mental representation, or a mechanism of motivation, that eludes capture by the explanation schemas characteristic of that theory. The metaphor of psychic energies is a useful reminder that, even if all motives are propositional attitudes in principle, some have motivational possibilities that cannot practically be formalized in spoken or written propositions.

Another idea that I want to borrow from Freud is that drives can take on a specific direction by "leaning" on some other, more specific motive. According to Freud, the infantile libido leans on and takes direction from the motive of hunger, with the result that the nutritive activity of sucking becomes a source of sensual pleasure, and the breast becomes a sexual object. Similarly, I think, aggression can take direction from more specific motives, such as professional ambition or athletic competitiveness. Aggressive energy is then invested in professional or athletic pursuits, which in turn take on an aggressive character.

The spirit of my kicks in Tae Kwon Do can thus be explained by the aggression from which they drew some of their motivation. Yet the explanation can hardly end here. The aggressiveness of my kicks was not like the aggressiveness of my driving, for example, which emerges without my knowledge and even despite my efforts to contain it. The aggressiveness of my kicks was knowing and intentional, because I was engaged in a fight. And yet I had no motives for, and many motives against, literally fighting my opponents. I was behaving aggressively in this case because I was engaged in fictional aggression, and so an explanation of my behavior requires an account of the operative fiction.

A martial art typically relies on a story – indeed, on a story-within-a-story, especially for students in the West. The "inner" story is a story of combat. At the founding of the discipline, this story may have been about combat on the battlefield, but in the modern *dojang* it is often about being attacked on the proverbial street. Some students have actually lived through a version of this story, especially women who seek out the martial arts after surviving rape or domestic abuse. But even these students train under a fiction, insofar as they are not really being attacked by their fellow students.

The "outer" story of a martial art, which is usually a fiction only for beginning students and then only briefly, is that they are devotees of a venerable tradition, transmitted to them by a revered master and shared with others in a spirit of humility and mutual self-restraint. The beginning student acts out this story before it can possibly be true of him, by bowing to his instructor and fellow students, calling them "Sir" and "Ma'am," wearing ritual garments and reciting ritual phrases, all from the first moment of the first class. For some students this story always remains a fiction, in the sense that they are never more than playing at participation in the tradition; but for most it soon becomes a true story, and the phrases of Korean or Japanese that were at first only mouthed come to be sincerely meant.

The inner and outer stories of a martial art are in direct conflict. The ferocity with which one tries to disable or kill an attacker, according to the inner story, is the very opposite of the humble deference that, according to the outer story, one owes to the instructor who may be playing the attacker's role. This conflict is vividly demonstrated when someone is injured in competitive sparring. The competitor responsible for the injury, who a moment ago seemed intent on bloody murder, suddenly kneels with his back to his opponent, in a posture of passivity and penitence, because he has drawn a single drop of blood. The fiction of combat is instantly dispelled, leaving only the outer story of deferential self-restraint.

This scene illustrates two further claims that I want to make about motivation, in addition to my prior claim on behalf of drives. The first of these further claims is that our motives are often manifested in our behavior under the guidance of a story: how we act on them is determined by the story that we are enacting.

The most ambitious version of this claim, which I have defended elsewhere, is that all of our autonomous actions are the enactments of stories, most of which are true but all of which are made up.[3] At any particular time we have motives for taking various actions, and the action we take is usually the one whose story we have in mind to enact. We are therefore in a position to make up the story of our behavior as we go, in the assurance that we'll behave accordingly, provided that we confine ourselves

---

3 Of course, the "stories" enacted in our autonomous actions are not the stuff of novels: they can be as trivial as the story that goes "My leg itches, so I'm scratching it." For this view of autonomy, see Velleman (1989b); Velleman (2000c), Chapters 1, 2, 7, and 9; and Chapters 9, 10, and 11 in the present volume. My view of agency bears similarities to: Hollis (1977), Harré (1979), and Anscombe (2000).

to stories whose enactment could be fueled by motives that we actually have. And the story that we make up is true, not only in that we proceed to enact it, but also in that it represents our action as its own enactment – as the action that we are hereby setting ourselves to take.

My view is that this process depends on a motive that is almost always in the background, and rarely in the foreground, of our autonomous actions: the desire to make sense of what we're doing. This desire moves us to take actions that make sense to us, and the actions that make sense are the ones about which we have a story to tell. Thus, although we ultimately do what is favored by the overall balance of our motives, that balance has often been tipped by the inclusion of our motive for doing things that make sense to us – a motive that is purely formal and does not appear in our conscious story of what we're doing. That story may tell of other motives, in light of which the action makes sense to us; but we perform the action not only out of those narrated motives but also out of our motive for making sense, which is enlisted by the availability of the narrative itself.

When a story renders an action intelligible to us, it becomes a *rationale* for the action. And when we are thereby led to perform the action, as the intelligible thing to do, we act on the basis of the story in its capacity as *rationale*. In other words, we act for a reason.

Thus, when I entered the *do jang* on a particular evening, I thought of myself as continuing my martial arts training, which I thought of myself as pursuing for the sake of cardiovascular fitness and fun. These thoughts were not just an idle commentary on my behavior; they constituted a story that I was in the process of enacting, with actions that I would not have taken in the absence of a story to tell about them. That I was seeking to continue my training out of desires for fitness and fun – that story was the *rationale* under which I entered the *do jang*. It was my reason for walking in the door.

Yet when I kicked an opponent in Tae Kwon Do, the story I enacted wasn't true, since it was a story of fending off a mortal attack. My behavior was therefore an enactment in the thespian sense – or, if you like, a game of make-believe.

I have argued elsewhere that the term 'make-believe' means "mock-belief," because it refers to a fantasy or imagining that stands in for a belief by playing its motivational role.[4] My examples on that occasion

---

[4] "On the Aim of Belief," in Velleman (2000c), 244–81.

were primarily imaginings that play the role of ordinary instrumental beliefs – such as the belief that I can communicate with someone by speaking to him, which is ordinarily one of the motives behind my verbal behavior. When I address remarks to other drivers on the road, however, or to the referees of a sporting event on television, I am not moved by the belief that I can thereby communicate with them; I'm moved instead by imagining that I can. Because imagining here plays the motivational role of a belief, it qualifies as "mock-belief," and I can be described as making believe. I'm making believe that I can communicate with these people, because I am acting on a mock-belief to that effect.

In the present context, I want to consider imaginings that substitute for beliefs in a slightly different motivational role. If I really believed myself to be under attack, that belief would serve as a narrative premise under which some courses of action would make sense and others would not, and I would be guided accordingly as I improvised my part in the encounter. Strictly speaking, this belief would be functioning as an instrumental motive, since it would influence me by causing some steps but not others to appear intelligible and hence conducive to making sense of what I do, which is a desired outcome. But this outcome is not an end-in-view – not, that is, an end-in-the-story, something whose pursuit I would enact. It's just something that I want, conduciveness to which makes actions attractive to me. And what it makes attractive to me, in particular, are actions about which I have a story to tell.

I think that fantasy and imagining can play this motivational role as well. When I imagined that I was facing an attack in Tae Kwon Do, I was thereby led to imagine some steps as making sense and others as making none, and I was guided accordingly as I improvised my part in the ensuing fights – make-believe fights, guided by a mock-belief. I then enacted a story that was fictional in every sense, since it was not only made up but also untrue.

Part of the story, of course, was that I fought out of a desire to disable or kill my opponent, and in reality I didn't have any such desire to draw on. What I drew on instead, I have argued, is a labile fund of aggression, which leaned in this case, not on any desire to harm my opponent, but on the motivational force lent to the story itself by my inclination to do what made sense in light of that story. I may actually have imagined the felt thrust of aggression to be a desire to harm my opponent, much as I was obliged, in self-defense drills, to imagine wooden batons to be knives. (In that case, my aggression served as a "prop," in the sense defined by

Kendall L. Walton.)[5] In reality, however, my aggression's being focused upon my opponent was due to my conceiving of it as a desire to harm him, rather than the other way around. That is, imagining it as a desire to harm my opponent lent intelligibility to the act of kicking, thus giving me a motive for kicking, on which my aggression could lean.

The game of make-believe was thus fueled by two elements – a drive and an imagining – and the game would fail if either element was missing. Some students of the martial arts don't have much aggression to draw on, and they consequently aren't fully equipped to play the game. Merely imagining that they are under attack isn't enough to make them fight, in the absence of a drive that could supply the force of their imagined desires with respect to an attacker. So their threatening yells always sound like peeps, and their blows really are no more than taps. Other students seem to have sufficient aggression but to be inhibited from entering into the requisite make-believe, at least in some circumstances. For example, some men simply can't bring themselves to imagine that they are trying to kill or disable a woman. Though capable of fighting other opponents aggressively, they can't muster the imagining that would bring their aggression to bear on these opponents, and so they merely go through the motions.

Of course, none of us actually tried to kill or disable an opponent. We were restrained by our sense of mutual respect and deference. But I do not think that the motive of deference simply combined with aggression to yield an intermediate vector-sum – a deferential aggression, or aggressive deference, or whatever. To pull a punch is not simply to strike at half-strength, out of some lukewarm mixture of hot and cold motives. This is my second of my further claims about motivation.

In making this claim, I do not mean to reject the principle that a person's behavior flows from the combined force of his motives; I mean only to point out that, because of the motivational force exerted by an agent's self-conception, there are two distinct ways in which his other motives can combine.

One way requires the agent to think of himself as acting on both motives at once and hence to be guided, not only by their combined forces, but also by his conception of how those forces combine. In this case, the agent is consciously engaged in a mixed activity – restrained hostilities, or perhaps hostile self-restraint. The agent's behavior is determined partly by the combined forces of his motives and partly by his

[5] Walton (1993).

conception of what would make sense for him to do in light of their combination, his story of how he is acting on both at once.

Another way for motives to combine is for the agent to conceive of himself as acting on only one of them, while the other tacitly modifies this activity. Thus, for example, an agent's desire to avoid bodily harm steers him away from obstacles even when he is single-mindedly engaged in vigorous activity and not consciously exercising caution. What makes for the difference between these two ways of mixing motives is the motivational role of the agent's self-conception, which is not epiphenomenal on his behavior, not just an idle commentary. In one case, the agent deliberately acts on both motives, by enacting a story of both; in the other case, the agent enacts the story of one motive, while this enactment is subject to unheralded modification by the other.

When we think about the mixing of motives, we usually have the former process in mind, because we assume that people are simultaneously aware of the various motives vying for control of their behavior. We may therefore assume that if students of the martial arts are both mutually deferential and mutually hostile, they must conceive of themselves in both terms at the same time. But such a conflicted self-conception would result in sparring that could only be described as half-assed. In fact, students imagine themselves entirely as hostile opponents while they are sparring, but this role is externally constrained by their deferential motives as colleagues.

Consider what happens when a participant in make-believe gets "carried away." Sometimes students do get carried away in sparring, especially new students who haven't yet learned how to manage the conflicting stories that they are supposed to enact. The reason why it's possible to get carried away, I think, is that a participant in make-believe puts his real identity and his real relations to other participants temporarily out of mind. In order to enact his fictional identity and his fictional relations to others, he must devote his mind to the fiction. In doing so, however, he trusts that the motives he has put out of mind will nevertheless hold him back from excesses, or will pull him up short if things get out of hand. His knowledge of who the participants really are, and his inclinations toward those real people, are motives that stand by and supervise, as it were, either by setting boundaries to the game of make-believe, within which they are not in view, or by forcing their way into view and breaking up the game, if it goes too far. The agent gets carried away when this external supervision fails and the game proceeds headlong, without either restraint or interruption.

Getting carried away often leads to irrational action. When someone gets carried away in a philosophical debate, for example, he presses his point at the expense of other people's feelings and his own reputation for collegiality, both of which he cares about, on balance, more than the question under dispute. In some cases, of course, intellectual enthusiasm may have blinded the agent to the undesirable consequences of his behavior; but in others, he sees those consequences yet presses on with the argument regardless.

From the agent's point-of-view, his motives may appear to wax and wane as circumstances change. In the heat of the argument, the prospect of securing his point consumes all of his attention and interest; whereas in a cooler moment, the philosophical point may seem unimportant. But this introspectable change need not be a change in the agent's desires themselves; it may instead be a change as to which desire is reinforced by the agent's conception of what he is doing. In the heat of the argument, the agent thinks of himself exclusively as pressing his point, and this self-conception provides reinforcement exclusively to his motives for doing so. Even if the agent notices the annoyance of his interlocutor, he doesn't think of it as something that he currently wants to avoid or to mitigate. Managing his relations with colleagues is not something toward which he thinks of himself as currently motivated, and so his potential motives for that activity are not bolstered by his interest in self-understanding.

These motives are nevertheless present, and as I have suggested, they have two chances to prevent him from getting carried away, corresponding to the two ways in which motives can combine. First, the desire for good relations with colleagues can leave the agent's pursuit of the argument uninterrupted while restraining it from the outside, in the same way as the desire to avoid bodily harm restrains his physical activities even when he isn't deliberately being cautious. And then, if unreflective restraint fails, the agent's desire for good relations with colleagues can obtrude itself on his attention, so that his concentration on the argument is broken and he comes to think of himself, under the circumstances, as having more than one end at stake.

These modes of restraint look quite different, both from the agent's perspective and from the perspective of observers. Some philosophers can throw themselves into an argument without fear of giving offense, because they will be unreflectively restrained from going too far. These philosophers are said to trust themselves in the heat of an argument, where the "selves" they trust are not reflective selves who might be trusted to make the right choice in deliberation but rather motives that can be trusted to restrain them without reflection or deliberation. Other philosophers never fully commit themselves to the point they're trying to make, because they are busy monitoring the expressions of their listeners and interjecting polite qualifications. Because they can't rely on their collegial motives for implicit restraint, they must explicitly adopt self-restraint as an additional activity whenever they get into an argument.

The same contrast applies to participants in the martial arts. If a student can't trust himself in sparring, he must consciously ride two horses at once, both his aggression and his self-restraint. If a student can trust himself, then he can ride his aggression wholeheartedly and count on his self-restraint to run alongside on its own. If the latter strategy fails, the student may be forced to adopt the former – not exactly to switch horses in midstream but to shift part of his weight onto the second horse. And part of what he counted on from his self-restraint, at the outset, was that it would force itself into his activity in this manner if it failed to steer him adequately from the outside.

Both forms of restraint are exemplified in an agent's behavior most of the time. Because moments of true single-mindedness are rare, an agent is often consciously multitasking, and yet he is also influenced by additional motives that remain out of view. Bustling down the street on several errands at once, he implicitly trusts himself not to step into potholes or bowl over fellow pedestrians – which is to say, he knows that various latent motives of his will either restrain his conscious pursuits or interrupt them if tacit restraint should fail.

An agent's self-conception thus separates his motives into two groups. One group comprises motives that the agent manifests in the process of consciously enacting them; the other comprises motives that manifest themselves primarily by externally modifying such enactments. The former are the motivational horses that the agent is riding, as I have put it, and the latter are relegated to the role of hemming him in or cutting him off as necessary.

The process becomes further complicated if the agent imagines himself to have motives that he doesn't actually have. The agent may be moved to enact this imaginative self-conception, especially if he has motivational resources that can mimic the force of the imagined motives, such as aggression that can be focussed onto a particular person by being conceived as a desire to kill or disable him. The agent's actual motives are then divided into those on which he is acting under a mistaken or imaginary guise, and those which are relegated to hemming in or cutting off that game of make-believe.

An extreme form of this motivational division may account for various dissociative phenomena, such as multiple personality disorder (or dissociative identity disorder, as it is now called). What seem like distinct personalities may in fact be distinct self-conceptions enacted by the agent at different times. The self-conceptions involved in DID would have to differ in various respects from ordinary self-conceptions, including those involved in make-believe. They would have to be full-blown delusions – that is, conscious fantasies not recognized as such by the agent – and they would have to resist external restraint or interruption to the point that the agent had no access to the motives that he wasn't currently enacting. The resulting division in the agent's motives would be deeper than that in the motives of a sane and sober agent. But it would be a deeper version of the same fundamental division, between the motives that are being enacted and the motives that can at most modify that enactment.

As we have seen, this division in an agent's motives can lead to action that is irrational in relation to the totality of his desires and interests, as when it lets him get carried away in a debate, to his subsequent regret. But I think that the temporary irrationality of getting carried away can sometimes be exploited for more permanent gains in rationality. For an agent can get carried away with the better of his motives as well as the worse.

A colleague who studies rational choice tells me that he could never have quit smoking without indulging in some irrationality.[6] Although the long-run costs of smoking outweighed the long-run benefits, he says, the costs of smoking the next cigarette never outweighed the benefits of smoking that one cigarette, since he could always decide to quit after the next cigarette rather than before. In order to stop smoking in the long run, of course, he had to forego the next cigarette at some point, at an obvious sacrifice of utility. The only way for him to stop was thus to do something irrational. How did he manage to do it?

The answer, he tells me, was *not to think of himself as a smoker.* At the beginning, of course, not to think of himself as a smoker was incorrect, since he was still addicted to smoking, both physically and psychologically. I suggest, then, that he resorted to make-believe. He imagined that he was not addicted – that he didn't like the taste of cigarettes, wasn't

[6] Thanks to Jim Joyce for this example.

in the habit of smoking them, had no craving for them – and he then enacted what he was imagining, pretending to be the non-smoker that he wanted to be. And I suggest that this make-believe succeeded because it excluded the smoker's tastes, habits, and cravings from the story that he was enacting. That story lacked the narrative background that would have made it intelligible for him to buy, light, or smoke the next cigarette.

I suggest, further, that my colleague got carried away with this make-believe, and that getting carried away was essential to his success at kicking the habit. His motives for smoking were relegated to externally constraining his enactment of a non-smoker's story. Those motives had proved irresistible when they were available at center-stage to motivate the next episode in the story; but when they were written out of the plot and left to operate, as it were, *ex machina*, they were unable to deflect the story from its natural conclusion.

I suggest, finally, that when my colleague got carried away with enacting an image of himself as a non-smoker, he was being motivated by an ideal. That's what an ideal is: the image of another person, or a currently untrue image of oneself, that one can get carried away with enacting.[7] To imagine oneself in that image, and to act accordingly, is to identify with and emulate the ideal.

An alternative to my conception of ideals would be to think of them as descriptions or images that motivate by way of one's desire to satisfy them and one's realistic beliefs about how to do so. According to this alternative conception, taking another person as one's ideal entails wanting to resemble him, which directly motivates behavior like his, conceived as a constitutive means to the desired resemblance. I doubt whether the motivational force of an ideal flows directly from such a desire in most cases.[8]

Suppose that one idealizes a person for his generosity and wants to resemble him in this respect.[9] Insofar as this desire directly moves one to do generous things, those acts will not in fact be motivated by generosity, after all, and so one's attempted imitation of the ideal will be an obvious failure. Indeed, one would be unlikely to acquire or to learn

---

7 By "an untrue image of oneself," I mean a self-image that would not be true even if one enacted it. Of course, my colleague eventually became a non-smoker by pretending to be one, but at the outset his pretense was false.

8 For background to this section, see "On the Aim of Belief," in Velleman (2000c), pp. 256–72.

9 See Aristotle's discussion at *Nicomachean Ethics* 1105a ff.

generosity through acts motivated in this way. The desire to mold oneself in the image of a generous person will meet with better success if it moves one first to imagine being a generous person and then to enact this self-image, making believe that one is generous and using as props whatever motives one has that can be cast in the role of generosity. (Such props might be drawn from that fund of tenderness that Freud calls the libido.) Emulating generosity in this fashion, one comes closer to being and to feeling generous, and one has a better chance of becoming really generous, by gradually working one's way into the role. One can thus gradually adopt or assume the motive of generosity in a way that one never could by imitating it from the outside.

The desire to resemble an ideal can initiate this process only by motivating a deliberate turn toward make-believe; other attitudes can initiate it directly, because they already engage the imagination. In the former case, the desire to resemble an ideal depends for its motivational force on an assessment of how one falls short of the ideal and what one must do to close the gap. The desire may ultimately favor a process of conjuring up and enacting an idealized self-image, but only on the basis of a realistic calculation that the process will be conducive to a resemblance not yet attained. Now consider an attitude like respect or admiration for the ideal. Precisely because these attitudes are not goal-oriented motives, they tend to favor wishful thinking over purposeful activity. Admiring someone isn't a motive for bringing about anything in particular, and so it doesn't call for an instrumental calculation of the steps required to bring anything about. But admiring someone can naturally motivate wishfully picturing oneself in his image. Emulation therefore flows directly out of admiration.

When a smoker draws on an ideal for motivation to quit, his behavior is in some respects irrational. He ignores various facts that would be relevant to fair-minded deliberation: the fact that he would enjoy the taste of a cigarette, that he is in habit of smoking, that he is even now craving a smoke, and so on. And he acts instead on various considerations that are figments of his imagination: that he feels fine without a cigarette, that he wouldn't enjoy one, that lighting up would be an uncharacteristic thing for him to do.

Yet his make-believe world is a world of make-believe reasons. His imaginative considerations guide him in the manner of reasons for acting, just as the facts would guide him if he acted on realistic grounds. These imaginative considerations serve as narrative premises in light of which only some actions make sense as the continuation of his story. And when an agent does what makes sense in light of a narrative premise, or *rationale*, he is acting for a reason, albeit one that isn't true.

What's more, this make-believe reasoning enables the agent to become more rational in the long run. For by pretending to be a non-smoker, he actually becomes a non-smoker, which is a more rational sort of person to be. As a smoker, he was deeply conflicted: his reasons for smoking were at odds with all of his other reasons for acting, although they were strong enough to prevail in a review of what he had reason to do next. He therefore chose to smoke, but always at the sacrifice of the many countervailing reasons that had been outweighed. In kicking the habit, he lost his reasons for smoking, leaving the field to his countervailing reasons, which can now guide his actions unopposed. Because his actual reasons have become less conflicted, he sacrifices less in doing what he actually has most reason to do.[10]

Indeed, the agent may have had sufficient reason to identify with a non-smoking ideal, even when he lacked sufficient reason to forego his next cigarette. Foregoing his next cigarette in his story as a smoker would have left the resulting discomforts and inconveniences at center-stage, as salient repercussions to be faced. The second act of this story would have been "The Smoker Copes with Withdrawal" – an episode that's difficult to improvise without ending up in a third act entitled "The Smoker's Relapse." The difficulty of charting an intelligible course through the story of quitting as a smoker is what made for the rationality of continuing to smoke instead. The point of identifying with the ideal of a non-smoker was precisely to gain access to a different story, presenting a different set of reasons. That alternative story entailed not smoking the next cigarette, of course, but not smoking that cigarette was a different option for a non-smoker than it was for a smoker. For a smoker, not smoking that cigarette was a matter of changing course and facing the consequences; for a non-smoker, it was a matter of going on as usual. To be sure, the non-smoker in this case would be a merely make-believe non-smoker, who would experience twinges and shakes of what was in reality nicotine withdrawal. But those discomforts would not be expected repercussions to be faced and overcome; they would be inexplicable irritations to be ignored, if possible. And the smoker who wants to quit has good reason to prefer facing the consequent discomforts under the guise of irritations

---

[10] I discuss these issues further in "Willing the Law" (Chapter 12 in the present volume).

to be ignored rather than expected repercussions to be faced. Hence he had good reason for undertaking the pretense of being a non-smoker.

The smoker who wants to quit is like other agents who have reason to make themselves temporarily irrational – warriors who have reason to work themselves into a frenzy in order to frighten the enemy, or negotiators who have reason to become obstinate in order to win concessions. Unlike the warrior or the negotiator, however, the smoker does not have reason to arrange for something to interfere with his faculty for practical reasoning. On the contrary, the irrationality that the smoker has reason to cultivate requires the exercise of an intact deliberative faculty; it merely requires that faculty to operate on input from the agent's imagination rather than on his knowledge of the facts. When the agent's deliberative faculty operates in this way, he becomes insensitive to considerations that are genuine reasons for him to act, and so he becomes dispositionally irrational. And because he thereby neglects reasons against the action that he performs, he may end up performing an irrational action.

I have now argued, on the one hand, that it was rational for the smoker to undertake the activity of pretending to be a non-smoker, that this activity involved an exercise of an intact rational faculty, and that it resulted in the smoker's becoming a more rational agent. On the other hand, I have argued that the activity of pretending to be a non-smoker was irrational in the sense that it made the smoker insensitive to some of the reasons that actually applied to him, and consequently led him to do something that wasn't supported by the balance of actual reasons.

I think that such irrationality is often involved when an agent is motivated by a personal ideal – including the overarching ideals that embody Hume's general perspective or the Aristotelian virtues. Whether one is emulating an impartial observer or a virtuous human being, one may be engaged in make-believe and hence in an activity that's irrational in the respects described earlier.

Note, however, that I have not included Kant's Categorical Imperative in the list of moral ideals whose emulation tends to require make-believe.[11] The reason is that, in my view, Kantian moral theory manages to kick away that particular ladder.

---

[11] For my interpretation of the Categorical Imperative, see Chapters 5 and 6 in the present volume.

The Categorical Imperative is an ideal image of the will, as acting on only those maxims which it can simultaneously will to be universal laws. But what moves this ideal will to act only on universalizable maxims? The answer is that it is restrained from acting on other maxims by respect for the law. And respect for the law is just respect for the Categorical Imperative, which is an ideal image of the will as acting only on universalizable maxims. To act out of respect for this ideal is therefore to emulate a will that acts out of respect for the very same ideal.

In the case of the Kantian ideal, then, emulation tends to rise to the level of attainment. What is ideal about the person we emulate is precisely that he is moved by an ideal, and indeed the same ideal by which we are moved. Hence to emulate him is already and really to resemble him, and so it is unlike emulating him with respect to a motive that doesn't rely on emulation. To do generous things by emulating a generous person is not yet to be generous, though it may be a means of learning generosity. But to do the moral thing by emulating a moral person really is to be moral, since enacting a moral image of oneself is what being a moral person consists in.

So we are not enacting a false conception of ourselves in emulating the Categorical Imperative, because we are making that conception true just by emulating it. Of course, we could get carried away with enacting that self-conception, by losing sight of our countervailing motives, so that they lapse into abeyance for want of reinforcement from our self-conception. Wouldn't we then be acting on a false self-conception and hence irrationally? Not necessarily. After all, the Categorical Imperative could be – come to think of it, I'm sure that it is – the image of a will that gets carried away with enacting that very self-image. The motivational division that underlies make-believe – the division between enacted motives and motives that externally modify such enactments – remains essential to our acting on the Categorical Imperative; but what gets enacted is not a false self-conception.

Insofar as we are Kantian moral agents, then, we are not just pretending. When we dream of our morally better selves, our dreams really can come true.

14

Identification and Identity

When Harry Frankfurt chose a title for the first volume of his essays, he must have been thinking of the direction in which his work was going rather than the direction from which it had come. Retrospect would have led him to the titles of the founding essays in his research program, such as "Freedom of the Will and the Concept of a Person" or "Identification and Externality." Instead he named the volume after the essay that set the theme for his future work, "The Importance of What We Care About."[1] In the years since the publication of that volume, Frankfurt has explored many topics suggested by its wonderfully resonant title: how our caring about things makes them important to us; how the process of caring about them is important to us; and how important a matter it is which things we care about.

What I most admire about Frankfurt's essays on these topics is their candor in reporting one man's efforts to understand life as he finds it. Reading this work, one has the sense of receiving dispatches from an

[1] *The Importance of What We Care About* (Cambridge: Cambridge University Press, 1987).

This chapter originally appeared in *The Contours of Agency: Essays on Themes from Harry Frankfurt*, eds. Sarah Buss and Lee Overton (Cambridge, MA: MIT Press, 2001), 91–123. It is reprinted by permission of MIT Press. For comments on earlier drafts of this essay, I am grateful to Nomy Arpaly, Linda Wimer Brakel, Michael Bratman, Sarah Buss, Jennifer Church, and Connie Rosati. The essay was presented to a conference on autonomy organized by Joel Anderson and Sigurdur Kristinsson, to the Philosophy Department of Kansas State University, and to the Contemporary Philosophy Workshop at the University of Chicago. Work on the essay was supported by a fellowship from the John Simon Guggenheim Memorial Foundation, together with matching grants from the Department of Philosophy and the College of Literature, Science, and the Arts, University of Michigan.

examined life. Frankfurt's reflections on caring, in particular, are clearly an expression of what the author cares about, and as such they command a respect that transcends any disagreement.

Disagreement there is bound to be, however, when philosophy cuts so close to the bone. In this essay I am going to disagree with Frankfurt's view on the last of the topics mentioned above, the importance of which things we care about. Which things we care about is important, according to Frankfurt, because our cares and concerns define our individual essences as persons: what we care about determines who we are. I don't believe that we have motivational essences of this sort, though I agree that we sometimes seem to have them. I want to look for the source of this misleading appearance.

Frankfurt's New Conception of the Self

Ever since "Freedom of the Will and the Concept of a Person," Frankfurt has sought to draw a distinction among motives as internal or external to the self. The need for this distinction was first suggested to Frankfurt by cases in which an agent lacks autonomy because he is actuated by motives from which he is alienated. These motives seem to assail the agent from without and to compete with him for control of his behavior. Such cases suggest that being autonomous, or self-governed, is a matter of being governed from within – that is, by motives internal to the self. The question is what makes some motives internal in this sense.

Frankfurt's initial answer relied on the concept of identification. He suggested that motives are internal to the self when the subject identifies with them, by reflectively endorsing them as determinants of his behavior. An agent is autonomous, Frankfurt concluded, when he is actuated in ways that he reflectively endorses. This analysis of autonomy elicited a number of objections, which have been the subject of an extensive literature, leading to various revisions on Frankfurt's part.[2] More recently, however, Frankfurt has made a revision that is not obviously prompted by objections: it appears to express a further intuition about the boundaries of the self.

[2] I discuss some of the relevant literature in "What Happens When Someone Acts?" in *The Possibility of Practical Reason* (Oxford: Oxford University Press, 2000). For a more recent discussion, and a promising alternative to Frankfurt's view, see Michael Bratman, "Identification, Decision, and Treating as a Reason," in *Faces of Intention* (Cambridge: Cambridge University Press, 1999), 185–206.

What Frankfurt now says about autonomy is this: "A person acts autonomously only when his volitions derive from the essential character of his will."[3] Frankfurt goes on to explain that inessential characteristics of a person's will are "separable" from it, and in that sense "external" to it, so that their governance of the person's behavior amounts to heteronomy rather than autonomy. Thus, Frankfurt still conceives of autonomy as governance by motives internal to the self, but he has adopted a new criterion of internality. Motives are internal to the self, according to the new criterion, when they are essential to the subject's volitional nature.

Frankfurt disavows what might be perceived as Kantian overtones in this statement. Kant would gladly join Frankfurt in saying that a person is autonomous when his behavior is determined by his essential nature. But what Kant would mean by this statement is that autonomy consists in being determined by practical reason, which places every agent under the same, universal laws.

Frankfurt explicitly rejects this Kantian reading of the relation between autonomy and personal essence. For he is loath to equate the self of self-governance with the anonymous faculty of practical reason:

[T]his *pure will* is a very peculiar and unlikely place in which to locate an indispensable condition of individual autonomy. After all, its purity consists precisely in the fact that it is wholly untouched by any of the contingent personal features that make people distinctive and that characterize their specific identities.... The pure will has no individuality whatsoever. It is identical in everyone, and its volitions are everywhere exactly the same. In other words, the pure will is thoroughly *impersonal*. The commands that it issues are issued by no one in particular.[4]

---

[3] Harry Frankfurt, "Autonomy, Necessity, and Love," in *Necessity, Volition, and Love* (Cambridge, Cambridge University Press, 1999), 132. Frankfurt first made this claim, though less explicitly, in the paper "Rationality and the Unthinkable," in *The Importance of What We Care About*, 178: "With respect to a person whose will has no fixed determinate character, it seems that the notion of autonomy or self-direction cannot find a grip."

[4] Frankfurt, "Autonomy, Necessity, and Love," 132. This remark about Kant's conception of the person as a subject of autonomy bears a striking resemblance to remarks often made about Kant's conception of the person as an object of moral concern. In Kant's view, a person is worthy of moral concern insofar as he is an instance of rational nature, which is the proper object of respect. Many critics reply that concern for someone as an instance of rational nature is concern for no one in particular, since the same generic nature is instantiated in everyone alike. As Robin Dillon puts it: "In Kantian-respecting someone, there is a real sense in which we are not paying attention to *her*, for it makes no difference to how we respect her that she is who she is and not some other individual. Kantian respect is thus not a 'respecter of persons,' in the sense that it does not discriminate or distinguish among persons." Robin Dillon, "Respect and Care: Toward Moral Integration," *Canadian Journal of Philosophy* 22 (1992): 105–132, at 121. See also Elizabeth Spelman,

In Frankfurt's view, the self whose governance constitutes self-governance, or autonomy, must be a thoroughly *personal* self: it must be someone in particular. Frankfurt therefore conceives of personal essences as comprising features of the very sort that Kant purified out of the will – that is, "contingent personal features that make people distinctive and that characterize their specific identities."

Such features, which are contingent to the nature of personhood, can still be essential to an individual person, in Frankfurt's view. "Even though a person's interests are contingent," Frankfurt says, "they can belong to the essential nature of his will."[5] A person can thus have a volitional essence that consists in perfectly idiosyncratic concerns.

What makes contingent interests essential to the nature of a person's will? The answer to this question is best developed in stages, through which an initial intuition is gradually modified.

Frankfurt's initial intuition is that the essence of an agent comprises what is volitionally necessary for him, just as the essence of a triangle comprises what is conceptually necessary for a triangle. Volitional necessity differs from conceptual necessity, however, in that it doesn't constrain how the person can be classified or described: "Volitional necessity constrains the person himself, by limiting the choices he can make."[6] It thus involves the inability to choose some things or to refrain from choosing others.

As Frankfurt goes on to note, however, such an inability may be due to an overwhelming aversion or compulsion of the sort that is alien to the self, constraining the will from without. If an inability is to be constitutive of the self, it ought to constrain the will from within and hence autonomously. Volitional necessity must therefore be a voluntary or willing inability of the will. And Frankfurt believes that the will can indeed

---

"On Treating Persons as Persons," *Ethics* 88 (1977): 150–161; Robert Paul Wolff, "There's Nobody Here but Us Persons," in *Women and Philosophy: Toward a Theory of Liberation*, eds. Carol C. Gould and Marx W. Wartofsky (New York: G.P. Putnam's Sons, 1976), 128–144; Seyla Benhabib, "The Generalized and the Concrete Other: The Kohlberg-Gilligan Controversy and Moral Theory," in *Women and Moral Theory*, eds. Eva Feder Kittay and Diana T. Meyers (Totowa, NJ: Rowman and Littlefield, 1987), 154–177; Edward Johnson, "Ignoring Persons," in *Respect for Persons*, ed. O. H. Green, *Tulane Studies in Philosophy* 31 (1982): 91–105. I discuss Dillon's statement in "Love as a Moral Emotion" (Chapter 4 in the present volume).

5 Frankfurt, "Autonomy, Necessity, and Love," 135.

6 Frankfurt, "On the Necessity of Ideals," in *Necessity, Volition, and Love*, 113; see also "Autonomy, Necessity, and Love," 138.

be subject to willing inabilities, such as the subject may express by calling an act unthinkable or saying that he cannot bring himself to perform it. To explain how an inability to will can be voluntary, Frankfurt modifies his initial intuition, by reintroducing the concept of identification. An inability becomes voluntary, Frankfurt explains, when it is due to a motive with which the subject identifies by means of a reflective endorsement.[7] If the motive's effectiveness in constraining his will is due in part to his reflective endorsement of it, then "the constraint is itself imposed by his will."[8]

Yet if the agent could potentially withhold his reflective endorsement from this constraint, then it isn't imposed by his will essentially. Hence more than reflective endorsement is required for the volitional necessities that define the subject's volitional essence. Frankfurt's initial intuition is therefore modified once again, to require not only that the agent endorse the motive constraining his will but that he be unable to help endorsing it. In such a case, the agent has a second-order inability: the inability to will any change in his inability to will. And for reasons already noted, this higher-order inability must itself be of the willing variety, by virtue of receiving a higher level endorsement, and so on. The subject's inability to alter his will thus appears to resound through higher and higher levels of the motivational hierarchy.[9] The subject finds that "it is not only unthinkable for him to perform the action in question; it is also unthinkable for him to form an effective intention to become willing to perform it."[10] Compound inabilities of this sort are what define the subject's essential nature, in Frankfurt's view.

Frankfurt describes these inabilities as "contingent volitional necessities by which the will of the person is as a matter of fact constrained."[11] They are contingent in the sense that they are not logically entailed by the subject's being a person or having a will. But they do have a quasi-conceptual consequence. By constraining the subject's will, they

---

[7] Frankfurt, "On the Necessity of Ideals," 111–12; see also "Autonomy, Necessity, and Love," 136–38; and "Rationality and the Unthinkable," 182–183.

[8] Frankfurt, "On the Necessity of Ideals," 112.

[9] The image is Frankfurt's: see, e.g., "Freedom of the Will and the Concept of a Person," in *The Importance of What We Care About,* 21; "Identification and Wholeheartedness," in *The Importance of What We Care About,* 168.

[10] Ibid. See also "Rationality and the Unthinkable," 187. Presumably then, the person must endorse his inability to will any change in his inability to will. Here the threat of a regress reappears.

[11] Frankfurt, "Autonomy, Necessity, and Love," 138.

also define his essence as an individual, and so they give rise to a further constraint – namely, that he could not alter them while remaining the same person.

Frankfurt makes this point most clearly as follows:

> Agamemnon at Aulis is destroyed by an inescapable conflict between two equally defining elements in his own nature: his love for his daughter and his love for the army he commands. . . . When he is forced to sacrifice one of these, he is thereby forced to betray himself. Rarely, if ever, do tragedies of this sort have sequels. Since the volitional unity of the tragic hero has been irreparably ruptured, there is a sense in which the person he had been no longer exists. Hence, there can be no continuation of *his* story.[12]

The necessitating concerns that make up Agamemnon's essence as a person, as Frankfurt conceives it, cannot be deduced from any of the generic concepts that apply to him, but they are necessary to his individual identity, to his being the particular person who he is. When Agamemnon sacrifices some of these concerns, he becomes a different person, and his former self ceases to exist.

Frankfurt makes the same point in several other ways. For example, he says that if someone is free of any volitional limits, then he has "no essential nature or identity,"[13] and he consequently suffers "a diminution, or even a dissolution, of the reality of the self."[14] A similar dissolution can be caused by boredom, which Frankfurt conceives as a lack of any compelling cares or interests. This state "threatens the extinction of the active self," and our dislike of it can be understood accordingly as an expression of our instinct for self preservation – "in the sense of sustaining not the *life* of the organism but the *persistence of the self*."[15] Yet a third threat to the self, as conceived by Frankfurt, comes from ambivalence, which guarantees that one or another element of the self will have to be sacrificed when a choice is made.[16] If the self is to have a chance of remaining whole, it must be wholehearted, in the sense of being unequivocal in its essential concerns.

---

[12] Ibid., 139, n. 8.
[13] Frankfurt, preface to *The Importance of What We Care About*, vii–ix, at ix. See also "Rationality and the Unthinkable," 188; and "On the Necessity of Ideals."
[14] Frankfurt, "Rationality and the Unthinkable," 179.
[15] Frankfurt, "On the Usefulness of Final Ends," in *Necessity, Volition, and Love*, 89.
[16] Frankfurt, "Autonomy, Necessity, and Love," 139, n. 9.

Because these concerns can be sacrificed only at the cost of the self, in Frankfurt's view, they "possess not simply power but authority,"[17] derived from the imperative of self-preservation. The subject has compelling reason not to oppose them, because of the "drastic psychic injuries" that such opposition would entail.[18] What someone cares about is thus important because, by defining who he is, it determines what he must do in order for that person to survive.

These recent developments in Frankfurt's conception of autonomy have, in effect, yoked it to a conception of personal identity, which also involves the boundaries of the self.[19] And Frankfurt's conception of personal identity agrees with the currently prevailing, neo-Lockean conception propounded by Derek Parfit. In particular, Frankfurt's conception of identity agrees with Parfit's in respects that, in turn, distinguish Parfit's conception from Locke's. Since the differences between Parfit and Locke have not been not widely discussed, I want to pause a moment to review them.

Parfit follows Locke in thinking that what makes for the survival of a person is his psychological relation to past and future selves.[20] But Parfit differs from Locke on the nature of the relevant relation, and he thereby makes room for motivational essences of the sort that Frankfurt envisions.

Locke thinks that the psychological relation making for a person's survival is exclusively a relation of memory: one's past selves are those whose experiences one remembers first-personally, and one's future selves are those who will first-personally remember one's experiences. A natural extension of Locke's theory applies this definition recursively, so that one's past and future selves include not only those who are linked to one by memory but also anyone similarly linked to them, and so on. In

---

[17] Ibid., 138.

[18] Ibid., 139.

[19] In "The Necessity of Ideals," 113, Frankfurt says: "The idea that the identity of a thing is to be understood in terms of conditions that are essential for its existence is one of the oldest and most compelling of the philosophical principles that guide our efforts to clarify our thought. To grasp what a thing is, we must grasp its essence – viz., those characteristics without which it is not possible for it to be what it is. Thus, the notions of necessity and identity are intimately related."

[20] Parfit denies that the relevant connections constitute a relation of identity, because they can branch in such a way as to connect a person to two distinct selves existing at one time. I will use the term "selves" to denote those person-stages to whom one bears the survival-relation that matters, whether or not they are stages of a single person.

either version, Locke's theory implies that one may share virtually no motivational characteristics with one's past or future selves. One may in the past have possessed vastly different attitudes and traits of character, so long as one remembers being the person who possessed them (or being someone who remembers being that person, and so on); and one may yet have vastly different attitudes and traits in the future, so long as the person possessing them remembers being oneself (or being someone who remembers being oneself, and so on). Not only can a prince and a cobbler end up inhabiting one another's bodies, according to Locke's theory; they can also end up possessing one another's beliefs, desires, ideals, loves, projects, and so on.

Parfit thinks that some of the latter characteristics are in fact relevant to survival.[21] Part of what makes for one's survival, in Parfit's view, is the persistence of attitudes and traits of character.[22] And for this purpose, some attitudes and traits are more important than others. Characteristics that differentiate one from other people tend to be more important to one's survival, as Parfit conceives it, than those which one shares with everyone else;[23] characteristics that one values in oneself may also be more important than those that one wishes to shed.[24] Parfit's theory thus allows for the possibility that some cluster of desires and intentions might be so distinctive of a person, and so valued by him, that he would be as good as dead without them. Sacrificing these attitudes would be the end of him, and so they would derive authority from the imperative of self-preservation, just as Frankfurt believes.[25]

The recent developments in Frankfurt's conception of autonomy have thus brought it into harmony with the distinctively un-Lockean strain in Parfit's otherwise Lockean conception of personal identity. Like Parfit,

---

[21] In this discussion, I gloss over many other differences between Locke and Parfit. Most important, perhaps, is that Parfit distinguishes survival from strict identity through time. Parfit thinks that survival, unlike identity, admits of degrees and intransitivities.

[22] Derek Parfit, *Reasons and Persons* (Oxford: Oxford University Press, 1984), 205–206; see also 301–302.

[23] Ibid., 300–301. See also 515, n. 6.

[24] Ibid., 299.

[25] This consequence of Parfit's view is confirmed by his discussion of "The Nineteenth Century Russian" in *Reasons and Persons*, 327–328. This idealistic nobleman bequeaths his land to the peasants, in a document that can be revoked only by his wife. He then makes his wife promise that she won't revoke the document, even if he later asks her to. Parfit comments, "The young Russian socialist regards his ideals as essential to his present self. He asks his wife to promise to this present self not to act against these ideals. And, on this way of thinking, she can never be released from her commitment. The self to whom she is committed would, in trying to release her, cease to exist."

but unlike Locke, Frankfurt believes that one may have to retain particular motives in order to remain oneself. And he believes that motives essential to the self in this sense are the motives whose governance of one's behavior constitutes one's self-governance, or autonomy.

A Critique of Frankfurt's New Conception

Even if I believed that a person had a motivational essence of this kind, I would not infer that his being governed by this essence was what made him autonomous. Being governed by such an essence might amount to authenticity, perhaps, but not autonomy.

To see the difference, consider the paradigm case of inauthenticity, the person who manifests what D. W. Winnicott called a "False Self."[26] This person laughs at what he thinks he is supposed to find amusing, shows concern for what he thinks he is supposed to care about, and in general conforms himself to the demands and expectations of others. The motives that his behavior is designed to simulate are motives that he doesn't genuinely have. And the overriding motive that he does have – namely, to satisfy the expectations of others – is hardly a motive that he cannot help endorsing; on the contrary, he doesn't even acknowledge this motive, much less endorse it. Hence neither the motives that he simulates nor the motive on which he thereby acts belong to his essential nature, as Frankfurt conceives it.

But is this person lacking in self-control, self-governance, or autonomy? To be sure, he has a problem with autonomy, but his problem is one of excess: he is overly self-controlled, overly deliberate; his grip on the reins of his behavior is too tight, not too loose. His failure to be motivated from within his true self makes him inauthentic, but it seems to result from his being all too autonomous.[27]

So if I believed in a person's motivational essence, I still wouldn't identify it as the source of autonomy; but I don't believe in a motivational

---

[26] "Ego Distortion in Terms of True and False Self," in *Collected Papers: Through Paediatrics to Psycho-analysis* (London: Tavistock Publications, 1958).

[27] One might be tempted to say that the exaggerated self-control of such a person is only an imitation of real self-control, amounting only to pseudo-autonomy. See David Shapiro, *Autonomy and Rigid Character* (New York: Basic Books, 1981), 74–75. But even if this person has only pseudo-autonomy, the reason is not that he is only pretending to be autonomous; it's rather that he's somehow misapplying the self-control that would otherwise count as very real autonomy. His pseudo-autonomy consists in the misdirected self-control by which he holds himself to a pretense; but the pretense is one of authenticity. Autonomy is not what the agent simulates but what he misuses in mounting the simulation.

essence. I am inclined to say of the essential self posited by Frankfurt what the psychoanalyst Jeffrey Rubin has recently said of the True Self posited by Winnicott:

> The process of searching for one's True Self, regarded as a singular entity waiting to be found, is a quixotic enterprise that may promote self-restriction and self-alienation.... [S]ingular notions like the True Self subjugate selfhood's possibilities by obscuring and limiting its multidimensionality. Facets of self-experience that do not fit into preexisting images of who one *really* is are neglected or not assimilated into one's sense of identity.... Not only is a monolithic sense of self limiting, but psychological health may involve access to, and comfort with, our multidimensionality. From this perspective, a sense of the complexity, multidimensionality, and polyvalency of the self is a developmental milestone and achievement.[28]

With these words in mind, I turn to a critique of Frankfurt's new conception of the self.

I have argued elsewhere against the notion that there must be motivational constancy between a person and his past or future selves. Specifically, I've argued that a person has past and future selves in virtue of psychological connections that give him first-personal access to past and future points-of-view – connections that can be forged by memory and anticipation but not by the retention of motives or traits of character.[29]

I don't deny that some of our concerns are authoritative for us because they are somehow central to our personalities; nor do I deny the temptation to describe these concerns as essential to who we are, integral to ourselves, definitive of our identities, and so on. At the end of this essay, I'll explain how I think we should understand these descriptions. For now,

[28] "Does the True Self Really Exist? A Critique of Winnicott's True Self Concept," in *A Psychoanalysis for our Time: Exploring the Blindness of the Seeing "I"* (New York: New York University Press, 1998), 109. Also relevant here is Erik Erikson's discussion of the difference between "wholeness" and "totalism," in *Identity, Youth, and Crisis* (New York: W. W. Norton, 1968), 74–90. Erikson concludes: "To have the courage of one's diversity is a sign of wholeness in individuals and in civilizations" (90). See also John D. W. Andrews, *The Active Self in Psychotherapy: An Integration of Therapeutic Styles* (Boston: Allyn & Bacon, 1991), 7–8, 35; Roderick Anscombe, "The Myth of the True Self," 52 *Psychiatry* 209–17 (1989); Mark Epstein, *Thoughts Without a Thinker: Psychotherapy From a Buddhist Perspective* (New York: Basic Books, 1995), 71–73.

[29] "Self to Self" (Chapter 8 in the present volume), especially note 5, p. 173. I do include long-range intentions among the mental states that connect the self to itself through time. Hence a person's plans and policies are part of what make him (in Locke's phrase) "self to himself" from one time to another, in my view. But I do not believe that particular plans and policies can play a privileged role simply because of their distinctiveness or importance to the subject.

I want to argue only that we shouldn't take them literally by claiming that the defense of our central concerns is a matter of self-preservation, a matter of life or death for the self. Such literalism can easily lead to absurdity.

Consider this passage, which is sometimes cited with approval by critics of impartial morality:

I am not a person who just happens accidentally and irrelevantly, to be a man, forty years old, the husband of a professor of English literature, the son of two aging and sick parents, the father of two small boys six and four, a comfortably well-off member of the upper middle class, American-Jewish, born and raised in New York. I am *essentially* such a man.[30]

Can a man be essentially forty years old, essentially the father of young children, or essentially the son of elderly parents? One cannot read this statement without wondering whether the author still believes it, now that he is in his sixties, his parents have passed away, and his children are grown.

Of course, Frankfurt would not include most of these attributes in a person's essential nature. But if we read this enumeration of attributes as an expression of the associated concerns – of the author's love for his wife and children; pity for his ailing parents; pride in his masculinity, his American-Jewish heritage, or his home town of New York – then we arrive at a personal essence that Frankfurt might recognize. And we can still wonder whether the author would be a different person simply because of having become estranged from his parents or having fallen for someone other than his wife.

According to Frankfurt, such crises may have no sequels, because their protagonist ceases to exist. But surely estrangements and betrayals are precisely what set the stage for a sequel. The Agamemnon legend would lose much of its power if the man who sacrificed his daughter at the beginning didn't survive to be murdered by his wife in the end. If a crisis like the one at Aulis necessarily put an end to its protagonist, we wouldn't

---

[30] Robert Paul Wolff, "There's Nobody Here But Us Persons," 136–137. This passage is quoted by Johnson, "Ignoring Persons," 97. Another author who thinks that the authority of our concerns can be traced to their place in our identity, and hence to the imperative of self-preservation, is Christine Korsgaard. See *The Sources of Normativity* (Cambridge: Cambridge University Press, 1996). For a critique of Korsgaard on this point, see David Copp, "Korsgaard on Normativity, Identity, and the Ground of Obligation," in *Rationality, Realism, Revision: Proceedings of the Third International Congress of the Society for Analytical Philosophy*, vol. 23 of *Perspektiven der Analytischen Philosophie*, ed. Julian Nida-Rümelin (Berlin: de Gruyter, 1999), 572–581. I discuss Korsgaard's version of this view in "Willing the Law," (Chapter 12 in the present volume).

just be lacking sequels to particular stories: we wouldn't have the concept of a sequel at all.

In light of how implausible the notion of personal essences can be when applied to particular cases, we have to wonder why it remains so attractive. Frankfurt never offers us a convincing example of someone who ceases to be the same person because of abandoning a project, betraying a commitment, or undergoing some other change of heart; nor does he offer any argument for thinking that motivational changes can have such momentous results. He simply asserts that our projects and commitments are sometimes essential to who we are. We welcome his assertion, but not as something of which he has convinced us; we welcome it as something that we, too, want to say about ourselves. The question is why we want to say it. In the absence of examples or arguments to show that we have motivational essences, what moves us to apply this self-description?

My worry is that believing ourselves to have motivational essences is a case of wishful thinking on our part. We'd like to have motivational essences, and so we're happy to agree when someone says that we do.

Now, a conception of the self cannot be faulted simply for being associated with wishes. Any conception of how we are constituted will yield implications about what it is for us to be well constituted. A conception of the self will thus entail an ideal of the self, to which holders of the conception will naturally aspire. What's crucial, however, is the logical order between conception and aspiration. We are justified in wishing to embody an ideal implicit in our self-conception; but our self-conception should not be tailored to suit our antecedent wishes. My worry is that Frankfurt's conception of the self appeals to us only because its implicit ideal represents us as we wish we could be.

The ideal implicit in Frankfurt's conception of the self is the ideal of wholeheartedness. Frankfurt reasons that if the self is constituted out of irresistible motives, then it had better be constituted out of motives that are in concert rather than conflict, so that it will not be divided against itself. He therefore concludes that the well-constituted self is wholehearted rather than ambivalent.

Frankfurt's term "wholeheartedness" does not denote the complete absence of conflicting motives. A person can be wholehearted in Frankfurt's sense while retaining desires that conflict, so long as he has decisively identified with one of the desires and dissociated himself from the other. This process "involves a radical *separation* of the competing desires, one of which is not merely assigned a relatively less favored position but extruded entirely as an outlaw."³¹ The motivational conflict is not thereby eliminated. Rather, "the conflict between the *desires* is in this way transformed into a conflict between *one* of them and the *person* who has identified himself with its rival."³²

Frankfurt compares and contrasts this process with "the self-reparative activities of the body":

> When the body heals itself, it *eliminates* conflicts in which one physical process (say, infection) interferes with others and undermines the homeostasis, or equilibrium, in which health consists. A person who makes up his mind also seeks thereby to overcome or to supersede a condition of inner division and to make himself into an integrated whole. But he may accomplish this without actually eliminating the desires that conflict with those on which he has decided, as long as he dissociates himself from them.³³

Thus, ambivalence is a disease of the self, to which wholeheartedness stands as the contrasting state of health. What cures the disease, and restores us to health, is the process of dissociating ourselves from unwelcome desires, a process that expels them from the self without necessarily eliminating them entirely.

This prescription for self-health is undeniably attractive. The question is whether it attracts us by articulating what would in fact be ideal for us, given how we are constituted. I suspect that it attracts us for other reasons.

Frankfurt is not alone in thinking of ambivalence as a disease of the self. One of the most famous discussions of ambivalence casts it literally as an agent of disease – specifically, the mental illness suffered by a patient of Freud's who has come to be known as the Rat Man.³⁴

---

³¹ Frankfurt, "Identification and Wholeheartedness," in *The Importance of What We Care About*, 170.

³² Ibid., 172. See also Frankfurt, "The Faintest Passion" in *Necessity, Volition, and Love*, 100: "Wholeheartedness does not require that a person be altogether untroubled by inner opposition to his will. It just requires that, with respect to any such conflict, he himself be fully resolved. This means that he must be resolutely on the side of one of the forces struggling within him and not on the side of any other."

³³ Frankfurt, "Identification and Wholeheartedness," 173–174. In "The Faintest Passion," Frankfurt quotes Saint Augustine as calling ambivalence "'a disease of the mind' from which we suffer in punishment for Original Sin" (100). Frankfurt himself calls it here "a disease of the will."

³⁴ Sigmund Freud, "Notes Upon a Case of Obsessional Neurosis," *The Standard Edition of the Complete Psychological Works of Sigmund Freud*, ed. James Strachey et al. (London: Hogarth Press and the Institute of Psycho-Analysis 1953–1974), Vol. X, 153–249.

Freud diagnoses the Rat Man's problem as "a splitting of the personality"[35] resulting from "a battle between love and hate [that] was raging in [his] breast"[36] with respect to one and the same person. The Rat Man desperately loved and violently hated his father, and his personality was consequently divided, according to Freud, into distinct loving and hating selves.[37] Freud cites this division to explain the Rat Man's symptoms, which often involved repeatedly doing and undoing an action, or thinking and contradicting a thought.

At first glance, then, Freud seems to agree that ambivalence is a disease of the self, a disease whose cure requires the attainment of wholeheartedness. A second look reveals, however, that the Rat Man's problem was not so much ambivalence as his response to it. What caused the Rat Man's neurosis, according to Freud, was the means by which he sought to cope with the battle between love and hatred within him – namely, by repressing his hatred and acknowledging only his love. This repression is what allowed the two emotions to survive unmixed and hence to continue pulling the patient so violently in opposite directions. Freud concludes, "We may regard the repression of his infantile hatred of his father as the event which brought his whole subsequent career under the dominion of the neurosis."[38]

The Rat Man's strategies of repression were not the ones with which we are familiar from Freud's more accessible writings. Most of the Rat Man's thoughts and feelings, both loving and hostile, were available to his consciousness; he simply disconnected them and reconnected them in such a way as to conceal their true significance.[39] Thus, for example, he frequently had thoughts of harm befalling his father, but he had disconnected those thoughts from their wishful affect. He insisted that they were merely "trains of thought" rather than hostile wishes.[40] Conversely, his hostile feelings were displaced from their true objects onto others, including his psychoanalyst[41] and himself.[42]

The Rat Man's repression thus consisted in a concerted practice of self-misinterpretation. And what motivated this misinterpretation was

[35] Ibid., 177.
[36] Ibid., 191; see also 180–183; 237–41.
[37] For the image of two selves, see Freud, "Notes Upon a Case," 177.
[38] Ibid., 238.
[39] Ibid., 196–7; see also 175–176; 231–232.
[40] Ibid., 178–180, 222.
[41] Ibid., 209.
[42] Ibid., 188–189.

precisely the desire to dissociate himself from his own hatred and hostility. Thus, Freud tells us that on the occasion when the Rat Man first divulged the hostile thought that became the centerpiece of his case history (and the source of his analytic moniker), "He broke off his story in order to assure me that these thoughts were entirely foreign and repugnant to him."[43] On another occasion, the Rat Man said "that he would like to speak of a criminal act, whose author he did not recognize as himself, though he quite clearly recollected committing it."[44] His hatred was thus something that he had alienated from himself, so that he no longer regarded its resultant thoughts and actions as his.

We might even say that the Rat Man's hatred had been repressed by being "extruded as an outlaw" – but then we would be quoting Frankfurt rather than Freud.[45] Conversely, Freud's discussion of this case begins with a statement that might easily have been written by Frankfurt. Referring to an erotic wish felt by the Rat Man in childhood, Freud says: "This wish corresponds to the later obsessional or compulsive idea; and if the quality of compulsion was not yet present in the wish, this was because the ego had not yet placed itself in complete opposition to it and did not yet regard it as something foreign to itself."[46] The theory expressed in this statement is that a wish becomes a compulsion when the ego comes to regard it as foreign – which is close to what Frankfurt believes as well.

Unfortunately, this point of agreement between Freud and Frankfurt suggests that the Rat Man suffered, not from the disease of ambivalence, but from something like Frankfurt's cure. What made him ill was his effort to dissociate himself from one of his emotions, which is just what Frankfurt prescribes for cases of ambivalence. The "radical separation of . . . competing desires" recommended by Frankfurt ultimately led to the "splitting of the personality" diagnosed by Freud.[47]

Of course, Frankfurt does not recommend separating desires by repressing some of them. Although Frankfurt's view implies that the Rat Man was right to expel his hatred, it also implies that he was wrong about where to expel it from. He expelled it from his self-awareness or

[43] Ibid., 167.
[44] Ibid., 184.
[45] Quoted at note 31.
[46] Ibid., 162–163.
[47] These expressions are quoted at notes 32 and 36, respectively. See Andrews, *The Active Self*, 29.

self-understanding; whereas Frankfurt's view implies that he should have consciously rejected it and thereby expelled it from the self.[48]

Yet the suspicion remains that this prescription, though different from what caused the Rat Man's illness, would hardly have been more healthy. Surely, what the Rat Man should have done was to accept his filial hostility as part of himself, to accept *himself* as ambivalent toward his father.[49] The Rat Man's mistake was indeed his attempt to separate competing desires by expelling one of them, not the specific form of expulsion by which he tried to separate them.

We can draw this moral from the Rat Man's story without relying on any distinctively Freudian hypotheses – childhood sexuality, the Oedipus complex, or even repression. Beneath these overlays of psychoanalytic theory is a story intelligible to pure common sense.

To begin with, the species of ambivalence attributed to the Rat Man is familiar to all of us. Almost all of us love our parents, but most of us also retain sources of deep hostility toward them – sore spots that can be inflamed into powerful anger or even hate. Other elements of the Rat Man's history may seem weird or incredible, but the element of filial ambivalence is not extraordinary in the least.

---

[48] Morris Eagle has argued that expulsion from the self is the ultimate aim of repression, and that expulsion from consciousness is adopted as a means to that aim. "Psychoanalytic Conceptions of the Self," in *The Self: Interdisciplinary Approaches* (New York: Springer-Verlag, 1991), 49–65. Eagle writes: "[T]he logic of Freudian theory, particularly the clinical logic, points to the expulsion of mental contents from *self-organization* as the significant aspect of repression. Or, to put it more fully, it is the *disowning or disavowal* of mental contents, the rejection of these contents as one's own, that is the clinically (and theoretically) significant aspect of repression. According to the view I am suggesting, expulsion from conscious awareness is mainly *a means*, albeit the most frequently employed means, toward the end of rendering certain mental contents as an impersonal 'it,' as not mine, as ego alien. But it is the disowned ego-alien status that is the critical element in dealing with mental contents incompatible with one's self-structure" (55). See note 66. See also Morris Eagle, "Psychoanalysis and the Personal," in *Mind, Psychoanalysis and Science*, eds. P. Clark and C. Wright (Oxford: Blackwell, 1988), 91–111.

[49] In other words, the Rat Man needed to attain the "developmental milestone" that Rubin describes as "access to, and comfort with, [his] multidimensionality," or "a sense of the complexity, multidimensionality, and polyvalency of the self" (quoted at note 28). Compare here Eagle's interpretation of psychotherapeutic change, as expressed in Freud's formula "where id was, there should ego be": "Freud is defining psychotherapeutic change, not in terms of consciousness and understanding, but in terms of alterations in self-structure. That is, he is saying that real change is marked by an enlargement of the self." Eagle, "Psychoanalytic Conceptions of the Self," 61.

Second, beneath the theoretical apparatus of Freud's account lies a piece of folk wisdom about dealing with mixed emotions. When we are angry with someone we love, the first step toward dealing with our anger is to let it mingle with, and be modified by, our other emotions toward the same person. Isolating our hostility from our other feelings is a way of not dealing with it, of allowing it to remain undigested, a lasting source of inner strife and outer impulsiveness. Of course, new-age common sense about the importance of "processing" problematic emotions is derivative of Freudian theory; but Freudian theory about the return of the repressed is, in turn, derivative of a common sense that is ageless, as Freud himself was the first to point out. When Freud explains why repression brought the Rat Man "under the dominion of the neurosis," his explanation strongly implies, on commonsensical grounds, that any attempt by the Rat Man to segregate his emotions would have been equally harmful.

A third piece of common sense in this case history is that allowing our emotions to mingle with their opposites is difficult, daunting, even terrifying. The Rat Man chose to regard his hatred as foreign because he was afraid of letting it into his emotional life, even though doing so was his only chance of domesticating it. All of us are like the Rat Man at least to this extent, that we feel threatened by various emotions that would introduce conflict into our lives. We consequently wish that our commitments were not tinged with regret, that our projects were not fraught with doubts, that our loves were not complicated by hate. We wish, in short, that we could be wholehearted.

What has now emerged is that wholeheartedness is an object of wishes that do not necessarily represent a healthy trend in our thought. Our attraction to the idea of being wholehearted is one manifestation of the fears that move us to defend ourselves against our own emotions. Hence our affinity for Frankfurt's ideal may not indicate that he's right about the constitution of the self; it may indicate no more than our own defensiveness.

Conceiving of ourselves to have motivational essences can serve the same defensive purpose. What's threatening about our hostility toward loved ones is that it might efface our love for them and move us to do things that love would never allow us to do.[50] Our love therefore entails

---

[50] See Freud, "Notes Upon a Case," 226–227, 233–236. Freud's view was that we fear the magical fulfillment of our hostile wishes, via the "omnipotence of thoughts."

a fear of its own obliteration. How comforting it would be to think that our love was indelibly written into our nature, so that we didn't have to protect it from exposure to contrary feelings. Are we attracted to this thought because it is true or because it is comforting?

A similar question can be asked about the very notion of an inner self. When we defend ourselves against unwelcome emotions, we would like to think that we are expelling, excluding, or (in Frankfurt's term) "extruding" them from ourselves. We are trying to neutralize troublesome elements of our psyches, and one way to neutralize troublemakers is to banish them beyond some enforceable boundary. When we picture the inner sanctuary of the self, we are picturing a defensible territory – which is precisely what's needed for successful defenses. Given our wish for this safe haven, however, our belief in its existence may be another case of wishful thinking.

Indeed, there is also a defensive way of applying Frankfurt's term "identification." I'm sure that Frankfurt didn't intend the term to be applied in this way, but I wonder whether we as readers haven't departed from his intentions. The term "identification" has an ordinary meaning, different from Frankfurt's, whose substitution into our interpretation of Frankfurt's theory would further suit our defensive purposes.

A Digression on Identification

Frankfurt is responsible for bringing the term "identification" into widespread use among contemporary philosophers and for shaping their intuitions about it. Following Frankfurt, philosophers have come to speak of identification as primarily reflective and evaluative – as a process of endorsing some parts or aspects of ourselves.[51] But the term "identification" ordinarily stands for a process that is not, in the first instance, either reflective or evaluative.[52] I want to examine what we ordinarily mean by

---

[51] There is at least one passage in which Frankfurt uses the term in a different sense: "A person who cares about something is, as it were, invested in it. By caring about it, he makes himself susceptible to benefits and vulnerable to losses depending upon whether what he cares about flourishes or is diminished. We may say that in this sense he *identifies* himself with what he cares about." Frankfurt, "On the Necessity of Ideals," 111. Here the target of identification is, not one of the subject's own motives, but the external object of those motives.

[52] For a related argument, see Nomy Arpaly and Timothy Schroeder, "Alienation and Externality," *Canadian Journal of Philosophy* 29 (1999): 371–387.

"identification" and then to consider the possibility that we can be misled by that meaning in our reading of Frankfurt.

In ordinary parlance we are more likely to speak of identifying with other people than with parts of ourselves. The remark "I can identify with that" is a way of saying that we have experienced what someone else is going through and that we empathize with his reaction to it. We speak of identifying with fictional characters or with their actions and reactions in particular scenes.[53] We also describe ourselves as identifying with authority figures and role models in our lives. Identifying is thus something that we do, in the first instance, with people other than ourselves.

In the case of role models, identification involves a positive evaluation: identifying with these people goes hand-in-hand with admiring them and wanting to emulate them. But in other cases, identification can be evaluatively neutral or even negative. "I can identify with that" may be our response to someone's self-depreciating tale of ineptitude or weakness. What elicits our identification may be another person's rendition of that which we find most disappointing or embarrassing in ourselves. Fiction would lack much of its educative force if it couldn't induce us to identify with characters whom we don't admire or wish to emulate. Our identification with these characters may soften our judgment of them, but only because it makes us empathize with them, not because it involves any judgment in their favor.

Perhaps the most extreme example of identification without positive evaluation is the phenomenon that Anna Freud called "identification with the aggressor."[54] When a child plays at being a hungry lion or an angry teacher, he may be identifying with what he most fears, so as to escape from being the target of its aggression. The same mechanism may be at work when an adult directs at others the very sort of criticism to which he feels most vulnerable himself. This person doesn't necessarily

---

[53] We also use the term "identification" to describe a person's sense of affiliation with a social group or movement; but this context usually calls for a different construction. What a person usually does with respect to a group or movement is, not simply to identify with it, but rather to identify *himself* with it – which is a slightly different maneuver. Frankfurt tends to use the constructions "to identify with" and "to identify oneself with" interchangeably.

[54] Anna Freud, *The Ego and the Mechanisms of Defense* (London: Hogarth Press, 1937), 109–121; reprinted in *Pivotal Papers on Identification*, ed. George H. Pollock (Madison, CT: International Universities Press, 1993), 105–114. On the variety of motives for identification, see Roy Schafer, *Aspects of Internalization* (New York: International Universities Press, 1968), chap. 1.

admire his critics or want to be like them; he would just prefer being the critic to being the object of criticism.

If identification doesn't necessarily involve a favorable evaluation, then what do instances of identification have in common? The nature of identification can only be obscured, I think, by a moral psychology confined to the categories of belief and desire, or belief and pro-attitude. If identification must sit with either the beliefs or the pro-attitudes, it will sit more comfortably with the latter, in the form of an endorsement or a desire to emulate. Yet to insist on placing identification in the matrix of belief and pro-attitude is to miss the fact that it involves, above all, an exercise of the imagination.[55]

To identify with someone, you have to imagine that you are he, or that he is you. Such an exercise of imagination isn't sufficient for identification: you can imagine that you are Caligula or Lady Macbeth even though you can't identify with them. But identifying with someone can be characterized, I think, as a particular way of imagining that you are he, with particular psychological consequences.

One respect in which identification exceeds merely imagining that you are someone else is that it must be spontaneous. You can deliberately conjure up the thought of being Lady Macbeth, but unless you were spontaneously affected by that thought, you wouldn't be said to identify with her. Another difference is that when you deliberately conjure up the thought of being Lady Macbeth, it occupies the focus of your awareness, while knowledge of your real identity is pushed into the background. When you identify with someone, the position is reversed: the thought of being that person is in the background – perhaps so far in the background as to be unconscious – while actual identities remain salient.

Finally, deliberately imagining that you are someone else doesn't necessarily affect your realistic attitudes – that is, your attitudes toward the world as you believe it to be rather than as you have imagined it. The activity of imagining that you are Caligula may leave no traces on your thoughts and feelings about the real world, including yourself and the historical figure of Caligula. But when you identify with someone, the thought of being that person, though outside the focus of awareness, somehow colors your attitudes toward yourself or him, toward your individual situations or shared relationship. Your attitudes toward the actual

---

55 See Richard Wollheim, "Imagination and Identification," in *On Art and the Mind* (Cambridge, MA: Harvard University Press, 1974), 73ff.

world are modified by your having spontaneously though perhaps unconsciously imagined a world in which you are he.

The most common way to imagine that you are someone else is to imagine being that person, by imagining the world as experienced by him – as seen through his eyes and traveled in his shoes.[56] This sort of imagining is also the most common means of identification. Identifying with someone is usually a matter of having your view of reality colored by a spontaneous image of how things are for him.

This image is of necessity incomplete, in that it doesn't represent every facet of the other person's perspective. Sometimes it can be so incomplete as to represent no more than a single sensation. Watching a sweaty jogger lift a drink to his lips, you may suddenly imagine a cool draught in your own throat; watching a couple pause to embrace on the street, you may spontaneously imagine a warm breath against your own face; seeing someone catch his finger in a car door, you may imagine a shooting pain in your own finger. These brief and fragmentary identifications have only an ephemeral impact on your view of the world, but they exemplify the same psychological process as identifications that are more consequential.[57]

---

[56] I discuss this claim at length in "Self to Self," (Chapter 8 in the present volume).

[57] In addition to imagining that you are someone else, you can also imagine that he is you, by regarding him externally and thinking "That's me," as you might think in reference to a photograph or a reflection of yourself in a shop window. Can you identify with someone by means of this external sort of imagining?

Imagining an external figure to be oneself may not seem like a compelling way of identifying with him. But consider the universal phenomenon of dreaming about oneself from a perspective outside one's own body, a perspective from which one sees oneself as an external figure. This phenomenon suggests that representing an external figure as oneself is deeply entrenched in the representational idiom of the imagination. And imaginatively representing another person as one represents oneself in dreams ought to be a compelling way of identifying with him.

But how exactly does a dream represent which figure is oneself? As the dream unfolds, one doesn't suddenly focus on one of the characters and think "That's me," as one does when recognizing oneself in a home movie. It's implicit from the outset of the dream that a particular figure is oneself, and so it never gets formulated explicitly in thought. The question is how one's identity among externally represented figures can be implicit in the dream.

Maybe one's identity is implicit in the emotional structure of the dream. Although one sees and hears all of the characters from the outside, one reacts emotionally to the dreamed events from the perspective of one character in particular, fearing whatever threatens him in the dream, resenting whoever insults him, and so on. Indeed, one doesn't so much react emotionally to dreamed events as one dreams them emotionally, to begin with: one fearfully dreams threats to a character and resentfully dreams insults to him. One thus dreams the dream from the emotional perspective of a particular

One consequence of imagining things from someone else's perspective is a tendency to empathize with him. Picturing the world as seen through his eyes or heard through his ears, you feel first-personal emotions on his behalf.[58] A further consequence of identification is insight into the other person's thinking and behavior. You are better able to anticipate the thoughts and actions of someone with whom you identify, because you have imaginatively simulated his situation, either consciously or unconsciously.

Another consequence of identifying with someone is a tendency to behave like him, partly because of empathizing with him but also because of the direct motivational force of the imagination. On the one hand, you tend to do what the other person does or would do because you feel the way he does or would feel. Loving his friends, you tend to favor them; hating his enemies, you tend to oppose them; and so on. On the other hand, you tend to pick up the person's behavioral style – his accent, his idiom, and his body-language as well – as if you were impersonating him.

The latter mechanism is similar to that of deliberate pretending or make-believe. When you played make-believe as a child, you did not just copy the behavior of the character or creature you were pretending to be; you imagined being that character or creature, and your imagination moved you to behave accordingly.[59] Similarly, when you identify with someone, the image of being that person leads you to move as if inside his body, to speak as if with his voice, even to think and feel as if

character, and this structural feature of the dream may be what implicitly casts him in the role of one's dream-self.

If so, then dreaming of an external figure as oneself is not very different, after all, from dreaming of being that person. Although the dream doesn't represent things as seen or heard by him, it does represent them as emotionally felt by him, and its so representing them is what casts him in the first-personal role. The emotions experienced in the dream are a partial image of being that person, just as a feeling imagined in the throat can be a partial image of being someone who is seen taking a drink. Thus all identification may involve imagining from within the other's perspective in some respect.

[58] On the effects of first-personal imagining, see Wollheim, "Imagination and Identification"; and *The Thread of Life* (Cambridge, MA: Harvard University Press, 1984), chap. 3. I think that empathy itself may be a mode of identification, in which we imagine the world as experienced by someone else emotionally rather than perceptually. My thought here is that the emotions we feel on behalf of the other person play the same role as the sensations that we feel on behalf of the drinking jogger described earlier. To develop this thought, however, I would need to offer a theory of the emotional imagination, explaining how we can feel imaginary emotions in the way that we can taste an imaginary drink. For some remarks in this direction, see my "On the Aim of Belief," in *The Possibility of Practical Reason* (Oxford: Oxford University Press, 2000), 270, n. 51.

[59] I defend this claim at length in "On the Aim of Belief."

with his sensibilities. Your identification with him may thereby become recognizable to observers, if they can detect these echoes of his behavior in yours.

What would happen if we interpreted Frankfurt's term "identification" as referring to this phenomenon, identification as ordinarily understood? Frankfurt's claim that we identify with some of our attitudes would then seem to describe us as imagining ourselves to *be* those attitudes. To identify with a desire or emotion would be to imagine being the desire or emotion. But how could we imagine being one of our own mental states, a proper part of ourselves?[60] How could we identify, in this sense, with something that isn't a whole person?

Come to think of it, there is a famous description of just this process. It goes like this:

> Let us consider this waiter in the café. His movement is quick and forward, a little too precise, a little too rapid. He comes toward the patrons with a step a little too quick. He bends forward a little too eagerly; his voice, his eyes express an interest a little too solicitous for the order of the customer. . . . All his behavior seems to us a game. He applies himself to chaining his movements as if they were mechanisms, the one regulating the other; his gestures and even his voice seem to be mechanisms; he gives himself the quickness and pitiless rapidity of things. He is playing, he is amusing himself. But what is he playing? We need not watch long before we can explain it: he is playing *at being* a waiter in a café.[61]

When Sartre says that this waiter is playing at being a waiter, he means that the waiter is playing at being less than a whole person – a waiter-on-tables and nothing more. The waiter imagines that he is nothing but the nexus of motives and skills exercised in his waiting on tables; that he is, not a person choosing to exercise those motives and skills, but a mechanism wholly composed of them; that he is, so to speak, a waiting machine. The waiter thus identifies with a proper part of himself.

This waiter is Sartre's prime specimen of bad faith, which is a mode of defensive thinking. Of course, the defenses diagnosed by Sartre are fueled by a different anxiety from the defenses diagnosed by Freud: they are fueled by a fear of our radical freedom rather than our threatening emotions. But the strategy of defense described by Sartre is available to the latter anxiety as well. If we are afraid of hating our parents, we can imagine being identical with our love for them – parent-lovers and

---

[60] This question is also raised by Arpaly and Schroeder.
[61] Jean-Paul Sartre, *Being and Nothingness: An Essay on Phenomenological Ontology*, trans. by Hazel E. Barnes (New York: Philosophical Library, 1956), 59.

nothing more. We can imagine shrinking to occupy the loving aspect of our personalities, just as the waiter imagines shrinking to occupy his waiterly motives and skills. Once we have imaginatively retreated to within the boundaries of our love, we can hope to keep our hatred at bay.

When Frankfurt describes us as identifying with some of our motives and alienating others, his description rings true, I suspect, because it accurately describes this common defensive fantasy. We do indeed identify with some of our motives, but we thereby engage not in self-definition but self-deception. We identify with some of our motives by imagining ourselves as *being* those motives, to the exclusion of whatever might complicate or conflict with them.

To repeat, I do not believe that Frankfurt uses the term "identification" in this ordinary sense. I think that he initially introduced the term by stipulation, with the intention that it would carry a new, philosophical meaning. "Identification" was meant to describe the psychological process by which a person empowers some of his motives to implicate him in causing behavior, so that whatever they motivate will be attributable to him, as his doing. The attention that Frankfurt has drawn to the process of identification, so defined, has greatly advanced the philosophy of action over the past twenty years. But I think that Frankfurt's own notion of identification has turned out to involve some assumptions that ought to be reexamined, in light of the conclusions at which he has now arrived.

Frankfurt assumed from the outset that identification works by incorporating motives into something called the self, so that behavior governed by those motives qualifies as self-governed, or autonomous. This assumption is harmless, I think, so long as it leaves open the sense in which the term "self" is being used. The reason some behavior counts as autonomous action, attributable to the subject as his doing, is that it is governed by motives constitutive of something deserving to be called the self in some sense of the word. What has emerged in Frankfurt's recent work, however, is the further assumption that the sense of the word "self" used in an account of autonomy will be the same one that is used in accounts of other phenomena that merit philosophical attention.

Thus, Frankfurt conceives of the self as an inner core or kernel comprising that *in* the person which really *is* the person and whose impact on the world is therefore his. The self so conceived underlies not just autonomy but personal identity as well. It is not just that part of a person whose participation in causing behavior is necessary and sufficient for his participating; it's that part of a person whose existence is necessary and sufficient for his existing. Indeed, it is the former precisely because it is the latter – the source of the person's autonomy because it is the basis of his identity, causing what he can be said to cause by virtue of being what he is.

Similarly, Frankfurt conceives of the self as that to which a person must be true in order to be true to himself, or that which he must not betray lest he be guilty of self-betrayal. Motives constitutive of the self therefore carry a special authority in the subject's practical reasoning. They exercise not only the force of his autonomy but also the claim of his self-worth, and for the same reason – namely, that they constitute what he is.

An Alternative Conception of the Self

I don't believe in the self, so conceived. That is, I don't believe that a person has a proper part that is both the source of his autonomy and the target of his self-regard because of being the basis of his identity. Expounding my own views is not the purpose of this essay, but I want to state them briefly in order to illustrate that believing in the self is optional.[62]

In my view, "self" is just a word used to express reflexivity – that is, the coincidence of object and subject, either of a verb or of the activity that it represents. ("She accidentally cut herself.") In many philosophical contexts, "self" expresses the reflexivity of representations, especially their notional reflexivity, the property they possess when they represent their object *as* their subject. ("He's always talking about himself.") In this sense, "self" is used to report indirectly a thought or utterance that originally contained a first-person pronoun. We use "self" to report a thought or utterance containing "I" just as we use "present" to report a thought or utterance containing "now."

As a word expressing reflexivity, "self" has various uses in various contexts, including several contexts that are of interest to philosophy. "Self" can express the reflexivity of the control that an autonomous agent exerts over his own behavior; the reflexivity of the memories and anticipations that link a temporally extended person to his past and future; or the reflexivity of any first-personal attitudes that he may hold. Although "self" expresses reflexivity in each of these contexts, there is no single entity to which it refers in all of them. We shouldn't assume, in other words, that there is something called The Self that governs a person's behavior when

[62] The views stated in this section are developed more fully in my "What Happens When Someone Acts?"

it is self-governed, persists so long as the person remains himself, and is the object of his self-concept or self-image.

I want to explain briefly how I understand the term "self" in these philosophical contexts. I begin with the context of personal identity.

I think that a person's past or future selves are just the past or future persons whom he can pick out with thoughts that are notionally reflexive, or first-personal.[63] There is no kernel or core whose presence in past or future persons makes them selves of his; there are only the psychological connections that mediate his reflexive references to them, thus enabling him to think of them first-personally. Locke was right to name experiential memory as the psychological medium connecting a person to his past selves, because replaying past experiences is how the person naturally and without contrivance thinks of past individuals as "me." I would merely add that there are experiential forms of anticipation that can mediate first-personal reference to future persons as "me," thus linking the subject to his future selves.

This conception of selfhood implies that a philosophical theory of the self should have as little substance as a philosophical theory of the present. We can theorize about the reflexive aspect of things, just as we can theorize about their present aspect, but we must avoid reifying the present or the self.[64]

If a person's relation to past and future selves doesn't depend on a shared subset of attributes and attitudes, then it doesn't depend on anything that might be the object of his self-regard. The self for whom the person may have esteem, and with whom he can keep or break faith, is not an inner core of traits and states that he must retain in order to remain himself.

In this latter usage, I think, the term "self" refers – not to the person, or a part of the person, represented reflexively – but to the person's own reflexive representations, which make up his self-image or self-conception.[65] This sense of the word "self" crops up frequently in

---

[63] This paragraph summarizes the thesis of my "Self to Self" (Chapter 8 in the present volume). Also relevant here is Rom Harré's contrast between the self as a point-of-view and the self as a bundle of personal qualities in *The Singular Self: An Introduction to the Psychology of Personhood* (London: Sage Publications, 1998).

[64] Here again see Rubin's critique of Winnicott's "True Self Concept."

[65] See, e.g., Frederic J. Levine and Robert Kravis, "Psychoanalytic Theories of the Self: Contrasting Clinical Approaches to the New Narcissism," in *The Book of the Self: Person, Pretext, and Process*, eds. Polly Young-Eisendrath and James A. Hall (New York: New York

the field known as self-psychology, where it is often paired with a corresponding sense of the word "identity." When someone suffers an identity crisis, as we call it, what is threatened is not his identity as a person but his conception of himself as a person, which might also be called his sense of identity or his sense of who he is.

In this context, I am happy to say that particular cares and concerns can be definitive of a person's identity or essential to the self.[66] That he has these motives may be a fundamental, organizing principle of a person's self-understanding, without which the rest of his self-image would no longer cohere. If he had to stop thinking of himself as having these motives, he would temporarily lack any coherent conception of himself as a person, and so he might be described as no longer knowing who he was. But the fact that jettisoning the representation of these motives from his current self-image would result, temporarily, in his no longer knowing who he was – this fact doesn't mean that jettisoning the motives themselves would result in his never again being who he is. These motives are essential to his self, or identity, in the sense that refers to his self-conception, which can in time be revised or replaced if his actual motives should change.[67]

This abstract distinction may be clarified by an example. A philosopher recently told me that when he discusses same-sex marriage in his Introduction to Political Philosophy, the fundamentalist Christians in the class find the subject threatening to their identities.[68] Frankfurt might explain

University Press, 1987), 306–330; J. F. Kihlstrom and N. Cantor, "Mental Representations of the Self," in *Advances in Experimental and Social Psychology*, ed. L. Berkowitz (New York: Academic Press, 1984), vol. 17, 2–40.

[66] This sense of the word also allows us to say that the Rat Man's strategies of repression were strategies of expelling unwelcome emotions from the self. For as I explained earlier, the Rat Man repressed his hatred by writing it out of his self-conception. (See "Notes Upon a Case," 194, and my note 48.)

[67] Frankfurt sometimes speaks of a person's "sense" or "grasp" of his identity, or "the clarity with which he comprehends who he is" ("On the Necessity of Ideals," 108–109; see also "Rationality and the Unthinkable, 177). But he doesn't adequately distinguish the person's grasp of his identity from the identity so grasped. He thus slides from the statement that "extensive proliferation of [a person's] options may weaken his grasp of his own identity" ("Rationality and the Unthinkable," 177; see also "On the Necessity of Ideals," 109: "Extensive growth in the variety of a person's options may weaken his sense of his identity") to the statement that "an excess of freedom gives rise to a diminution, or even to a dissolution, of the reality of the self" ("Rationality and the Unthinkable," 179; see also "On the Necessity of Ideals," 110: "With total freedom, there can be no individual identity").

[68] Thanks to John Exdell for this useful example.

this phenomenon by pointing out that the doctrinal commitments of these students involve various volitional necessities, such as an inability to condone homosexuality or even to wish that they could condone it, or a similarly structured inability to question the dictates of scripture. If the students allow these essential aspects of their natures to change, they would bring their current selves to an end – a "drastic psychic injury," in Frankfurt's view.[69] Frankfurt's view thus seems to imply that these students are justified to resist any change of mind on the issue, on grounds of self-preservation.

I would say that a commitment to religious doctrines is essential to these students' identities only in the sense that it is central to their self-conceptions. They think of themselves as Christians first and foremost, and much else that they believe about themselves is based on this premise. If they had to question their faith in the doctrines that they regard as essential to Christianity, they would have to question most of what they currently believe about themselves. Changing their minds on doctrinal matters is therefore threatening to their identities because it threatens to enforce a major revision in their self-conceptions. They would still be themselves after changing their minds, but they would have temporarily lost their grasp of who they are. Some resistance to such radical change may well be justified, but not as much as would be justified for the sake of literal self-preservation.

I have now explained what an aspectual interpretation of "self" implies for discourse about personal identity and self-regard. In discourse about personal identity, "self" refers to those past or future persons whom the subject can denote reflexively, as "me"; in discourse about self-regard, it denotes the subject's reflexive representation, his self-concept or self-image. I turn, finally, to discourse about autonomy, or self-governance. My aspectual interpretation of "self" doesn't require me to deny that a person has a source of autonomy that might be called his essential self: the source of a person's autonomy can be his essential self in an aspectual sense.[70]

Suppose that a person has a part that he is unable to regard non-reflexively, a part on which he cannot attain a truly detached, third-personal perspective. That part of him will be essentially "self" to him,

---

[69] Quoted at note 18.
[70] I discuss this claim in the introduction to *The Possibility of Practical Reason.*

in the sense that it is inalienably "me" from his perspective. Its being his essential self won't mean that it is essential to his identity; only that it always presents a reflexive aspect to his thinking.

Maybe an analogy would help. Consider that spot, right between your eyes, which is at the origin of your visual perspective – the vertex of all the angles that your visual images subtend. That spot is your visual location, or visual standpoint, in the sense that you always see things as projected onto that point. Of course, you can look at yourself in the mirror and refer to the relevant point in space as "over there," in the mirror. But even when you look at it "over there," you are still looking at it *from* that point, and so it remains "back here" as well.

Now, is your visual standpoint an essential part of your visual apparatus? No. Indeed, it isn't a part of your visual apparatus at all. It's just a part of you that always presents a particular aspect to you – the aspect of being visually "here," at the geometric origin of your visual perspective.[71] Surely, we would be making a mistake to regard this point as the origin of your vision in any other sense.

If there is a part of your personality with which you necessarily think about things, then it will be your mental standpoint, always presenting a reflexive aspect to your thought. You will be able to think about this part of your personality as "it," but only from a perspective in which it continues to function as the thinking "I" – just as you can find a reflection of your visual location "over there" only from a perspective in which it is also "back here."

I believe that this phenomenon is what Aristotle had in mind when he said that "each person seems to be his understanding."[72] A person can never conceive of his own conceptual capacity from a purely third-personal perspective, because he can conceive of it only *with* that capacity, and hence from a perspective in which it continues to occupy first-person position. Just as the person cannot attain a visual perspective from which the point between his eyes isn't "here," so he cannot attain a cognitive perspective from which his understanding isn't "I." That's why the person seems to be his understanding.

---

[71] As Dan Dennett demonstrates in his paper "Where Am I?" your visual standpoint can migrate out of your body with the help of prosthetic sense-organs. In *Brainstorms: Philosophical Essays on Mind and Psychology* (Cambridge, MA: MIT Press, 1981), 310–23. I take myself to be making the same point as Dennett – namely, that your visual location is a merely aspectual matter.

[72] *Nicomachean Ethics*, 1178a.

This Aristotelian observation does not imply that a person's understanding is his essence or the basis of his identity through time. On the contrary, it comports best with the view that his past and future selves are determined aspectually, too, as the past and future persons whom he can think of first-personally, as "me." Their being his past and future selves need have nothing to do with whether they preserve some component of his psyche.

I believe that a person's understanding makes a distinctive contribution to just those behaviors which count as his autonomous actions. Roughly speaking, my view is that autonomous action is behavior motivated in part by the understanding. How the understanding motivates is a question beyond the scope of this essay. What's relevant here is that this part of a person can be the locus of his autonomy, and by virtue of being his essential self, without necessarily constituting his essence or identity as a person. Autonomy can be an aspectual matter, a matter of whether behavior originates in a part of the person that inevitably presents a reflexive aspect to him.[73]

This conception of autonomy remains deeply indebted to Frankfurt. The guiding insight of Frankfurt's work is that a person's capacity to act autonomously rests on his capacity to reflect on aspects of his personality and to feel a special relation to some of them. My aspectual conception of autonomy is little more than a reinterpretation of this insight.

In fact, my aspectual conception of autonomy is just a reinterpretation of a statement from Frankfurt's most recent work on the subject. What Frankfurt now says, in part, is that autonomous behavior is motivated by parts of the subject with which he cannot help identifying.[74] If "identification" is read as a term for first-personal thinking – for thinking

---

[73] My claim that selfhood is an aspectual matter does not apply to personhood. What makes someone a person is not merely that he presents a particular aspect to himself; what makes him a person includes various other facts about him, including the fact that he is autonomous. Of course, his autonomy consists in the fact that his behavior is governed partly by his understanding, which inevitably presents a reflexive aspect to him, thus qualifying as his essential self; and being governed by such a self is part of what makes him a person; but the self by which he is governed must not be conflated or confused with the person he thus becomes.

In "Self to Self" (Chapter 8 in the present volume), I argue for a similar distinction between selfhood and personhood in the discussion of personal identity. A person's past and future selves are those past and future persons who present a particular aspect to him, but they need not be the same person.

[74] See the quotations at note 10.

of something as "me" or "mine" – then Frankfurt's statement simply becomes the aspectual thesis.

Like much philosophy of action over the past twenty years, then, my view can be expressed as a commentary on Frankfurt – specifically, on what Frankfurt meant, or should have meant, by "identification." I agree with Frankfurt that autonomous action is guided by a part of us with which we cannot help identifying; I disagree mainly with his claim that our identifying with a part of ourselves incorporates it into something called the self.

Bibliography

Allison, Henry E., *Kant's Theory of Freedom* (Cambridge: Cambridge University Press, 1990).

Anderson, Elizabeth, *Value in Ethics and Economics* (Cambridge, MA: Harvard University Press, 1993).

Andrews, John D.W., *The Active Self in Psychotherapy: An Integration of Therapeutic Styles* (Boston: Allyn & Bacon, 1991).

Annas, Julia, "Personal Love and Kantian Ethics in *Effi Briest*," in *Friendship: A Philosophical Reader*, ed. Neera Kapur Badhwar (Ithaca, NY: Cornell University Press, 1993), 155–73.

Anscombe, Elizabeth, "The First Person," in her *Metaphysics and the Philosophy of Mind: Collected Papers* (Oxford: Blackwell, 1981), 21–36.

Anscombe, Elizabeth, *Intention* (Ithaca, NY: Cornell University Press, 1957); reprinted (Cambridge, MA: Harvard University Press, 2000).

Anscombe, Roderick, "The Myth of the True Self," *Psychiatry* 52 (1989): 209–17.

Aristotle, *Nichomachean Ethics*.

Aronson, E., "Dissonance theory: Progress and problems," in *Theories of Cognitive Consistency: A Sourcebook*, ed. Robert P. Ableson, Elliot Aronson, William J. McGuire, Theodore M. Newcomb, Milton J. Rosenberg, and Percy H. Tannenbaum (Chicago: Rand McNally, 1968), 5–27.

Aronson, E., "The Theory of Cognitive Dissonance: a Current Perspective, *Advances in Experimental Social Psychology* 4 (1969): 1–34.

Aronson, E., "The Return of the Repressed: Dissonance Theory Makes a Comeback," *Psychological Inquiry* 3 (1992): 303–311.

Aronson, E., and Carlsmith, J.M., "Performance expectancy as a determinant of actual performance," *Journal of Abnormal and Social Psychology* 65 (1962): 178–82.

Arpaly, Nomy, and Schroeder, Timothy, "Alienation and Externality," *Canadian Journal of Philosophy* 29 (1999): 371–387.

Augustine, St., *The City of God*, transl. Marcus Dods (New York: The Modern Library, 1950).

Aune, Bruce, "Speaking of Selves," *Philosophical Quarterly* 44 (1994): 279–93.

Badhwar, Neera Kapur, "Friends as Ends in Themselves," *Philosophy and Phenomenological Research* 48 (1987): 1–25.

Badhwar, Neera Kapur (listed as Kapur, Neera Badhwar), "Why It Is Wrong to Be Always Guided by the Best: Consequentialism and Friendship," *Ethics* 101 (1991): 483–504.

Baier, Annette, "The Moral Perils of Intimacy," in *Pragmatism's Freud: The Moral Disposition of Psychoanalysis*, ed. Joseph H. Smith and William Kerrigan (Baltimore: Johns Hopkins University Press, 1986), 93–101.

Baron, Marcia, "On Admirable Immorality," *Ethics* 96 (1986): 557–66.

Baron, Marcia, "Impartiality and Friendship," *Ethics* 101 (1991): 836–57.

Baron, Marcia, *Kantian Ethics Almost without Apology* (Ithaca, NY: Cornell University Press, 1995).

Baumann, Paul, and Betzler, Monika (eds.), *Practical Conflicts: New Philosophical Essays* (Cambridge: Cambridge University Press, 2004).

Bem, D.J., "Self-perception theory," in *Advances in Experimental Social Psychology*, Vol. 6, ed. Leonard Berkowitz (New York: Academic Press, 1972), 1–62.

Benhabib, Seyla, "The Generalized and the Concrete Other: The Kohlberg-Gilligan Controversy and Moral Theory," in *Women and Moral Theory*, ed. Eva Feder Kittay and Diana T. Meyers (Totowa, NJ: Rowman and Littlefield, 1987), 154–177.

Berkowitz, L., "Mood, self-awareness, and willingness to help," *Journal of Personality and Social Psychology* 52 (1987): 721–29.

Berkowitz, L., & Turner, C., "Perceived anger level, instigating agent, and aggression," in *Cognitive Alteration of Feeling States*, ed. H. London and R.E. Nisbett (Chicago: Aldine, 1974), 174–89.

Bermúdez, José Luis, *The Paradox of Self-Consciousness* (Cambridge, MA: MIT Press, 1998).

Bettelheim, Bruno, *Freud and Man's Soul* (New York: Vintage, 1984).

Blackburn, Simon, "Has Kant Refuted Parfit?" in *Reading Parfit*, ed. Jonathan Dancy (Oxford: Blackwell, 1997) 180–202.

Blackburn, Simon, *Ruling Passions* (Oxford: Clarendon Press, 1998).

Blum, Lawrence A., *Friendship, Altruism and Morality* (London: Routledge & Kegan Paul, 1980).

Blum, Lawrence, "Iris Murdoch and the Domain of the Moral," *Philosophical Studies* 50 (1986): 343–67.

Boër, Stephen E., and Lycan, William G., *Knowing Who* (Cambridge, MA: MIT Press, 1986).

Borch-Jacobsen, Mikkel, *The Freudian Subject*, transl. Catherine Porter (Stanford: Stanford University Press, 1988).

Brakel, Linda, "Phantasy and Wish: A Proper Function Account for Human A-Rational Primary Process Mediated Mentation," *Australasian Journal of Philosophy* 80 (2002): 1–16.

Branden, Nathaniel, "Love and Psychological Visibility," in *Friendship: A Philosophical Reader*, ed. Neera Kapur Badhwar (Ithaca, NY: Cornell University Press, 1993), 64–72.

Bratman, Michael, *Intention, Plans, and Practical Reason* (Cambridge, MA: Harvard University Press, 1987).

Bratman, Michael, "Identification, Decision, and Treating as a Reason," in his *Faces of Intention* (Cambridge: Cambridge University Press, 1999), 185–206.

Bratman, Michael, "Reflection, Planning, and Temporally Extended Agency," *Philosophical Review* 109 (2000): 35–61.

Brewer, Bill, "Self-Location and Agency," *Mind* 101 (1992): 17–34.

Brodt, S.E., and Zimbardo, P.G., "Modifying shyness-related social behavior through symptom misattribution," *Journal of Personality and Social Psychology* 41 (1981): 437–49.

Buss, Sarah, and Overton, Lee (eds.) *Contours of Agency: Essays on Themes from Harry Frankfurt* (Cambridge, MA: MIT Press, 2002).

Calhoun, Cheshire, "An Apology for Moral Shame" (forthcoming in the *Journal of Political Philosophy*).

Campbell, John, "The Reductionist View of the Self," in *Reduction, Explanation, and Realism*, ed. David Charles and Kathleen Lennon, (Oxford: Clarendon Press, 1992), 380–419.

Campbell, John, "Self-Reference and Self-Knowledge," in *Past, Space, and Self* (Cambridge, MA: MIT Press, 1994), Chapter 4.

Cantor, J.R., Zillman, D., and Bryant, J., "Enhancement of experienced sexual arousal in response to erotic stimuli through misattribution of unrelated residual excitation," *Journal of Personality and Social Psychology*, 32 (1975): 69–75.

Cavell, Marcia, "Knowing and Valuing: Some Questions of Genealogy," in *Psychoanalysis, Mind and Art: Perspectives on Richard Wollheim*, ed. Jim Hopkins and Anthony Saville (Oxford: Blackwell, 1992), 68–86.

Cavell, Stanley, "The Avoidance of Love: A Reading of *King Lear*," in his *Must We Mean What We Say? A Book of Essays* (Cambridge: Cambridge University Press, 1976), 267–353.

Cohen, G.A., "Reason, Humanity, and the Moral Law," in *The Sources of Normativity*, ed. Onora O'Neill (Cambridge: Cambridge University Press, 1996) 167–70.

Coltart, Nina, "Attention," in her *Slouching towards Bethlehem* (New York: Guildford, 1992), 176–93.

Conly, Sarah, "The Objectivity of Morals and the Subjectivity of Agents," *American Philosophical Quarterly* 22 (1985): 275–86.

Conly, Sarah, "Utilitarianism and Integrity," *Monist* 66 (1983): 298–311.

Cooper, J., Zanna, M.P., and Taves, P.A., "Arousal as a necessary condition for attitude change following induced compliance," *Journal of Personality & Social Psychology* 36 (1978): 1101–1106.

Copp, David, "Korsgaard on Normativity, Identity, and the Ground of Obligation," in *Rationality, Realism, Revision: Proceedings of the Third International Congress of the Society for Analytical Philosophy*, vol. 23 of *Perspektiven der Analytischen Philosophie*, ed. Julian Nida-Rümelin (Berlin: de Gruyter, 1999), 572–581.

Cottingham, John, "Ethics and Impartiality," *Philosophical Studies* 43 (1983): 83–99.

Cross, S.E., and Markus, H.R., "The Willful Self," *Personality and Social Psychology Bulletin* 16 (1990): 726–42.

Darwall, Stephen L., "Two Kinds of Respect," *Ethics* 88 (1977): 36–49.

Darwall, Stephen L., *The British Moralists and the Internal 'Ought' 1640–1740* (Cambridge: Cambridge University Press, 1995), Chapter 9.

Darwall, Stephen L., "Self-Interest and Self-Concern," *Social Philosophy and Policy* 14 (1997): 158–78.

Darwall, Stephen L., "Empathy, Sympathy, Care," *Philosophical Studies* 89 (1998): 261–82.

Davidson, D., *Essays on Actions and Events* (Oxford: Clarendon Press, 1980).

Deci, E.L., and Ryan, R.M., "A motivational approach to self: Integration in Personality," *Perspectives on Motivation, Nebraska Symposium on Motivation 1990*, ed. Richard Dienstbier (Lincoln: University of Nebraska Press, 1991), 237–88.

Deigh, John, "Shame and Self-Esteem: A Critique," *Ethics* 93 (1983): 225–45.

Deigh, John, "Freud, Naturalism, and Modern Moral Philosophy," in his *The Sources of Moral Agency: Essays in Moral Psychology and Freudian Theory* (Cambridge: Cambridge University Press, 1996a), Chapter 6.

Deigh, John, "Remarks on Some Difficulties in Freud's Theory of Moral Development," in his *The Sources of Moral Agency: Essays in Moral Psychology and Freudian Theory* (Cambridge: Cambridge University Press, 1996b), Chapter 4.

Delaney, Neil, "Romantic Love and Loving Commitment: Articulating a Modern Ideal," *American Philosophical Quarterly* 33 (1996): 339–56.

Dennett, Daniel, "Where Am I?" in his *Brainstorms: Philosophical Essays on Mind and Psychology* (Cambridge, MA: MIT Press, 1981), 310–23.

Dennett, Daniel, "The Origins of Selves," *Cogito* 3 (1989): 163–73.

Dennett, Daniel, "The Reality of Selves," in his *Consciousness Explained* (Boston: Little, Brown and Company, 1991), Chapter 13.

Dennett, Daniel, "The Self as a Center of Narrative Gravity," in *Self and Consciousness: Multiple Perspectives*, ed. Frank S. Kessel, Pamela M. Cole, and Dale L. Johnson (Hillsdale, NJ: Erlbaum Associates, 1992) 103–115.

Dennett, Daniel, with Humphrey, Nicholas, "Speaking for Our Selves," in his *Brainchildren: Essays on Designing Minds* (Cambridge, MA: MIT Press, 1998), 31–58.

Dent, N.J.H., "Duty and Inclination," *Mind* 83 (1974): 552–70.

Dillon, Robin S., "Respect and Care: Toward Moral Integration," *Canadian Journal of Philosophy* 22 (1992a): 105–32.

Dillon, Robin S., "Toward a Feminist Conception of Self-Respect," *Hypatia* 7 (1992b): 52–69.

Dipboye, R.L., "A critical review of Korman's self-consistency theory of work motivation and occupational choice," *Organizational Behavior and Human Performance* 18 (1977): 108–26.

Downie, R.S., and Telfer, Elizabeth, *Respect for Persons* (New York: Shocken, 1970).

Dr. Seuss, *Horton Hears a Who!* (New York: Random House, 1954).

Dr. Seuss, *Happy Birthday to You!* (New York: Random House, 1959).

Eagle, Morris, "Psychoanalysis and the Personal," in *Mind, Psychoanalysis and Science*, ed. P. Clark and C. Wright (Oxford: Blackwell, 1988), 91–111.

Eagle, Morris, "Psychoanalytic Conceptions of the Self," in *The Self: Interdisciplinary Approaches*, ed. J. Strauss and G.R. Goethals (New York: Springer-Verlag, 1991), 49–65.

Eisenberg, N., Cialdini, R.B., McCreath, H., and Shell, R., "Consistency-based compliance: When and why do children become vulnerable?" *Journal of Personality and Social Psychology* 52 (1987): 1174–81.

Eisenberg, N., Cialdini, R.B., McCreath, H., and Shell, R., "Consistency-based compliance in children: When and why do consistency procedures have immediate effects?" *International Journal of Behavioural Development* 12 (1989): 351–67.

Eliot, George, *Felix Holt* (London: Penguin, 1995).

Elliot, A.J., and Devine, P.G., "On the motivational nature of cognitive dissonance: Dissonance as psychological discomfort," *Journal of Personality and Social Psychology* 67 (1994): 382–94.

Ellison, Ralph, *Invisible Man* (New York: New American Library, 1952).

Elster, Jon, *Strong Feelings: Emotion, Addiction, and Human Behavior* (Cambridge, MA: MIT Press, 1999).

Epstein, Mark, *Thoughts Without a Thinker: Psychotherapy From a Buddhist Perspective* (New York: Basic Books, 1995).

Epstein, S., "The Self-Concept Revisited; Or a Theory of a Theory," *American Psychologist* 28 (1973): 404–416.

Epstein, S., "The Unity Principle Versus the Reality and Pleasure Principles, *Or* the Tale of the Scorpion and the Frog," in *Self-Concept: Advances in Theory and Research*, ed. M.D. Lynch, A.A. Norem-Hebeisen, and K.J. Gergen (Cambridge, MA: Ballinger, 1981).

Erikson, Erik, *Identity, Youth, and Crisis* (New York: W.W. Norton, 1968), 74–90.

Evans, Gareth, *The Varieties of Reference* (Oxford: Oxford University Press, 1982).

Fairbairn, W.R.D., *Psychoanalytic Studies of the Personality* (London: Routledge, 1990).

Fazio, R.H., Zanna, M.P., and Cooper, J., "Dissonance and self-perception: An integrative view of each theory's proper domain of application," *Journal of Experimental Social Psychology* 13 (1977): 464–479.

Festinger, L., and Carlsmith, J.M., "Cognitive Consequences of Forced Compliance," *Journal of Abnormal and Social Psychology* 58 (1959), 203–11.

Flanagan, Owen, "Multiple Identity, Character Transformation, and Self-Reclamation," in *Philosophical Psychopathology*, eds. G. Graham and Lynn Stephens, (Cambridge, MA: MIT Press, 1994), Chapter 7; reprinted in his *Self Expressions* (Oxford: Oxford University Press, 1996), 65–87.

Foot, Philippa, "Are Moral Considerations Overriding?" in her *Virtues and Vices* (Berkeley: University of California Press, 1978a), 181–88.

Foot, Philippa, "Morality as a System of Hypothetical Imperatives," in her *Virtues and Vices* (Berkeley: University of California Press, 1978b), 157–73.

Frankena, William K., "The Ethics of Respect for Persons," *Philosophical Topics* 14 (1986): 149–67.

Frankfurt, Harry, "Identification and Wholeheartedness," in his *The Importance of What We Care About* (Cambridge: Cambridge University Press, 1988a), Chapter 12.

Frankfurt, Harry, "Rationality and the Unthinkable," in his *The Importance of What We Care About* (Cambridge: Cambridge University Press, 1988b), Chapter 13.

Frankfurt, Harry, *The Importance of What We Care About* (Cambridge: Cambridge University Press, 1988c).

Frankfurt, Harry, "Autonomy, Necessity, and Love," in *Vernunftbegriffe in der Moderne*, ed. Hans Friedrich Fulda and Rolf-Peter Horstmann (Klett-Cotta, 1994), 433–47; reprinted in his *Necessity, Volition, and Love* (Cambridge, Cambridge University Press, 1999).

Frankfurt, Harry, "Some Thoughts about Caring," *Ethical Perspectives* 5 (1998): 3–14.

Frankfurt, Harry, "On the Necessity of Ideals," in his *Necessity, Volition, and Love* (Cambridge: Cambridge University Press, 1999a), Chapter 9.

Frankfurt, Harry, "The Faintest Passion," in his *Necessity, Volition, and Love* (Cambridge: Cambridge University Press, 1999b), Chapter 8.

Frankfurt, Harry, *Necessity, Volition, and Love* (Cambridge: Cambridge University Press, 1999c).

Freedman, J.L., and Fraser, S.C., "Compliance without pressure: The foot-in-the-door technique," *Journal of Personality and Social Psychology* 4 (1966): 195–202.

Freud, Anna, *The Ego and the Mechanisms of Defense* (London: Hogarth Press, 1937), 109–121; reprinted in *Pivotal Papers on Identification*, ed. George H. Pollock (Madison, CT: International Universities Press, 1993), 105–14.

Freud, Sigmund, "Group Psychology and the Analysis of the Ego," in *S.E.*, vol. 18, 67–143.

Freud, Sigmund, "Instincts and Their Vicissitudes," in *S.E.*, vol. 14, 111–40.

Freud, Sigmund, "Notes Upon a Case of Obsessional Neurosis," in *S.E.*, vol. 10, 153–249.

Freud, Sigmund, "Observations on Transference-Love," in *S.E.*, vol. 12, 157–71.

Freud, Sigmund, "On Narcissism: An Introduction," in *S.E.*, vol. 14, 67–102.

Freud, Sigmund, "Psycho-Analysis," in *S.E.*, vol. 20, 261–70.

Freud, Sigmund, "Recommendations to Physicians Practicing Psycho-Analysis," in *S.E.*, vol. 12, 111–20.

Freud, Sigmund, "The Economic Problem of Masochism," in *S.E.*, vol. 19, 156–70.

Freud, Sigmund, "The Libido Theory," in *S.E.*, vol. 18, 255–59.

Freud, Sigmund, "Three Essays on the Theory of Sexuality," in *S.E.*, vol. 7, 125–243.

Freud, Sigmund, *An Autobiographical Study*, in *S.E.*, vol. 20, 3–74.

Freud, Sigmund, *Civilization and Its Discontents*, *S.E.*, vol. 21, 59–145.

Freud, Sigmund, *Five Lectures on Psychoanalysis*, in *S.E.*, vol. 11, 3–55.

Freud, Sigmund, *Group Psychology*, in *S.E.*, vol. 18, 69–143.

Freud, Sigmund, *Inhibitions, Symptoms and Anxiety*, in *S.E.*, vol. 20, 77–175.

Freud, Sigmund, *Introductory Lectures on Psychoanalysis*, in *S.E.*, vol. 16.

Freud, Sigmund, *Moses and Monotheism*, in *S.E.*, vol. 23, 3–137.

Freud, Sigmund, *New Introductory Lectures in Psychoanalysis*, in *S.E.*, vol. 22, 3–182.

Freud, Sigmund, *Outline of Psychoanalysis*, in *S.E.*, vol. 23, 141–207.

Freud, Sigmund, *The Ego and the Id*, in *S.E.*, vol. 19, 3–66.

Freud, Sigmund, *The Standard Edition of the Complete Psychological Works of Sigmund Freud*, ed. James Strachey et al. (London: Hogarth Press and the Institute of Psycho-Analysis, 1953–1974).

Freud, Sigmund, *Totem and Taboo*, in *S.E.*, vol. 13, ix–162.

Gewirth, Alan, "Ethical Universalism and Particularism," *Journal of Philosophy* 85 (1988): 283–302.

Gibbard, Allan, *Wise Choices, Apt Feelings: A Theory of Normative Judgment* (Cambridge, MA: Harvard University Press, 1990).

Gilbert, Margaret, *On Social Facts* (Princeton: Princeton University Press, 1992).

Goldman, M., Seever, M., and Seever, M., "Social labeling and the foot-in-the-door effect," *The Journal of Social Psychology* 117 (1982): 19–23.

Gorasini, D.R., and Olson, J.M., "Does self-perception change explain the foot-in-the-door effect?" *Journal of Personality and Social Psychology* 69 (1995): 91–105.

Green, O.H., *The Emotions: A Philosophical Theory* (Boston: Kluwer, 1992).

Green, O.H., "Is Love an Emotion?" *Love Analyzed*, ed. Roger E. Lamb (Boulder, CO.: Westview, 1997) 209–24.

Greenspan, Patricia, *Emotions and Reason: An Inquiry into Emotional Justification* (New York: Routledge, 1988).

Greenwald, A.G., Carnot, C.G., Beach, R., and Young, B., "Increasing Voting Behavior by Asking People if They Expect to Vote," *Journal of Applied Psychology* 72 (1987): 315–18.

Grusec, J.E., and Redler, E., "Attribution, reinforcement, and altruism: A developmental analysis," *Developmental Psychology* 16 (1980): 525–34.

Guyer, Paul, "The Possibility of the Categorical Imperative," *Philosophical Review* 104 (1995): 353–85.

Hamilton, Andy, "A New Look at Personal Identity," *The Philosophical Quarterly* 45 (1995): 332–49.

Hardcastle, Valerie Gray, and Flanagan, Owen, "Multiplex vs. Multiple Selves: Distinguishing Dissociative Disorders," *The Monist* 82 (1999): 645–57.

Harman, Gilbert, *Change in View: Principles of Reasoning* (Cambridge, MA: Bradford Books, 1986).

Harmon-Jones, E., and Mills, J. (eds.), *Cognitive Dissonance: Progress on a Pivotal Theory in Social Psychology* (Washington, DC: American Psychological Association, 1999).

Harré, Rom, *Social Being* (Oxford: Basil Blackwell, 1979).

Harré, Rom, *The Singular Self: An Introduction to the Psychology of Personhood* (London: Sage Publications, 1998).

Hatzimoysis, Anthony (ed.), *Philosophy and the Emotions* (New York: Cambridge University Press, 2003).

Hawthorne, Nathaniel, *The Scarlet Letter* (New York: Bantam Books, 1986).

Herman, Barbara, *The Practice of Moral Judgement* (Cambridge, MA: Harvard University Press, 1993).

Higgins, E.T., Rhodewalt, F., and Zanna, M.P., "Dissonance motivation: Its nature, persistence, and reinstatement," *Journal of Experimental Social Psychology* 15 (1979): 16–34.

Hill, Thomas E., Jr., "Humanity as an End in Itself," in his *Dignity and Practical Reason in Kant's Moral Theory* (Ithaca, NY: Cornell University Press, 1992), 38–57.

Hollis, Martin, *Models of Man* (Cambridge: Cambridge University Press, 1977).

Hussain, Nadeem, "The Guise of A Reason," 121 (2004) *Philosophical Studies*: 263–75.

Ishiguro, Hidé, "Imagination II," *Proceedings of the Aristotelian Society* Supp. Vol. 41 (1967): 37–56.

Jackson, Frank, "Decision-Theoretic Consequentialism and the Nearest and Dearest Objection," *Ethics* 101 (1991): 461–82.

Jensen, R.E., and Moore, S.G., "The effect of attribute statements on cooperativeness and competitiveness in school-age boys," *Child Development* 48 (1977): 305–07.

Jeske, Diane, "Friendship, Virtue, and Impartiality," *Philosophy and Phenomenological Research* 57 (1997): 51–72.

Johnson, Edward, "Ignoring Persons," in *Respect for Persons*, ed. O.H. Green, *Tulane Studies in Philosophy* 31 (1982): 91–105.

Jones, David H., "Freud's Theory of Moral Conscience," *Philosophy* 41 (1966): 34–57.

Jussim, L., Eccles, J., and Madon, S., "Social perception, social stereotypes, and teacher expectations: Accuracy and the quest for the powerful self-fulfilling prophecy," in *Advances in Experimental Social Psychology*, Vol. 28, ed. M.P. Zanna (New York: Academic Press, 1996), 281–388.

Jussim, L., Yen, H.J., and Aiello, J.R., "Self-consistency, self-enhancement, and accuracy in reactions to feedback," *Journal of Experimental and Social Psychology* 31 (1995): 322–56.

Kant, Immanuel, *Critique of Practical Reason*, transl. Lewis White Beck (Indianapolis: Bobbs-Merrill, 1956).

Kant, Immanuel, *Groundwork of the Metaphysic of Morals*, transl. H.J. Paton (New York: Harper and Row, 1964).

Kant, Immanuel, *Critique of Pure Reason*, transl. Norman Kemp Smith (New York: St. Martin's Press, 1965).

Kant, Immmanuel, "On the Proverb: That May be True in Theory, But Is of No Practical Use," in *Perpetual Peace and Other Essays*, transl. Ted Humphrey (Indianapolis: Hackett Publishing, 1983), 61–92.

Kant, Immanuel, *The Metaphysics of Morals*, transl. Mary Gregor (Cambridge: Cambridge University Press, 1996).

Kant, Immanuel, *Groundwork of the Metaphysics of Morals*, transl. Mary Gregor (Cambridge: Cambridge University Press, 1997).

Kavka, Gregory, "The Toxin Puzzle," *Analysis* 43 (1983): 33–36.

Kekes, John, "Morality and Impartiality," *American Philosophical Quarterly* 18 (1981): 295–303.

Kelley, H.H., "Attribution theory in social psychology," in *Nebraska Symposium on Motivation, 1967*, Vol. 15 of *Current Theory and Research in Motivation*, ed. David Levine (Lincoln: University of Nebraska Press, 1967), 192–238.

Kihlstrom, J.F., and Cantor, N., "Mental Representations of the Self," in *Advances in Experimental and Social Psychology*, ed. L. Berkowitz (New York: Academic Press, 1984), vol. 17, 2–40.

Korman, A.K., "Toward an Hypothesis of Work Behavior," 54 *Journal of Applied Psychology* 54 (1970): 31–41.

Korsgaard, Christine, "Skepticism about Practical Reason," *Journal of Philosophy* 83 (1986): 5–25.

Korsgaard, Christine, "An Introduction to the Ethical, Political, and Religious Thought of Kant," in her *Creating the Kingdom of Ends* (Cambridge: Cambridge University Press, 1996a), 3–42.

Korsgaard, Christine, "Kant's Analysis of Obligation: the Argument of *Groundwork I*," in her *Creating the Kingdom of Ends* (Cambridge: Cambridge University Press, 1996b), 43–76.

Korsgaard, Christine, "Kant's Formula of Universal Law," in her *Creating the Kingdom of Ends* (Cambridge: Cambridge University Press, 1996c), 77–105.

Korsgaard, Christine, (with G.A. Cohen, Raymond Geuss, Thomas Nagel, and Bernard Williams), *The Sources of Normativity*, ed. Onora O'Neill. (Cambridge: Cambridge University Press, 1996d).

Korsgaard, Christine, "The Normativity of Instrumental Reason, in *Ethics and Practical Reason*, ed. Garrett Cullity & Berys Gaut (Oxford: Oxford University Press, 1997), 213–54.

Korsgaard, Christine, "Self-Constitution in the Ethics of Plato and Kant," *Journal of Ethics* 3 (1999): 1–29.

Kraut, R.E., "Effects of social labeling on giving to charity," *Journal of Experimental Social Psychology* (1973): 551–62.

Kraut, Robert, "Love *De Re*," *Midwest Studies in Philosophy* 10 (1986): 413–30.

Lamb, Roger E., "Love and Rationality," in *Love Analyzed*, ed. Roger E. Lamb (Boulder, CO: Westview, 1997), 23–47.

Lampl-de Groot, Jeanne, "Ego Ideal and Superego," *The Psychoanalytic Study of the Child* 17 (1962): 94–106.

Lecky, P., *Self-Consistency: A Theory of Personality* (New York: Island Press, 1945).

Levine, Frederic J., and Kravis, Robert, "Psychoanalytic Theories of the Self: Contrasting Clinical Approaches to the New Narcissism," in *The Book of the Self: Person, Pretext, and Process*, ed. Polly Young-Eisendrath and James A. Hall (New York: New York University Press, 1987), 306–330.

Lewis, David, "Attitudes *De Dicto* and *De Se*," *The Philosophical Review* 88 (1979): 513–14.

Locke, John, *An Essay Concerning Human Understanding*, ed. Peter H. Nidditch (Oxford: Oxford University Press, 1975).

Lyons, William G., *Emotion* (Cambridge: Cambridge University Press, 1980).

Lycan, William G., *Consciousness* (Cambridge, MA: MIT Press, 1987).

Mackie, John, "The Transcendental 'I'," in *Philosophical Subjects: Essays Presented to P.F. Strawson*, ed. Zak van Straaten (Oxford: Clarendon Press, 1980), 48–61.

Madell, Geoffrey, "Personal Identity and the Idea of a Human Being," in *Human Beings*, ed. David Cockburn (Cambridge: Cambridge University Press, 1991), 127–42.

Malcolm, Janet, *Psychoanalysis: The Impossible Profession* (New York: Vintage Press, 1980).

Maracek, J., & Mettee, D.R., "Avoidance of continued success as a function of self-esteem, level of esteem certainty, and responsibility for success," *Journal of Personality and Social Psychology* 22 (1972): 98–107.

Martin, Raymond, "Having the Experience: The Next Best Thing to Being There," *Philosophical Studies* 70 (1993): 305–21.

Mason, Michelle, *Moral Virtue and Reasons for Action*, (Ph.D. diss.: University of Chicago, 2001).

McFall, Lynne, "Integrity," *Ethics* 98 (1987): 5–20.

McNulty, S.E., and Swann, W.B., Jr., "Psychotherapy, Self-Concept Change, and Self-Verification," in *The Relational Self: Theoretical Convergences in Psychoanalysis and Social Psychology*, ed. Rebecca C. Curtis (New York: Guildford Press, 1991), 213–37.

Mellor, D.H., "I and Now," *Proceedings of the Aristotelian Society* 89 (1989): 79–94; reprinted in his *Matters of Metaphysics* (Cambridge: Cambridge University Press, 1991).

Mezzacappa, E.S., Katkin, E.S., and Palmer, S.N., "Epinephrine, arousal, and emotion: A new look at two-factor theory," *Cognition and Emotion* 13 (1999): 181–99.

Midgley, Mary, "The Objection to Systematic Humbug," *Philosophy* 53 (1978): 147–69.

Miller, R.L., Brickman, P., and Bolen, D., "Attribution Versus Persuasion as a Means for Modifying Behavior," *Journal of Personality and Social Psychology* 31 (1975): 430–41.

Moran, Richard, *Authority and Estrangement: An Essay on Self-Knowledge* (Princeton: Princeton University Press, 2001).

Morris, Herbert, "The Decline of Guilt," in *Ethics and Personality: Essays in Moral Psychology*, ed. John Deigh (Chicago: University of Chicago Press, 1992), 117–31.

Murdoch, Iris, *The Sovereignty of Good* (New York: Routledge, 1970).

Nagel, Thomas, *The Possibility of Altruism* (Oxford: Clarendon Press, 1970); reprinted (Princeton: Princeton University Press, 1978).

Nagel, Thomas, "Subjective and Objective," in his *Mortal Questions* (Cambridge: Cambridge University Press, 1979), 196–213.

Nagel, Thomas, "The Limits of Objectivity," in *The Tanner Lectures on Human Values*, Vol. I, ed. S. McMurrin (Salt Lake City: University of Utah Press, 1980), 77–139.

Nagel, Thomas, "The Objective Self," in *Knowledge and Mind*, ed. Carl Ginet and Sydney Shoemaker (New York: Oxford University Press, 1983), 211–32.

Nagel, Thomas, *The View From Nowhere* (New York: Oxford University Press, 1986), Chapter 4.

Nagel, Thomas, "Concealment and Exposure," *Philosophy & Public Affairs* 27, no. 1 (Winter 1998): 3–30.

Nakhnikian, George, "Love in Human Reason," *Midwest Studies in Philosophy* 3 (1978): 286–317.

Neu, Jerome, "*Odi et Amo:* On Hating the Ones We Love," in *Freud and the Passions*, ed. John O'Neill (University Park: Pennsylvania State University Press, 1996), 53–72.

Nisbett, R.E., and Valins, S., "Perceiving the causes of one's own behavior," in *Attribution: Perceiving the Causes of Behavior*, ed. Edward E. Jones, David E. Kanouse, Harold H. Kelley, Richard E. Nisbett, Stuart Valins, and Bernard Weiner (Morristown, NJ: General Learning, 1972).

Nisbett, R.E., and Wilson, T.D., "Telling more than we can know: Verbal reports of mental processes," *Psychological Review* 84 (1977), 231–59.

Nozick, Robert, *Anarchy, State, and Utopia* (New York: Basic, 1974).

Nozick, Robert, *Philosophical Explanations* (Cambridge, MA: Harvard University Press, 1981).

Nozick, Robert, *The Examined Life* (New York: Simon & Schuster, 1989).

Nozick, Robert, *The Nature of Rationality* (Princeton: Princeton University Press, 1993).

Nussbaum, Martha C., " 'Finely Aware and Richly Responsible': Literature and the Moral Imagination," in *Anti-Theory in Ethics and Moral Conservatism*, ed. Stanley G. Clarke and Evan Simpson (Albany: SUNY, 1989), 111–34.

Nussbaum, Martha C., "Beatrice's 'Dante': Loving the Individual?" in *Virtue, Love, and Form: Essays in Memory of Gregory Vlastos*, ed. Terence Irwin and Martha C. Nussbaum (Edmonton: Academic Printing & Publishing, 1993), 161–78.

Nuttin, Joseph, *Motivation, Planning, and Action: a Relational Theory of Behavior Dynamics*, transl. Raymond P. Lorion and Jean E. Dumas (Hillsdale, NJ: Erlbaum, 1984).

O'Brien, Gerard, and Opie, Jonathan, "The Multiplicity of Consciousness and the Emergence of Self," in *The Self in Neuroscience and Psychiatry*, ed. Tilo Kirchner and Anthony David (Cambridge: Cambridge University Press, 2003) 107–120.

O'Brien, Lucy F., "Anscombe and the Self-Reference Rule," *Analysis* 54 (1994): 277–81.

O'Neill, Onora, *Acting on Principle: an Essay on Kantian Ethics* (New York: Columbia University Press, 1975).

O'Neill, Onora, "Consistency in Action," in her *Constructions of Reason: Explorations of Kant's Practical Philosophy* (Cambridge: Cambridge University Press, 1989a), 81–104.

O'Neill, Onora, "Universal Laws and Ends-in-Themselves," in her *Constructions of Reason: Explorations of Kant's Practical Philosophy* (Cambridge: Cambridge University Press, 1989b), 126–44.

Oldenquist, Andrew, "Loyalties," *Journal of Philosophy* 79 (1982): 173–93.

Olson, J.M., "Self-inference processes in emotion," in *Self-Inference Processes: The Ontario Symposium*, Vol. 6, ed. James M. Olson and Mark P. Zanna (Hillsdale, NJ: Erlbaum, 1990), 17–41.

Parfit, Derek, *Reasons and Persons* (Oxford: Clarendon Press, 1984).

Paton, H.J., "Kant on Friendship," *Proceedings of the British Academy* 42 (1956): 45–66.

Peacocke, Christopher, *Sense and Content: Experience, Thought, and their Relations* (Oxford: Clarendon Press, 1983).

Perry, John, *A Dialogue on Personal Identity and Immortality* (Indianapolis: Hackett, 1978); reprinted in *The Problem of the Essential Indexical and Other Essays* (New York: Oxford University Press, 1993).

Perry, John "Problem of the Essential Indexical," *Noûs* 13 (1979): 3–21; reprinted in his *The Problem of the Essential Indexical and Other Essays* (New York: Oxford University Press, 1993).

Perry, John, "Self-Notions," 11 *Logos: Philosophic Issues in Christian Perspective* (1990): 17–31; reprinted in his *The Problem of the Essential Indexical and Other Essays* (New York: Oxford University Press, 1993).

Perry, John, *The Problem of the Essential Indexical and Other Essays* (New York: Oxford University Press, 1993).

Perry, John, "Myself and 'I'," in *Philosophie in Synthetischer Absicht* (A festschrift for Dieter Heinrich), ed. Marcelo Stamm (Stuttgart: Klett-Cotta, 1998), 83–103.

Bibliography

Piper, Adrian M.S., "Moral Theory and Moral Alienation," *Journal of Philosophy* 84 (1987): 102–18.

Prislin, R., and Pool, G.J., "Behavior, consequences, and the self: Is all well that ends well?" *Personality and Social Psychology Bulletin* 22 (1996): 933–48.

Railton, Peter, "Alienation, Consequentialism, and the Demands of Morality," *Philosophy and Public Affairs* 13 (1984): 134–72.

Rawls, John, *A Theory of Justice* (Cambridge, MA: Harvard University Press, 1971).

Richardson, Henry S., *Practical Reasoning about Final Ends* (Cambridge: Cambridge University Press, 1994).

Rogers, C.R., *Client-Centered Therapy: It's Current Practice, Implications, and Theory* (New York: Houghton Mifflin, 1951).

Rorty, Amélie Oksenberg, "The Historicity of Psychological Attitudes: Love Is Not Love which Alters Not when It Alteration Finds," *Midwest Studies in Philosophy* 10 (1986): 399–412.

Rorty, Richard, "Freud, Morality, and Hermeneutics," *New Literary History* 12 (1980): 177–85.

Rovane, Carol, "Branching Self-Consciousness" *The Philosophical Review* 99 (1990): 355–95.

Rubin, Jeffrey, "Does the True Self Really Exist? A Critique of Winnicott's True Self Concept," in his *A Psychoanalysis for Our Time: Exploring the Blindness of the Seeing I* (New York: New York University Press, 1998).

Ruddick, Sara, "Maternal Thinking," in *Women and Values: Readings in Recent Feminist Philosophy*, ed. Marilyn Pearsall (Belmont, CA: Wadsworth, 1986), 340–51.

Sandler, Joseph, "On the Concept of the Superego," *The Psychoanalytic Study of the Child* 15 (1960): 128–62.

Sandler, Joseph, Holder, Alex, and Meers, Dale, "The Ego Ideal and the Ideal Self," *The Psychoanalytic Study of the Child* 18 (1963): 139–58.

Sartre, Jean-Paul, *Being and Nothingness: An Essay on Phenomenological Ontology*, transl. Hazel E. Barnes (New York: Philosophical Library, 1956).

Schachter, S., "The interaction of cognitive and physiological determinants of emotional state," *Advances in Experimental Social Psychology*, Vol. 1, ed. Leonard Berkowitz (New York: Academic Press, 1964).

Schachter, S., & Singer, J.E., "Cognitive, social and physiological determinants of emotional state," *Psychological Review* 69 (1962): 379–99.

Schafer, Roy, *Aspects of Internalization* (New York: International Universities Press, 1968).

Schapiro, Tamar, "What is a Child," *Ethics* 109 (1999): 715–38.

Scheffler, Samuel, "Naturalism, Psychoanalysis, and Moral Motivation," in *Psychoanalysis, Mind and Art: Perspectives on Richard Wollheim*, ed. Jim Hopkins and Anthony Savile (Oxford: Blackwell, 1992a), 86–109.

Scheffler, Samuel, "Reason, Psychology and the Authority of Morality," *Human Morality* (New York: Oxford University Press, 1992b), Chapter 5.

Scheler, Max, "Über Scham und Schamgefühle," in *Schriften aus dem Nachlass* (Bern: Francke Verlag, 1957).

Schreiber, Flora Rheta, *Sybil* (Chicago: Regnery,1973).

Scruton, Roger, *Sexual Desire: A Moral Philosophy of the Erotic* (New York: Free Press, 1986).

Setterlund, M.B., and Niedenthal, P.M., " 'Who am I? Why am I here?': Self-esteem, self-clarity, and prototype matching," *Journal of Personality and Social Psychology* 65 (1993): 769–80.

Shah, Nishi, "How Truth Governs Belief," *The Philosophical Review* 112(2003): 447–82.

Shapiro, David, *Autonomy and Rigid Character* (New York: Basic Books, 1981).

Sherman, S.J., "On the self-erasing nature of errors of prediction," *Journal of Personality and Social Psychology* 39 (1980): 211–21.

Shoemaker, Sydney, "Persons and Their Pasts," *American Philosophical Quarterly* 7 (1970): 269–85.

Shoemaker, Sydney, "Embodiment and Behavior," in *The Identities of Persons*, ed. Amélie Rorty (Berkeley: University of California Press, 1976), 109–37.

Sidgwick, Henry, *The Methods of Ethics* (Indianapolis: Hackett, 1981).

Simmel, Georg, "The Secret and the Secret Society," Part IV of *The Sociology of Georg Simmel*, transl. Kurt H. Wolff (Glencoe, IL: Free Press, 1950).

Slote, Michael, *Goods and Virtues* (Oxford: Clarendon Press, 1983).

Smith, Michael, "The Possibility of Philosophy of Action," in *Human Action, Deliberation and Causation*, ed. Jan Bransen and Stefaan Cuypers (Dordrecht: Kluwer Academic Publishers, 1998), 17–41.

Snyder, M., and Ebbesen, E.B., "Dissonance awareness: A test of dissonance theory versus self-perception theory," *Journal of Experimental Social Psychology* 8 (1972): 502–17.

Snygg, D., and Combs, A.W., *Individual Behavior: A Perceptual Approach to Behavior* (New York: Harper & Brothers, 1959).

Soble, Alan, *The Structure of Love* (New Haven, CT: Yale University Press, 1990).

Soble, Alan, "Union, Autonomy, and Concern," in *Love Analyzed*, ed. Roger E. Lamb (Boulder, CO: Westview, 1997).

Solomon, Robert C., "The Virtue of (Erotic) Love," *Midwest Studies in Philosophy* 13 (1988): 12–31.

Sommers, Christina Hoff, "Filial Morality," *Journal of Philosophy* 83 (1986): 439–56.

Spelman, Elizabeth, "On Treating Persons as Persons," *Ethics* 88 (1977): 150–161.

Stark, Cynthia A., "Decision Procedures, Standards of Rightness, and Impartiality," *Noûs* 31 (1997): 478–95.

Steele, C.M., & Liu, T.J., "Dissonance processes as self-affirmation," *Journal of Personality and Social Psychology* 45 (1983): 5–19.

Stocker, Michael, "The Schizophrenia of Modern Ethical Theories," *Journal of Philosophy* 73 (1976): 453–66.

Stocker, Michael, "Values and Purposes: The Limits of Teleology and the Ends of Friendship," *Journal of Philosophy* 78 (1981): 747–65.

Stocker, Michael, "Friendship and Duty: Some Difficult Relations," in *Identity, Character, and Morality: Essays in Moral Psychology*, ed. Owen Flanagan and Amélie Oksenberg Rorty (Cambridge, MA: MIT Press, 1990), 219–33.

Stocker, Michael, and Hegeman, Elizabeth, *Valuing Emotions* (Cambridge: Cambridge University Press, 1996).

Stone, J., Cooper, J., Wiegand, A.W., and Aronson, E., "When exemplification fails: Hypocrisy and the motive for self-integrity," *Journal of Personality and Social Psychology* 72 (1997): 54–65.

Strawson, P.F., *Subject and Predicate in Logic and Grammar* (London: Methuen, 1974).

Strawson, P.F., "Kant's Paralogisms: Self-Consciousness and the 'Outside Observer'," in *Theorie der Subjectivität*, ed. Konrad Cramer et al. (Frankfurt: Suhrkamp, 1987), 203–19.

Sullivan, Roger J., *Kant's Moral Theory* (Cambridge: Cambridge University Press, 1989).

Swann, W.B., Jr., "Self-Verification: Bringing Social Reality into Harmony with the Self," in *Psychological Perspectives on the Self*, Vol. 2, ed. J. Suls and A.G. Greenwald (Hillsdale, NJ: Erlbaum, 1983), 33–66.

Swann, W.B., Jr., "The Self as Architect of Social Reality," in *The Self and Social Life*, ed. Barry R. Schlenker (New York: McGraw-Hill, 1985), 100–25.

Swann, W.B., Jr., "To be adored or to be known? The interplay of self-enhancement and self-verification," in *Handbook of Motivation and Cognition: Foundations of Social Behavior*, Vol. 2, ed. E.T. Higgins and R.M. Sorrentino (New York: Guilford Press, 1986), 408–48.

Swann, W.B., Jr., *Self-Traps: The Elusive Quest for Higher Self-Esteem* (New York: W.H. Freeman, 1996).

Swann, W.B., Jr., and Brown, J.D., "From Self to health: Self-verification and identity disruption," in *Social Support: An Interactional View*, ed. Barbara R. Sarason, Irwin G. Sarason, and Gregory R. Pierce (New York: Wiley-Interscience, 1990), 150–72.

Swann, W.B., Jr., De La Ronde, C., and Hixon, G., "Embracing the bitter 'truth': Negative self-concepts and marital commitment," *Psychological Science* 3 (1992), 383–86.

Swann, W.B., Jr., De La Ronde, C., and Hixon, G., "Authenticity and positivity strivings in marriage and courtship," *Journal of Personality and Social Psychology* 66 (1994): 857–69.

Swann, W.B., Jr., and Ely, R.J., "A Battle of Wills: Self-Verification Versus Behavioral Confirmation," *Journal of Personality and Social Psychology* 46 (1984): 1287–1302.

Swann, W.B., Jr., and Hill, C.A., "When our identities are mistaken: Reaffirming self-conceptions through social interaction," *Journal of Personality and Social Psychology* 43 (1982): 59–66.

Swann, W.B., Jr., Hixon, G., Stein-Seroussi, A., and Gilbert, D.T., "The fleeting gleam of praise: Cognitive processes underlying behavioral reactions to self-relevant feedback," *Journal of Personality and Social Psychology* 59 (1990): 17–26.

Swann, W.B., Jr., Pelham, B.W., and Krull, D.S., "Agreeable fancy or disagreeable truth? Reconciling self-enhancement and self-verification," *Journal of Personality and Social Psychology* 57 (1989): 782–91.

Swann, W.B., Jr., and Predmore, S.C., "Intimates as agents of social support: Sources of consolation or despair?" *Journal of Personality and Social Psychology* 49 (1985): 1609–17.

Swann, W.B., Jr., and Read, S.J., "Acquiring Self-Knowledge: The Search for Feedback that Fits," *Journal of Personality and Social Psychology* 41 (1981a): 1119–1128.

Swann, W.B., Jr., and Read, S.J., "Self-Verification Processes: How We Sustain Our Self-Conceptions," *Journal of Experimental Social Psychology* 17 (1981b): 351–72.

Swann, W.B., Jr., Stein-Seroussi, A., and Giesler, R.B., "Why people self-verify," *Journal of Personality and Social Psychology* 62 (1992): 392–401.

Taylor, Charles, *Human Agency and Language* (Cambridge: Cambridge University Press, 1985).

Taylor, Charles, *Sources of the Self: The Making of the Modern Identity* (Cambridge, MA: Harvard University Press, 1989).

Taylor, Gabrielle, "Love," *Proceedings of the Aristotelian Society* 76 (1976): 147–64.

Taylor, Gabrielle, *Pride, Shame, and Guilt: Emotions of Self-Assessment* (Oxford: Clarendon Press, 1985).

Thibodeau, R., and Aronson, E., "Taking a Closer Look: Reasserting the Role of the Self-Concept in Dissonance Theory," *Personality and Social Psychology Bulletin* 18 (1992): 91–602.

Thigpen, Corbett H., and Cleckley, Hervey M., *The Three Faces of Eve* (New York: McGraw-Hill, 1957).

Thomas, Laurence, "Reasons for Loving," in *The Philosophy of (Erotic) Love*, ed. Robert C. Solomon and Kathleen M. Higgins (Lawrence: University of Kansas Press, 1991), 467–76.

Toner, I.J., Moore, L.P., and Emmons, B.A., "The effects of being labeled on subsequent self-control in children," *Child Development* 51 (1980): 618–21.

Torek, Paul, *Something to Look Forward To: Personal Identity, Prudence, and Ethics* (Ph.D. diss., University of Michigan, 1995).

Trzebinski, J., "Narrative Self, Understanding, and Action," in *The Self in European and North American Culture: Development and Processes*, ed. A. Oosterwegel and R.A. Wicklund (Dordrecht: Kluwer, 1995), 73–88.

Vallacher, R.R., and Wegner, D.M., *A Theory of Action Identification* (Hillsdale, NJ: Erlbaum, 1985).

Vallacher, R.R., and Wegner, D.M., "What Do People Think They're Doing? Action Identification and Human Behavior," *Psychological Review* 94 (1987): 3–15.

Velleman, J. David, "Epistemic Freedom," *Pacific Philosophical Quarterly* 70 (1989a): 73–97.

Velleman, J. David, *Practical Reflection* (Princeton: Princeton University Press, 1989b).

Velleman, J. David, "The Guise of the Good" *Noûs* 26 (1992a): 3–26; reprinted in his *The Possibility of Practical Reason* (Oxford: Oxford University Press, 2000), Chapter 5.

Velleman, J. David, "What Happens When Someone Acts?" *Mind* 101 (1992b): 461–81; reprinted in his *The Possibility of Practical Reason* (Oxford: Oxford University Press, 2000), Chapter 6.

Velleman, J. David, "The Story of Rational Action," *Philosophical Topics* 21 (1993): 229–53 (1993); reprinted in his *The Possibility of Practical Reason* (Oxford: Oxford University Press, 2000), Chapter 7.

Velleman, J. David, "The Possibility of Practical Reason," *Ethics* 106 (1996): 694–726; reprinted in his *The Possibility of Practical Reason* (Oxford: Oxford University Press, 2000), Chapter 8.

Velleman, J. David "Deciding How to Decide," in *Ethics and Practical Reason,* ed. Garrett Cullity and Berys Gaut (Oxford: Clarendon Press, 1997), 29–52; reprinted in his *The Possibility of Practical Reason* (Oxford: Oxford University Press, 2000), Chapter 10.

Velleman, J. David, "A Right of Self-Termination?" *Ethics* 109 (1999): 606–28.

Velleman, J. David, "How to Share an Intention," in his *The Possibility of Practical Reason* (Oxford: Oxford University Press, 2000a), Chapter 9.

Velleman, J. David, "On the Aim of Belief," in his *The Possibility of Practical Reason* (Oxford: Clarendon Press, 2000b), Chapter 11.

Velleman, J. David, *The Possibility of Practical Reason* (Oxford: Oxford University Press, 2000c).

Velleman, J. David, "Narrative Explanation," *The Philosophical Review* 112 (2003): 1–25.

Velleman, J. David, "Precis" and "Replies to Discussion" on *The Possibility of Practical Reason, Philosophical Studies* 121 (2004): 225–38, 277–98.

Vendler, Zeno, *The Matter of Minds* (Oxford: Clarendon Press, 1984).

Vlastos, Gregory, "Justice and Equality," in *Social Justice,* ed. Richard B. Brandt (Englewood Cliffs, N.J.: Prentice Hall, 1962), 31–72.

Vlastos, Gregory, "The Individual as an Object of Love in Plato," in his *Platonic Studies* (Princeton, N.J.: Princeton University Press, 1973), 3–42.

Walton, Kendall L., *Mimesis as Make-Believe: On the Foundations of the Representational Arts* (Cambridge, MA: Harvard University Press, 1993).

Wegner, D.M., and Bargh J.A., "Control and Automaticity in Social Life," in *The Handbook of Social Psychology,* 4th ed., Vol. 1, ed. Daniel T. Gilbert, Susan T. Fiske, and Gardner Lindzey (Boston: McGraw-Hill, 1998), 446–96.

Wegner, D.M., and Vallacher, R.R., "Action Identification," in *Handbook of Motivation and Cognition,* ed. Richard M. Sorrentino and E. Tory Higgins (New York: Guilford Press, 1986), 550–82.

Wegner, D.M., Vallacher, R.R., Kiersted, G.W., and Dizadji, D., "Action Identification in the Emergence of Social Behavior," *Social Cognition* 4 (1986): 18–38.

Weil, Simone, "Human Personality," in *The Simone Weil Reader,* ed. George A. Panichas (New York: David McKay, 1977), 313–39.

Westen, Drew, "The Superego: A Revised Developmental Model," *Journal of the American Academy of Psychoanalysis* 14 (1986): 181–202.

Whiting, Jennifer, "Impersonal Friends," *Monist* 74 (1991): 3–29.

Wiggins, David, *Identity and Spatio-Temporal Continuity* (Oxford: Basic Blackwell, 1967).

Williams, Bernard, "A Critique of Utilitarianism," in *Utilitarianism: For and Against,* J.J.C. Smart and Bernard Williams (Cambridge: Cambridge University Press, 1973a), 75–150.

Williams, Bernard, "Morality and the Emotions," in his *Problems of the Self* (Cambridge: Cambridge University Press, 1973b), 207–29.

Williams, Bernard, "The Imagination and the Self," in his *Problems of the Self* (Cambridge: Cambridge University Press, 1973c), 26–45.

Williams, Bernard, "The Self and the Future," in his *Problems of the Self* (Cambridge: Cambridge University Press, 1973d), 46–63.

Williams, Bernard, "Internal and External Reasons," in his *Moral Luck: Philosophical Papers 1973–1980* (Cambridge: Cambridge University Press, 1981a), 101–13.

Williams, Bernard, "Persons, Character and Morality," in his *Moral Luck: Philosophical Papers 1973–1980* (Cambridge: Cambridge University Press, 1981b), 1–19.

Williams, Bernard, *Shame and Necessity* (Berkeley: University of California Press, 1993).

Williams, Bernard, "Internal Reasons and the Obscurity of Blame," in his *Making Sense of Humanity and Other Philosophical Essays* (Cambridge: Cambridge University Press, 1995), 39–45.

Wilson, Stephen, *Feuding, Conflict, and Banditry in Nineteenth-Century Corsica* (Cambridge: Cambridge University Press, 1988).

Winnicott, D.W., "Ego Distortion in Terms of True and False Self," in *Collected Papers: Through Paediatrics to Psycho-analysis* (London: Tavistock Publications, 1958).

Winnicott, D.W., "Hate in the Countertransference," *Through Paediatrics to Psycho-analysis* (London: Hogarth Press, 1975), 194–203.

Winnicott, D.W., "Mirror-Role of Mother and Family in Child Development," in his *Playing and Reality* (New York: Routledge, 1989), 111–18.

Wittgenstein, Ludwig, *The Blue and Brown Books* (Oxford: Blackwell, 1972).

Wolf, Susan, "Moral Saints," *Journal of Philosophy* 79 (1982): 419–39.

Wolf, Susan, "Morality and Partiality," *Philosophical Perspectives* 6 (1992): 243–59.

Wolff, Robert Paul, "There's Nobody Here but Us Persons," in *Women and Philosophy: Toward a Theory of Liberation,* ed. Carol C. Gould and Marx W. Wartofsky (New York: G.P. Putnam's Sons, 1976), 128–144.

Wollheim, Richard, "Imagination and Identification," in his *On Art and the Mind* (Cambridge: Harvard University Press, 1974), 54–83.

Wollheim, Richard, *The Thread of Life* (Cambridge: Harvard University Press, 1984).

Wollheim, Richard, *Painting as an Art* (Princeton: Princeton University Press, 1987).

Wollheim, Richard, *On the Emotions* (New Haven: Yale University Press, 1999).

Yeats, W.B., "For Anne Gregory," in *The Collected Poems of W.B. Yeats* (New York: Macmillan, 1956), p. 240.

Zanna, M.P., and Cooper, J., "Dissonance and the pill: An attribution approach to studying the arousal properties of dissonance," *Journal of Personality & Social Psychology* 29 (1974): 703–709.

Zanna, M.P., Higgins, E.T., and Taves, P.A., "Is dissonance phenomenologically aversive?" *Journal of Experimental Social Psychology* 12 (1976): 530–538.

Zillman, D., "Attribution and misattribution of excitatory reactions," *New Directions in Attribution Research,* Vol. 2, ed. John H. Harvey, William Ickes, and Robert F. Kidd (Hillsdale, NJ: Erlbaum, 1978), 335–68.

Zillman, E., Johnson, R.C., and Day, K.D., "Attribution of apparent arousal and proficiency of recovery for sympathetic activation affecting excitation transfer to aggressive behavior," *Journal of Experimental Social Psychology* 10 (1974): 503–15.

Index

379